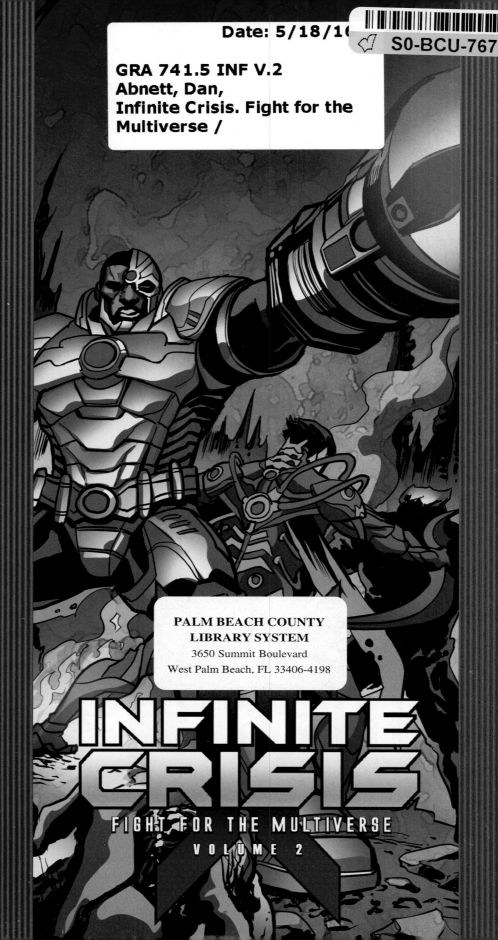

INFINITE CRISIS

FIGHT FOR THE MULTIVERSE

VOLUME 2

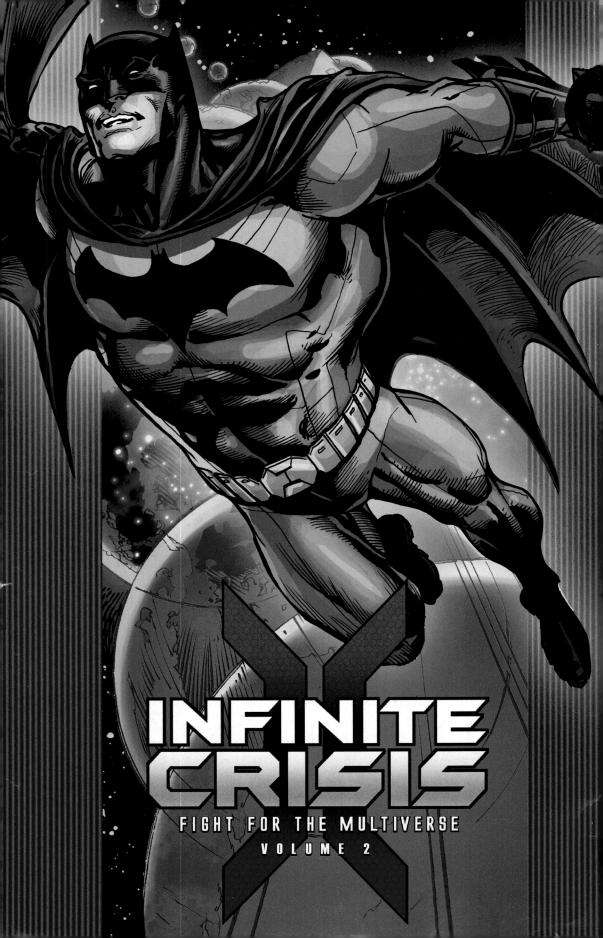

INFINITE CRISIS

FIGHT FOR THE MULTIVERSE

VOLUME 2

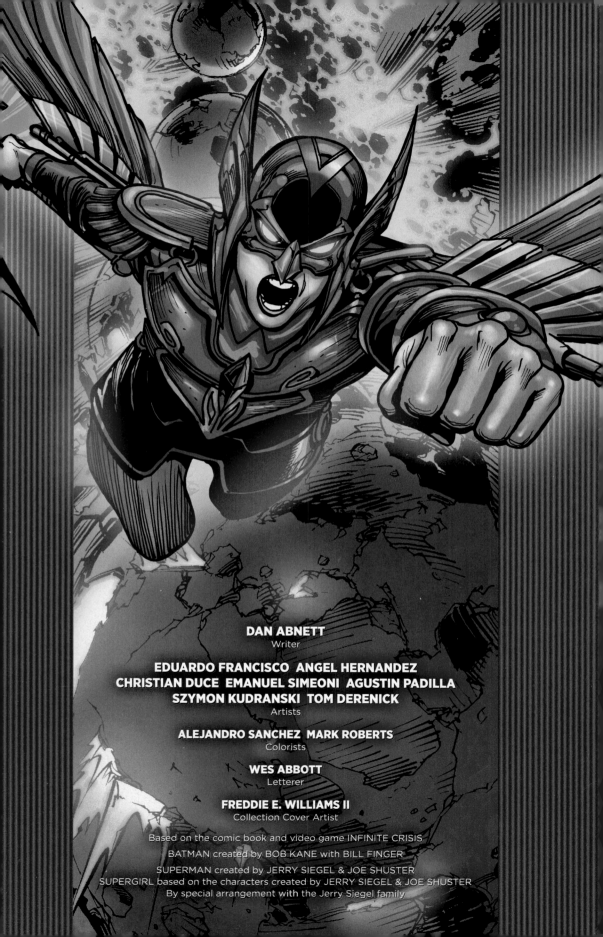

DAN ABNETT
Writer

EDUARDO FRANCISCO ANGEL HERNANDEZ
CHRISTIAN DUCE EMANUEL SIMEONI AGUSTIN PADILLA
SZYMON KUDRANSKI TOM DERENICK
Artists

ALEJANDRO SANCHEZ MARK ROBERTS
Colorists

WES ABBOTT
Letterer

FREDDIE E. WILLIAMS II
Collection Cover Artist

Based on the comic book and video game INFINITE CRISIS
BATMAN created by BOB KANE with BILL FINGER
SUPERMAN created by JERRY SIEGEL & JOE SHUSTER
SUPERGIRL based on the characters created by JERRY SIEGEL & JOE SHUSTER
By special arrangement with the Jerry Siegel family

Jim Chadwick Editor – Original Series

Aniz Ansari Assistant Editor – Original Series

Jeb Woodard Group Editor – Collected Editions

Liz Erickson Editor – Collected Edition

Curtis King Jr. Publication Design

Bob Harras Senior VP – Editor-in-Chief, DC Comics

Diane Nelson President

Dan DiDio and **Jim Lee** Co-Publishers

Geoff Johns Chief Creative Officer

Amit Desai Senior VP – Marketing & Global Franchise Management

Nairi Gardiner Senior VP – Finance

Sam Ades VP – Digital Marketing

Bobbie Chase VP – Talent Development

Mark Chiarello Senior VP – Art, Design & Collected Editions

John Cunningham VP – Content Strategy

Anne DePies VP – Strategy Planning & Reporting

Don Falletti VP – Manufacturing Operations

Lawrence Ganem VP – Editorial Administration & Talent Relations

Alison Gill Senior VP – Manufacturing & Operations

Hank Kanalz Senior VP – Editorial Strategy & Administration

Jay Kogan VP – Legal Affairs

Derek Maddalena Senior VP – Sales & Business Development

Jack Mahan VP – Business Affairs

Dan Miron VP – Sales Planning & Trade Development

Nick Napolitano VP – Manufacturing Administration

Carol Roeder VP – Marketing

Eddie Scannell VP – Mass Account & Digital Sales

Courtney Simmons Senior VP – Publicity & Communications

Jim (Ski) Sokolowski VP – Comic Book Specialty & Newsstand Sales

Sandy Yi Senior VP – Global Franchise Management

INFINITE CRISIS: FIGHT FOR THE MULTIVERSE VOLUME 2

Published by DC Comics. Compilation Copyright © 2015 DC Comics.
All Rights Reserved.

Originally published in single magazine form in INFINITE CRISIS:
FIGHT FOR THE MULTIVERSE 7-12 and online as INFINITE CRISIS:
FIGHT FOR THE MULTIVERSE Digital Chapters 19-36 Copyright ©
2015 DC Comics. All Rights Reserved. All characters, their distinctive
likenesses and related elements featured in this publication are
trademarks of DC Comics. The stories, characters and incidents
featured in this publication are entirely fictional. DC Comics does not
read or accept unsolicited ideas, stories or artwork.

DC Comics, 2900 West Alameda Ave., Burbank, CA 91505
Printed by RR Donnelley, Salem, VA, USA. 11/27/15. First Printing.
ISBN: 978-1-4012-5849-8

Library of Congress Cataloging-in-Publication Data

Abnett, Dan.
  Infinite Crisis : fight for the multiverse volume 2 / Dan Abnett,
Christian Duce, Eduardo Francisco.
    pages cm
  ISBN 978-1-4012-5849-8 (paperback)
  1. Graphic novels. I. Duce, Christian, illustrator. II. Francisco, Edu,
illustrator. III. Title.
  PN6728.I469A34 2016
  741.5'973—dc23
                                        2015034651

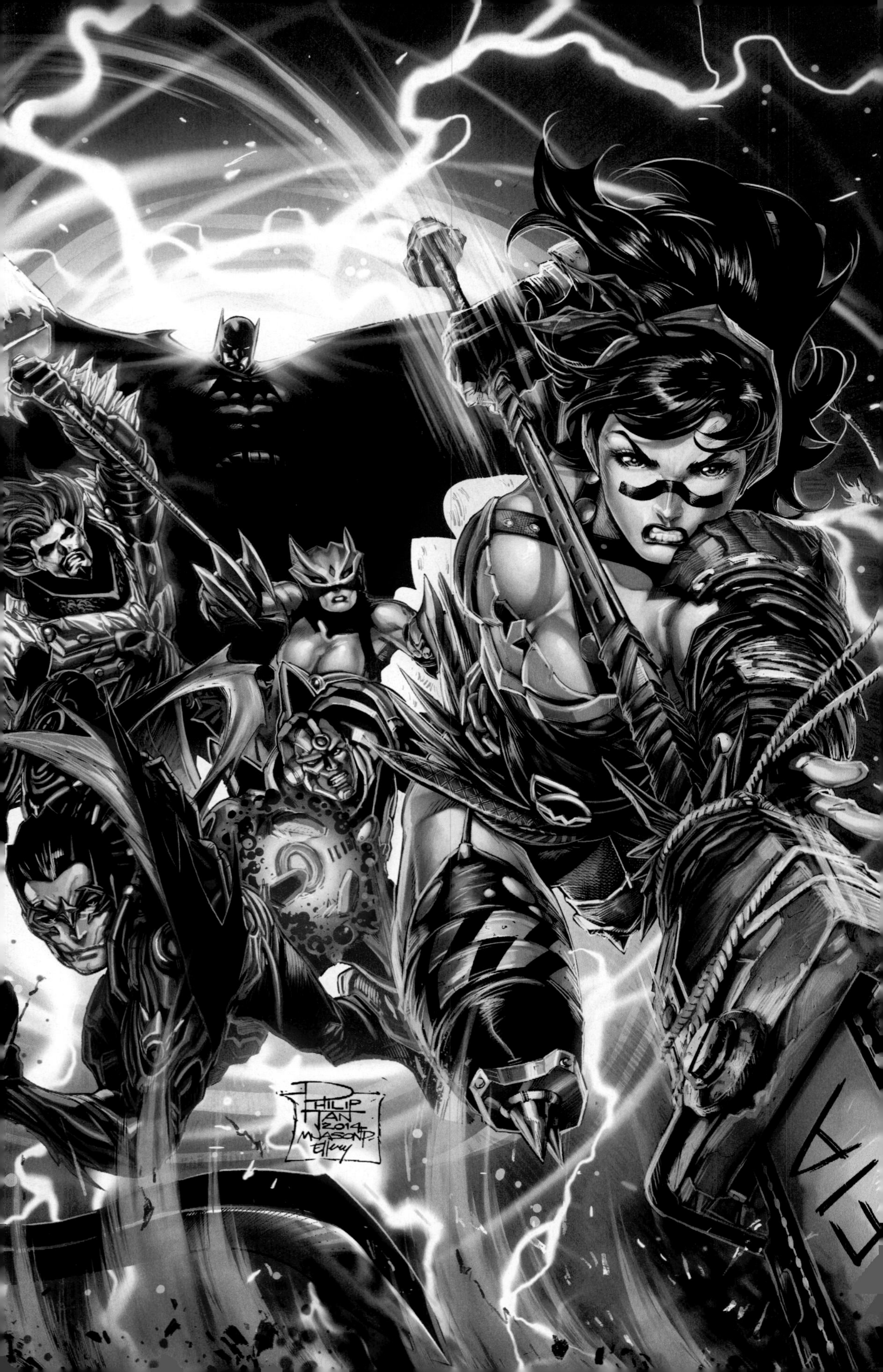
PHILIP TAN 2014

NIL

Emanuel Simeoni **Christian Duce** **Agustin Padilla** Artists
Alejandro Sanchez Colorist
Cover Art by **Philip Tan and Jason Paz with Ellery Santos**

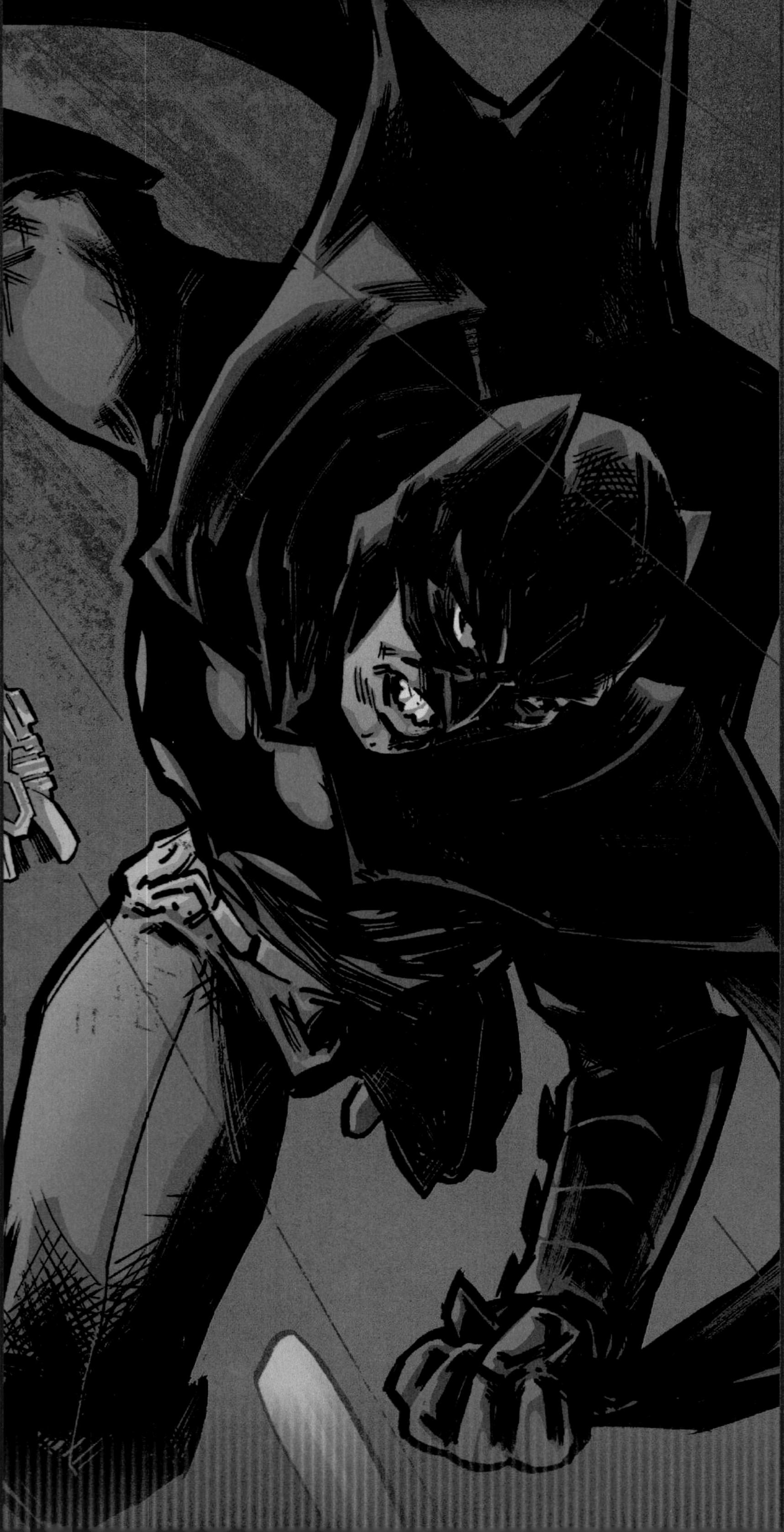

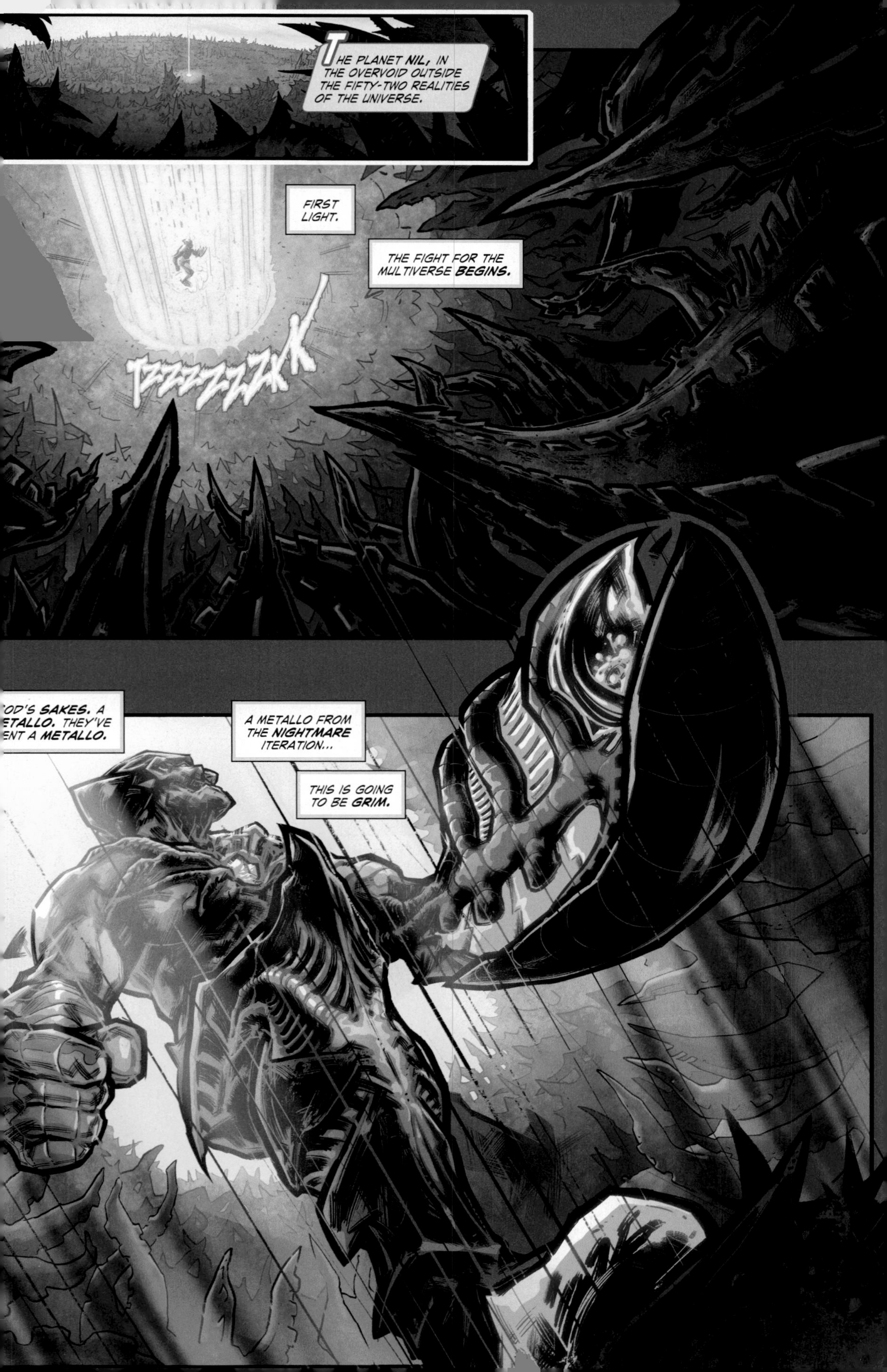
THE PLANET NIL, IN THE OVERVOID OUTSIDE THE FIFTY-TWO REALITIES OF THE UNIVERSE.
FIRST LIGHT.
THE FIGHT FOR THE MULTIVERSE BEGINS.
TZZZZZZZKK
OD'S SAKES. A ETALLO. THEY'VE ENT A METALLO.
A METALLO FROM THE NIGHTMARE ITERATION...
THIS IS GOING TO BE GRIM.

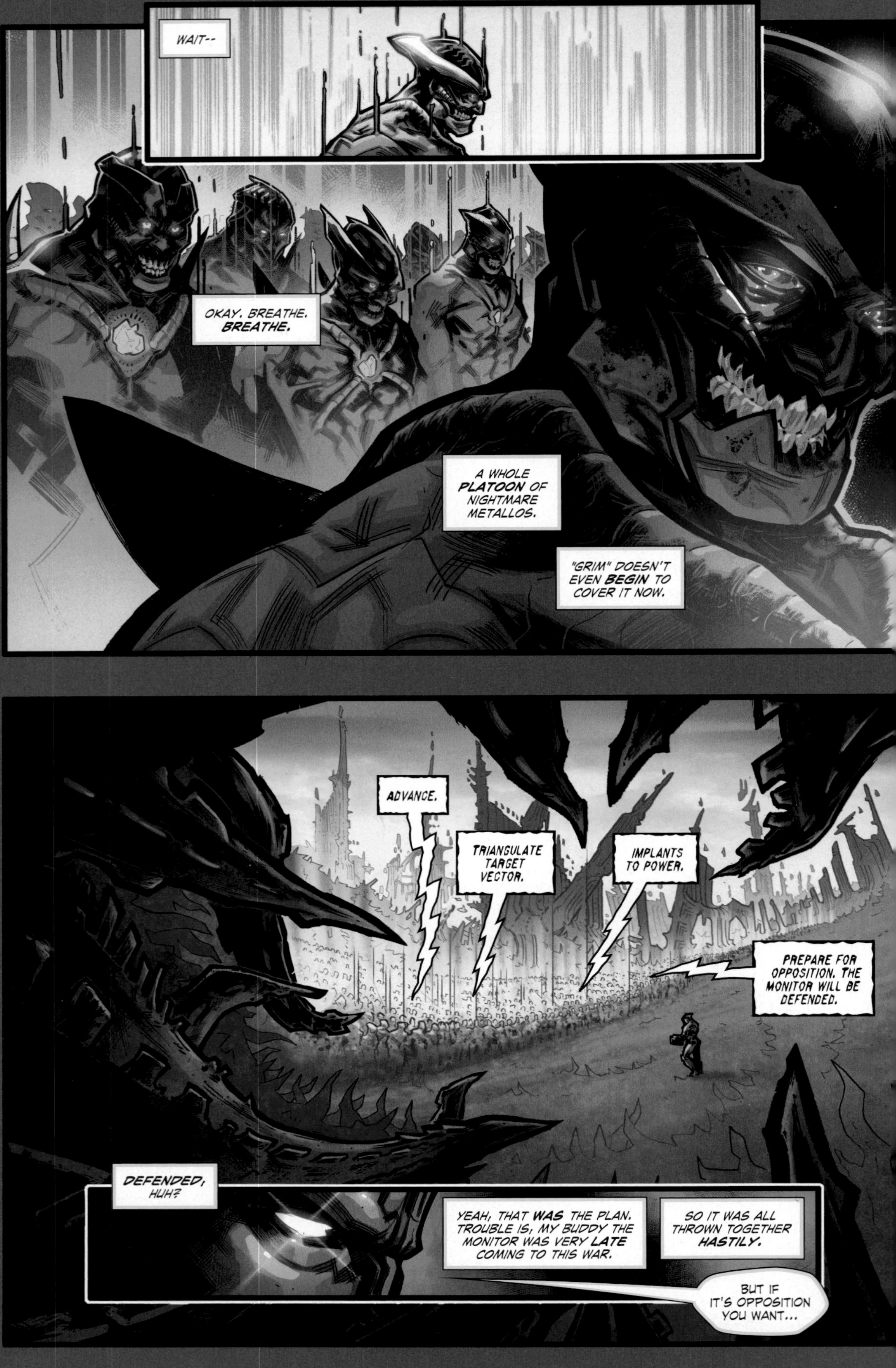
WAIT--
OKAY. BREATHE. BREATHE.
A WHOLE PLATOON OF NIGHTMARE METALLOS.
"GRIM" DOESN'T EVEN BEGIN TO COVER IT NOW.
ADVANCE.
TRIANGULATE TARGET VECTOR.
IMPLANTS TO POWER.
PREPARE FOR OPPOSITION. THE MONITOR WILL BE DEFENDED.
DEFENDED, HUH?
YEAH, THAT WAS THE PLAN. TROUBLE IS, MY BUDDY THE MONITOR WAS VERY LATE COMING TO THIS WAR.
SO IT WAS ALL THROWN TOGETHER HASTILY.
BUT IF IT'S OPPOSITION YOU WANT...

...COME AND GET IT!

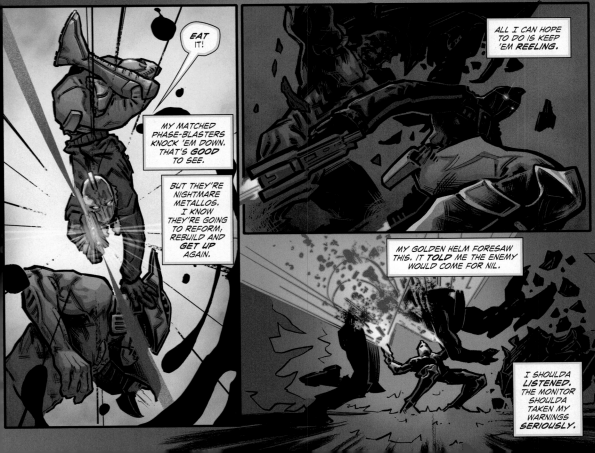

EAT IT!

MY MATCHED PHASE-BLASTERS KNOCK 'EM DOWN. THAT'S GOOD TO SEE.

BUT THEY'RE NIGHTMARE METALLOS. I KNOW THEY'RE GOING TO REFORM; REBUILD AND GET UP AGAIN.

ALL I CAN HOPE TO DO IS KEEP 'EM REELING.

MY GOLDEN HELM FORESAW THIS. IT TOLD ME THE ENEMY WOULD COME FOR NIL.

I SHOULDA LISTENED. THE MONITOR SHOULDA TAKEN MY WARNINGS SERIOUSLY.

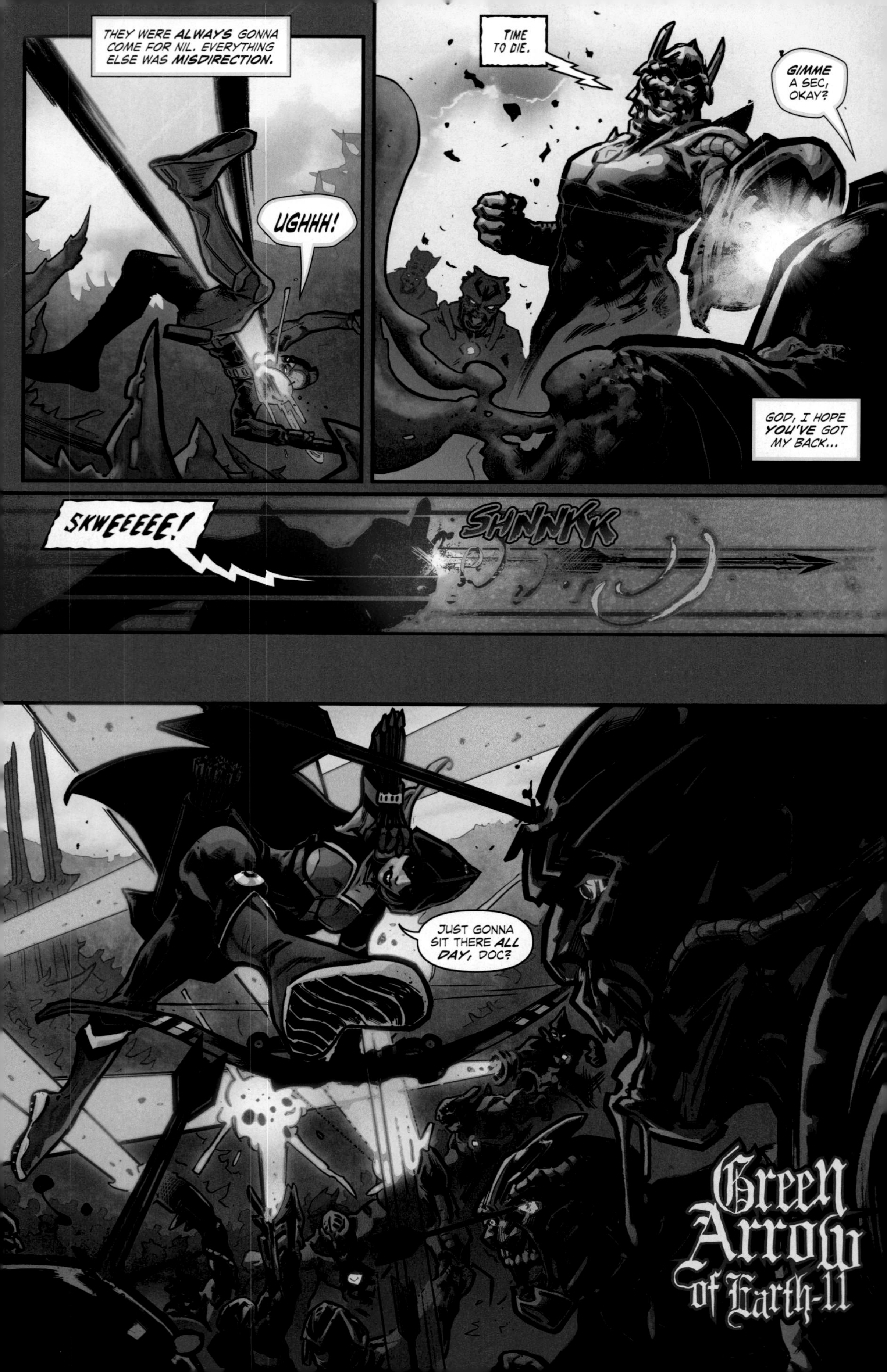
THEY WERE ALWAYS GONNA COME FOR NIL. EVERYTHING ELSE WAS MISDIRECTION.
UGHHH!
TIME TO DIE.
GIMME A SEC, OKAY?
GOD, I HOPE YOU'VE GOT MY BACK...
SKWEEEEE!
SHNNKK
JUST GONNA SIT THERE ALL DAY, DOC?
Green Arrow of Earth-11

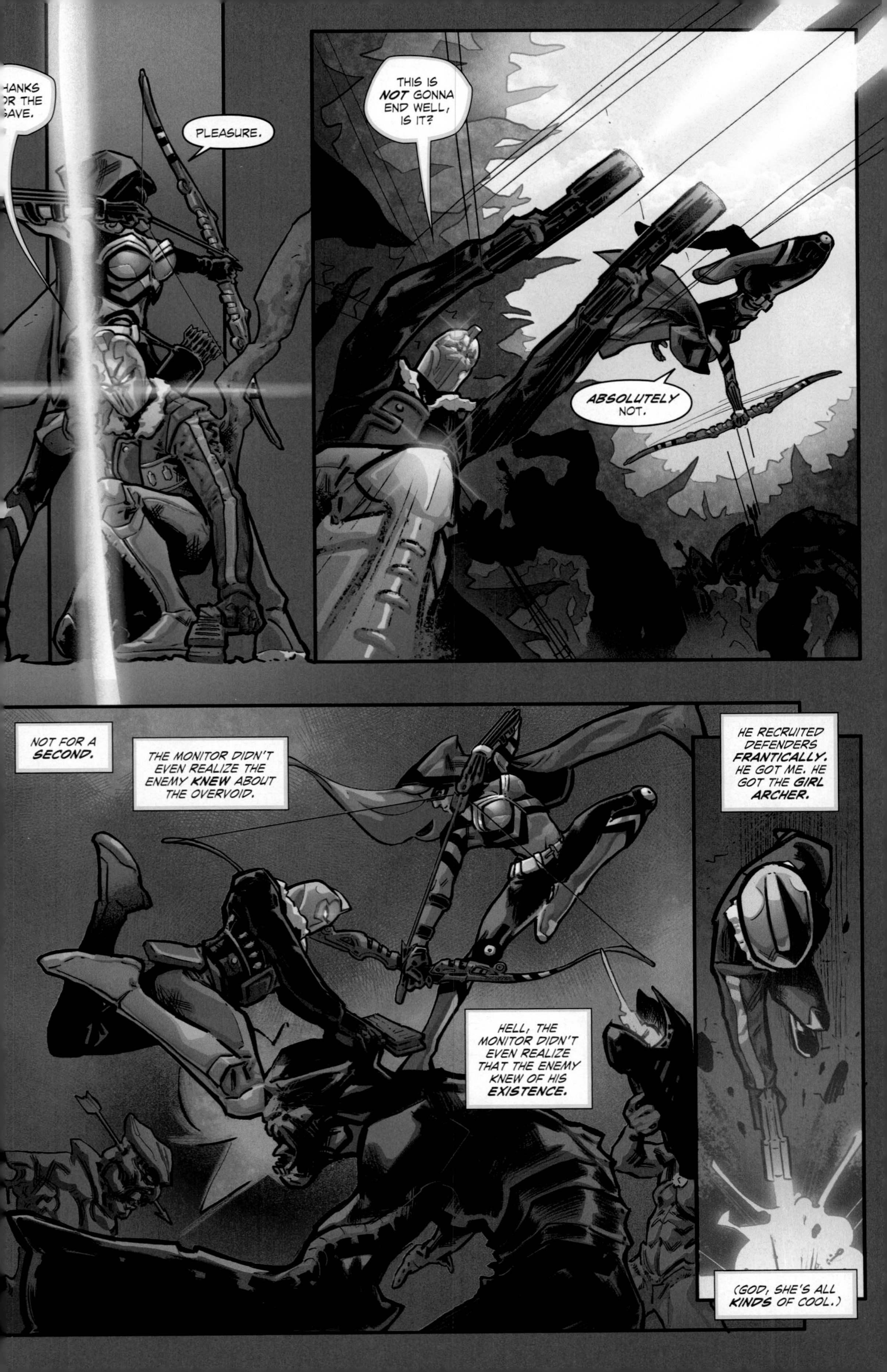
HANKS
OR THE
SAVE.
PLEASURE.
THIS IS NOT GONNA END WELL, IS IT?
ABSOLUTELY NOT.
NOT FOR A SECOND.
THE MONITOR DIDN'T EVEN REALIZE THE ENEMY KNEW ABOUT THE OVERVOID.
HELL, THE MONITOR DIDN'T EVEN REALIZE THAT THE ENEMY KNEW OF HIS EXISTENCE.
HE RECRUITED DEFENDERS FRANTICALLY. HE GOT ME. HE GOT THE GIRL ARCHER.
(GOD, SHE'S ALL KINDS OF COOL.)

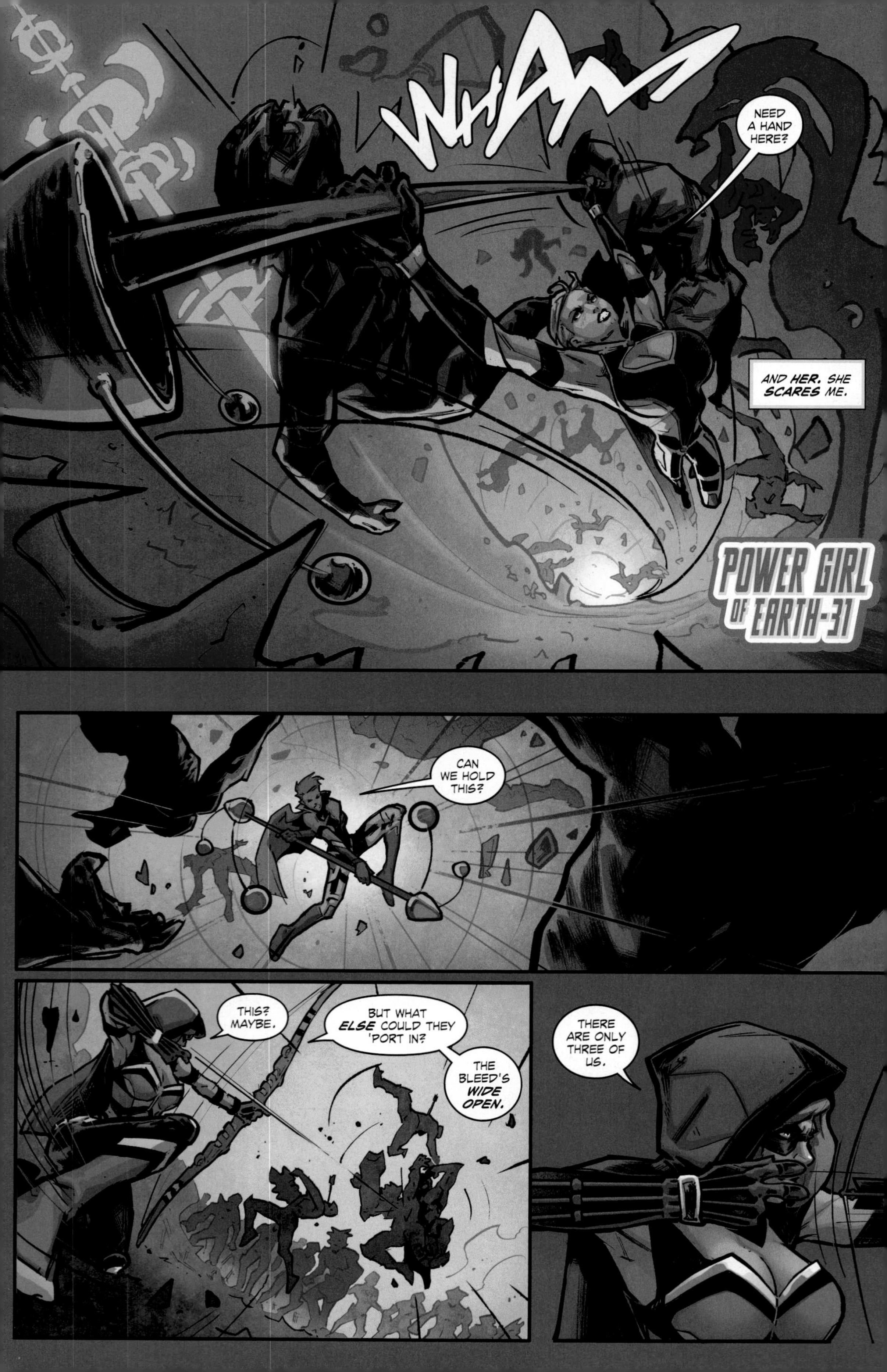

WHAM
NEED A HAND HERE?
AND HER. SHE SCARES ME.
POWER GIRL OF EARTH-31
CAN WE HOLD THIS?
THIS? MAYBE.
BUT WHAT ELSE COULD THEY 'PORT IN?
THE BLEED'S WIDE OPEN.
THERE ARE ONLY THREE OF US.

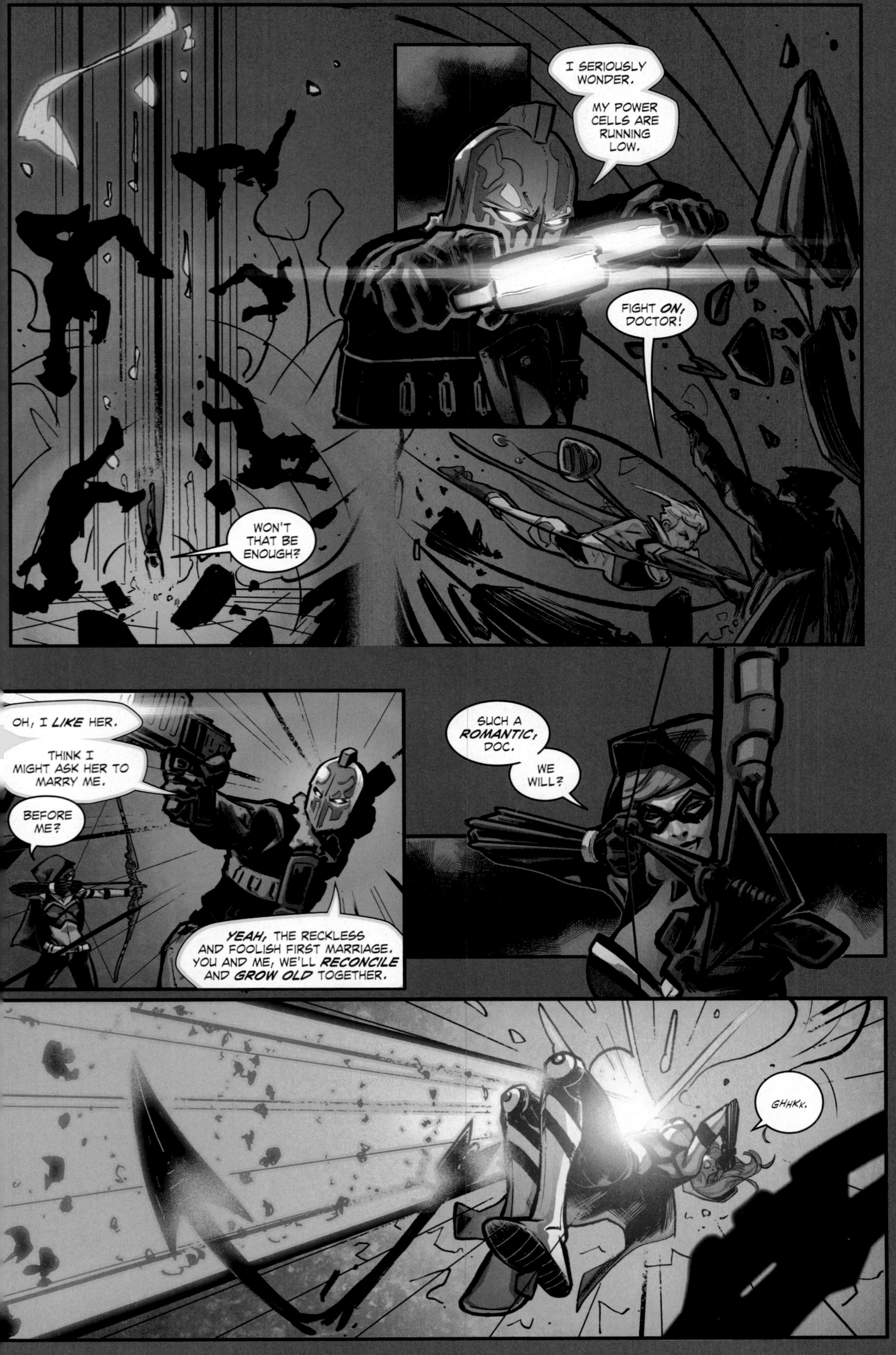

I SERIOUSLY WONDER.
MY POWER CELLS ARE RUNNING LOW.
FIGHT ON, DOCTOR!
WON'T THAT BE ENOUGH?
OH, I LIKE HER.
THINK I MIGHT ASK HER TO MARRY ME.
BEFORE ME?
YEAH, THE RECKLESS AND FOOLISH FIRST MARRIAGE. YOU AND ME, WE'LL RECONCILE AND GROW OLD TOGETHER.
SUCH A ROMANTIC, DOC.
WE WILL?
GHHKK.

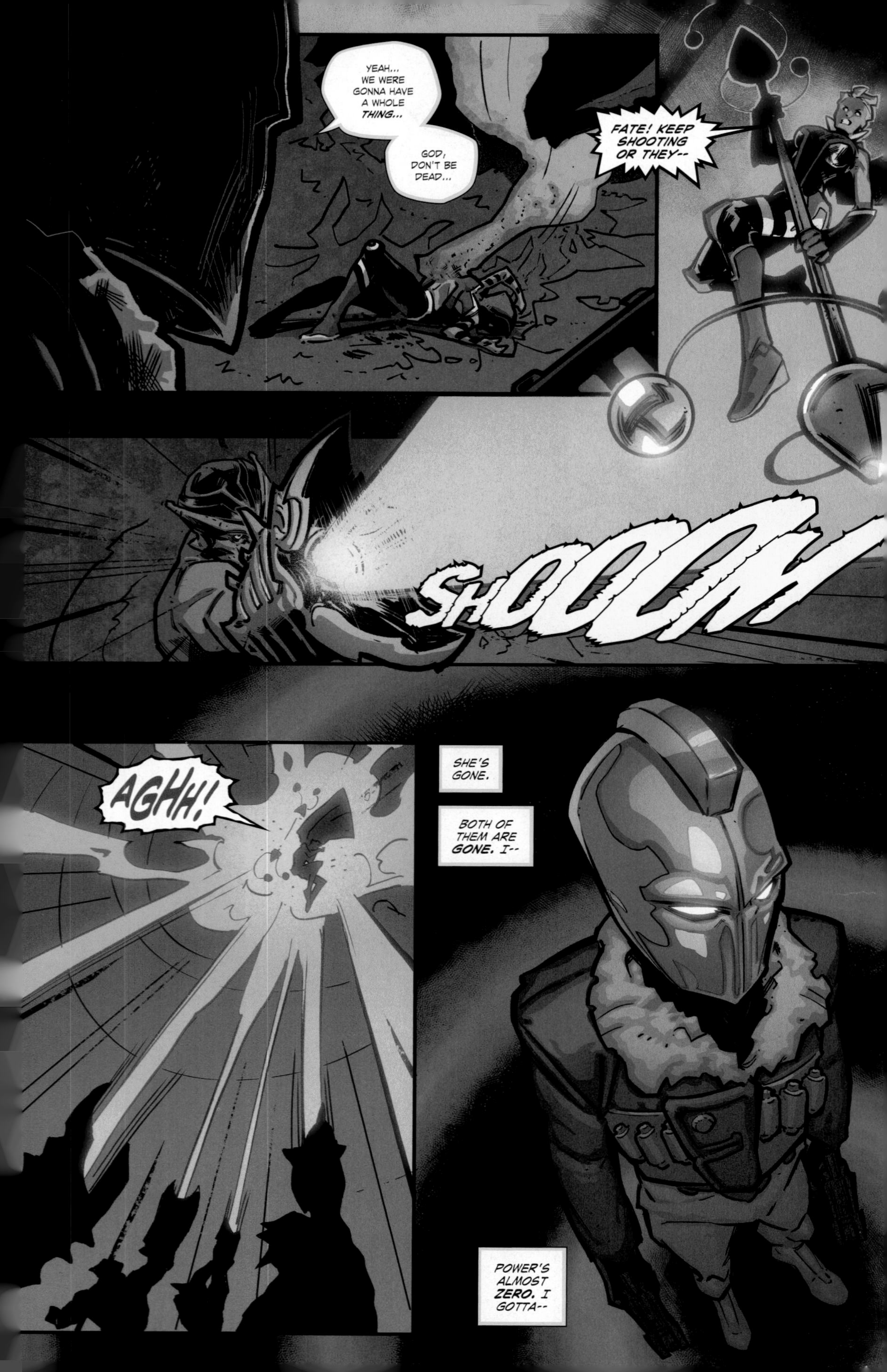
YEAH... WE WERE GONNA HAVE A WHOLE THING...
GOD, DON'T BE DEAD...
FATE! KEEP SHOOTING OR THEY--
SHOOOM
AGHH!
SHE'S GONE.
BOTH OF THEM ARE GONE. I--
POWER'S ALMOST ZERO. I GOTTA--

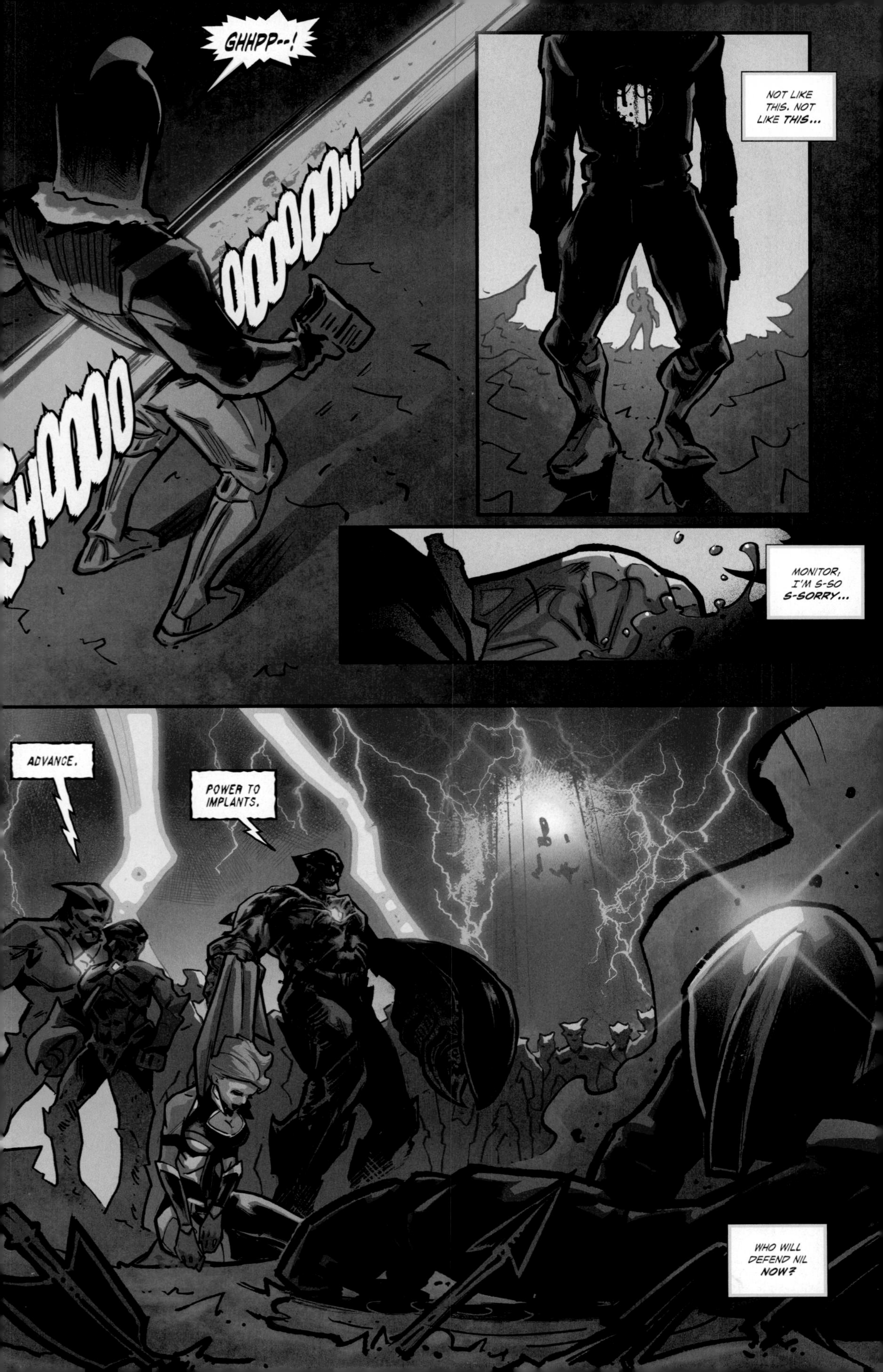
GHHPP--!
SHOOOO
OOOOOOM
NOT LIKE THIS. NOT LIKE THIS...
MONITOR, I'M S-SO S-SORRY...
ADVANCE.
POWER TO IMPLANTS.
WHO WILL DEFEND NIL NOW?

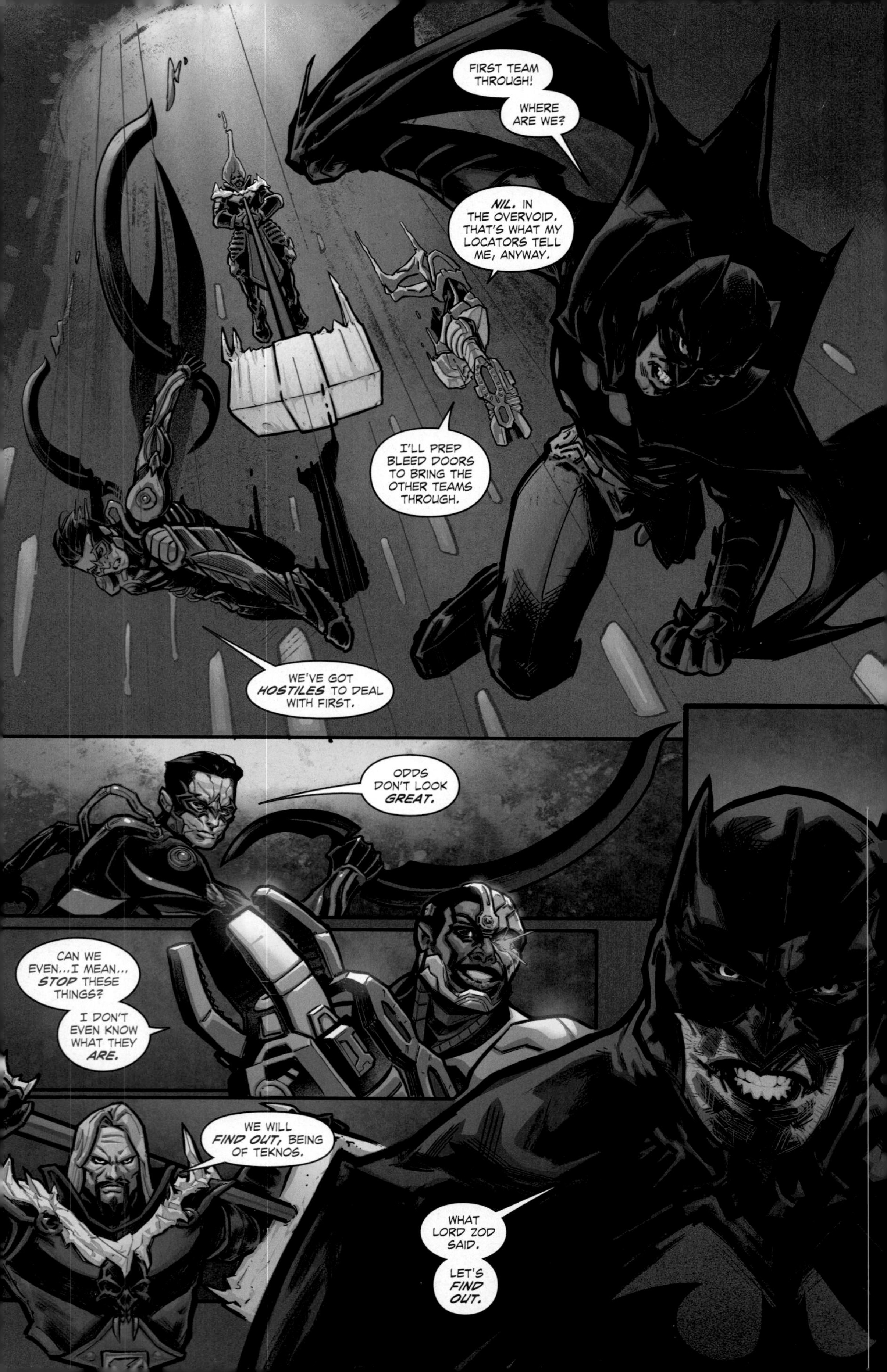
FIRST TEAM THROUGH!
WHERE ARE WE?
NIL. IN THE OVERVOID. THAT'S WHAT MY LOCATORS TELL ME, ANYWAY.
I'LL PREP BLEED DOORS TO BRING THE OTHER TEAMS THROUGH.
WE'VE GOT HOSTILES TO DEAL WITH FIRST.
ODDS DON'T LOOK GREAT.
CAN WE EVEN...I MEAN... STOP THESE THINGS?
I DON'T EVEN KNOW WHAT THEY ARE.
WE WILL FIND OUT, BEING OF TEKNOS.
WHAT LORD ZOD SAID.
LET'S FIND OUT.

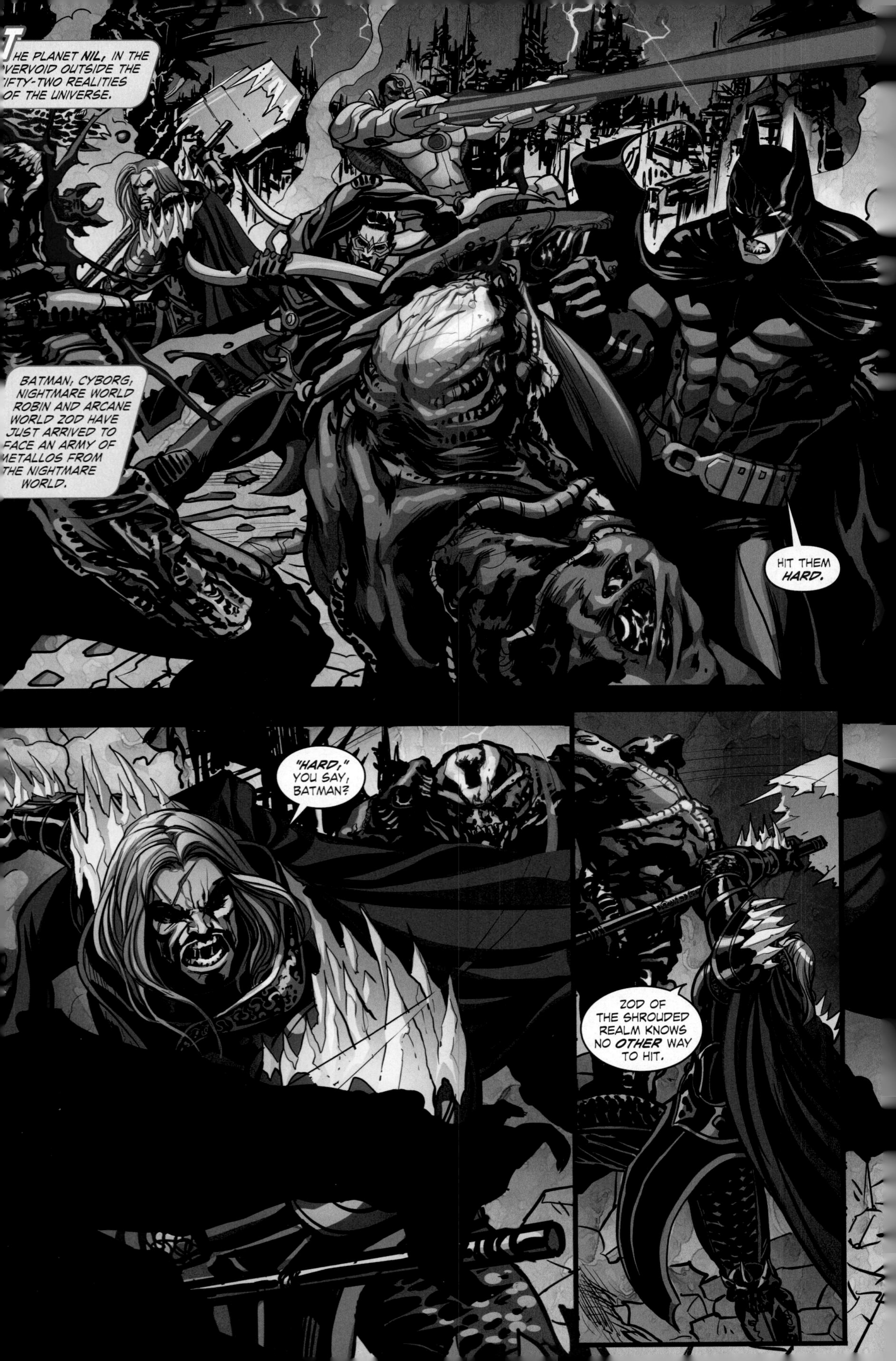
THE PLANET NIL, IN THE OVERVOID OUTSIDE THE FIFTY-TWO REALITIES OF THE UNIVERSE.
BATMAN, CYBORG, NIGHTMARE WORLD ROBIN AND ARCANE WORLD ZOD HAVE JUST ARRIVED TO FACE AN ARMY OF METALLOS FROM THE NIGHTMARE WORLD.
HIT THEM HARD.
"HARD," YOU SAY, BATMAN?
ZOD OF THE SHROUDED REALM KNOWS NO OTHER WAY TO HIT.

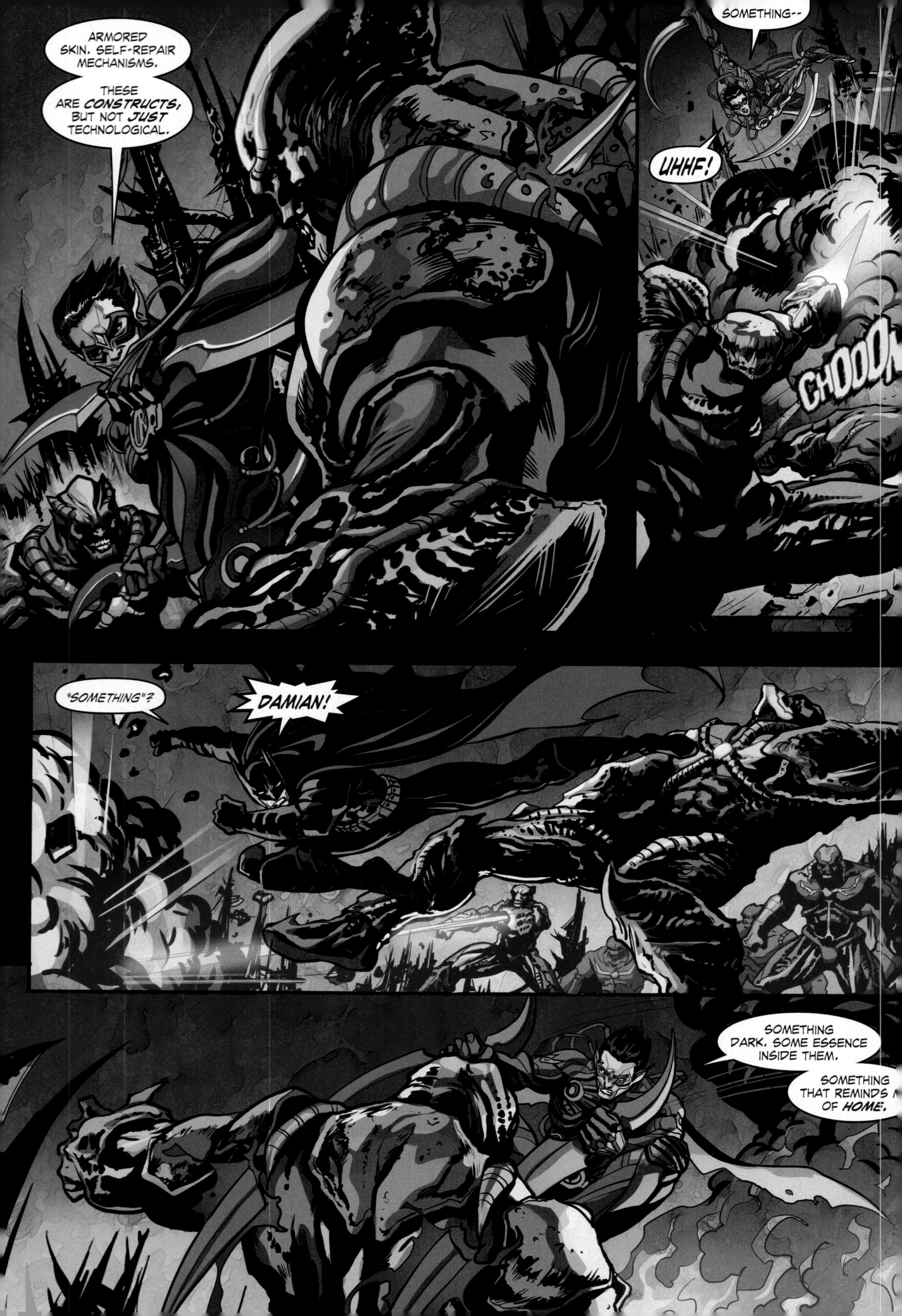
ARMORED SKIN. SELF-REPAIR MECHANISMS.
THESE ARE CONSTRUCTS, BUT NOT JUST TECHNOLOGICAL.
SOMETHING--
UHHF!
CHOOOM
"SOMETHING"?
DAMIAN!
SOMETHING DARK. SOME ESSENCE INSIDE THEM.
SOMETHING THAT REMINDS OF HOME.

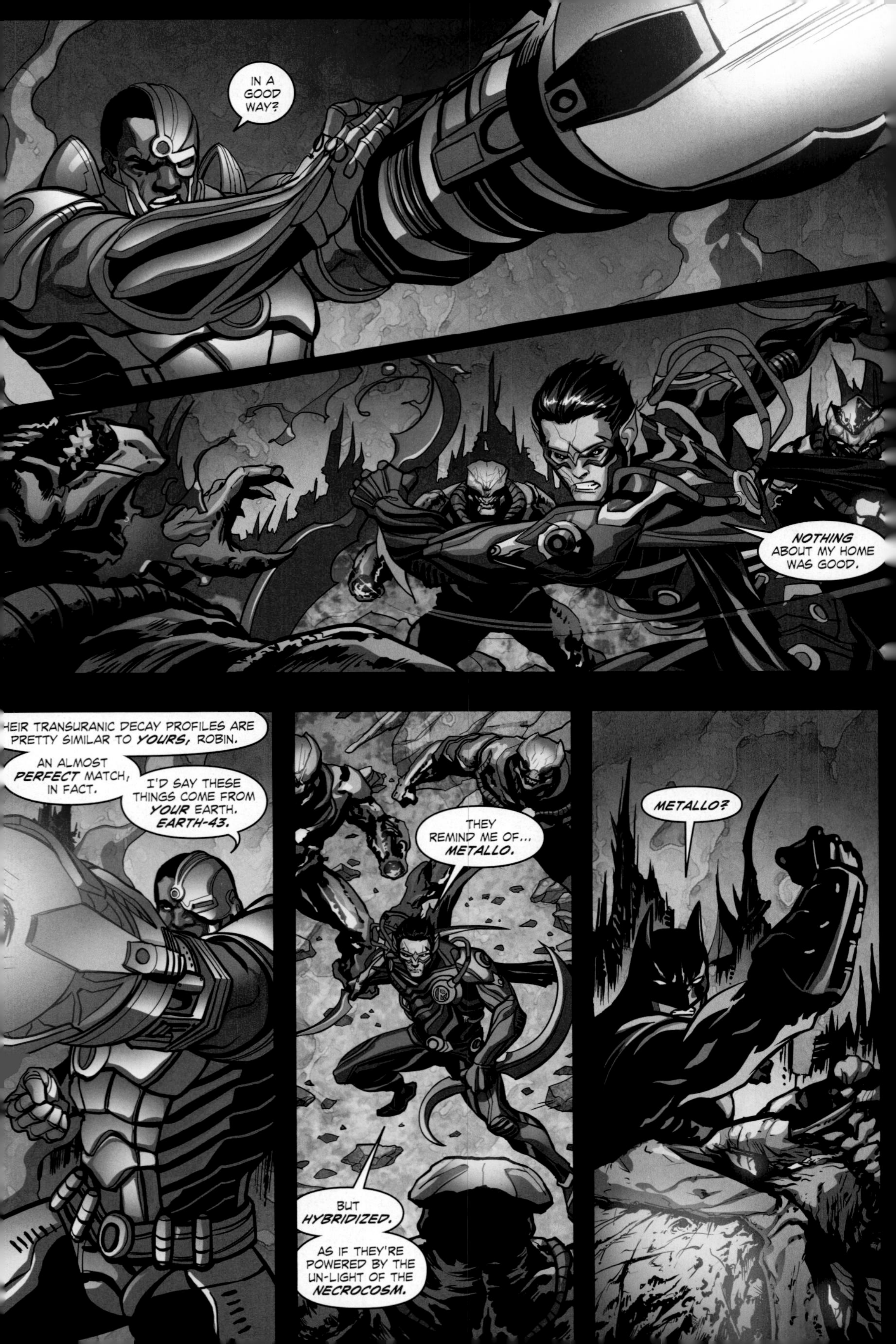
IN A GOOD WAY?
NOTHING ABOUT MY HOME WAS GOOD.
HEIR TRANSURANIC DECAY PROFILES ARE PRETTY SIMILAR TO YOURS, ROBIN.
AN ALMOST PERFECT MATCH, IN FACT.
I'D SAY THESE THINGS COME FROM YOUR EARTH. EARTH-43.
THEY REMIND ME OF... METALLO.
BUT HYBRIDIZED.
AS IF THEY'RE POWERED BY THE UN-LIGHT OF THE NECROCOSM.
METALLO?

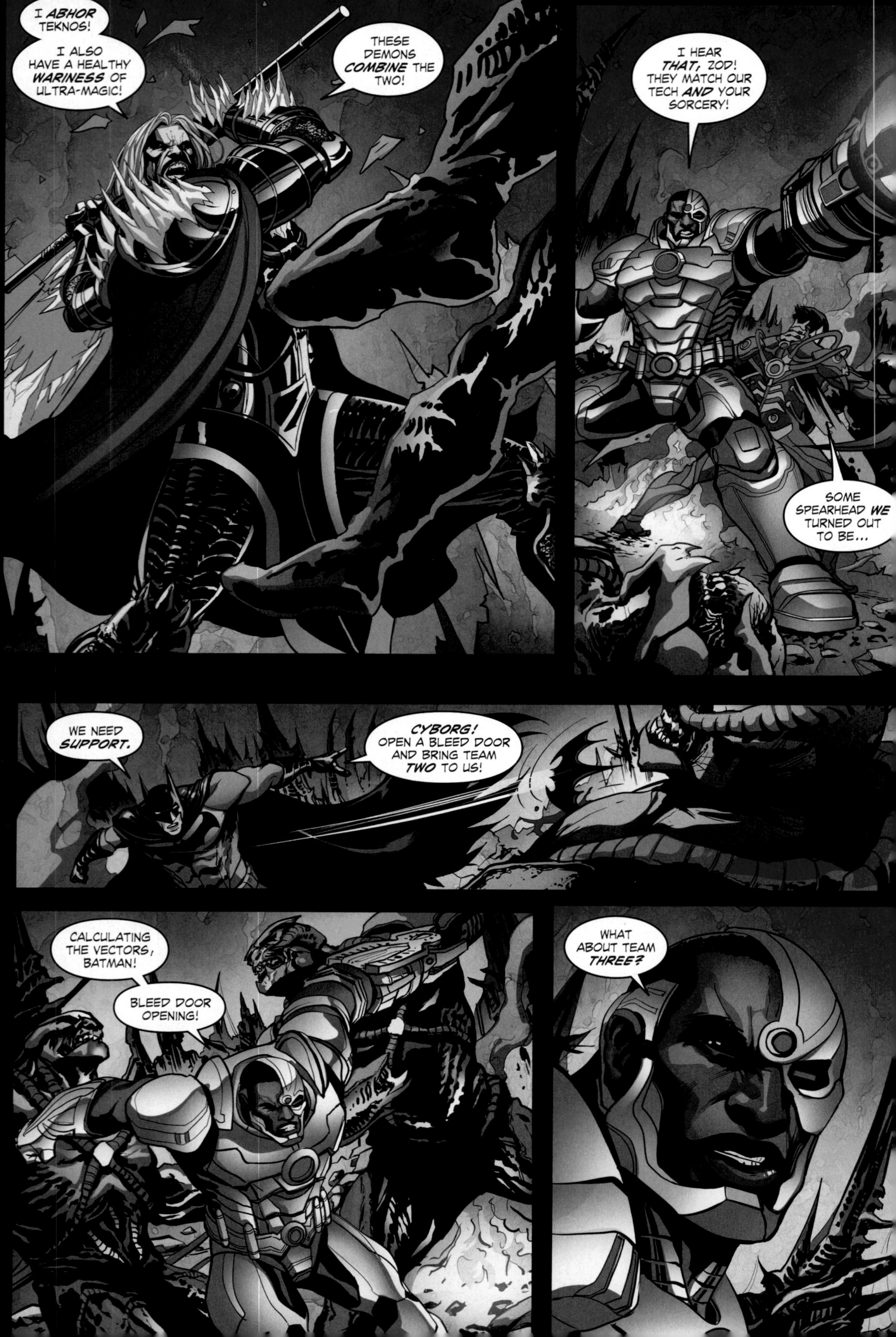
I ABHOR TEKNOS!
I ALSO HAVE A HEALTHY WARINESS OF ULTRA-MAGIC!
THESE DEMONS COMBINE THE TWO!
I HEAR THAT, ZOD! THEY MATCH OUR TECH AND YOUR SORCERY!
SOME SPEARHEAD WE TURNED OUT TO BE...
WE NEED SUPPORT.
CYBORG! OPEN A BLEED DOOR AND BRING TEAM TWO TO US!
CALCULATING THE VECTORS, BATMAN!
BLEED DOOR OPENING!
WHAT ABOUT TEAM THREE?

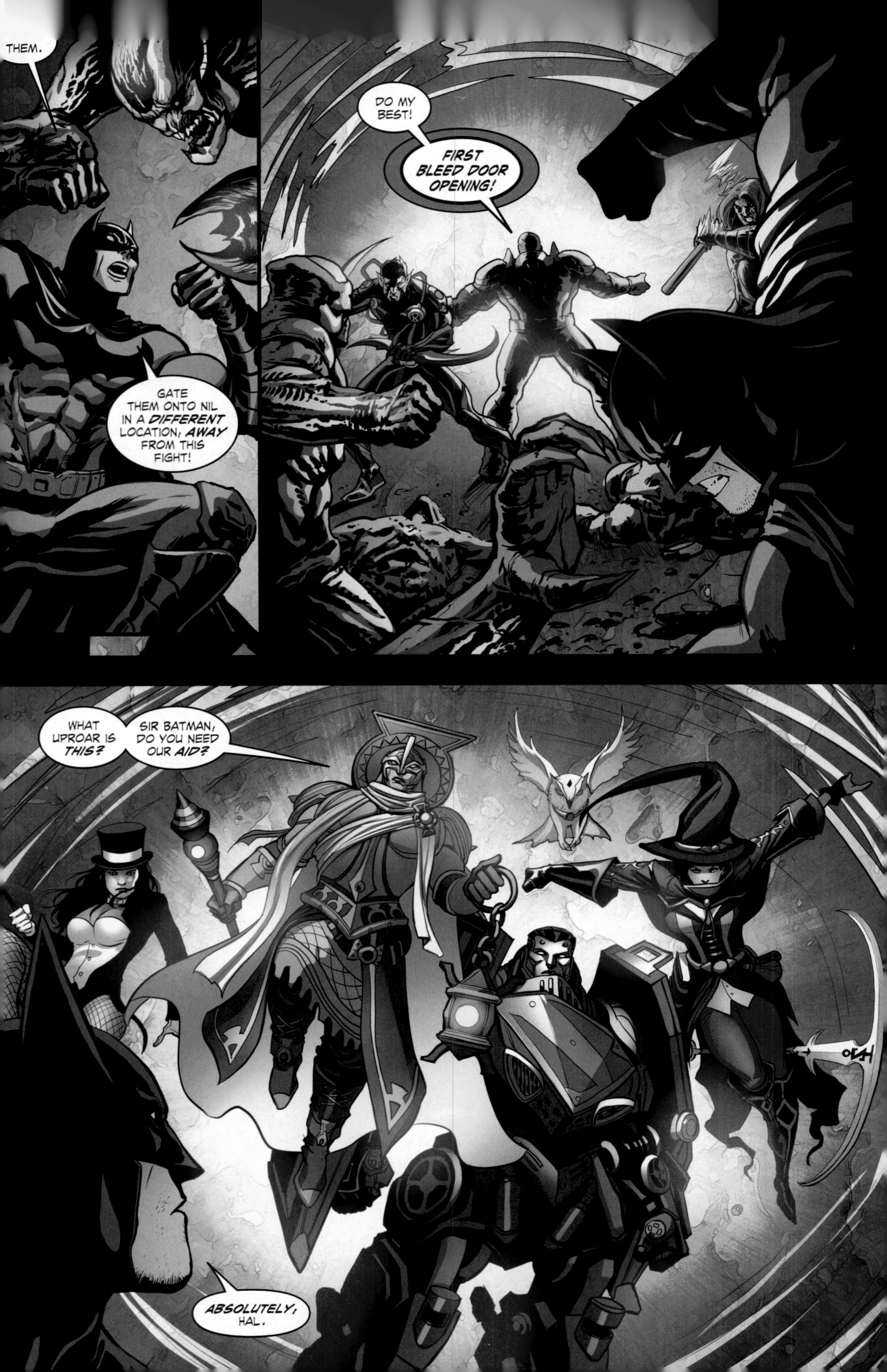
THEM.
DO MY BEST!
FIRST BLEED DOOR OPENING!
GATE THEM ONTO NIL IN A DIFFERENT LOCATION, AWAY FROM THIS FIGHT!
WHAT UPROAR IS THIS?
SIR BATMAN, DO YOU NEED OUR AID?
ABSOLUTELY, HAL.

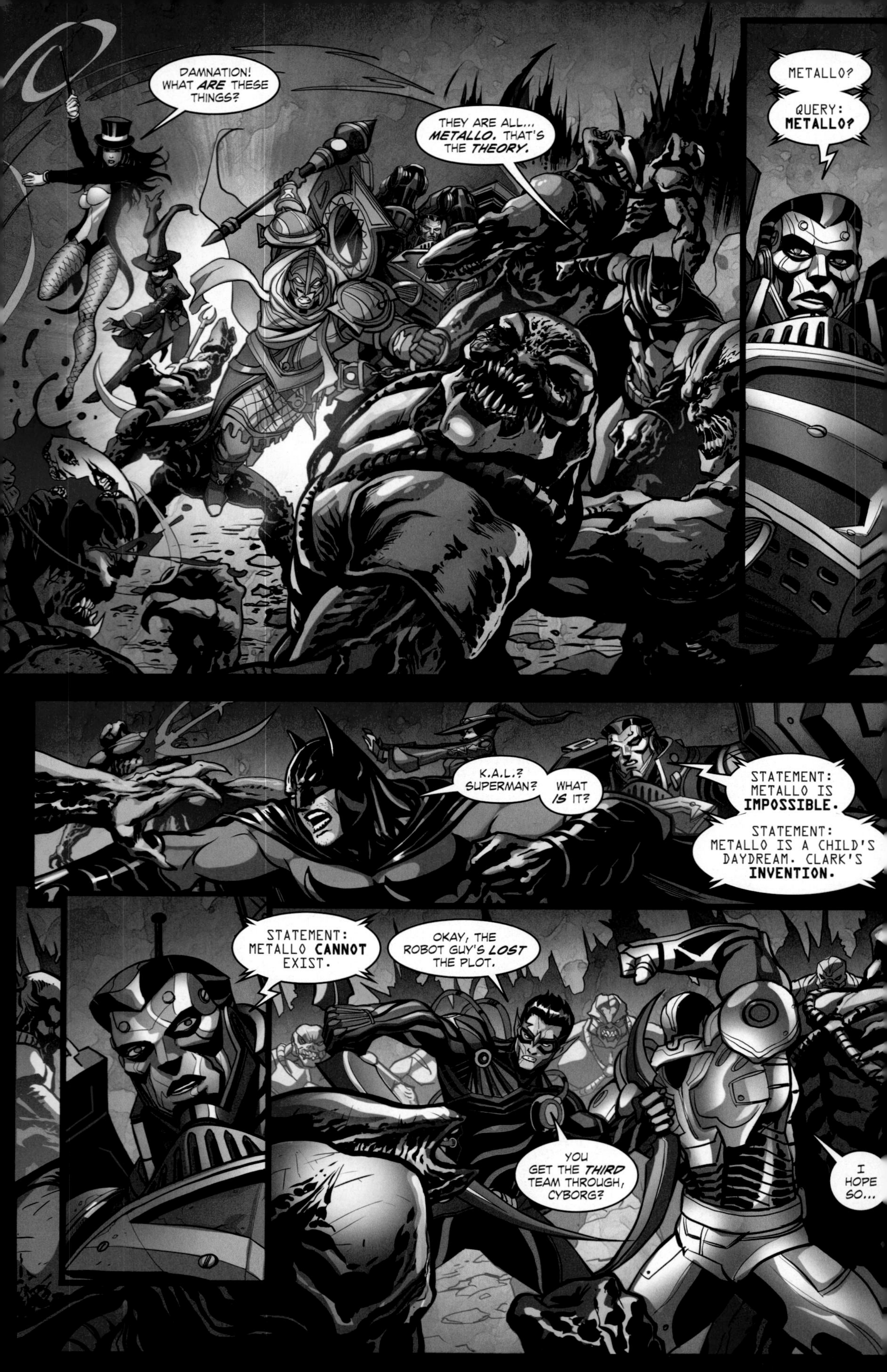
DAMNATION! WHAT ARE THESE THINGS?
THEY ARE ALL... METALLO. THAT'S THE THEORY.
METALLO?
QUERY: METALLO?
K.A.L.? SUPERMAN?
WHAT IS IT?
STATEMENT: METALLO IS IMPOSSIBLE.
STATEMENT: METALLO IS A CHILD'S DAYDREAM. CLARK'S INVENTION.
STATEMENT: METALLO CANNOT EXIST.
OKAY, THE ROBOT GUY'S LOST THE PLOT.
YOU GET THE THIRD TEAM THROUGH, CYBORG?
I HOPE SO...

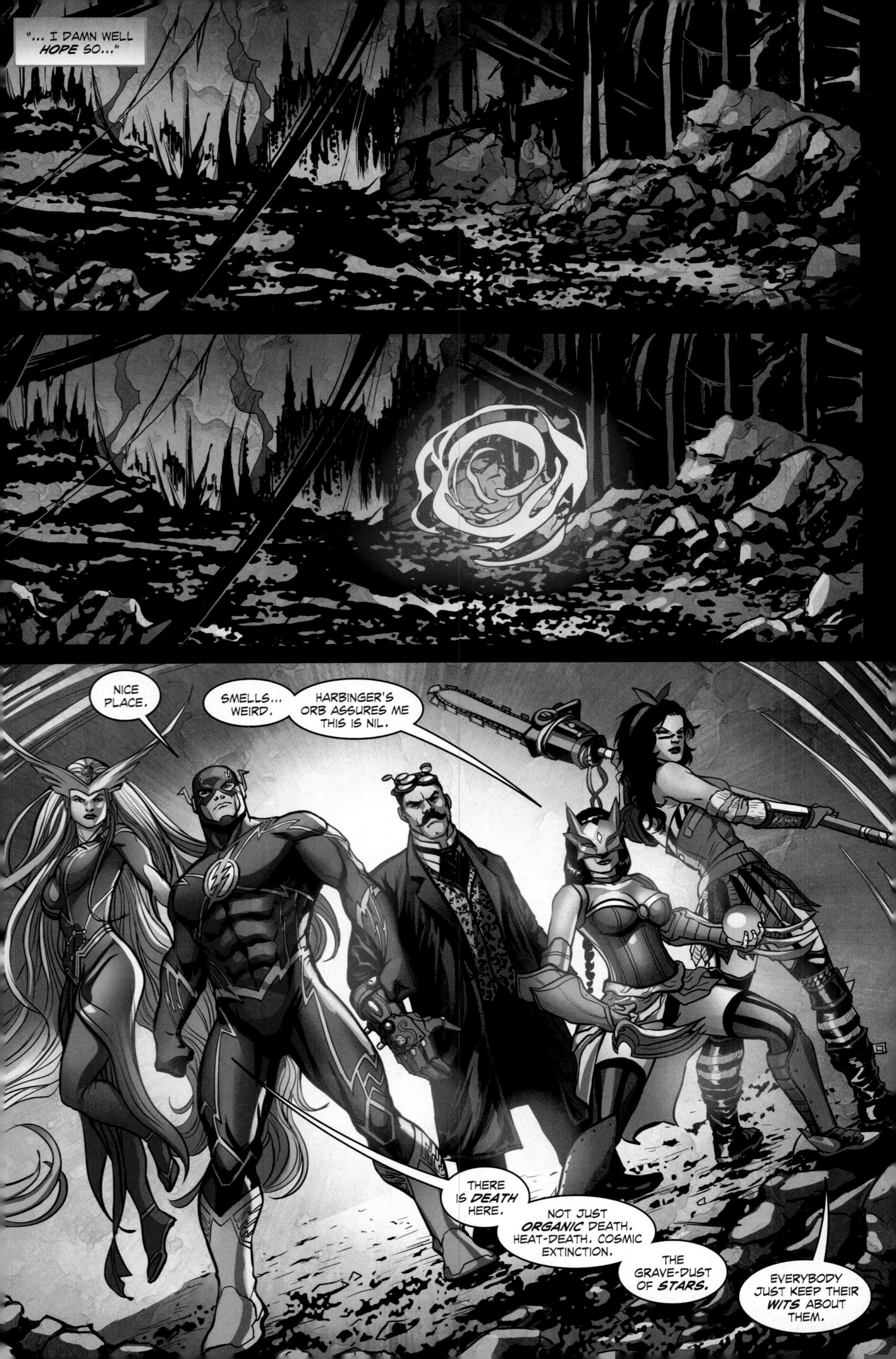
"... I DAMN WELL HOPE SO..."
NICE PLACE.
SMELLS... WEIRD.
HARBINGER'S ORB ASSURES ME THIS IS NIL.
THERE IS DEATH HERE.
NOT JUST ORGANIC DEATH. HEAT-DEATH. COSMIC EXTINCTION.
THE GRAVE-DUST OF STARS.
EVERYBODY JUST KEEP THEIR WITS ABOUT THEM.

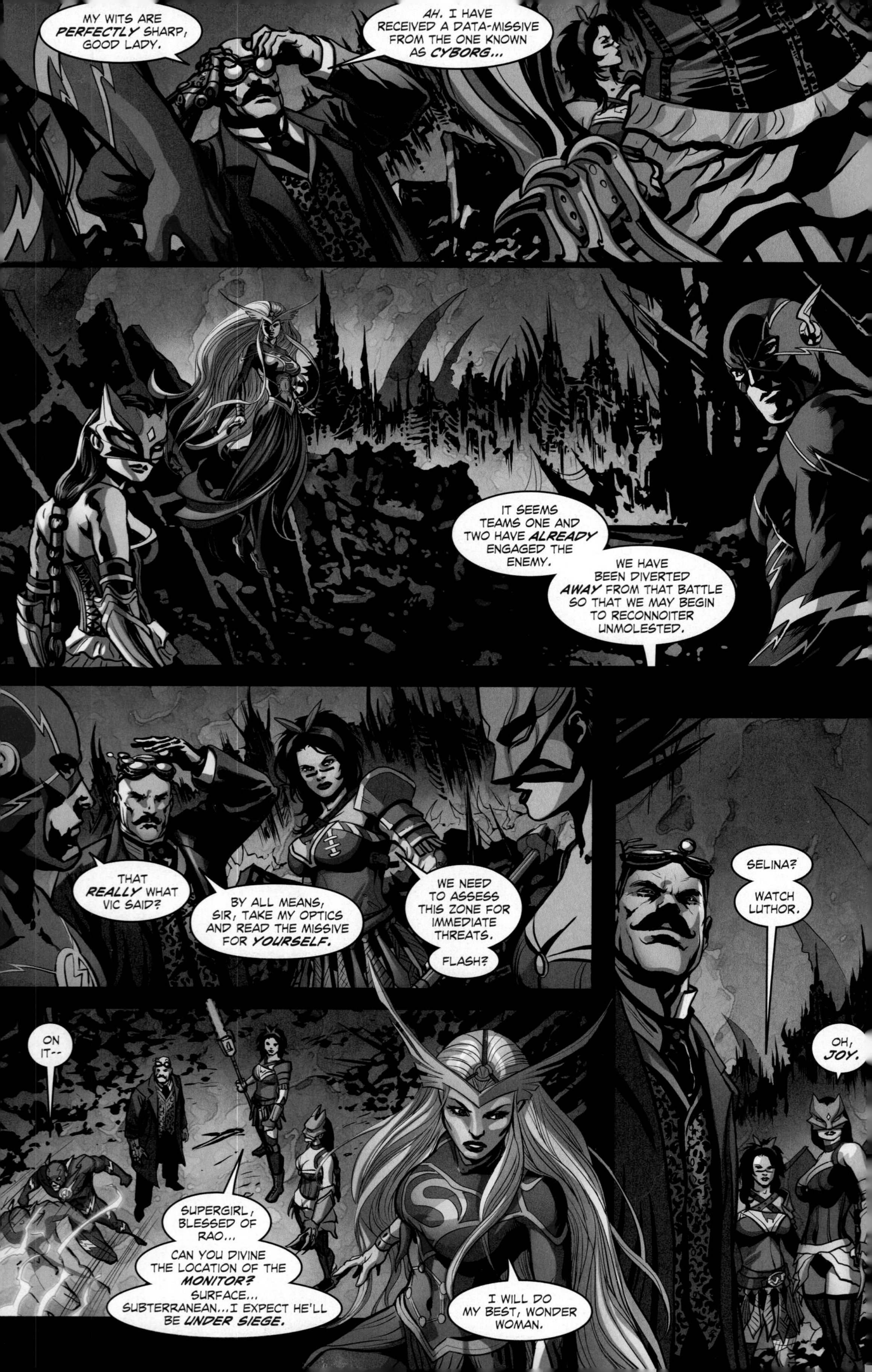
MY WITS ARE PERFECTLY SHARP, GOOD LADY.
AH. I HAVE RECEIVED A DATA-MISSIVE FROM THE ONE KNOWN AS CYBORG...
IT SEEMS TEAMS ONE AND TWO HAVE ALREADY ENGAGED THE ENEMY.
WE HAVE BEEN DIVERTED AWAY FROM THAT BATTLE SO THAT WE MAY BEGIN TO RECONNOITER UNMOLESTED.
THAT REALLY WHAT VIC SAID?
BY ALL MEANS, SIR, TAKE MY OPTICS AND READ THE MISSIVE FOR YOURSELF.
WE NEED TO ASSESS THIS ZONE FOR IMMEDIATE THREATS.
FLASH?
SELINA?
WATCH LUTHOR.
ON IT--
OH, JOY.
SUPERGIRL, BLESSED OF RAO...
CAN YOU DIVINE THE LOCATION OF THE MONITOR? SURFACE... SUBTERRANEAN...I EXPECT HE'LL BE UNDER SIEGE.
I WILL DO MY BEST, WONDER WOMAN.

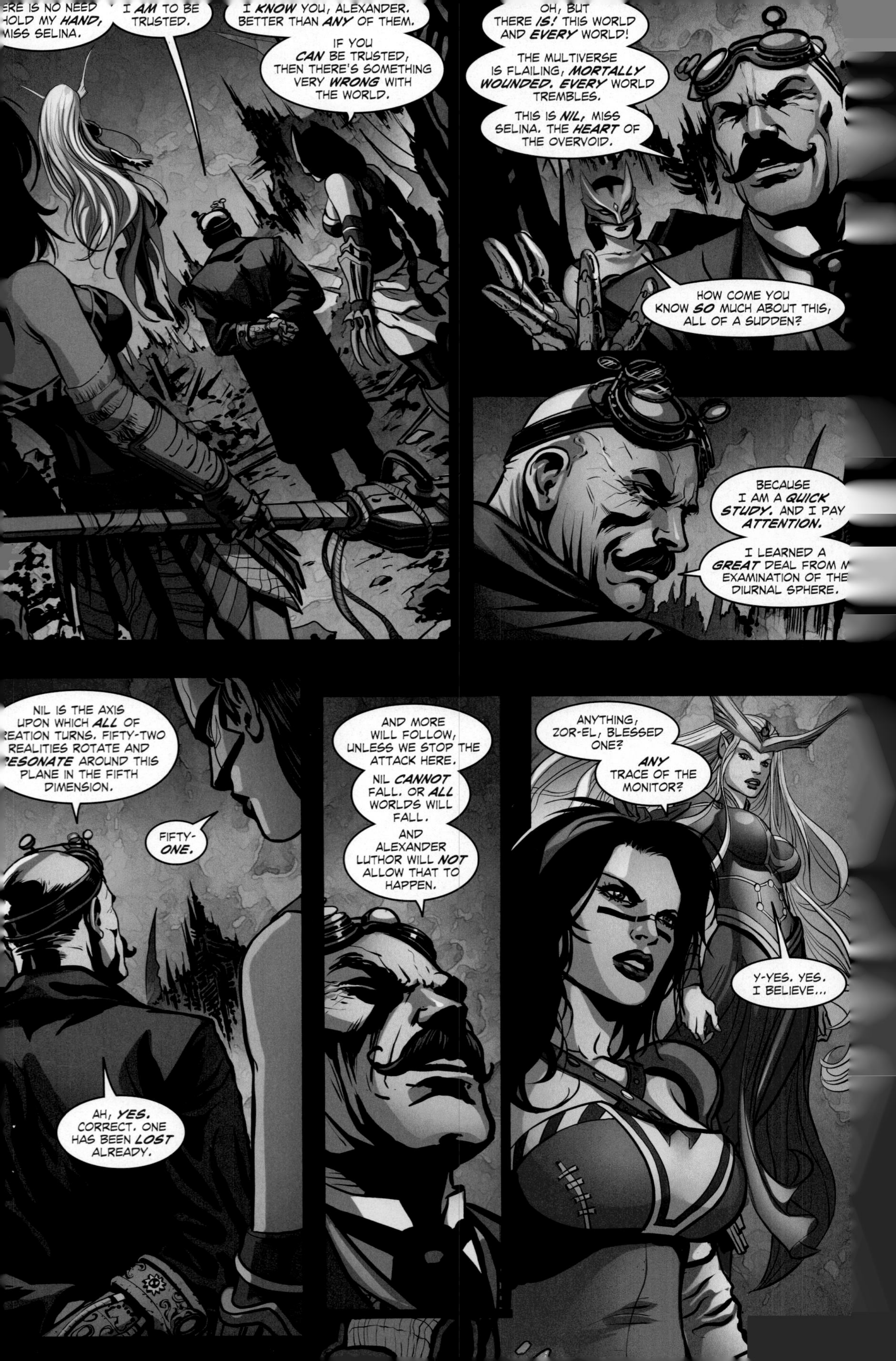

ERE IS NO NEED
HOLD MY HAND,
MISS SELINA.
I AM TO BE TRUSTED.
I KNOW YOU, ALEXANDER. BETTER THAN ANY OF THEM.
IF YOU CAN BE TRUSTED, THEN THERE'S SOMETHING VERY WRONG WITH THE WORLD.
OH, BUT THERE IS! THIS WORLD AND EVERY WORLD!
THE MULTIVERSE IS FLAILING, MORTALLY WOUNDED. EVERY WORLD TREMBLES.
THIS IS NIL, MISS SELINA. THE HEART OF THE OVERVOID.
HOW COME YOU KNOW SO MUCH ABOUT THIS, ALL OF A SUDDEN?
BECAUSE I AM A QUICK STUDY. AND I PAY ATTENTION.
I LEARNED A GREAT DEAL FROM M
EXAMINATION OF THE
DIURNAL SPHERE.
NIL IS THE AXIS UPON WHICH ALL OF
REATION TURNS. FIFTY-TWO REALITIES ROTATE AND
ESONATE AROUND THIS PLANE IN THE FIFTH DIMENSION.
FIFTY-ONE.
AH, YES. CORRECT. ONE HAS BEEN LOST ALREADY.
AND MORE WILL FOLLOW, UNLESS WE STOP THE ATTACK HERE.
NIL CANNOT FALL. OR ALL WORLDS WILL FALL.
AND ALEXANDER LUTHOR WILL NOT ALLOW THAT TO HAPPEN.
ANYTHING, ZOR-EL, BLESSED ONE?
ANY TRACE OF THE MONITOR?
Y-YES. YES. I BELIEVE...

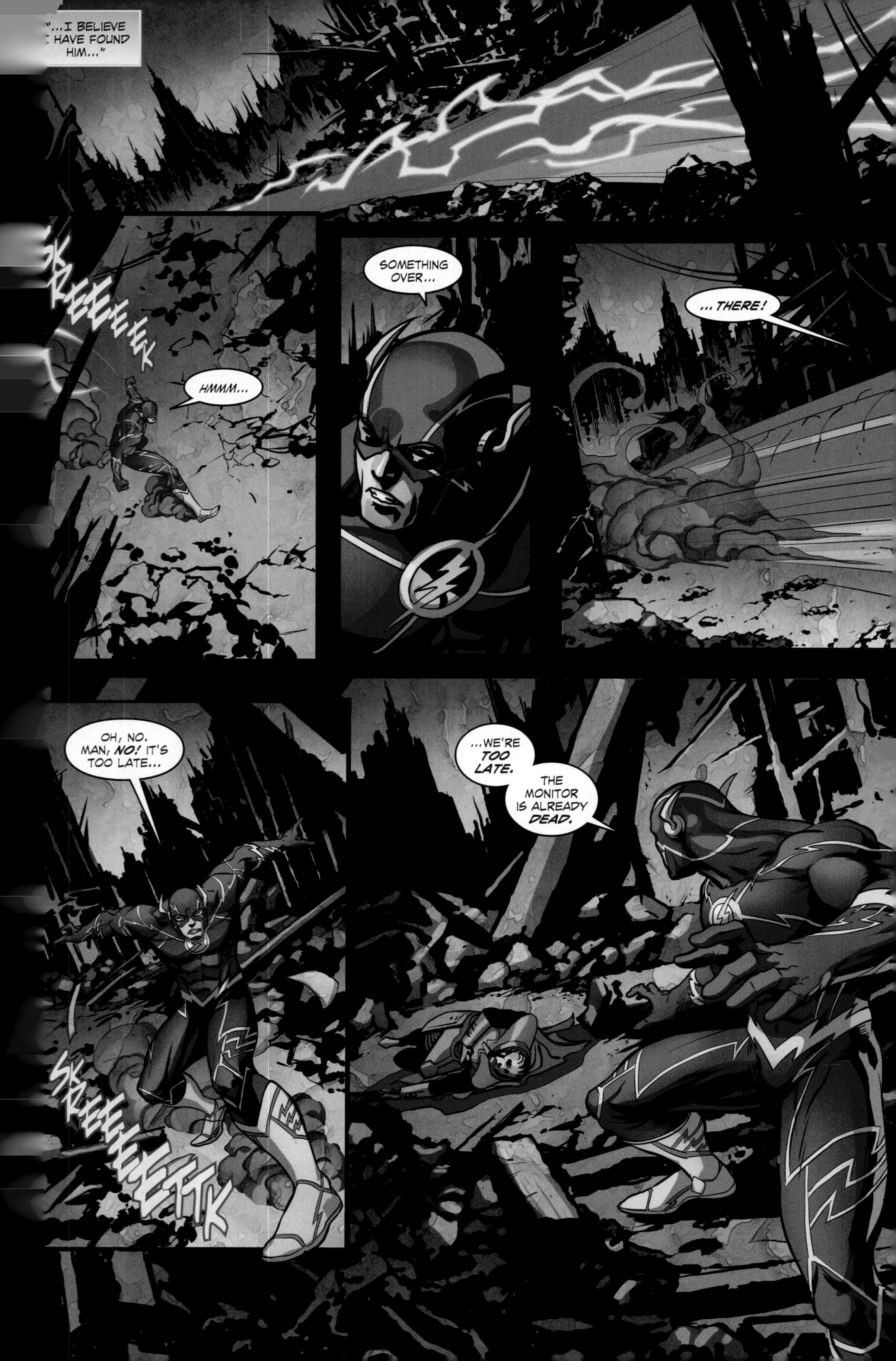
"...I BELIEVE
HAVE FOUND
HIM..."
KREEEEEK
HMMM...
SOMETHING OVER...
...THERE!
OH, NO. MAN, NO! IT'S TOO LATE...
SKREEEEEETTK
...WE'RE TOO LATE.
THE MONITOR IS ALREADY DEAD.

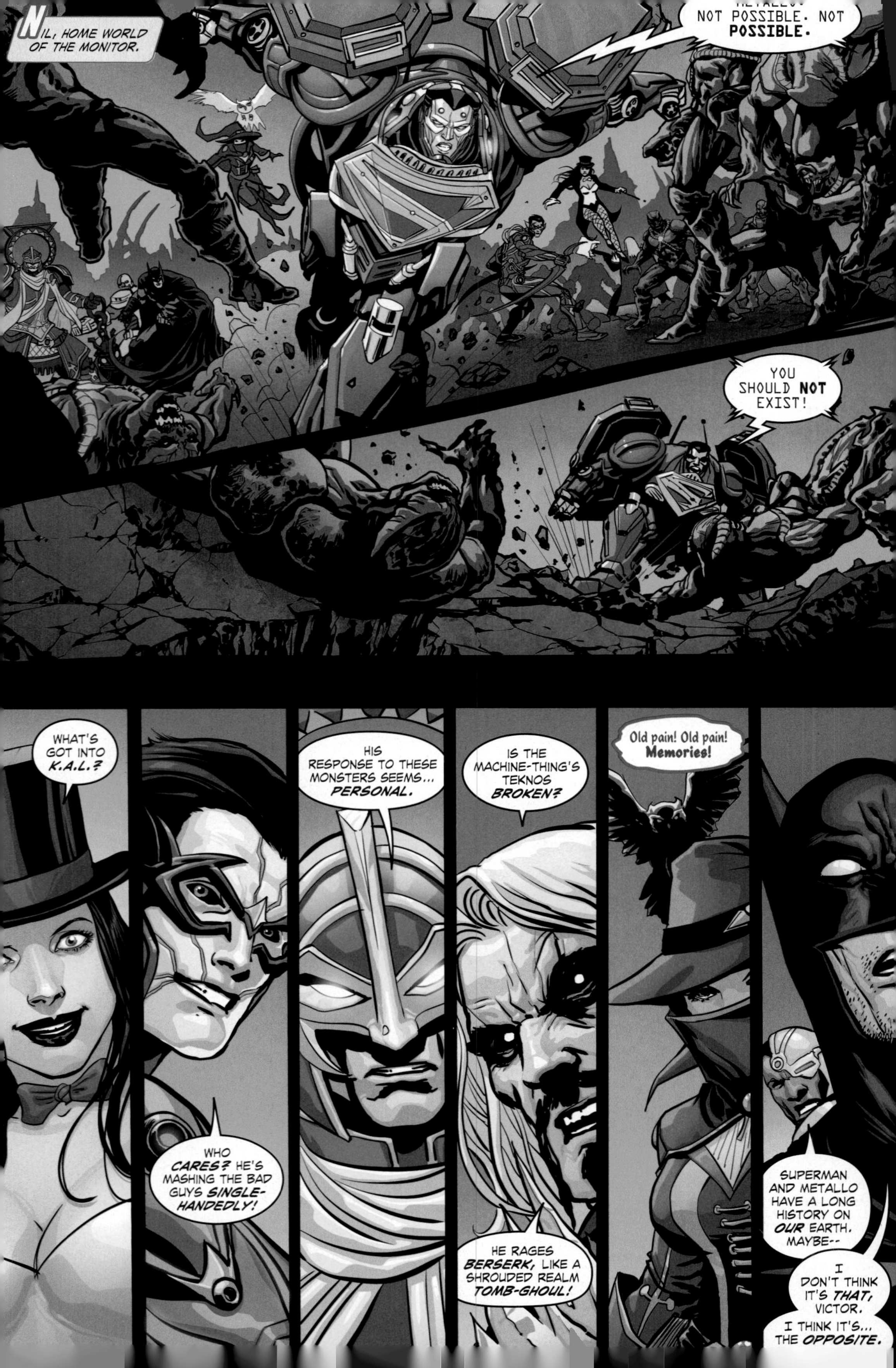
NIL, HOME WORLD OF THE MONITOR.
NOT POSSIBLE. NOT POSSIBLE.
YOU SHOULD NOT EXIST!
WHAT'S GOT INTO K.A.L.?
WHO CARES? HE'S MASHING THE BAD GUYS SINGLE-HANDEDLY!
HIS RESPONSE TO THESE MONSTERS SEEMS... PERSONAL.
IS THE MACHINE-THING'S TEKNOS BROKEN?
HE RAGES BERSERK, LIKE A SHROUDED REALM TOMB-GHOUL!
Old pain! Old pain! Memories!
SUPERMAN AND METALLO HAVE A LONG HISTORY ON OUR EARTH. MAYBE--
I DON'T THINK IT'S THAT, VICTOR.
I THINK IT'S... THE OPPOSITE.

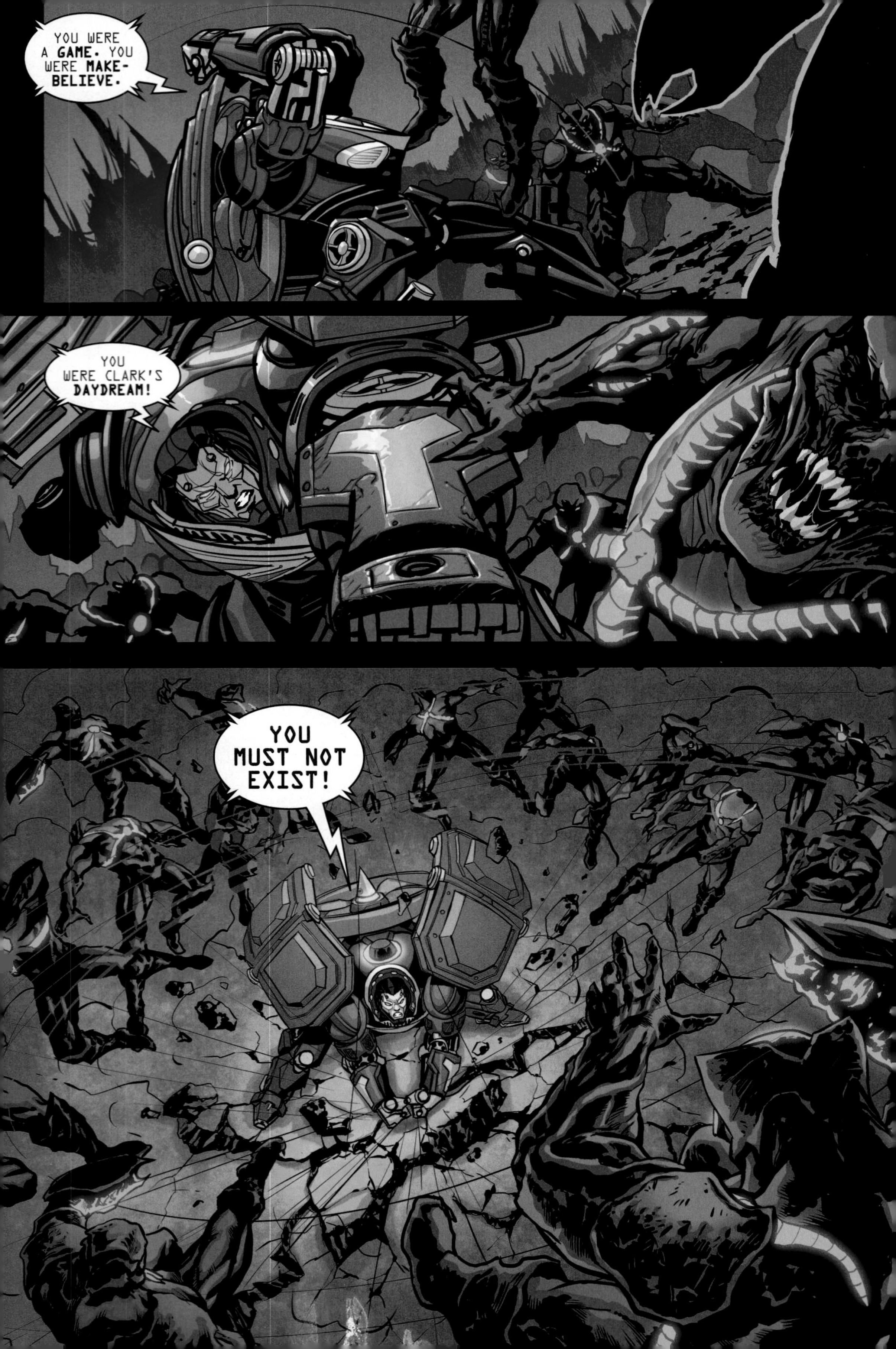
YOU WERE A GAME. YOU WERE MAKE-BELIEVE.
YOU WERE CLARK'S DAYDREAM!
YOU MUST NOT EXIST!

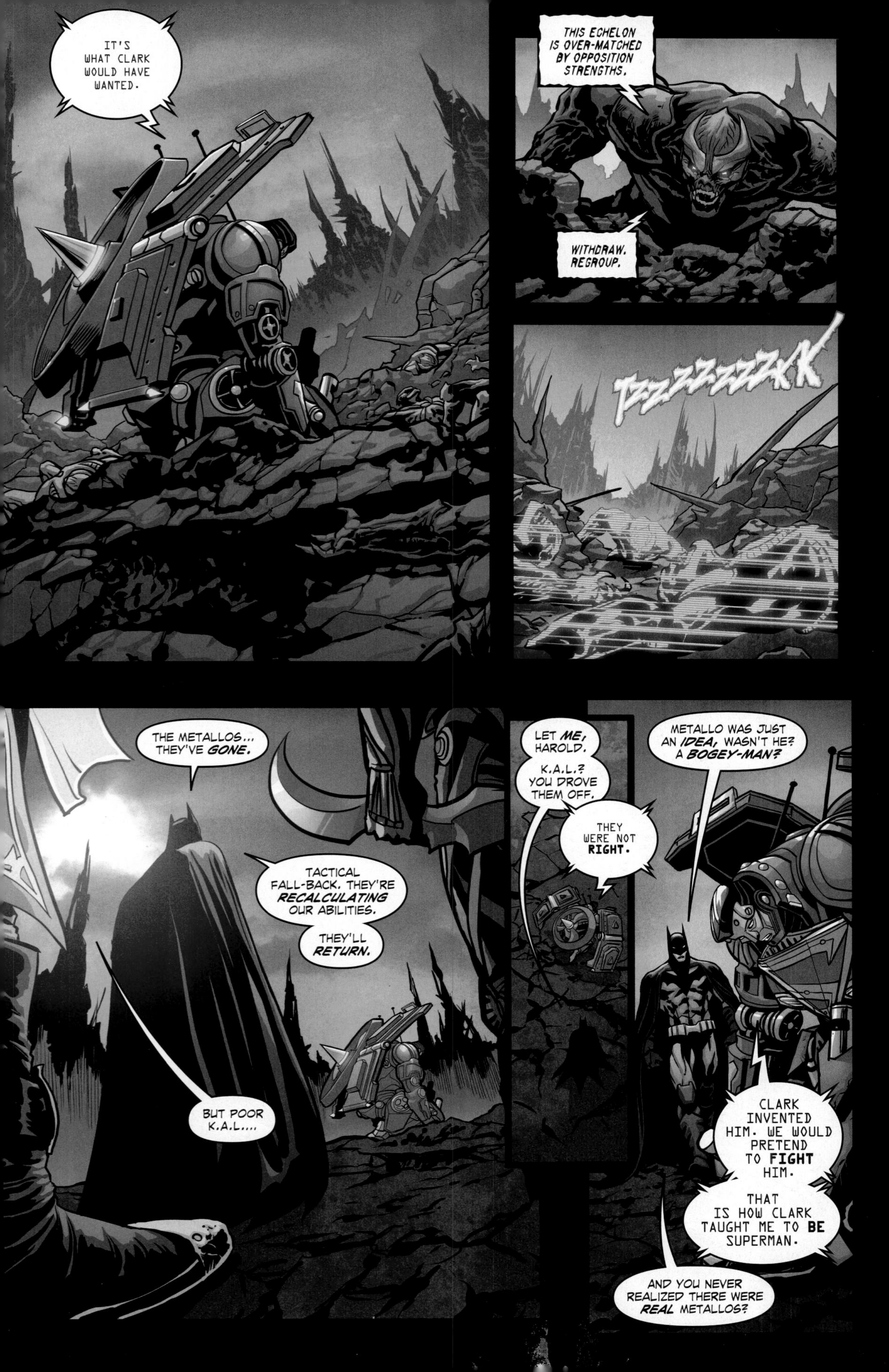
IT'S WHAT CLARK WOULD HAVE WANTED.
THIS ECHELON IS OVER-MATCHED BY OPPOSITION STRENGTHS.
WITHDRAW. REGROUP.
TZZZZZZZKK
THE METALLOS... THEY'VE GONE.
TACTICAL FALL-BACK. THEY'RE RECALCULATING OUR ABILITIES.
THEY'LL RETURN.
BUT POOR K.A.L....
LET ME, HAROLD.
K.A.L.? YOU DROVE THEM OFF.
THEY WERE NOT RIGHT.
METALLO WAS JUST AN IDEA, WASN'T HE? A BOGEY-MAN?
CLARK INVENTED HIM. WE WOULD PRETEND TO FIGHT HIM.
THAT IS HOW CLARK TAUGHT ME TO BE SUPERMAN.
AND YOU NEVER REALIZED THERE WERE REAL METALLOS?

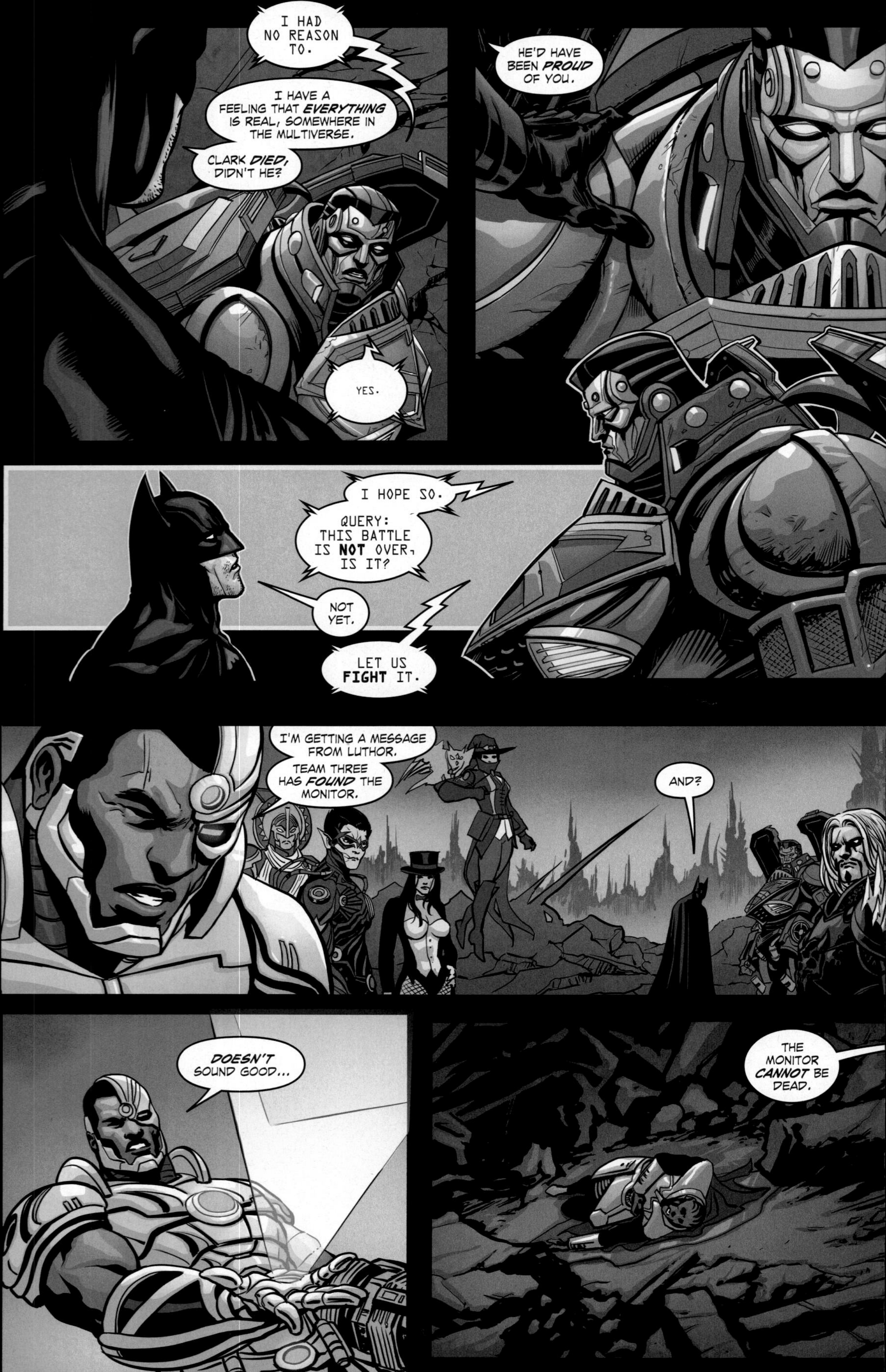
I HAD NO REASON TO.
I HAVE A FEELING THAT EVERYTHING IS REAL, SOMEWHERE IN THE MULTIVERSE.
CLARK DIED, DIDN'T HE?
YES.
HE'D HAVE BEEN PROUD OF YOU.
I HOPE SO.
QUERY: THIS BATTLE IS NOT OVER, IS IT?
NOT YET.
LET US FIGHT IT.
I'M GETTING A MESSAGE FROM LUTHOR.
TEAM THREE HAS FOUND THE MONITOR.
AND?
DOESN'T SOUND GOOD...
THE MONITOR CANNOT BE DEAD.

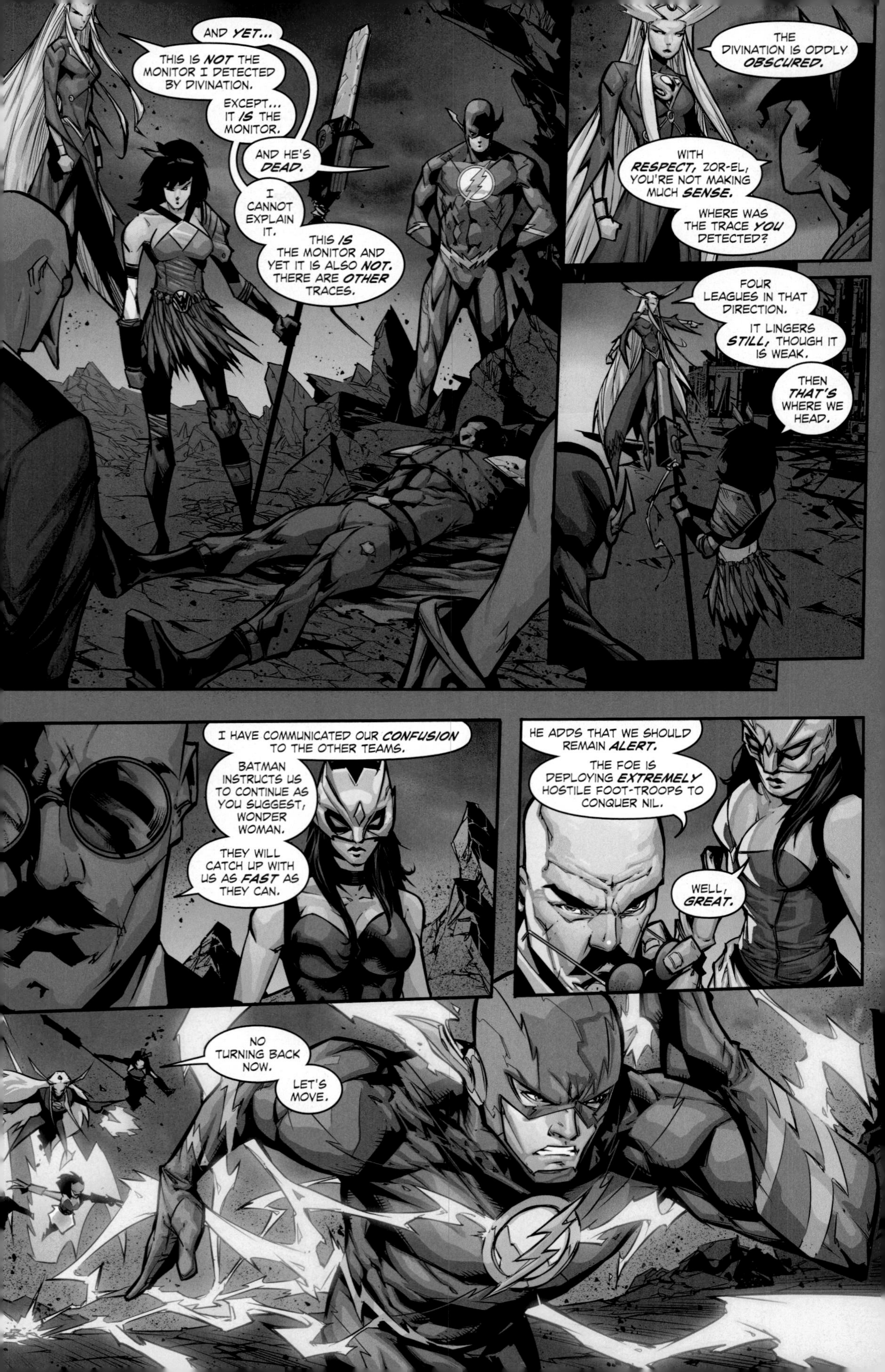
AND *YET...*
THIS IS *NOT* THE MONITOR I DETECTED BY DIVINATION.
EXCEPT... IT *IS* THE MONITOR.
AND HE'S *DEAD.*
I CANNOT EXPLAIN IT.
THIS *IS* THE MONITOR AND YET IT IS ALSO *NOT.* THERE ARE *OTHER* TRACES.
THE DIVINATION IS ODDLY *OBSCURED.*
WITH *RESPECT,* ZOR-EL, YOU'RE NOT MAKING MUCH *SENSE.*
WHERE WAS THE TRACE *YOU* DETECTED?
FOUR LEAGUES IN THAT DIRECTION.
IT LINGERS *STILL,* THOUGH IT IS WEAK.
THEN *THAT'S* WHERE WE HEAD.
I HAVE COMMUNICATED OUR *CONFUSION* TO THE OTHER TEAMS.
BATMAN INSTRUCTS US TO CONTINUE AS YOU SUGGEST, WONDER WOMAN.
THEY WILL CATCH UP WITH US AS *FAST* AS THEY CAN.
HE ADDS THAT WE SHOULD REMAIN *ALERT.*
THE FOE IS DEPLOYING *EXTREMELY* HOSTILE FOOT-TROOPS TO CONQUER NIL.
WELL, *GREAT.*
NO TURNING BACK NOW.
LET'S MOVE.

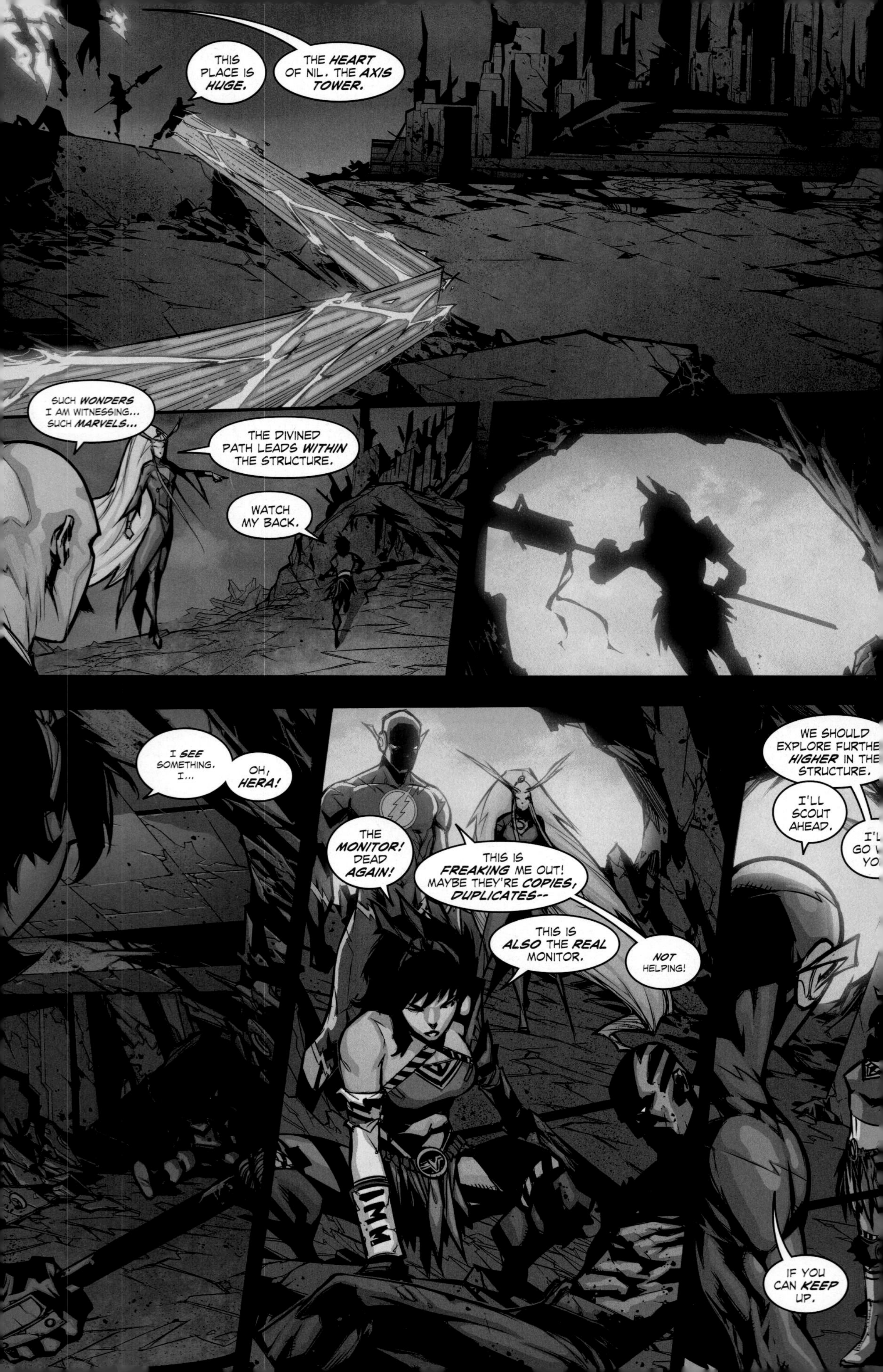

THIS PLACE IS HUGE.
THE HEART OF NIL. THE AXIS TOWER.
SUCH WONDERS I AM WITNESSING... SUCH MARVELS...
THE DIVINED PATH LEADS WITHIN THE STRUCTURE.
WATCH MY BACK.
I SEE SOMETHING. I...
OH, HERA!
THE MONITOR! DEAD AGAIN!
THIS IS FREAKING ME OUT! MAYBE THEY'RE COPIES, DUPLICATES--
THIS IS ALSO THE REAL MONITOR.
NOT HELPING!
WE SHOULD EXPLORE FURTHE HIGHER IN THE STRUCTURE.
I'LL SCOUT AHEAD.
IF YOU CAN KEEP UP.

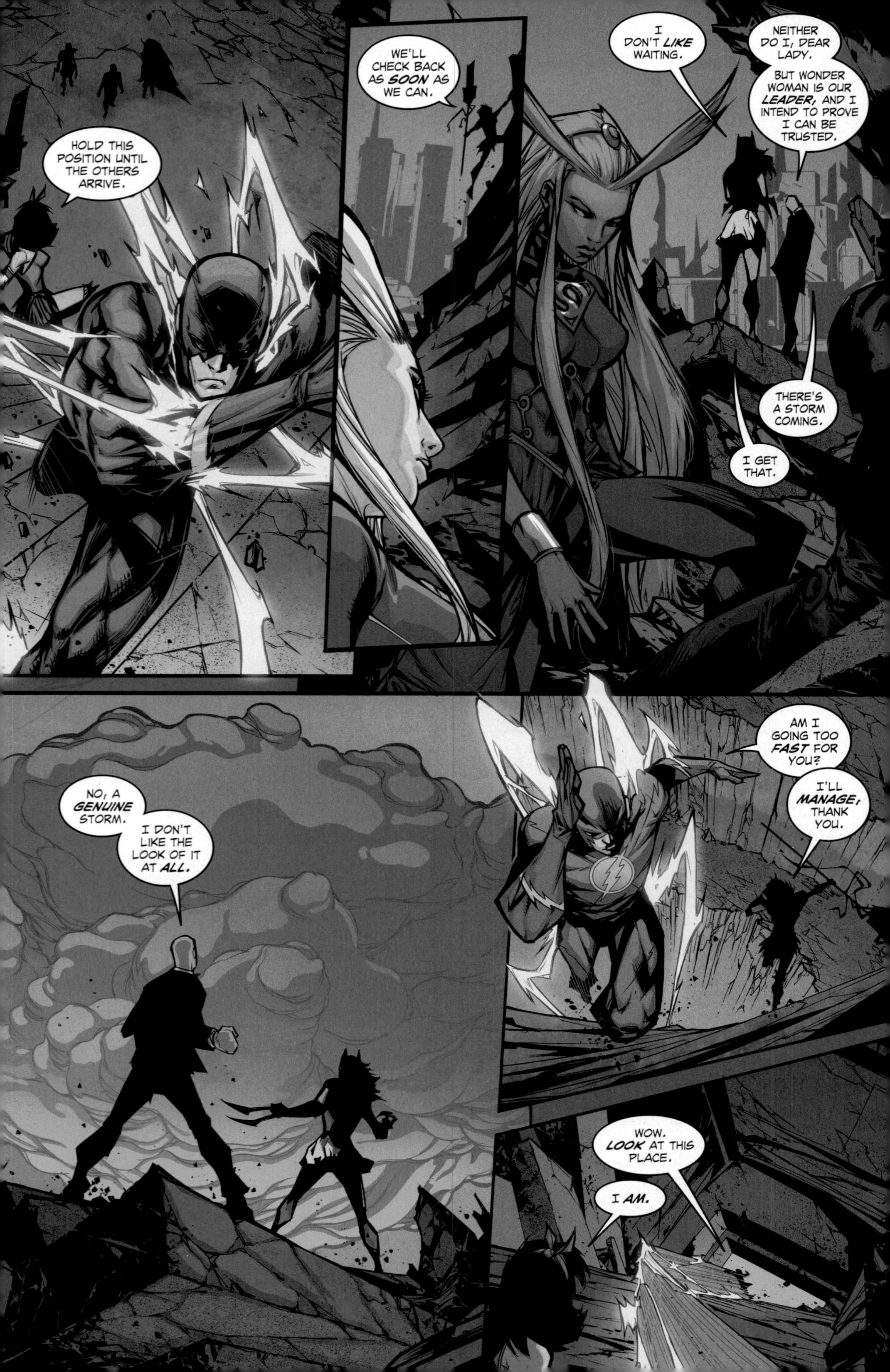
HOLD THIS POSITION UNTIL THE OTHERS ARRIVE.
WE'LL CHECK BACK AS SOON AS WE CAN.
I DON'T LIKE WAITING.
NEITHER DO I, DEAR LADY.
BUT WONDER WOMAN IS OUR LEADER, AND I INTEND TO PROVE I CAN BE TRUSTED.
THERE'S A STORM COMING.
I GET THAT.
NO, A GENUINE STORM.
I DON'T LIKE THE LOOK OF IT AT ALL.
AM I GOING TOO FAST FOR YOU?
I'LL MANAGE, THANK YOU.
WOW. LOOK AT THIS PLACE.
I AM.

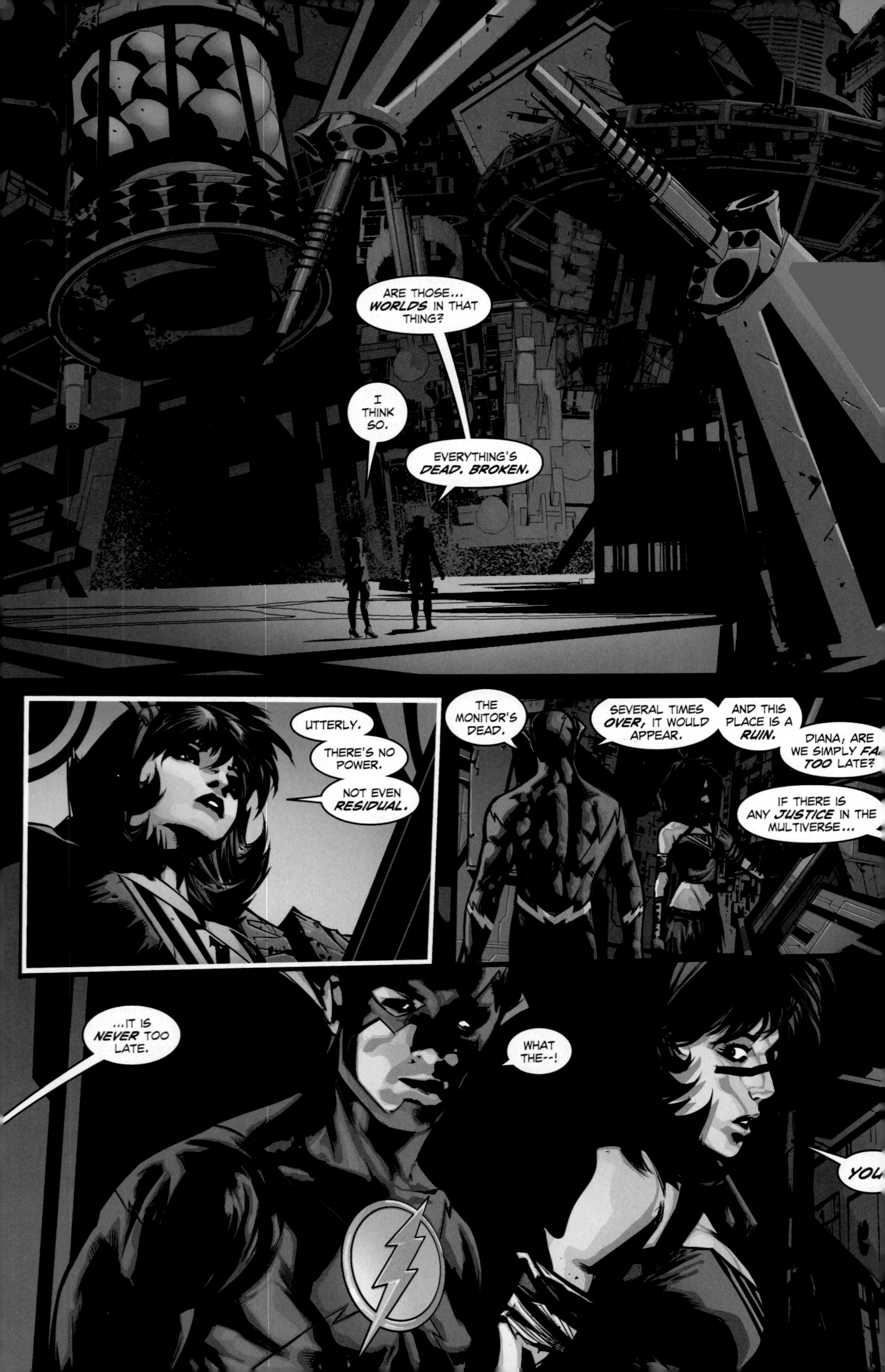
ARE THOSE... WORLDS IN THAT THING?
I THINK SO.
EVERYTHING'S DEAD. BROKEN.
UTTERLY.
THERE'S NO POWER.
NOT EVEN RESIDUAL.
THE MONITOR'S DEAD.
SEVERAL TIMES OVER, IT WOULD APPEAR.
AND THIS PLACE IS A RUIN.
DIANA, ARE WE SIMPLY FA TOO LATE?
IF THERE IS ANY JUSTICE IN THE MULTIVERSE...
...IT IS NEVER TOO LATE.
WHAT THE--!

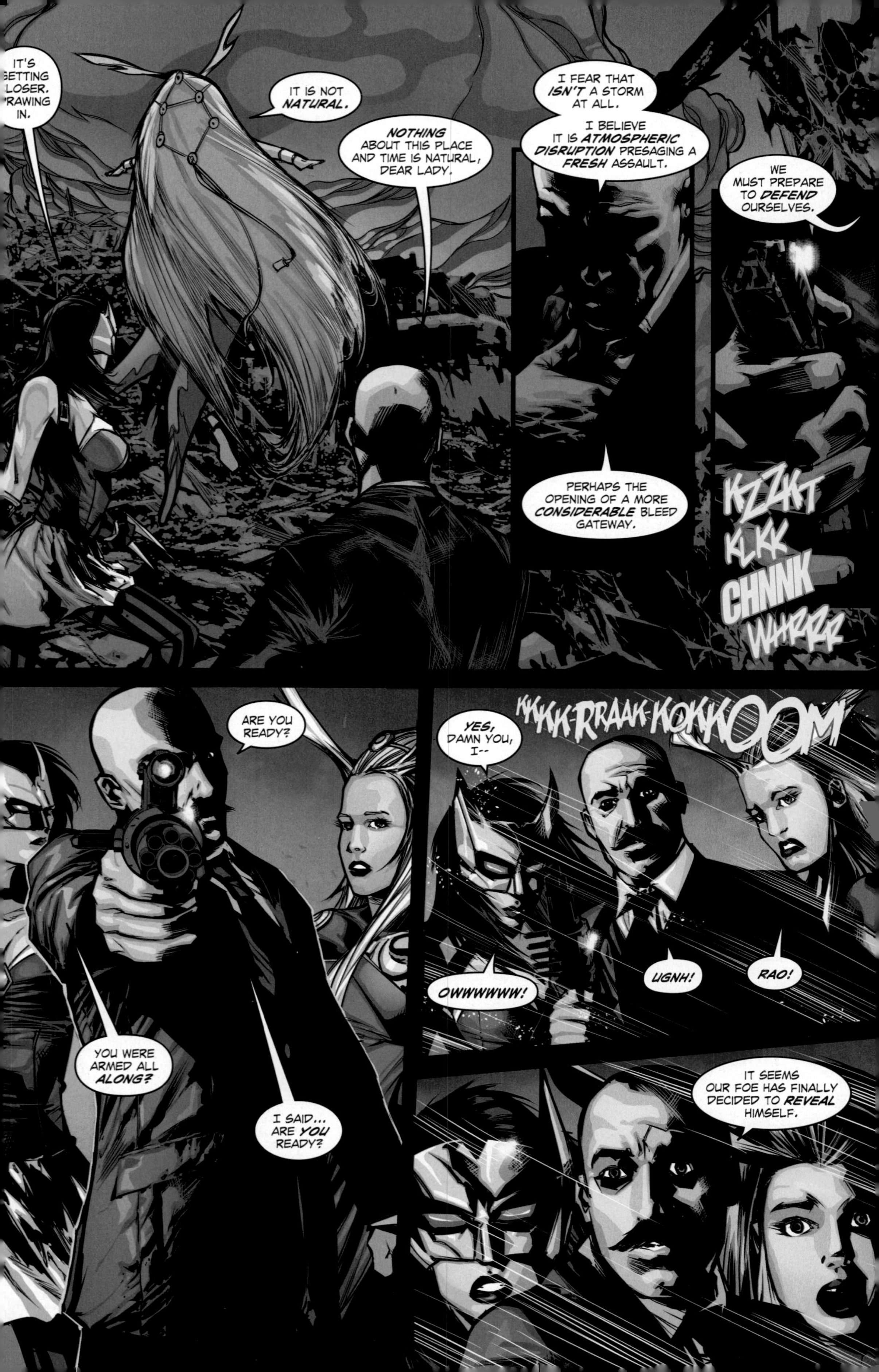
IT'S GETTING CLOSER. DRAWING IN.
IT IS NOT NATURAL.
NOTHING ABOUT THIS PLACE AND TIME IS NATURAL, DEAR LADY.
I FEAR THAT ISN'T A STORM AT ALL.
I BELIEVE IT IS ATMOSPHERIC DISRUPTION PRESAGING A FRESH ASSAULT.
PERHAPS THE OPENING OF A MORE CONSIDERABLE BLEED GATEWAY.
WE MUST PREPARE TO DEFEND OURSELVES.
KZZAKT
KLKK
CHNNK
WHRRR
ARE YOU READY?
YOU WERE ARMED ALL ALONG?
I SAID... ARE YOU READY?
KKKK-RRAAK-KOKKOOM
YES, DAMN YOU, I--
OWWWWWW!
UGNH!
RAO!
IT SEEMS OUR FOE HAS FINALLY DECIDED TO REVEAL HIMSELF.

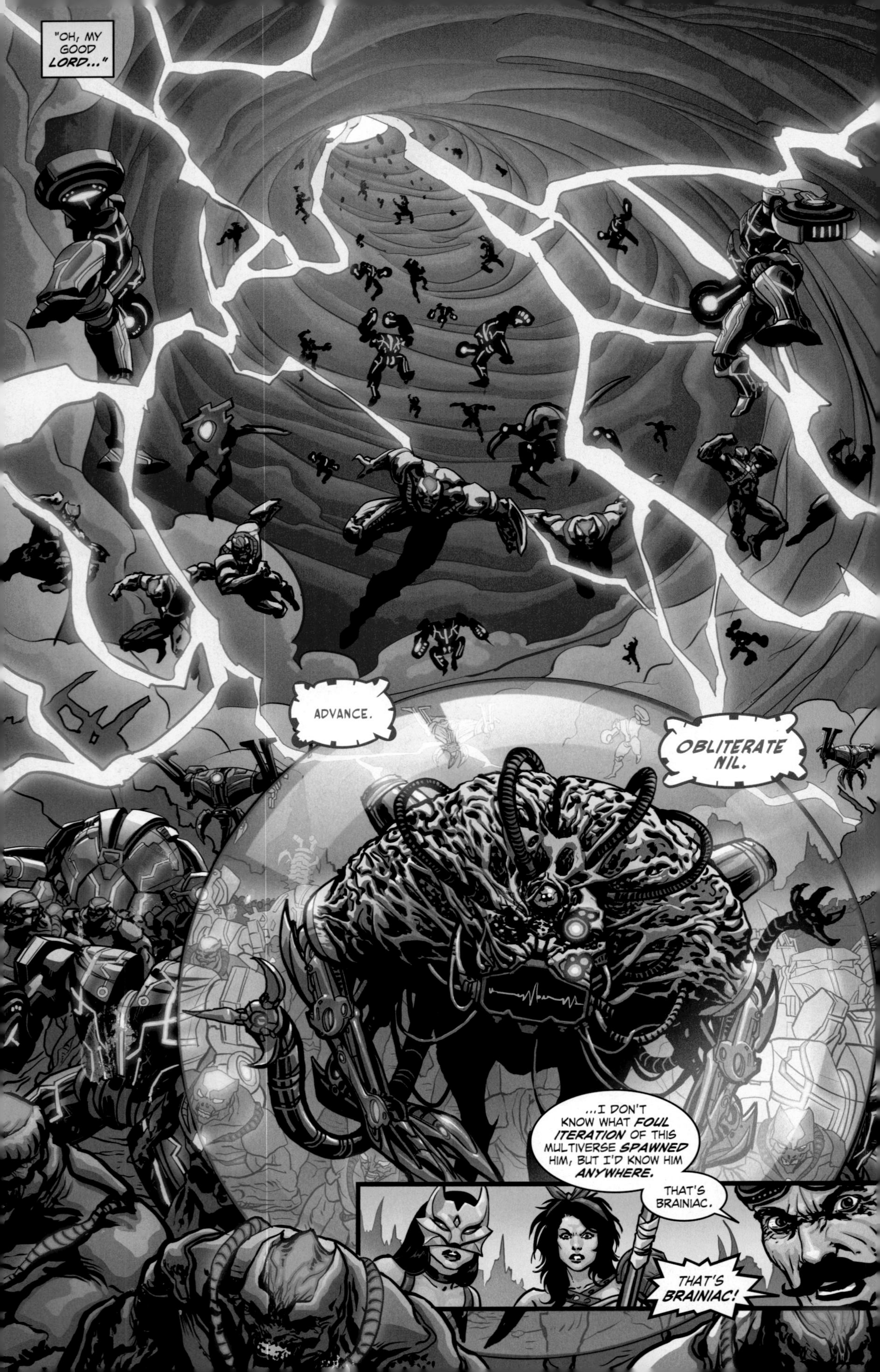
"OH, MY GOOD LORD..."
ADVANCE.
OBLITERATE NIL.
...I DON'T KNOW WHAT FOUL ITERATION OF THIS MULTIVERSE SPAWNED HIM, BUT I'D KNOW HIM ANYWHERE.
THAT'S BRAINIAC.
THAT'S BRAINIAC!

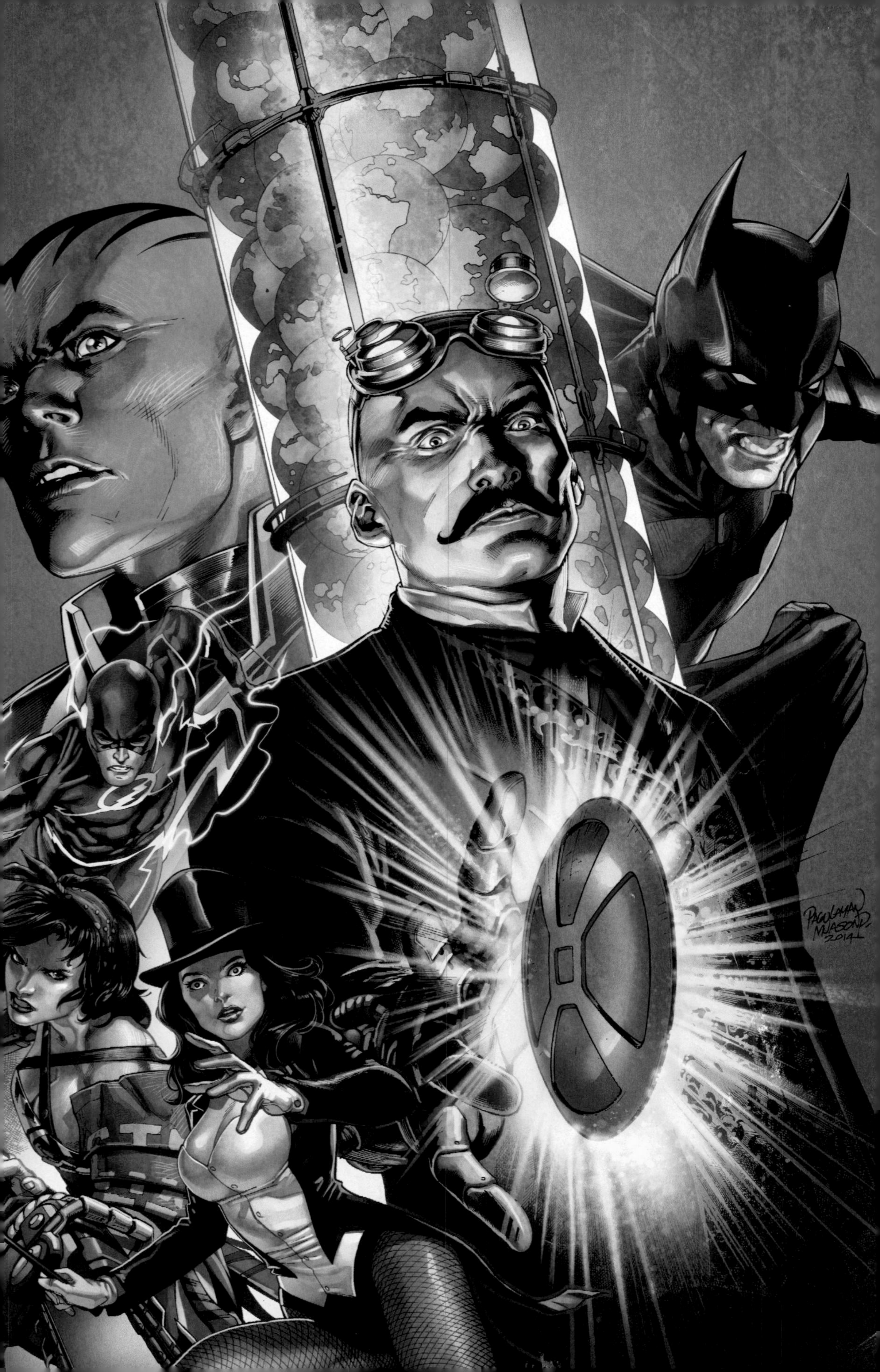

NIL PART 2

Eduardo Francisco Szymon Kudranski Christian Duce Artists
Mark Roberts Alejandro Sanchez Colorists
Cover Art by **Carlo Pagulayan and Jason Paz with Ellery Santos**

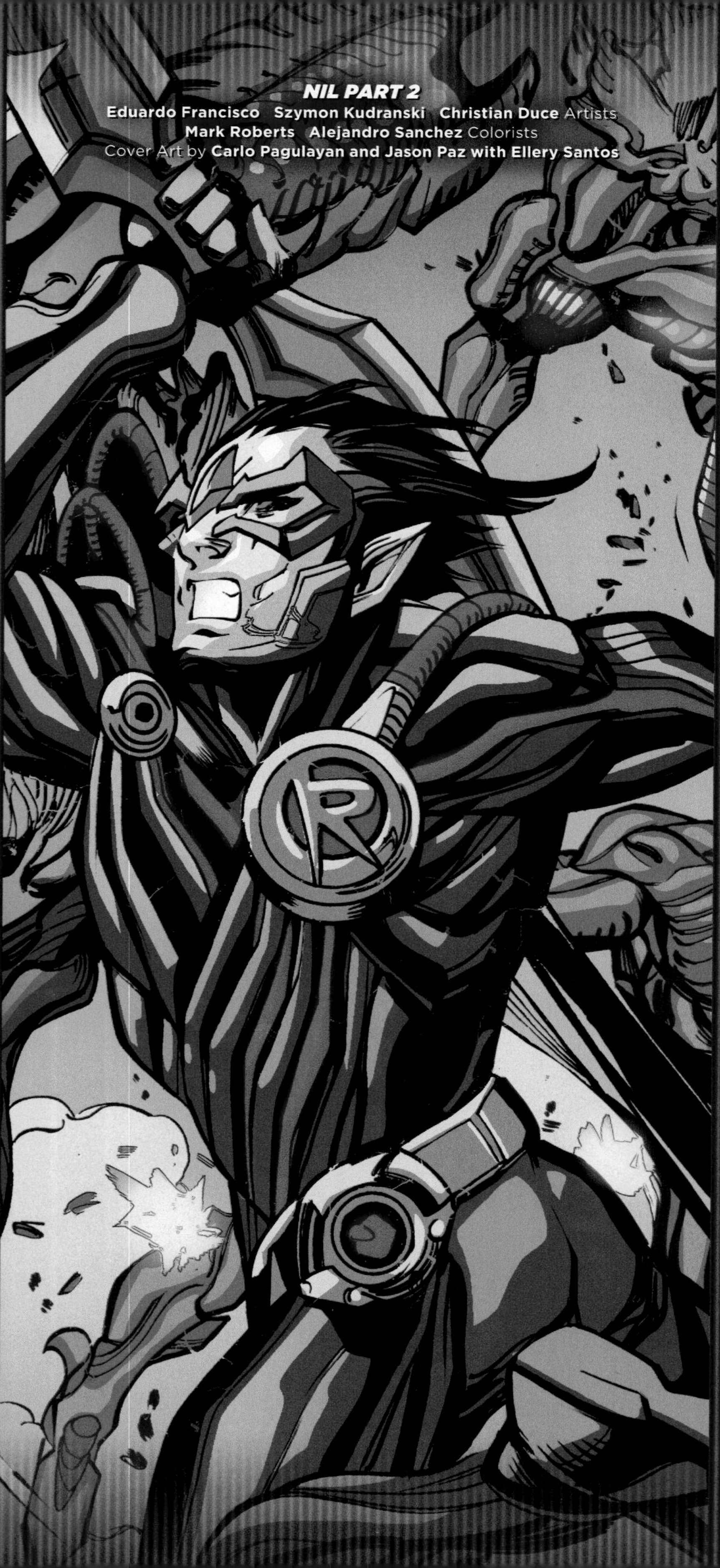

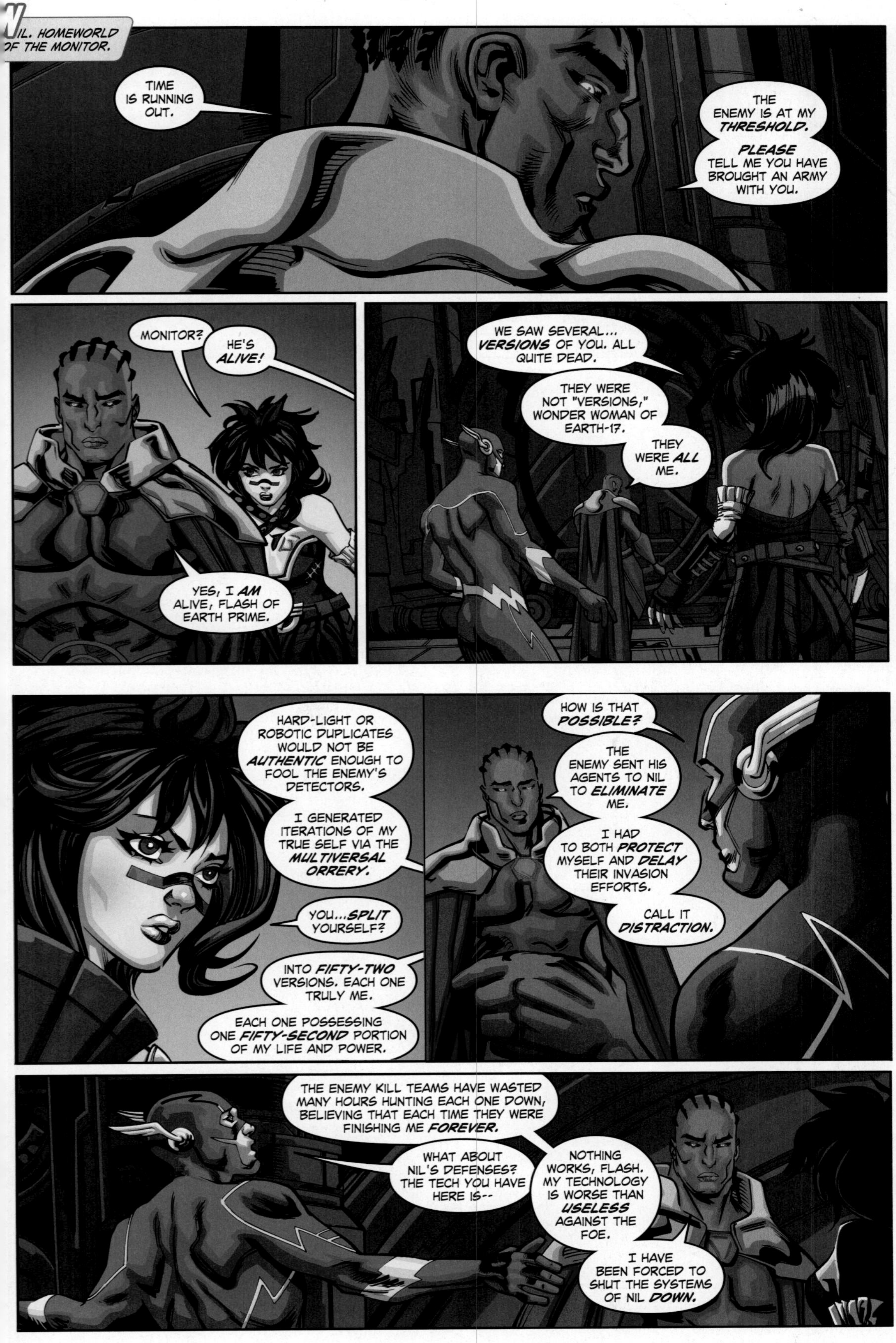
NIL. HOMEWORLD OF THE MONITOR.
TIME IS RUNNING OUT.
THE ENEMY IS AT MY THRESHOLD.
PLEASE TELL ME YOU HAVE BROUGHT AN ARMY WITH YOU.
MONITOR?
HE'S ALIVE!
YES, I AM ALIVE, FLASH OF EARTH PRIME.
WE SAW SEVERAL... VERSIONS OF YOU. ALL QUITE DEAD.
THEY WERE NOT "VERSIONS," WONDER WOMAN OF EARTH-17.
THEY WERE ALL ME.
HARD-LIGHT OR ROBOTIC DUPLICATES WOULD NOT BE AUTHENTIC ENOUGH TO FOOL THE ENEMY'S DETECTORS.
I GENERATED ITERATIONS OF MY TRUE SELF VIA THE MULTIVERSAL ORRERY.
YOU...SPLIT YOURSELF?
INTO FIFTY-TWO VERSIONS. EACH ONE TRULY ME.
EACH ONE POSSESSING ONE FIFTY-SECOND PORTION OF MY LIFE AND POWER.
HOW IS THAT POSSIBLE?
THE ENEMY SENT HIS AGENTS TO NIL TO ELIMINATE ME.
I HAD TO BOTH PROTECT MYSELF AND DELAY THEIR INVASION EFFORTS.
CALL IT DISTRACTION.
THE ENEMY KILL TEAMS HAVE WASTED MANY HOURS HUNTING EACH ONE DOWN, BELIEVING THAT EACH TIME THEY WERE FINISHING ME FOREVER.
WHAT ABOUT NIL'S DEFENSES? THE TECH YOU HAVE HERE IS--
NOTHING WORKS, FLASH. MY TECHNOLOGY IS WORSE THAN USELESS AGAINST THE FOE.
I HAVE BEEN FORCED TO SHUT THE SYSTEMS OF NIL DOWN.

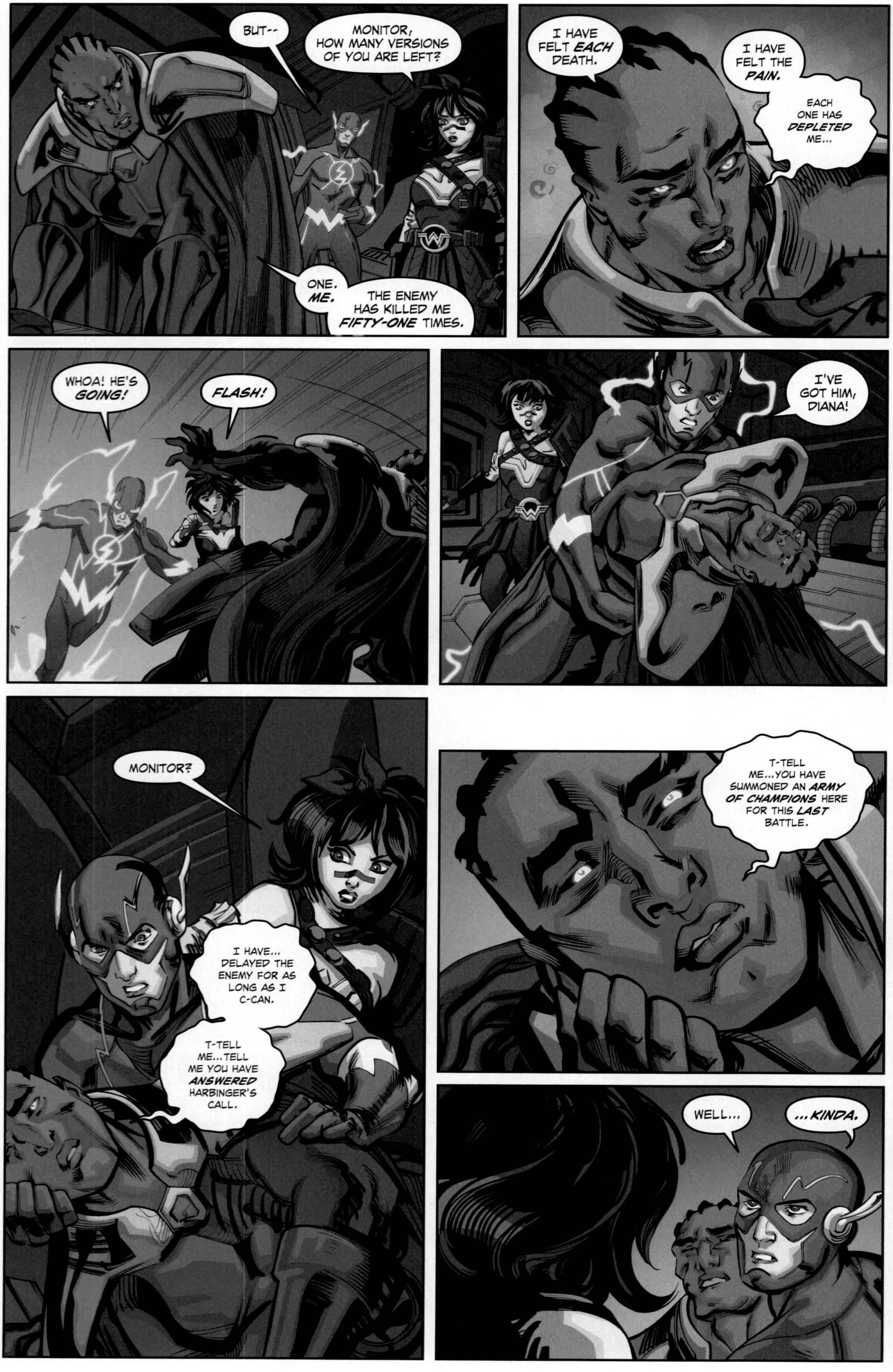

BUT--
MONITOR, HOW MANY VERSIONS OF YOU ARE LEFT?
ONE. ME.
THE ENEMY HAS KILLED ME FIFTY-ONE TIMES.
I HAVE FELT EACH DEATH.
I HAVE FELT THE PAIN.
EACH ONE HAS DEPLETED ME...
WHOA! HE'S GOING!
FLASH!
I'VE GOT HIM, DIANA!
MONITOR?
I HAVE... DELAYED THE ENEMY FOR AS LONG AS I C-CAN.
T-TELL ME...TELL ME YOU HAVE ANSWERED HARBINGER'S CALL.
T-TELL ME...YOU HAVE SUMMONED AN ARMY OF CHAMPIONS HERE FOR THIS LAST BATTLE.
WELL...
...KINDA.

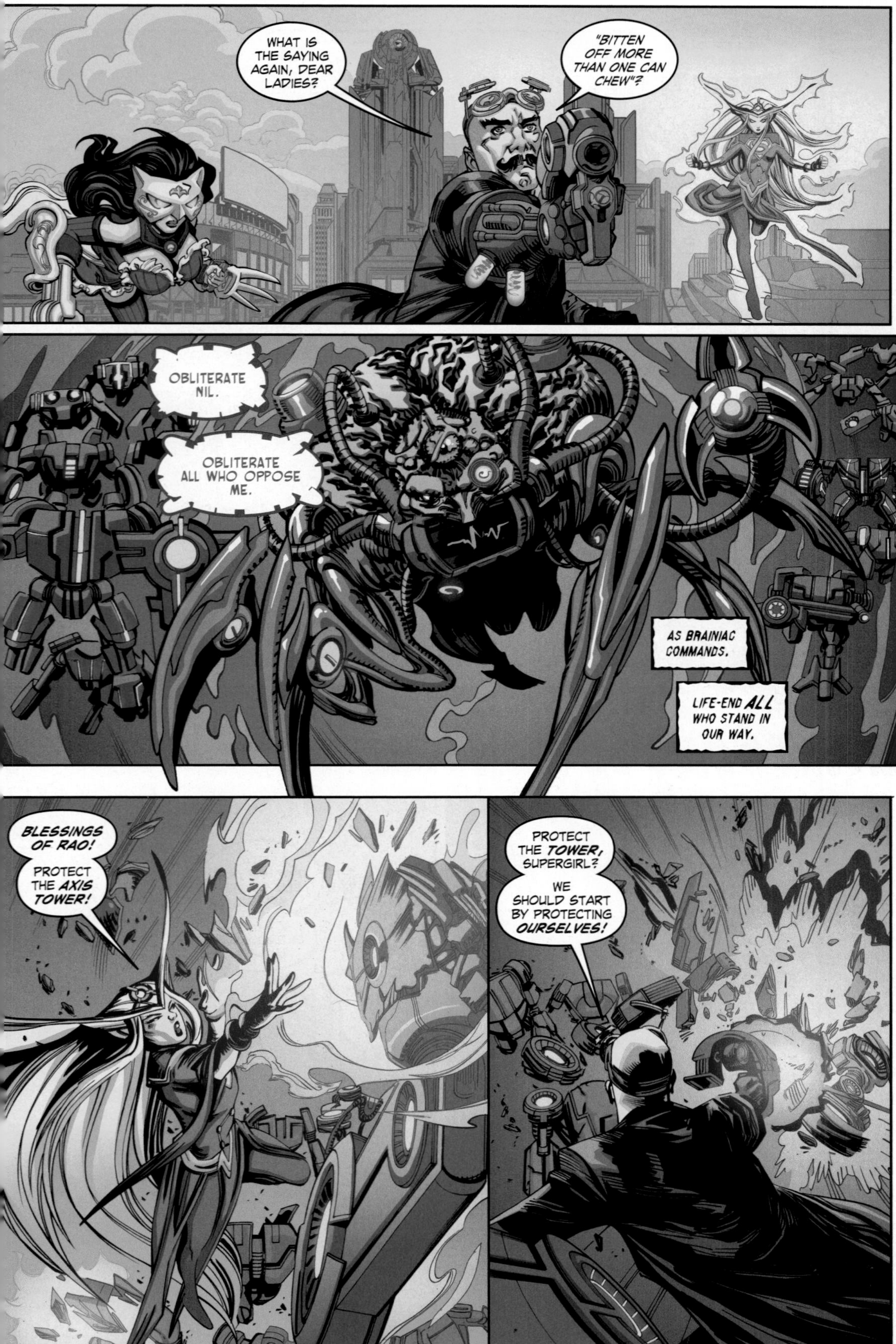
WHAT IS THE SAYING AGAIN, DEAR LADIES?
"BITTEN OFF MORE THAN ONE CAN CHEW"?
OBLITERATE NIL.
OBLITERATE ALL WHO OPPOSE ME.
AS BRAINIAC COMMANDS.
LIFE-END ALL WHO STAND IN OUR WAY.
BLESSINGS OF RAO!
PROTECT THE AXIS TOWER!
PROTECT THE TOWER, SUPERGIRL?
WE SHOULD START BY PROTECTING OURSELVES!

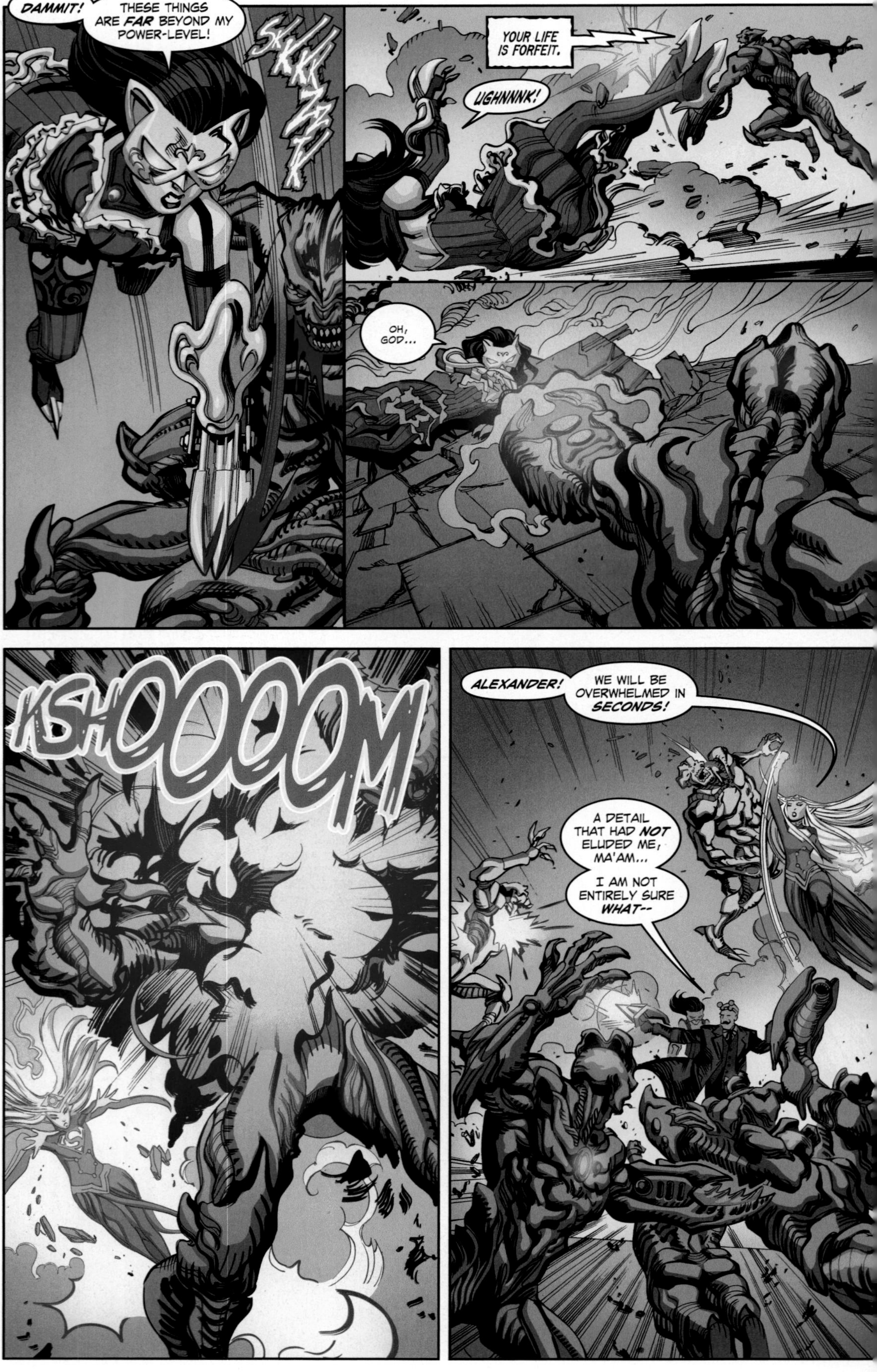
DAMMIT!
THESE THINGS ARE FAR BEYOND MY POWER-LEVEL!
SKKKZZTK
YOUR LIFE IS FORFEIT.
UGHNNNK!
OH, GOD...
KSHOOOOM
ALEXANDER!
WE WILL BE OVERWHELMED IN SECONDS!
A DETAIL THAT HAD NOT ELUDED ME, MA'AM...
I AM NOT ENTIRELY SURE WHAT--

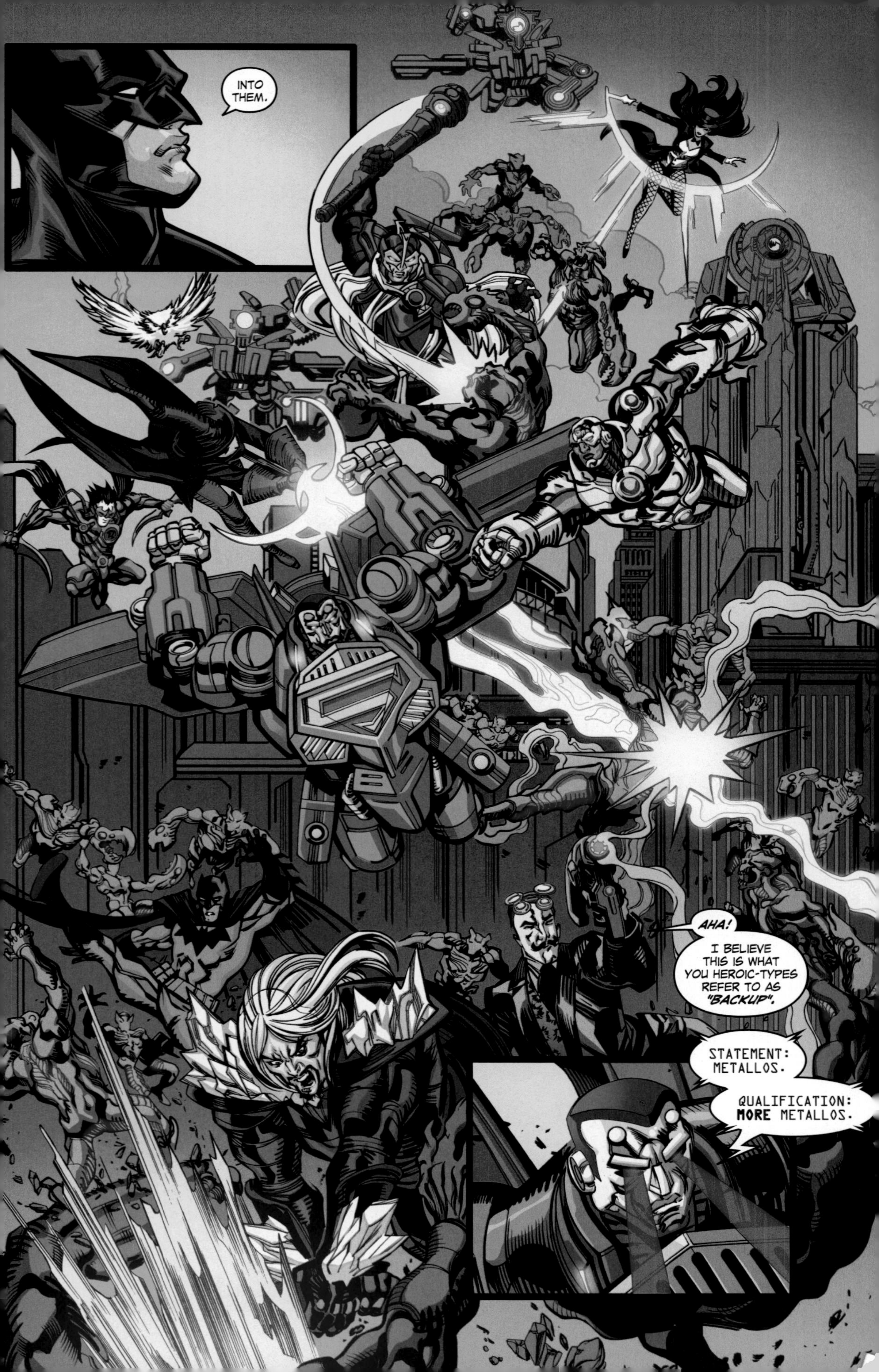
INTO THEM.
AHA!
I BELIEVE THIS IS WHAT YOU HEROIC-TYPES REFER TO AS "BACKUP".
STATEMENT: METALLOS.
QUALIFICATION: MORE METALLOS.

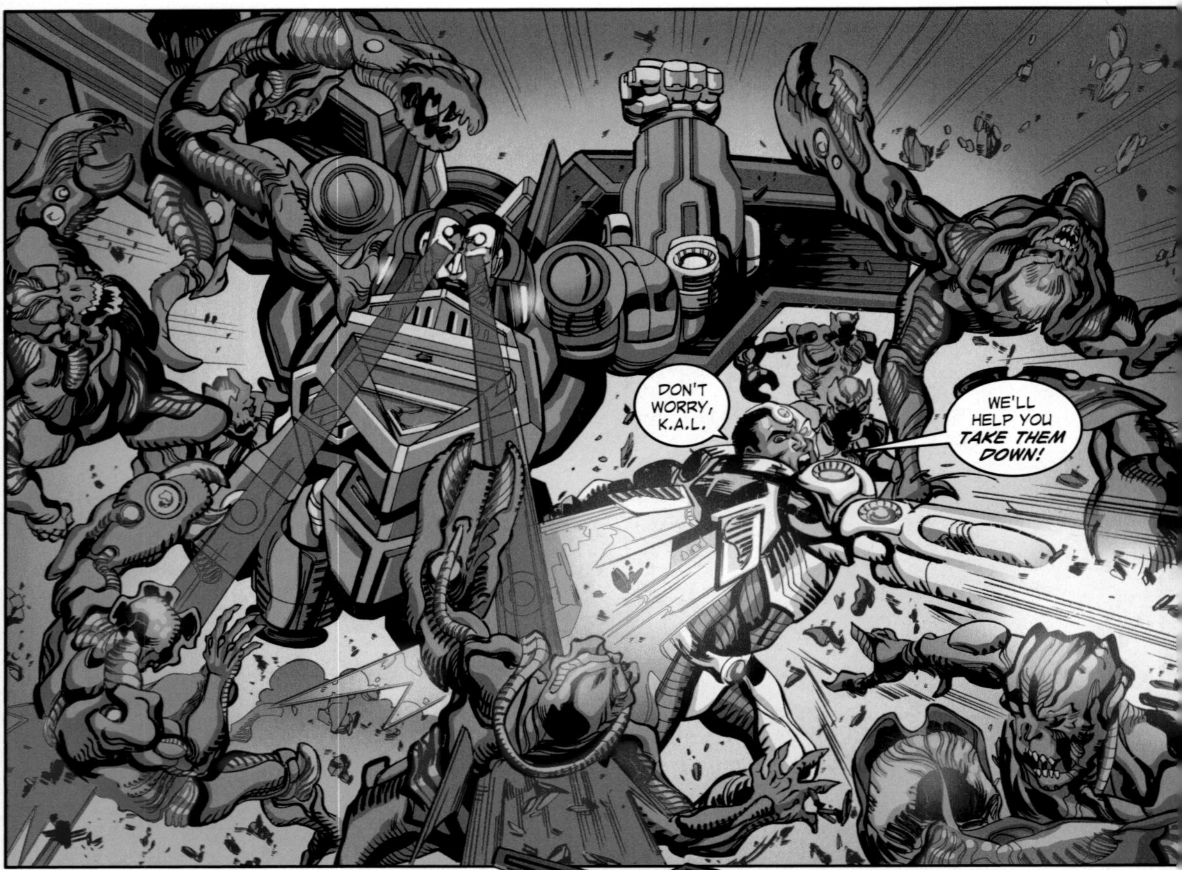
DON'T WORRY, K.A.L.
WE'LL HELP YOU TAKE THEM DOWN!

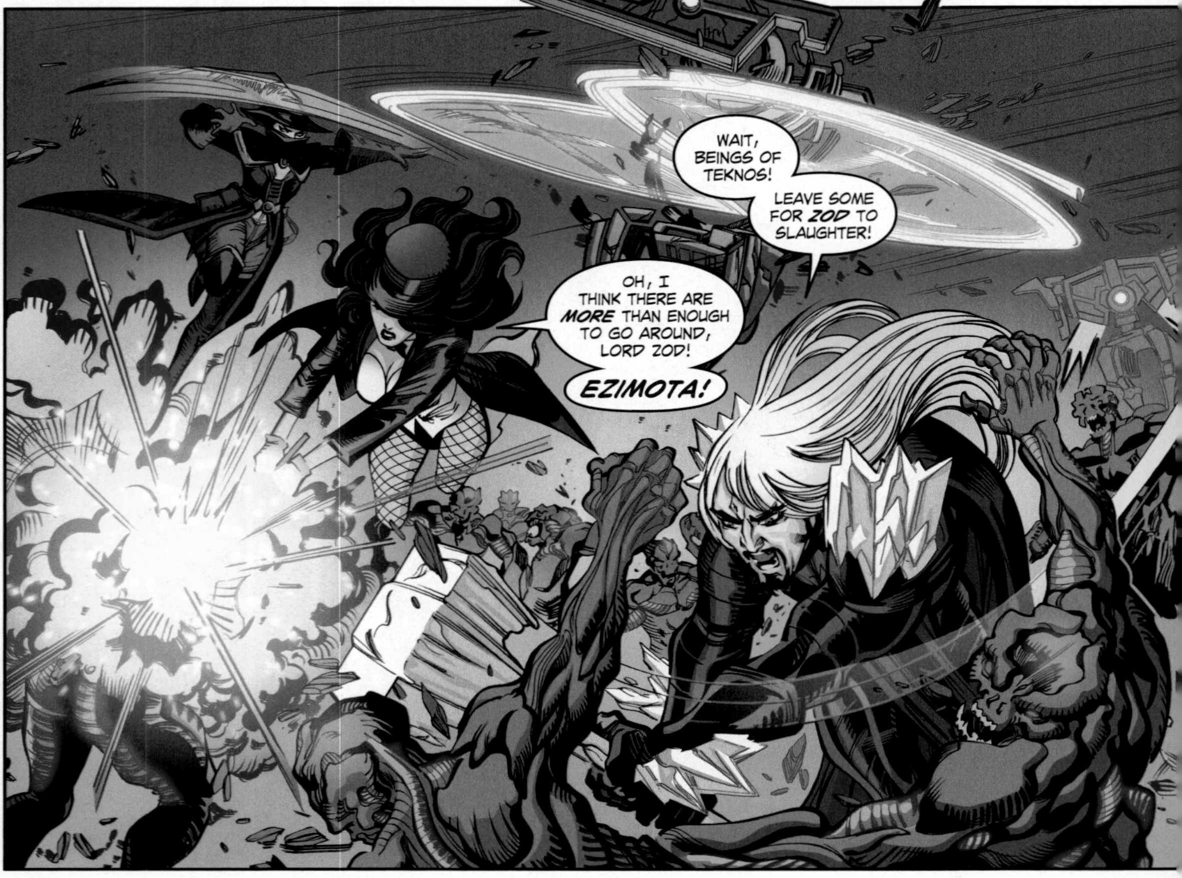
WAIT, BEINGS OF TEKNOS!
LEAVE SOME FOR ZOD TO SLAUGHTER!
OH, I THINK THERE ARE MORE THAN ENOUGH TO GO AROUND, LORD ZOD!
EZIMOTA!

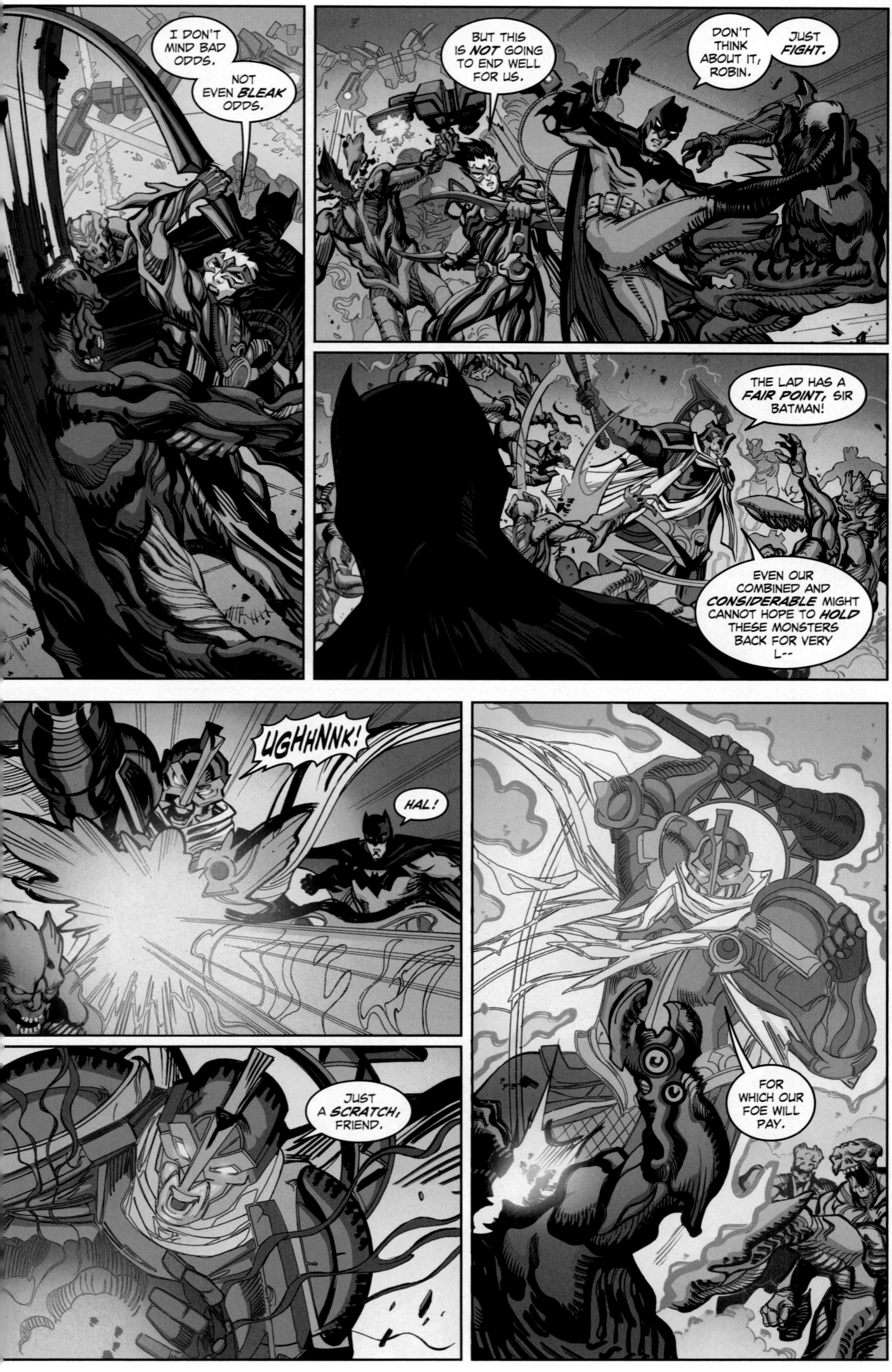
I DON'T MIND BAD ODDS.
NOT EVEN BLEAK ODDS.
BUT THIS IS NOT GOING TO END WELL FOR US.
DON'T THINK ABOUT IT, ROBIN.
JUST FIGHT.
THE LAD HAS A FAIR POINT, SIR BATMAN!
EVEN OUR COMBINED AND CONSIDERABLE MIGHT CANNOT HOPE TO HOLD THESE MONSTERS BACK FOR VERY L--
UGHHNNK!
HAL!
JUST A SCRATCH, FRIEND.
FOR WHICH OUR FOE WILL PAY.

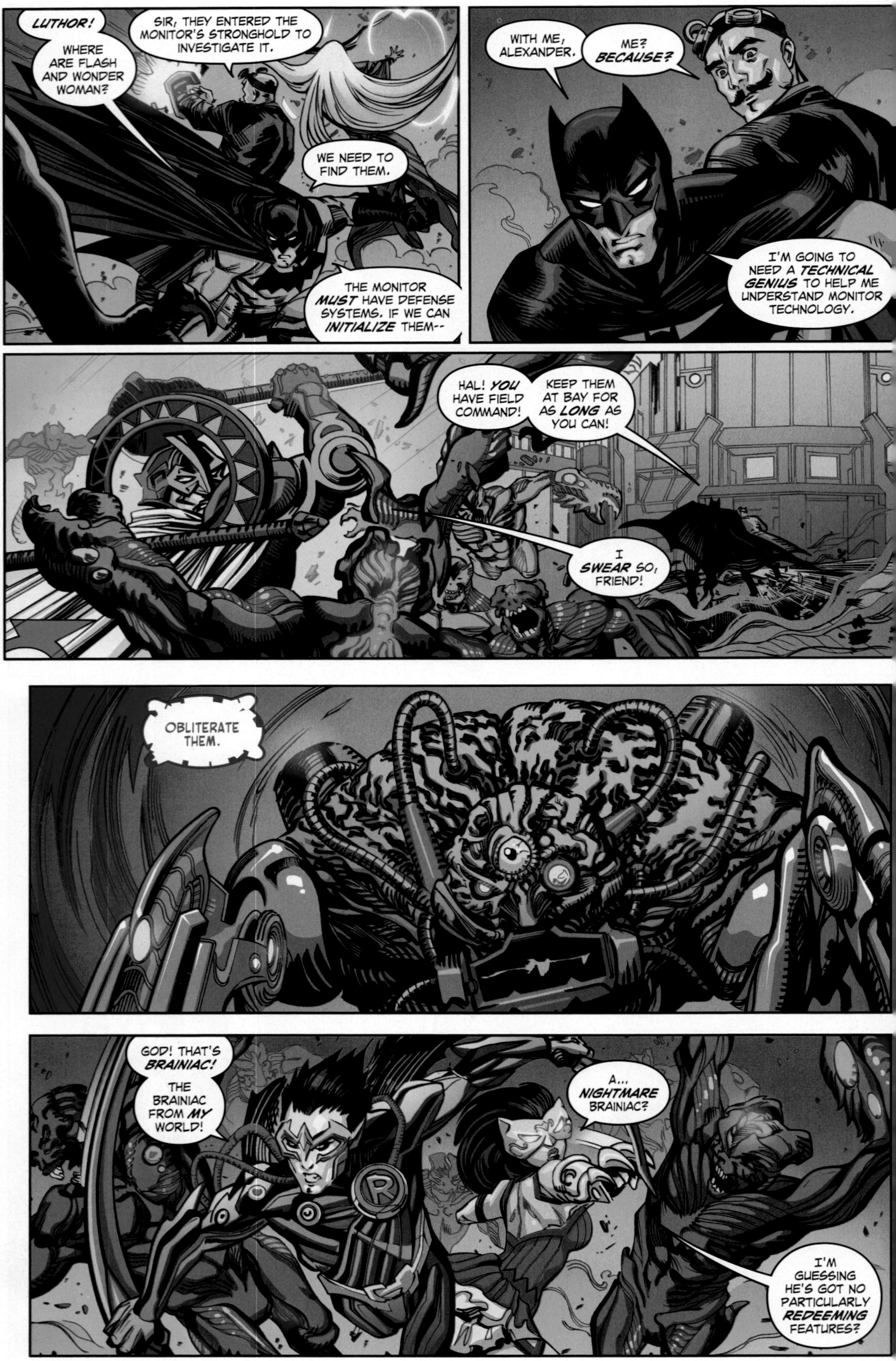
LUTHOR!
WHERE ARE FLASH AND WONDER WOMAN?
SIR, THEY ENTERED THE MONITOR'S STRONGHOLD TO INVESTIGATE IT.
WE NEED TO FIND THEM.
THE MONITOR MUST HAVE DEFENSE SYSTEMS. IF WE CAN INITIALIZE THEM--
WITH ME, ALEXANDER.
ME? BECAUSE?
I'M GOING TO NEED A TECHNICAL GENIUS TO HELP ME UNDERSTAND MONITOR TECHNOLOGY.
HAL! YOU HAVE FIELD COMMAND!
KEEP THEM AT BAY FOR AS LONG AS YOU CAN!
I SWEAR SO, FRIEND!
OBLITERATE THEM.
GOD! THAT'S BRAINIAC!
THE BRAINIAC FROM MY WORLD!
A... NIGHTMARE BRAINIAC?
I'M GUESSING HE'S GOT NO PARTICULARLY REDEEMING FEATURES?

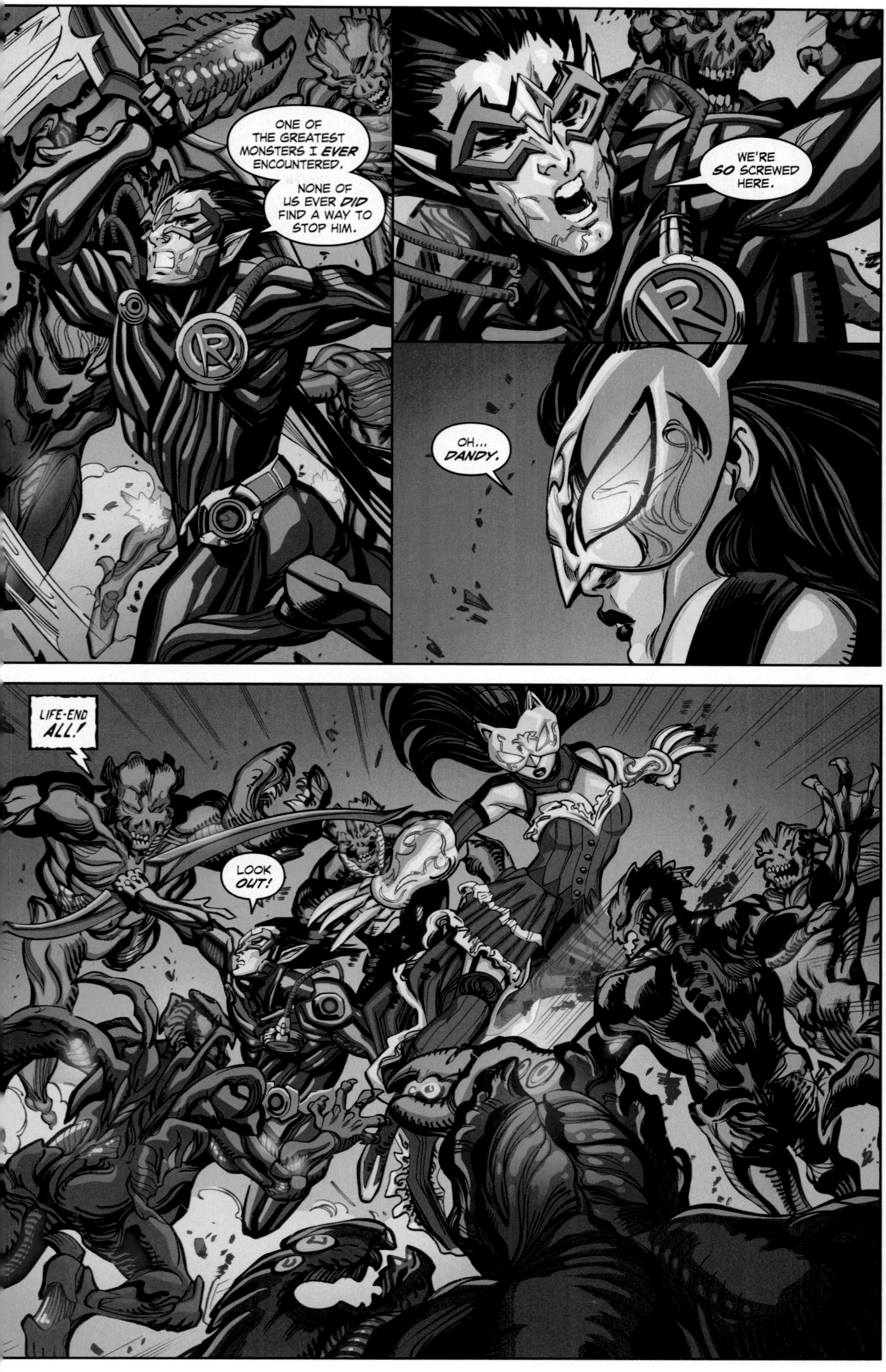
ONE OF THE GREATEST MONSTERS I *EVER* ENCOUNTERED.
NONE OF US EVER *DID* FIND A WAY TO STOP HIM.
WE'RE *SO* SCREWED HERE.
OH... *DANDY.*
LIFE-END *ALL!*
LOOK *OUT!*

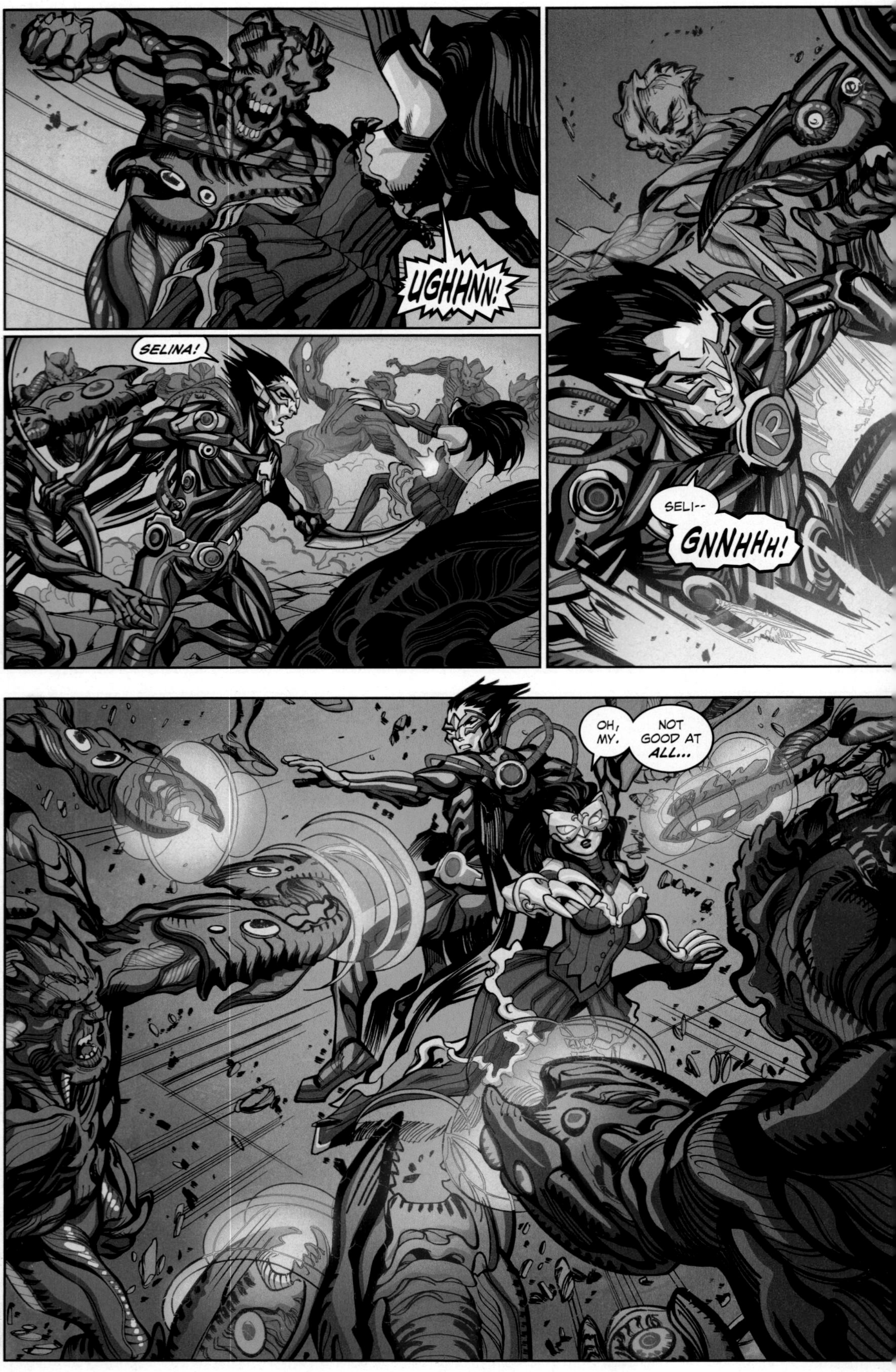
UGHHNN!
SELINA!
SELI--
GNHHHH!
OH, MY.
NOT GOOD AT ALL...

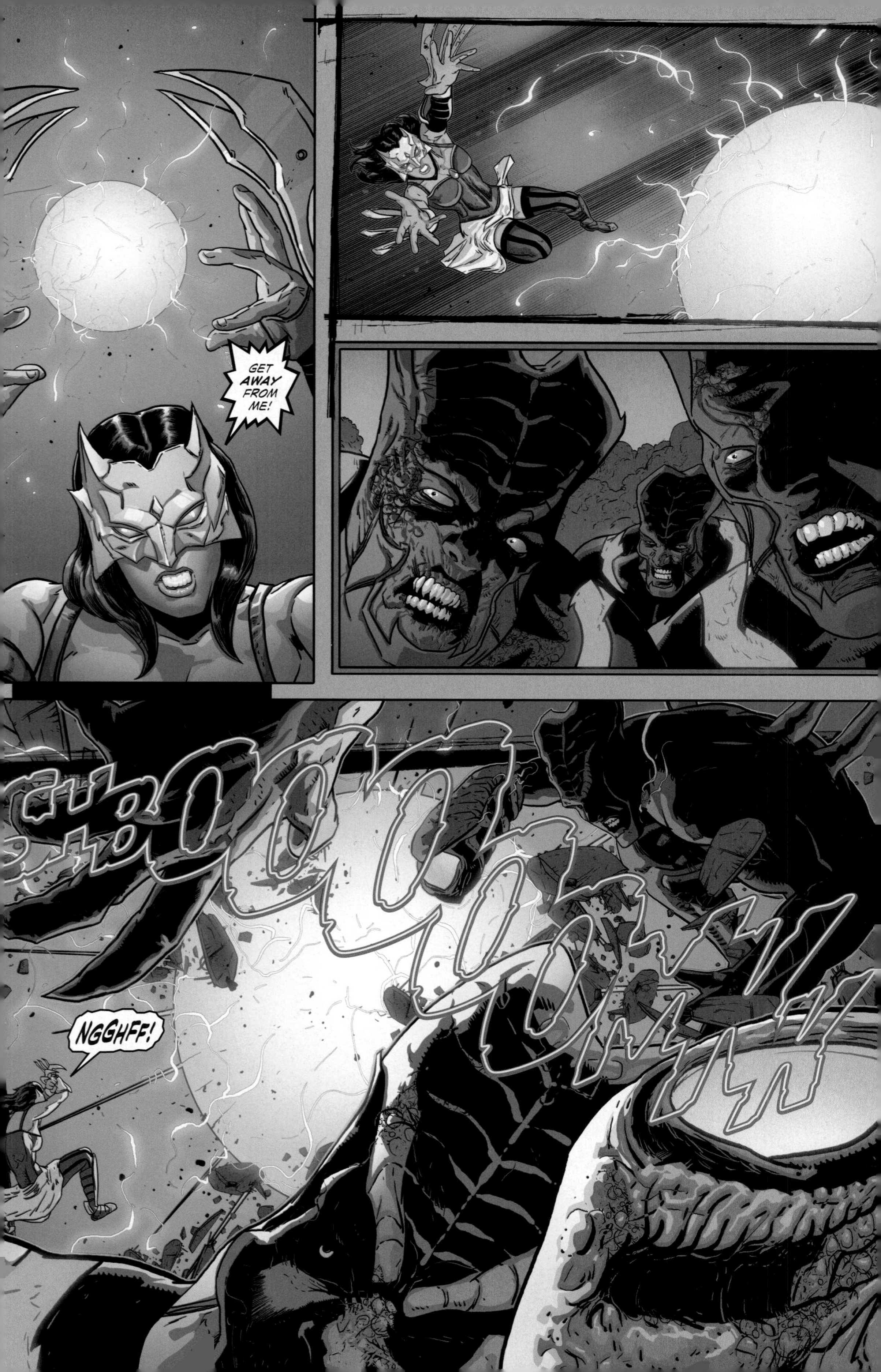
GET AWAY FROM ME!
NGGHFF!
SHBOOOOOOOOM

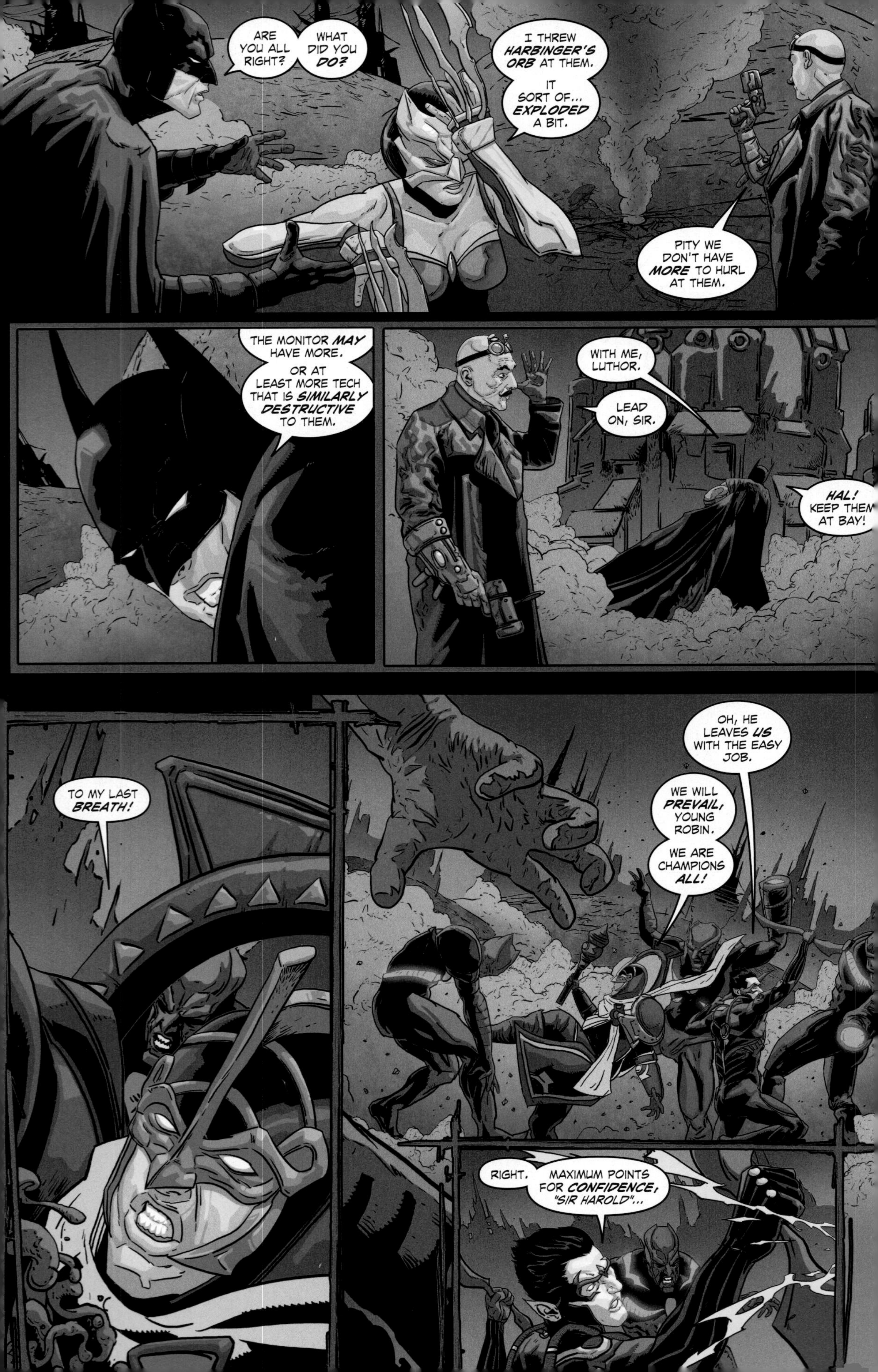
ARE YOU ALL RIGHT?
WHAT DID YOU DO?
I THREW HARBINGER'S ORB AT THEM.
IT SORT OF... EXPLODED A BIT.
PITY WE DON'T HAVE MORE TO HURL AT THEM.
THE MONITOR MAY HAVE MORE.
OR AT LEAST MORE TECH THAT IS SIMILARLY DESTRUCTIVE TO THEM.
WITH ME, LUTHOR.
LEAD ON, SIR.
HAL! KEEP THEM AT BAY!
TO MY LAST BREATH!
OH, HE LEAVES US WITH THE EASY JOB.
WE WILL PREVAIL, YOUNG ROBIN.
WE ARE CHAMPIONS ALL!
RIGHT.
MAXIMUM POINTS FOR CONFIDENCE, "SIR HAROLD"...

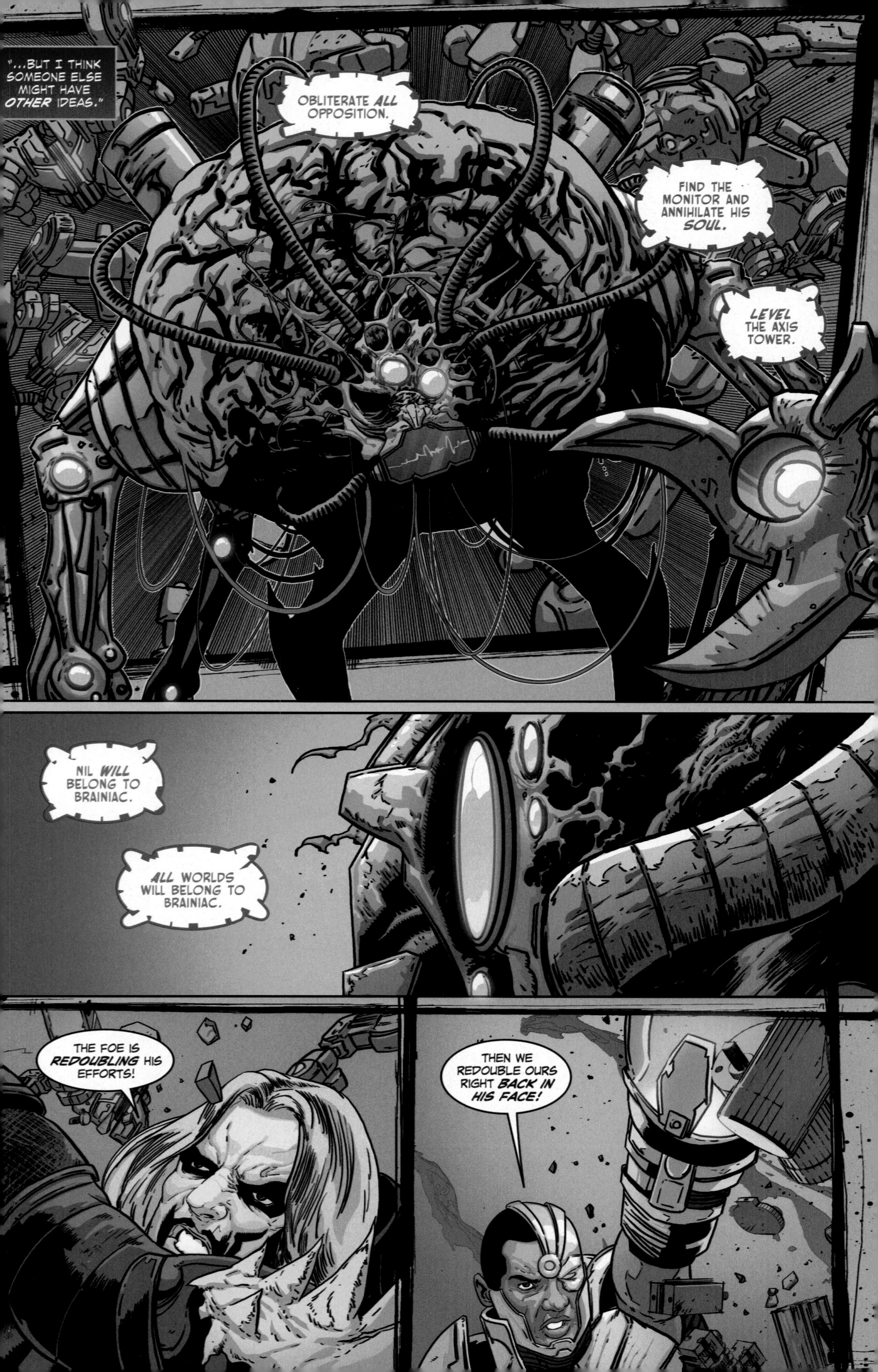
"...BUT I THINK SOMEONE ELSE MIGHT HAVE OTHER IDEAS."
OBLITERATE ALL OPPOSITION.
FIND THE MONITOR AND ANNIHILATE HIS SOUL.
LEVEL THE AXIS TOWER.
NIL WILL BELONG TO BRAINIAC.
ALL WORLDS WILL BELONG TO BRAINIAC.
THE FOE IS REDOUBLING HIS EFFORTS!
THEN WE REDOUBLE OURS RIGHT BACK IN HIS FACE!

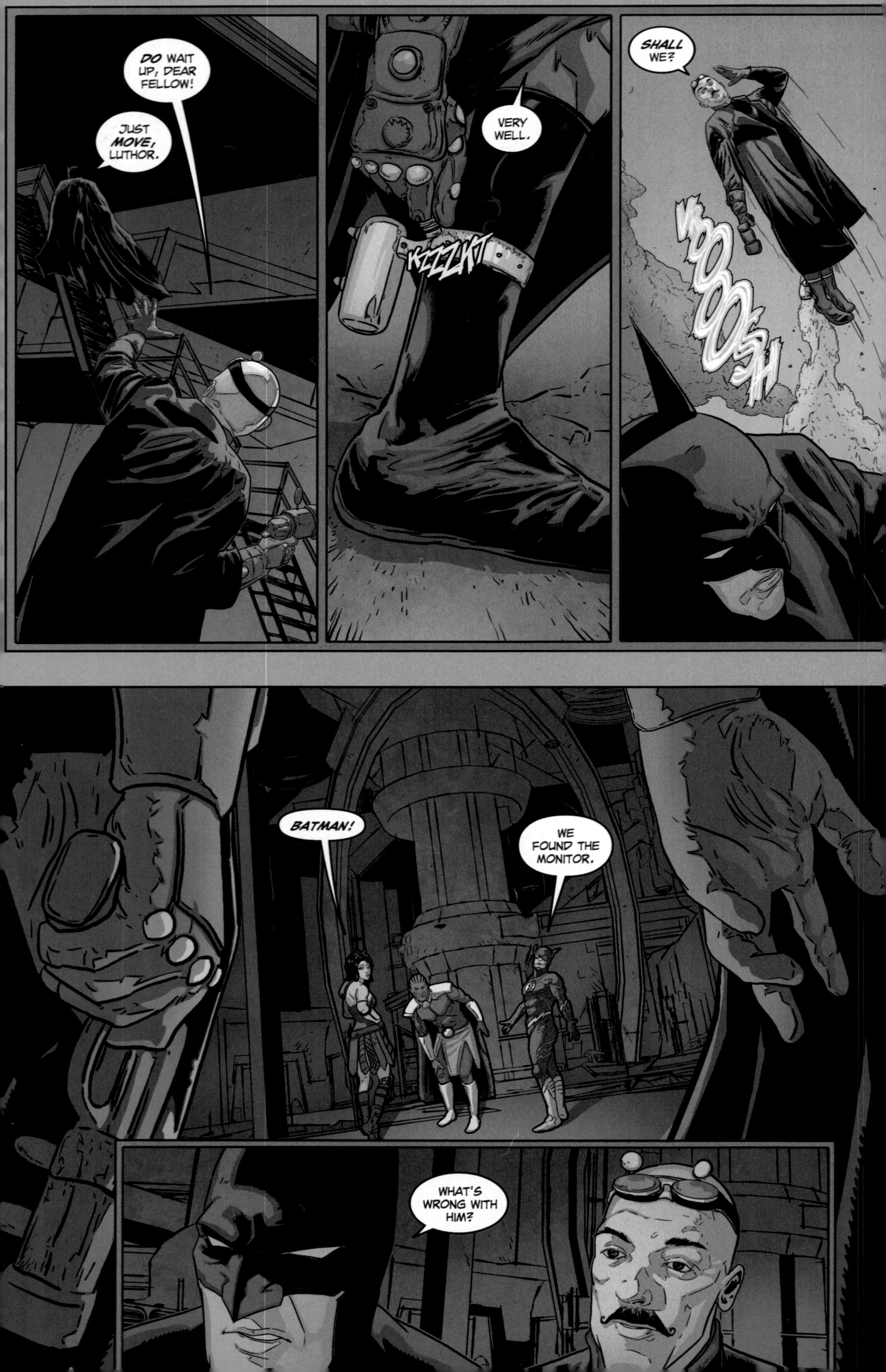
DO WAIT UP, DEAR FELLOW!
JUST MOVE, LUTHOR.
VERY WELL.
KZZZKT
SHALL WE?
VOOOOOSH
BATMAN!
WE FOUND THE MONITOR.
WHAT'S WRONG WITH HIM?

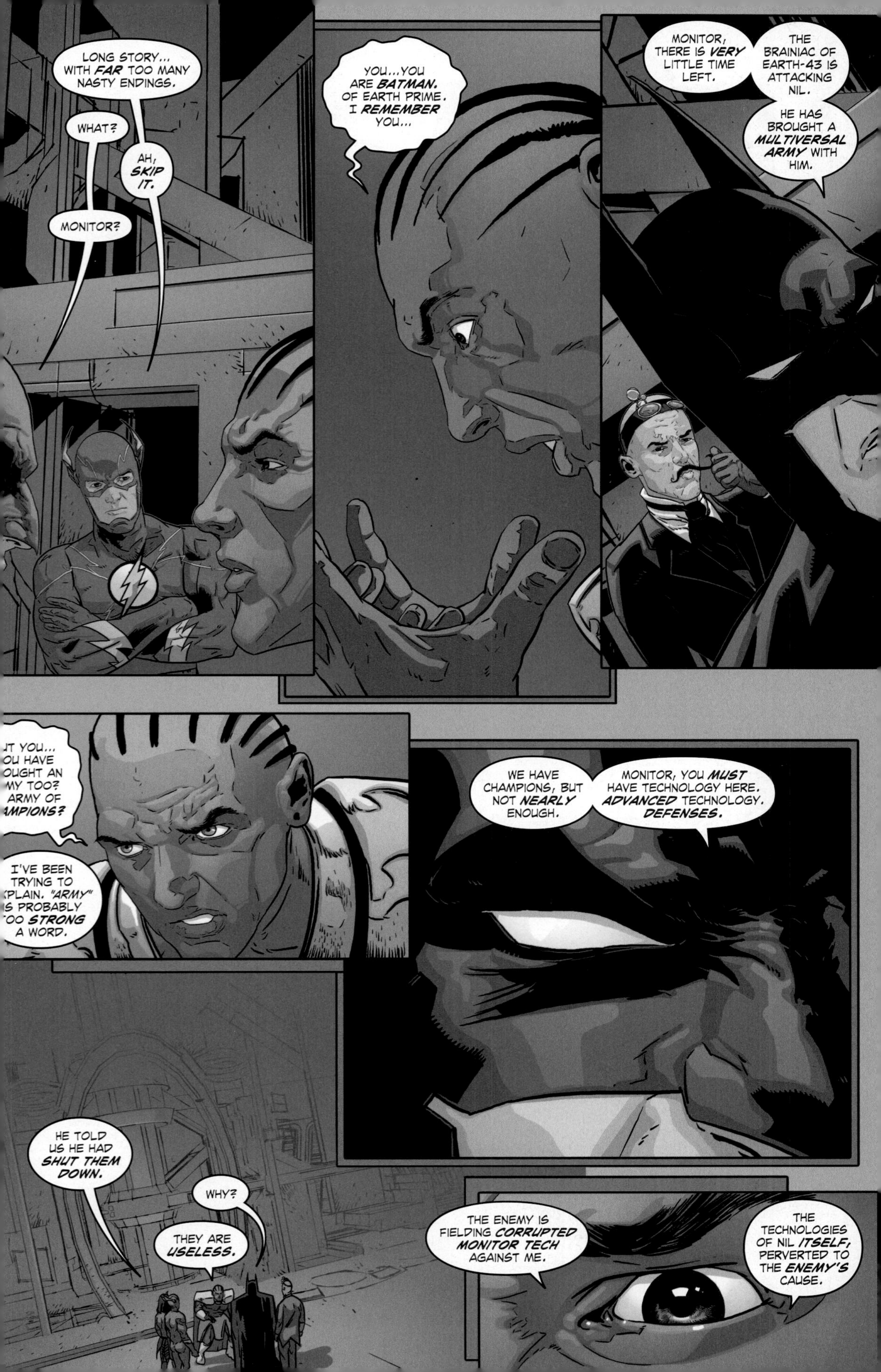
LONG STORY... WITH FAR TOO MANY NASTY ENDINGS.
WHAT?
AH, SKIP IT.
MONITOR?
YOU...YOU ARE BATMAN. OF EARTH PRIME. I REMEMBER YOU...
MONITOR, THERE IS VERY LITTLE TIME LEFT.
THE BRAINIAC OF EARTH-43 IS ATTACKING NIL.
HE HAS BROUGHT A MULTIVERSAL ARMY WITH HIM.
UT YOU... OU HAVE OUGHT AN MY TOO? ARMY OF AMPIONS?
I'VE BEEN TRYING TO XPLAIN. "ARMY" IS PROBABLY TOO STRONG A WORD.
WE HAVE CHAMPIONS, BUT NOT NEARLY ENOUGH.
MONITOR, YOU MUST HAVE TECHNOLOGY HERE. ADVANCED TECHNOLOGY. DEFENSES.
HE TOLD US HE HAD SHUT THEM DOWN.
WHY?
THEY ARE USELESS.
THE ENEMY IS FIELDING CORRUPTED MONITOR TECH AGAINST ME.
THE TECHNOLOGIES OF NIL ITSELF, PERVERTED TO THE ENEMY'S CAUSE.

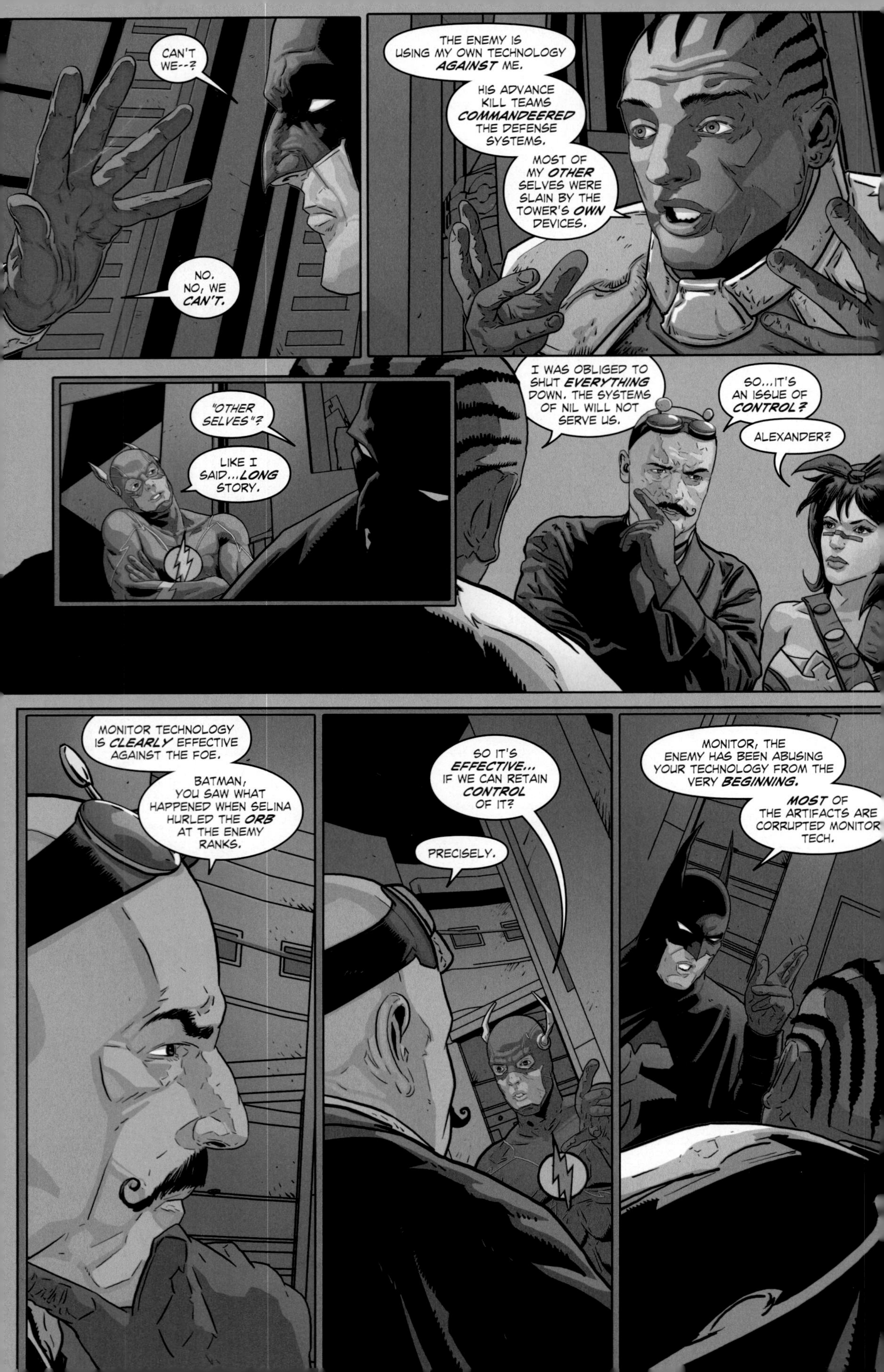
CAN'T WE--?
NO. NO, WE CAN'T.
THE ENEMY IS USING MY OWN TECHNOLOGY AGAINST ME.
HIS ADVANCE KILL TEAMS COMMANDEERED THE DEFENSE SYSTEMS.
MOST OF MY OTHER SELVES WERE SLAIN BY THE TOWER'S OWN DEVICES.
"OTHER SELVES"?
LIKE I SAID...LONG STORY.
I WAS OBLIGED TO SHUT EVERYTHING DOWN. THE SYSTEMS OF NIL WILL NOT SERVE US.
SO...IT'S AN ISSUE OF CONTROL?
ALEXANDER?
MONITOR TECHNOLOGY IS CLEARLY EFFECTIVE AGAINST THE FOE.
BATMAN, YOU SAW WHAT HAPPENED WHEN SELINA HURLED THE ORB AT THE ENEMY RANKS.
SO IT'S EFFECTIVE... IF WE CAN RETAIN CONTROL OF IT?
PRECISELY.
MONITOR, THE ENEMY HAS BEEN ABUSING YOUR TECHNOLOGY FROM THE VERY BEGINNING.
MOST OF THE ARTIFACTS ARE CORRUPTED MONITOR TECH.

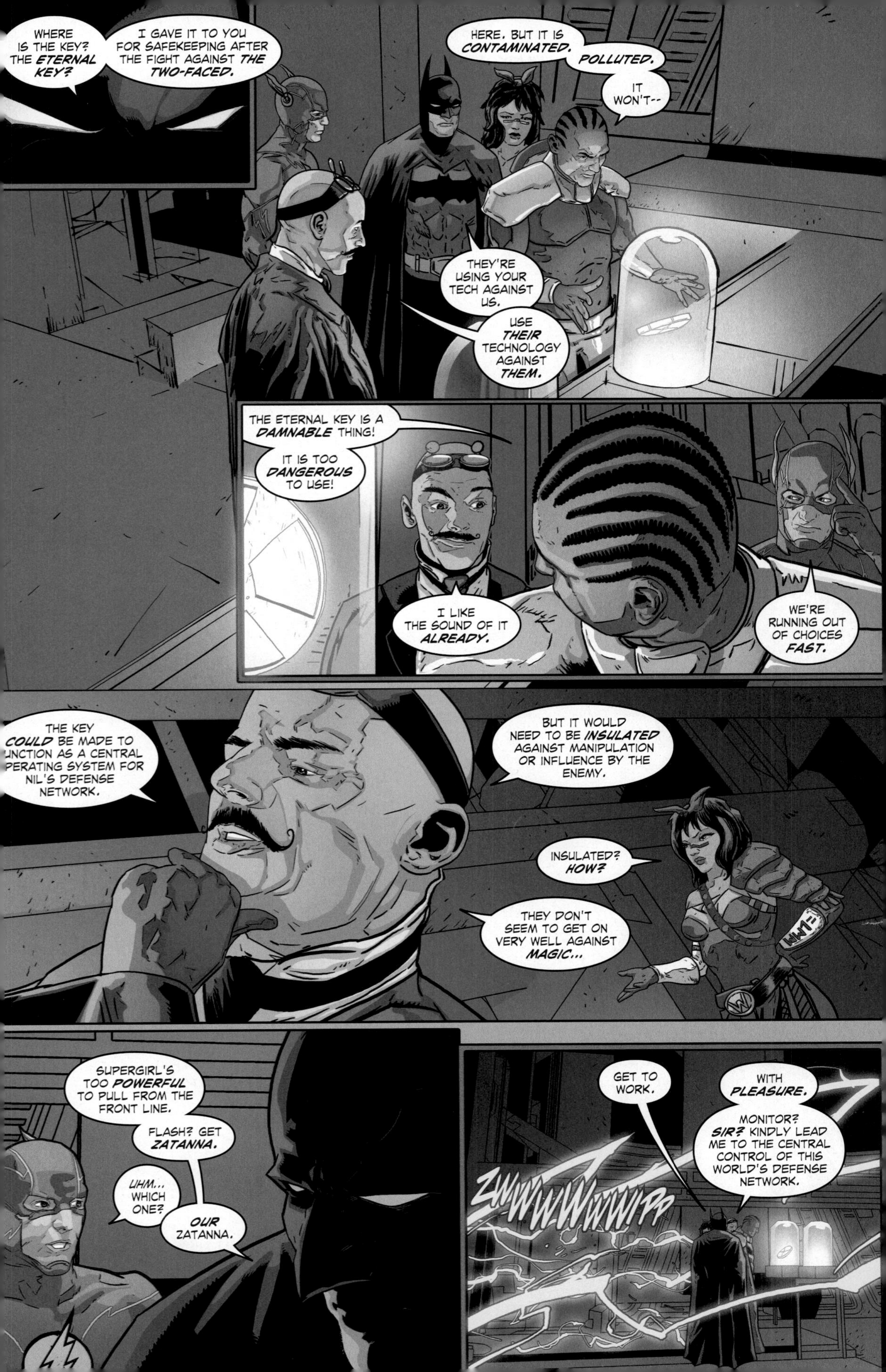
WHERE IS THE KEY? THE *ETERNAL KEY?*
I GAVE IT TO YOU FOR SAFEKEEPING AFTER THE FIGHT AGAINST *THE TWO-FACED.*
HERE. BUT IT IS *CONTAMINATED.*
POLLUTED.
IT WON'T--
THEY'RE USING YOUR TECH AGAINST US.
USE *THEIR* TECHNOLOGY AGAINST *THEM.*
THE ETERNAL KEY IS A *DAMNABLE* THING!
IT IS TOO *DANGEROUS* TO USE!
I LIKE THE SOUND OF IT *ALREADY.*
WE'RE RUNNING OUT OF CHOICES *FAST.*
THE KEY *COULD* BE MADE TO UNCTION AS A CENTRAL PERATING SYSTEM FOR NIL'S DEFENSE NETWORK.
BUT IT WOULD NEED TO BE *INSULATED* AGAINST MANIPULATION OR INFLUENCE BY THE ENEMY.
INSULATED? *HOW?*
THEY DON'T SEEM TO GET ON VERY WELL AGAINST *MAGIC...*
SUPERGIRL'S TOO *POWERFUL* TO PULL FROM THE FRONT LINE.
FLASH? GET *ZATANNA.*
UHM... WHICH ONE?
OUR ZATANNA.
GET TO WORK.
WITH *PLEASURE.*
MONITOR? *SIR?* KINDLY LEAD ME TO THE CENTRAL CONTROL OF THIS WORLD'S DEFENSE NETWORK.
ZWWWWWWWIPP

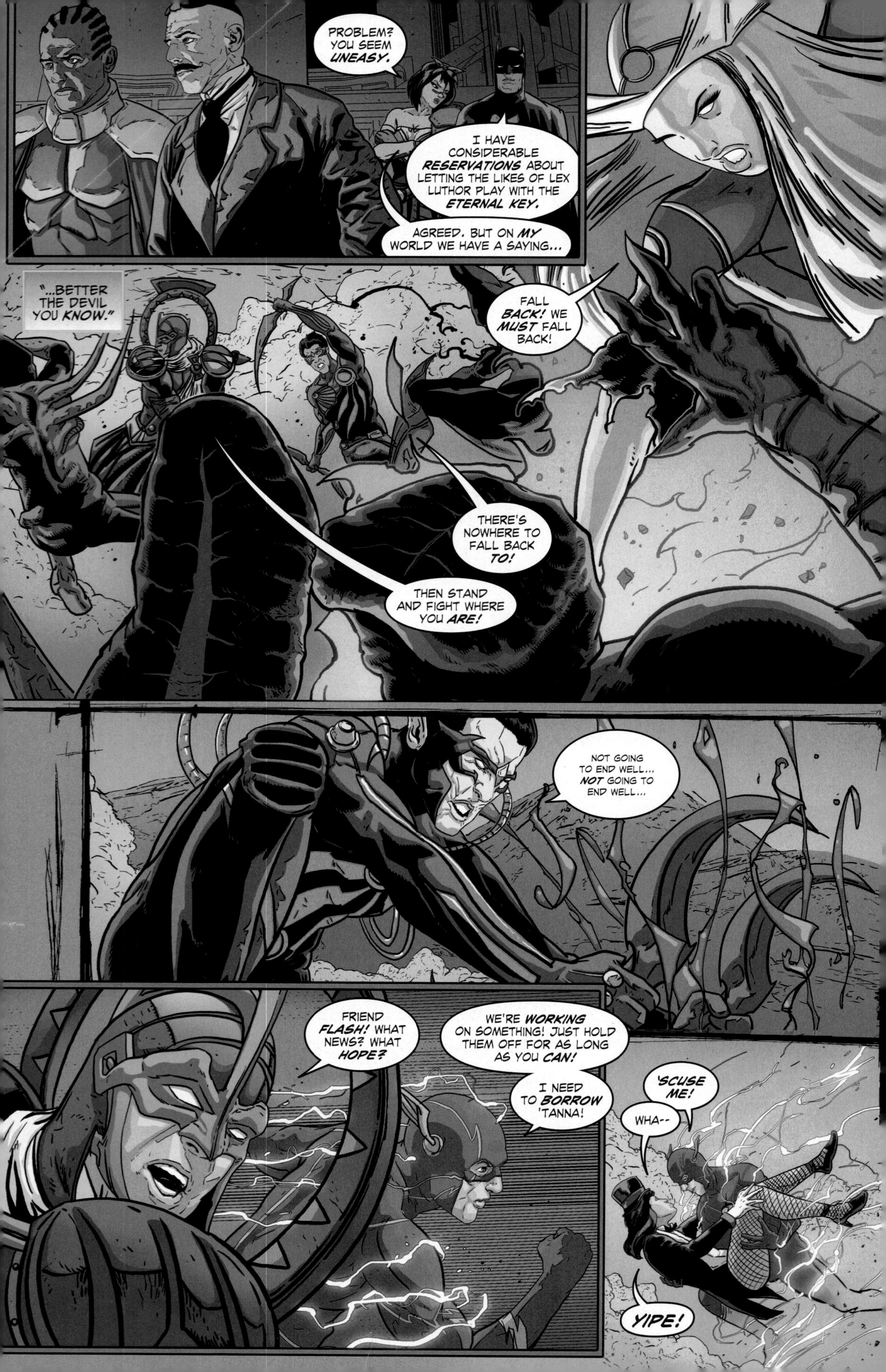
PROBLEM? YOU SEEM UNEASY.
I HAVE CONSIDERABLE RESERVATIONS ABOUT LETTING THE LIKES OF LEX LUTHOR PLAY WITH THE ETERNAL KEY.
AGREED. BUT ON MY WORLD WE HAVE A SAYING...
"...BETTER THE DEVIL YOU KNOW."
FALL BACK! WE MUST FALL BACK!
THERE'S NOWHERE TO FALL BACK TO!
THEN STAND AND FIGHT WHERE YOU ARE!
NOT GOING TO END WELL... NOT GOING TO END WELL...
FRIEND FLASH! WHAT NEWS? WHAT HOPE?
WE'RE WORKING ON SOMETHING! JUST HOLD THEM OFF FOR AS LONG AS YOU CAN!
I NEED TO BORROW 'TANNA!
'SCUSE ME!
WHA--
YIPE!

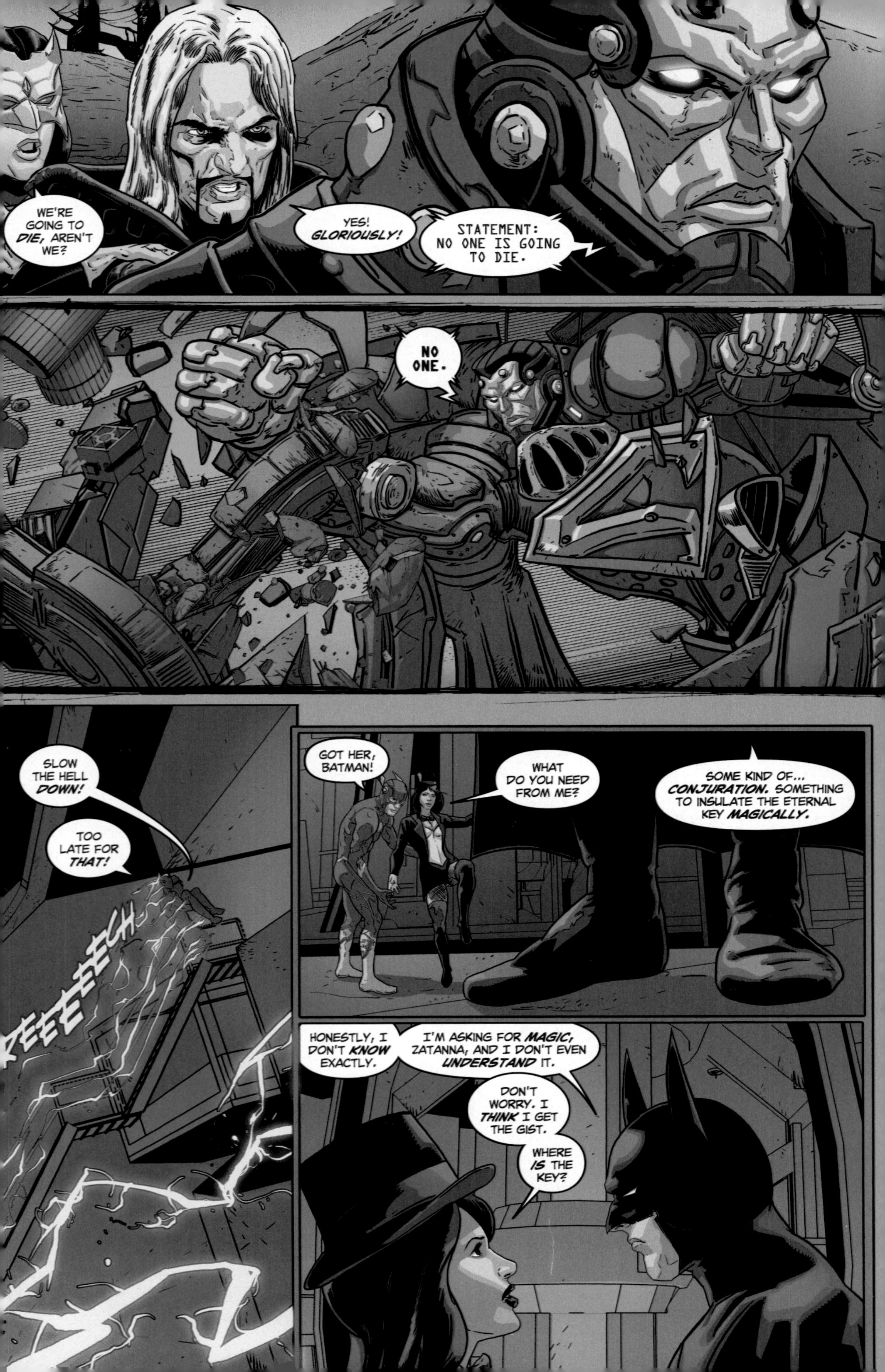

WE'RE GOING TO DIE, AREN'T WE?
YES! GLORIOUSLY!
STATEMENT: NO ONE IS GOING TO DIE.
NO ONE.
SLOW THE HELL DOWN!
TOO LATE FOR THAT!
SKREEEEECH
GOT HER, BATMAN!
WHAT DO YOU NEED FROM ME?
SOME KIND OF... CONJURATION. SOMETHING TO INSULATE THE ETERNAL KEY MAGICALLY.
HONESTLY, I DON'T KNOW EXACTLY.
I'M ASKING FOR MAGIC, ZATANNA, AND I DON'T EVEN UNDERSTAND IT.
DON'T WORRY. I THINK I GET THE GIST.
WHERE IS THE KEY?

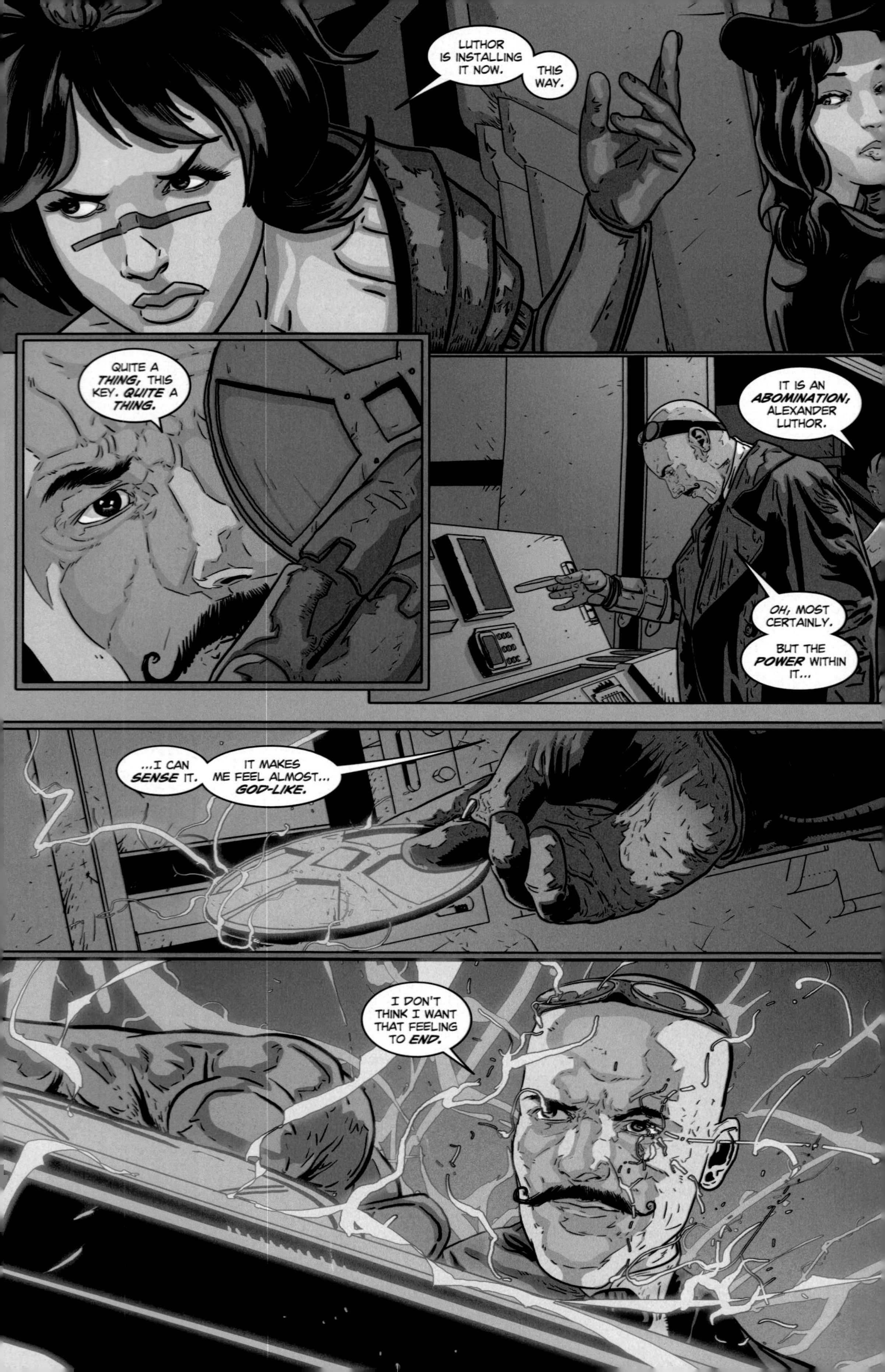
LUTHOR IS INSTALLING IT NOW.
THIS WAY.
QUITE A THING, THIS KEY. QUITE A THING.
IT IS AN ABOMINATION, ALEXANDER LUTHOR.
OH, MOST CERTAINLY.
BUT THE POWER WITHIN IT...
...I CAN SENSE IT.
IT MAKES ME FEEL ALMOST... GOD-LIKE.
I DON'T THINK I WANT THAT FEELING TO END.

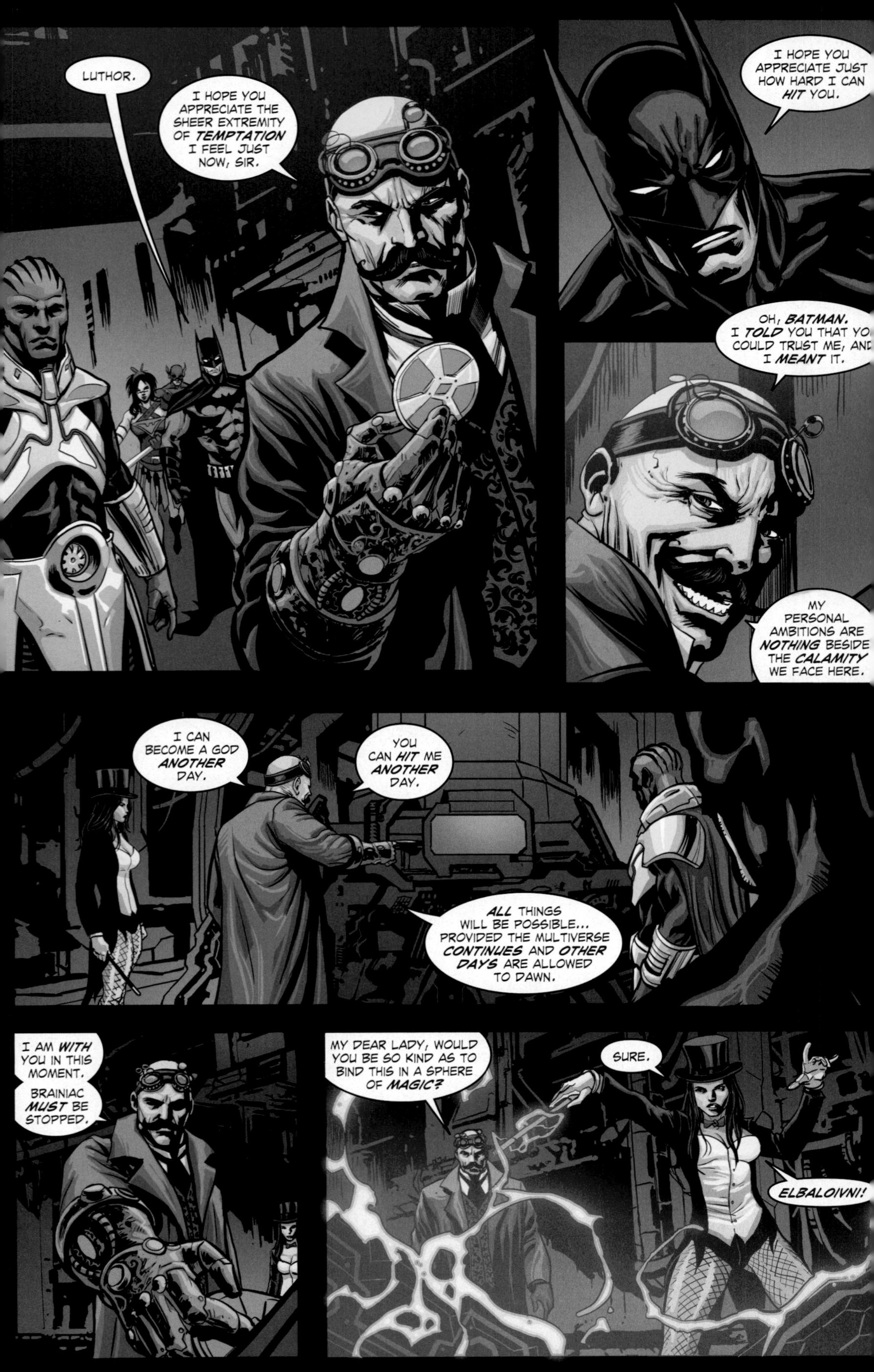
LUTHOR.
I HOPE YOU APPRECIATE THE SHEER EXTREMITY OF TEMPTATION I FEEL JUST NOW, SIR.
I HOPE YOU APPRECIATE JUST HOW HARD I CAN HIT YOU.
OH, BATMAN. I TOLD YOU THAT YO COULD TRUST ME, AND I MEANT IT.
MY PERSONAL AMBITIONS ARE NOTHING BESIDE THE CALAMITY WE FACE HERE.
I CAN BECOME A GOD ANOTHER DAY.
YOU CAN HIT ME ANOTHER DAY.
ALL THINGS WILL BE POSSIBLE... PROVIDED THE MULTIVERSE CONTINUES AND OTHER DAYS ARE ALLOWED TO DAWN.
I AM WITH YOU IN THIS MOMENT.
BRAINIAC MUST BE STOPPED.
MY DEAR LADY, WOULD YOU BE SO KIND AS TO BIND THIS IN A SPHERE OF MAGIC?
SURE.
ELBALOIVNI!

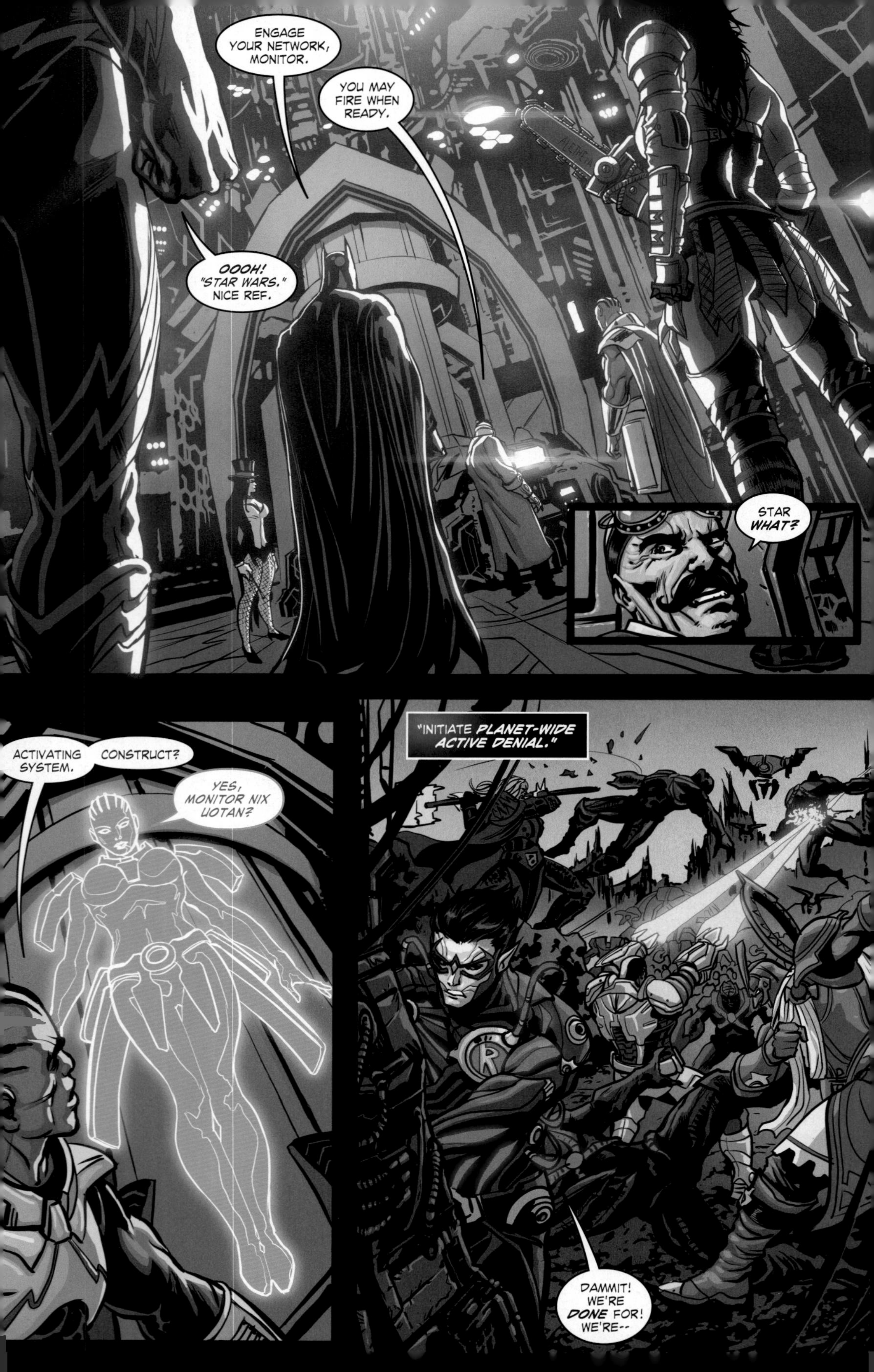
ENGAGE YOUR NETWORK, MONITOR.
YOU MAY FIRE WHEN READY.
OOOH! "STAR WARS." NICE REF.
STAR WHAT?
ACTIVATING SYSTEM.
CONSTRUCT?
YES, MONITOR NIX UOTAN?
"INITIATE PLANET-WIDE ACTIVE DENIAL."
DAMMIT! WE'RE DONE FOR! WE'RE--

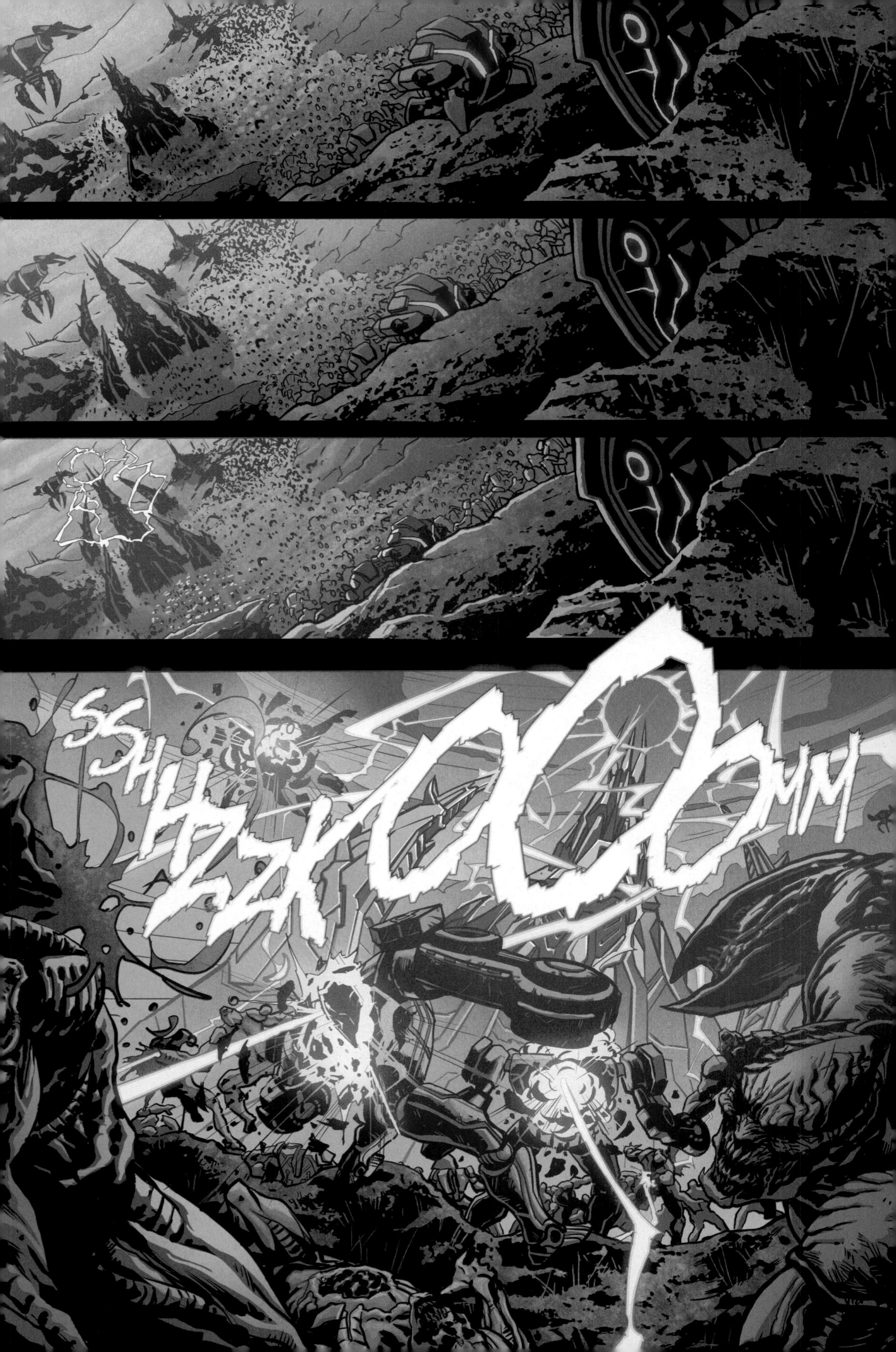
SCHHZKOOOMM

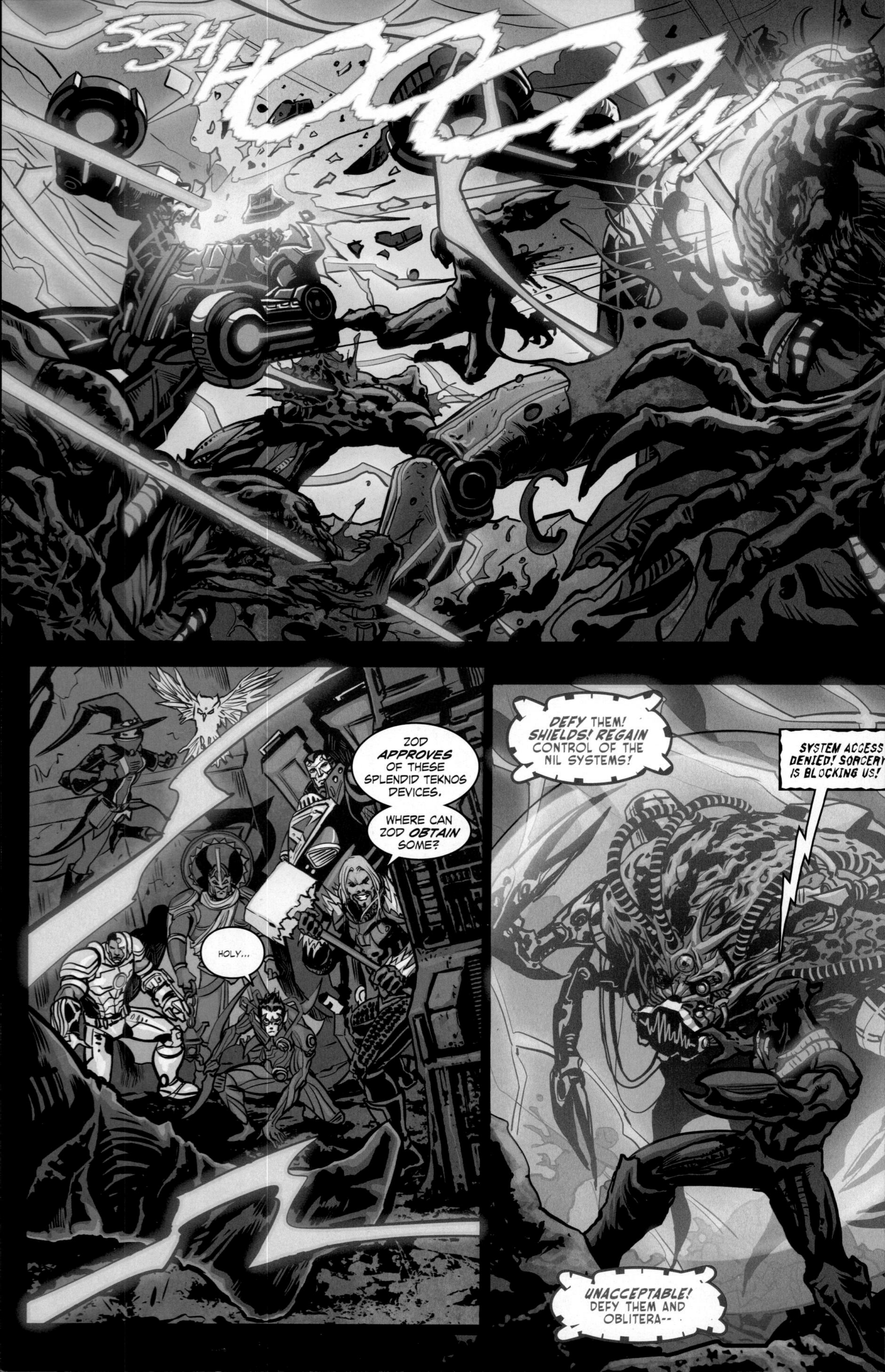
SSHHOOOOM
ZOD APPROVES OF THESE SPLENDID TEKNOS DEVICES.
WHERE CAN ZOD OBTAIN SOME?
HOLY...
DEFY THEM! SHIELDS! REGAIN CONTROL OF THE NIL SYSTEMS!
SYSTEM ACCESS DENIED! SORCERY IS BLOCKING US!
UNACCEPTABLE! DEFY THEM AND OBLITERA--

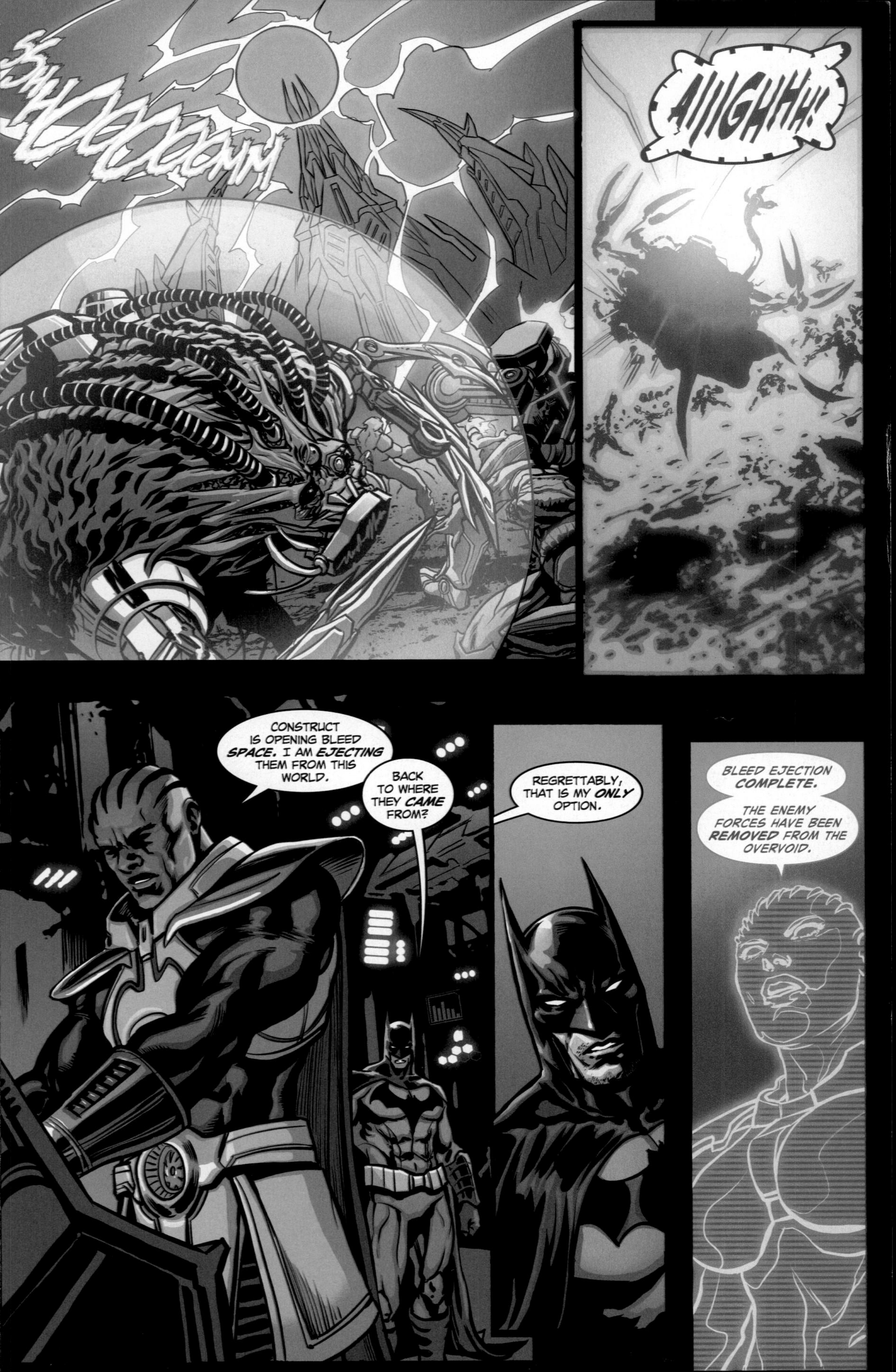
SSHHOOOOOOMM
AIIIGHHH!
CONSTRUCT IS OPENING BLEED SPACE. I AM EJECTING THEM FROM THIS WORLD.
BACK TO WHERE THEY CAME FROM?
REGRETTABLY, THAT IS MY ONLY OPTION.
BLEED EJECTION COMPLETE.
THE ENEMY FORCES HAVE BEEN REMOVED FROM THE OVERVOID.

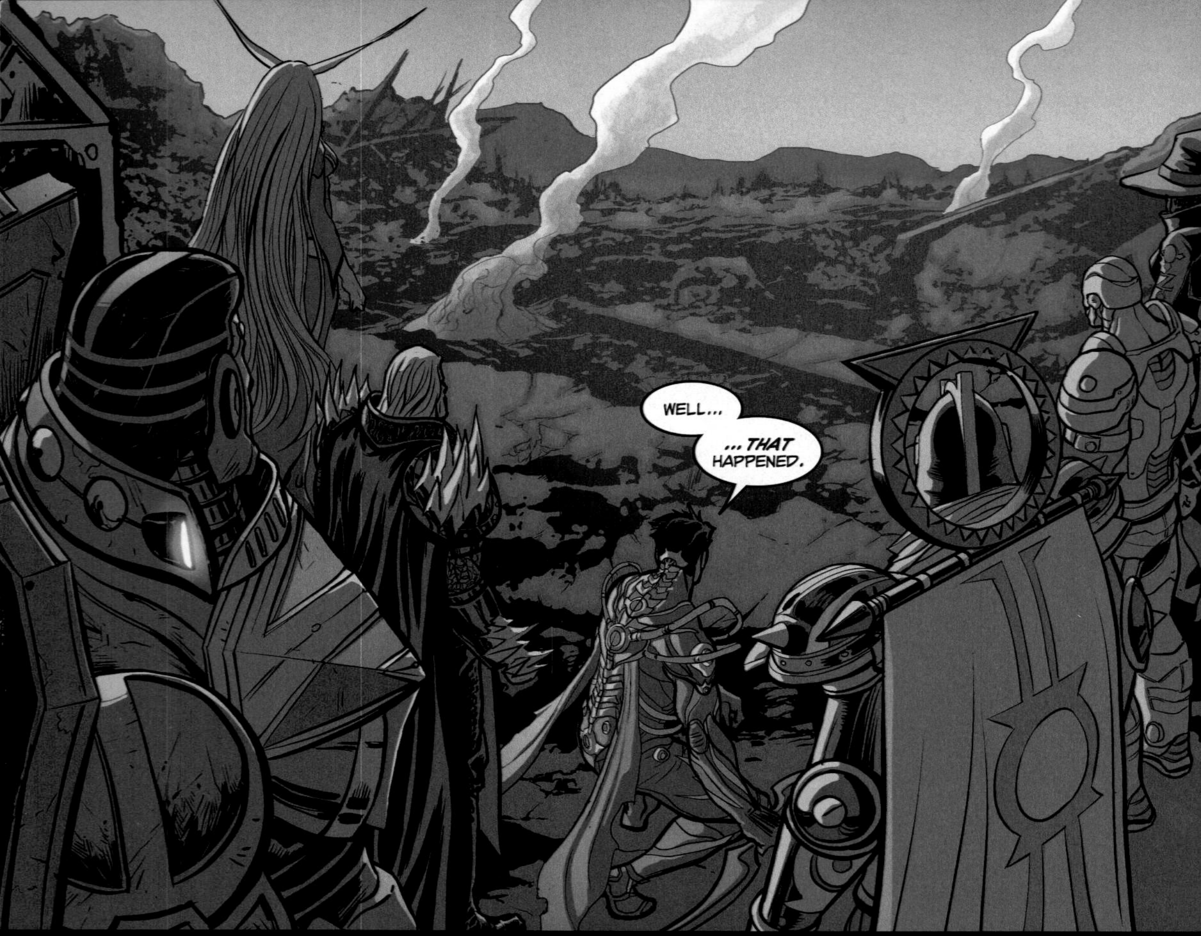
WELL...
...THAT HAPPENED.

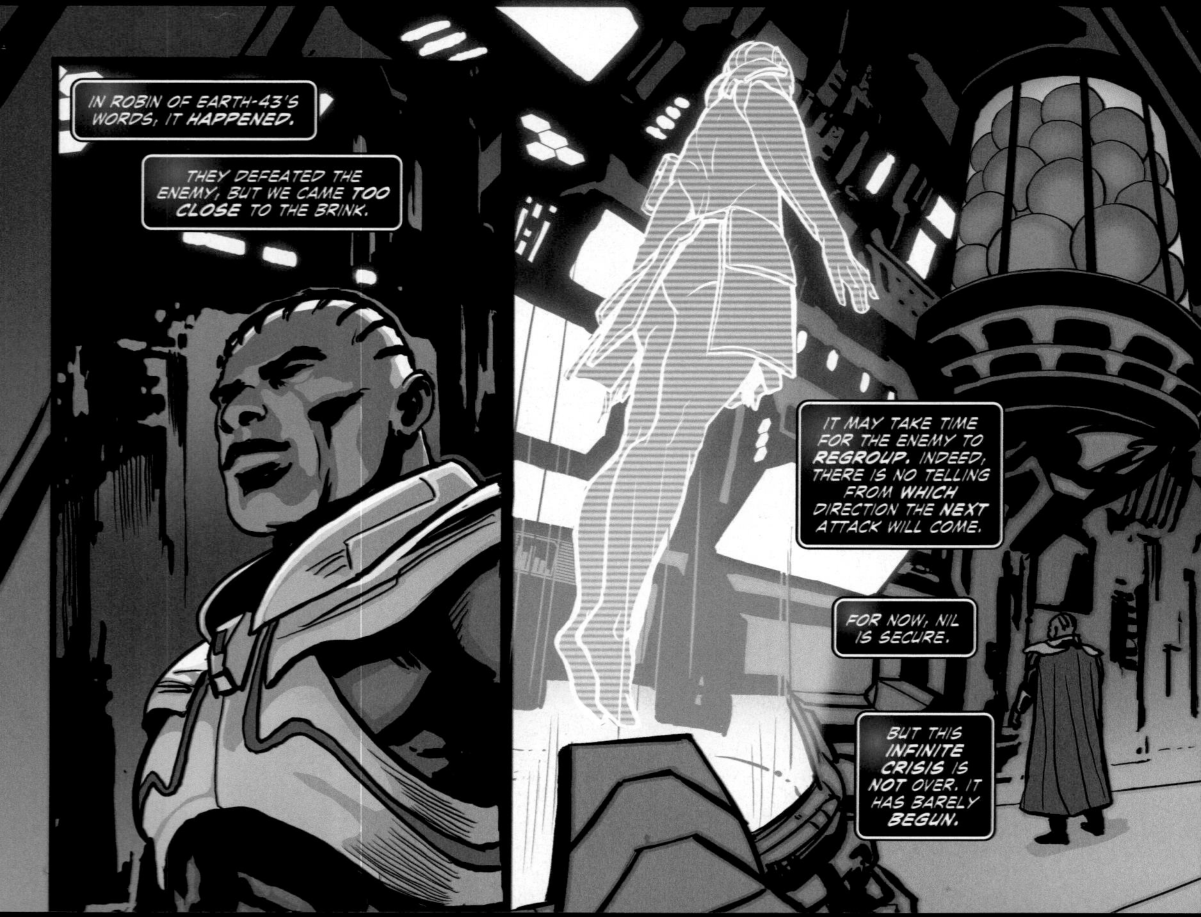
IN ROBIN OF EARTH-43'S WORDS, IT HAPPENED.
THEY DEFEATED THE ENEMY, BUT WE CAME TOO CLOSE TO THE BRINK.
IT MAY TAKE TIME FOR THE ENEMY TO REGROUP. INDEED, THERE IS NO TELLING FROM WHICH DIRECTION THE NEXT ATTACK WILL COME.
FOR NOW, NIL IS SECURE.
BUT THIS INFINITE CRISIS IS NOT OVER. IT HAS BARELY BEGUN.

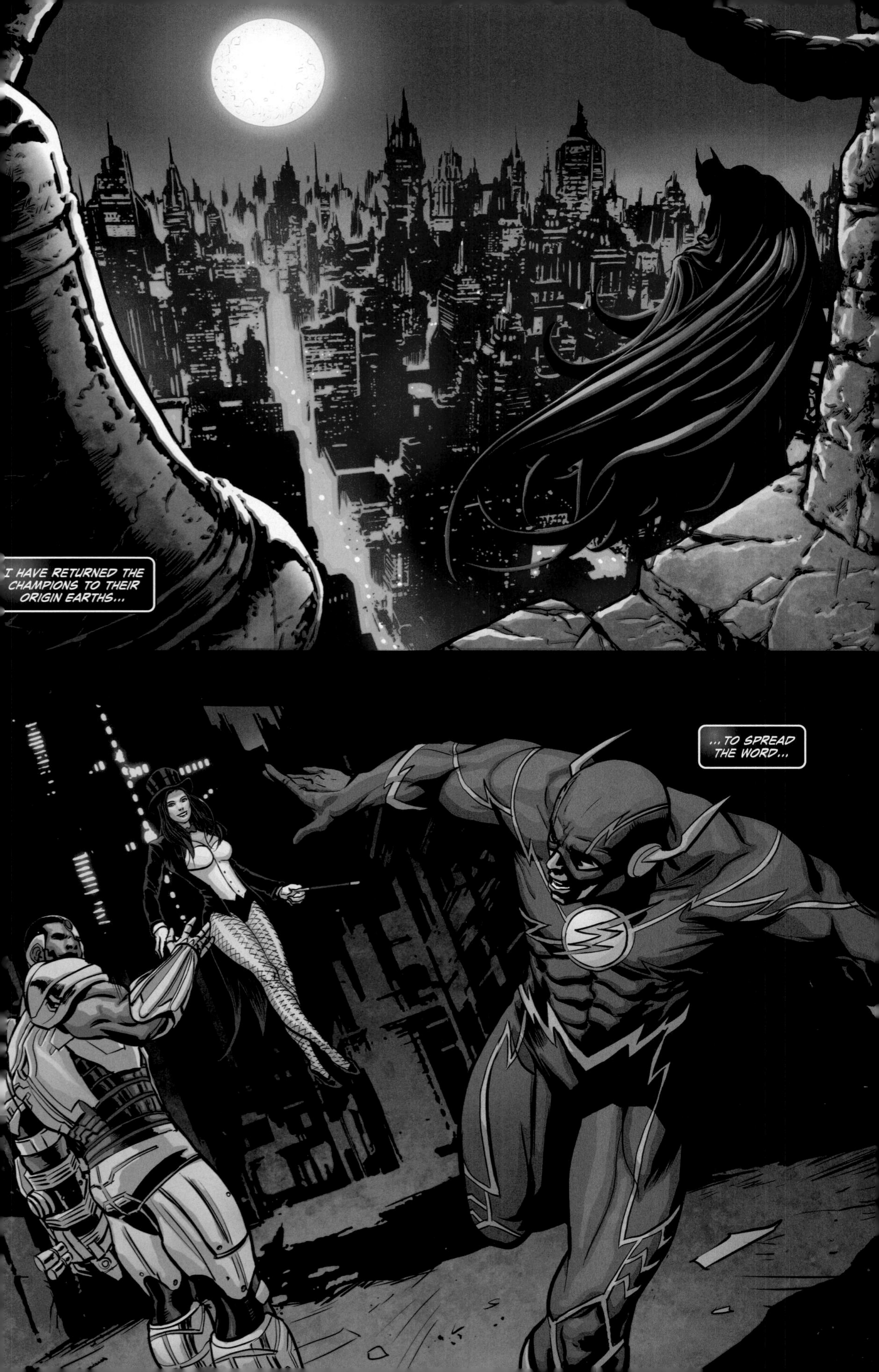
I HAVE RETURNED THE CHAMPIONS TO THEIR ORIGIN EARTHS...
...TO SPREAD THE WORD...

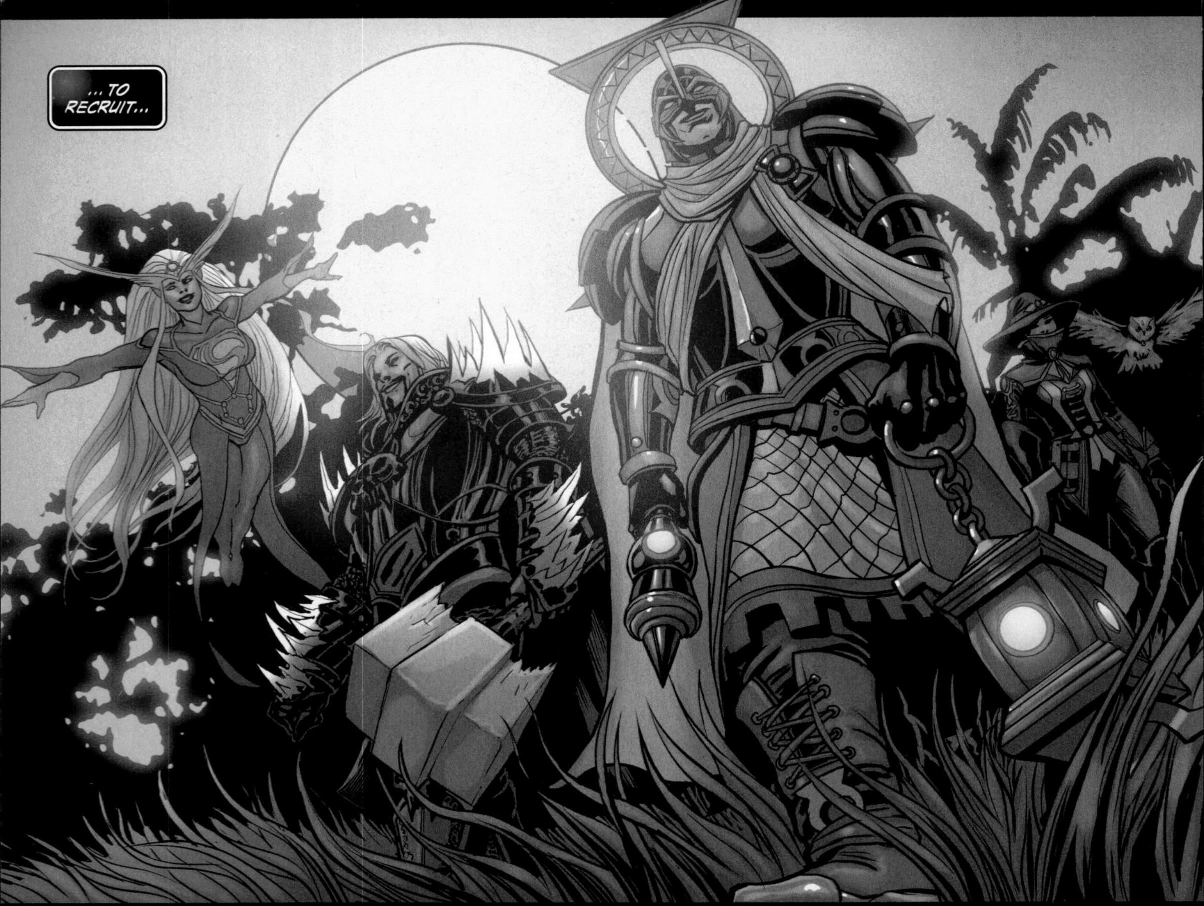
...TO RECRUIT...

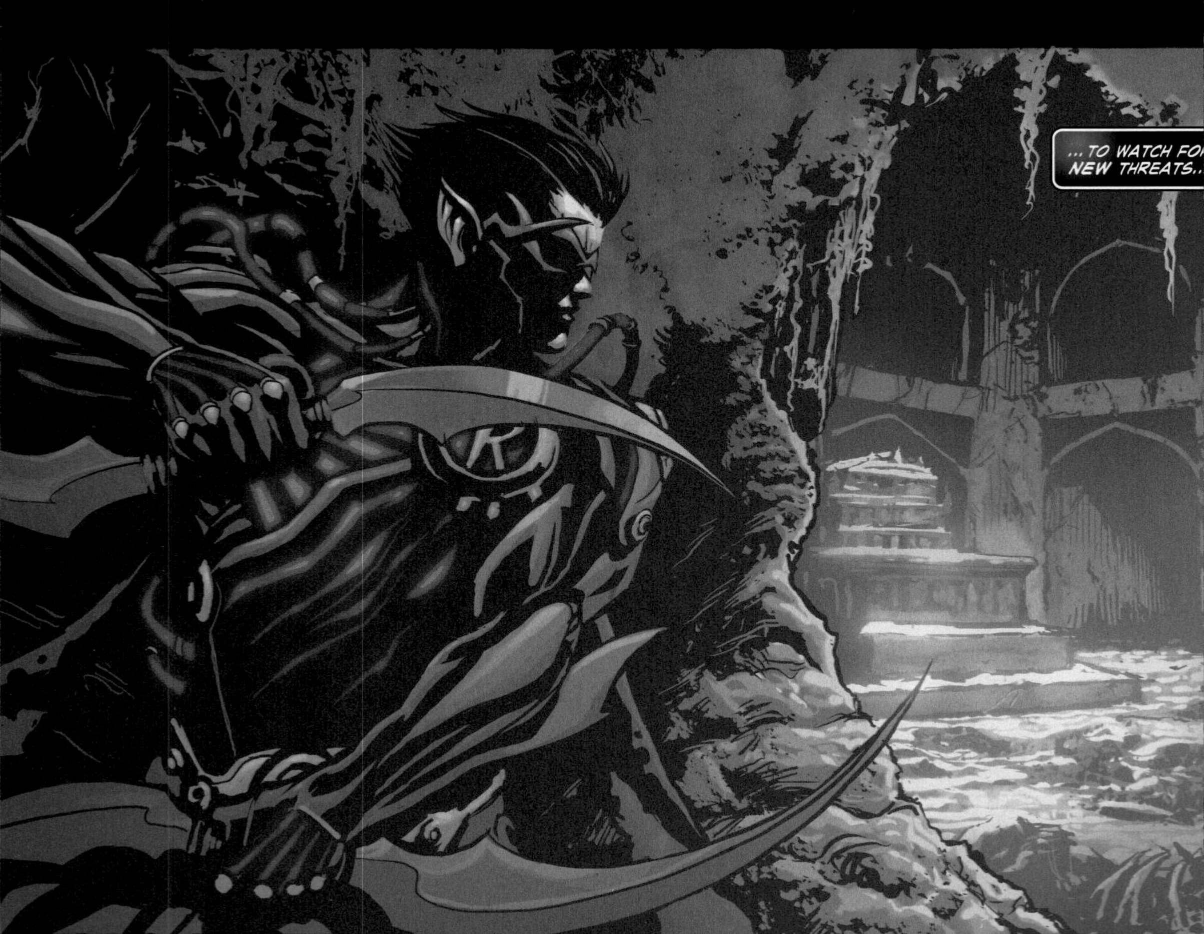
...TO WATCH FO
NEW THREATS..

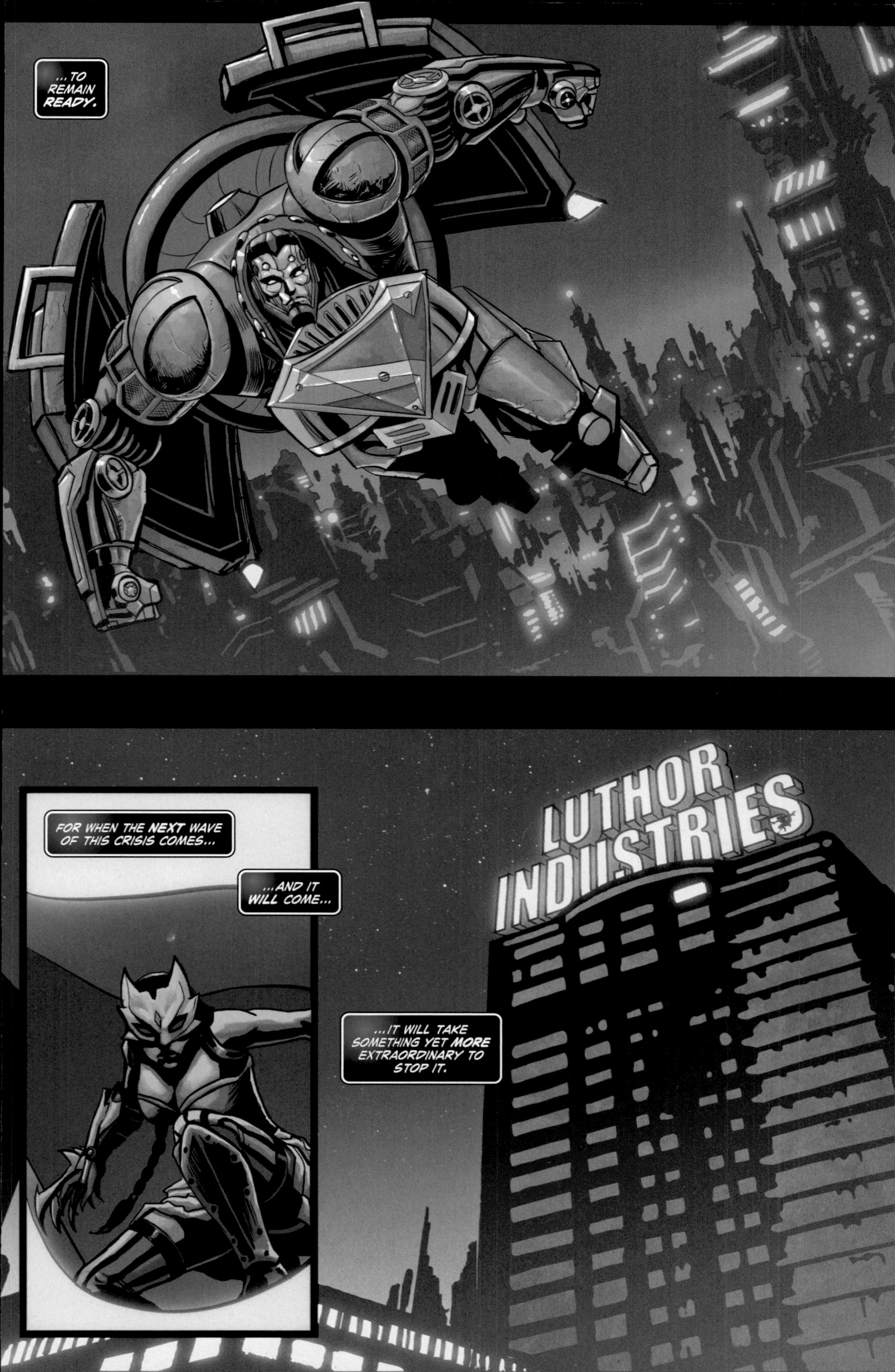
...TO REMAIN READY.
FOR WHEN THE NEXT WAVE OF THIS CRISIS COMES...
...AND IT WILL COME...
LUTHOR INDUSTRIES
...IT WILL TAKE SOMETHING YET MORE EXTRAORDINARY TO STOP IT.

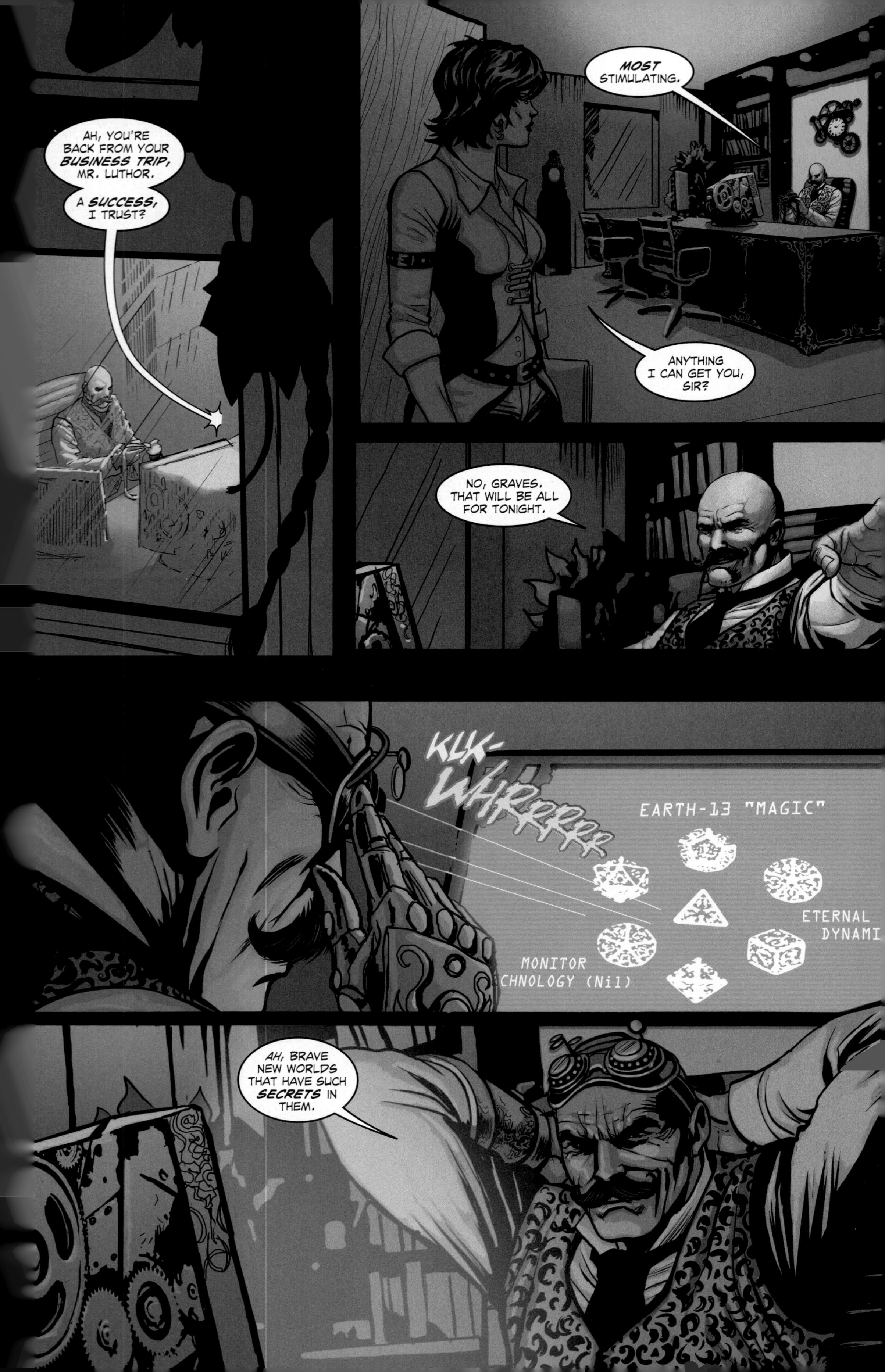
AH, YOU'RE BACK FROM YOUR BUSINESS TRIP, MR. LUTHOR.
A SUCCESS, I TRUST?
MOST STIMULATING.
ANYTHING I CAN GET YOU, SIR?
NO, GRAVES. THAT WILL BE ALL FOR TONIGHT.
KLK-WHRRRRR
EARTH-13 "MAGIC"
ETERNAL DYNAMI
MONITOR
CHNOLOGY (Nil)
AH, BRAVE NEW WORLDS THAT HAVE SUCH SECRETS IN THEM.

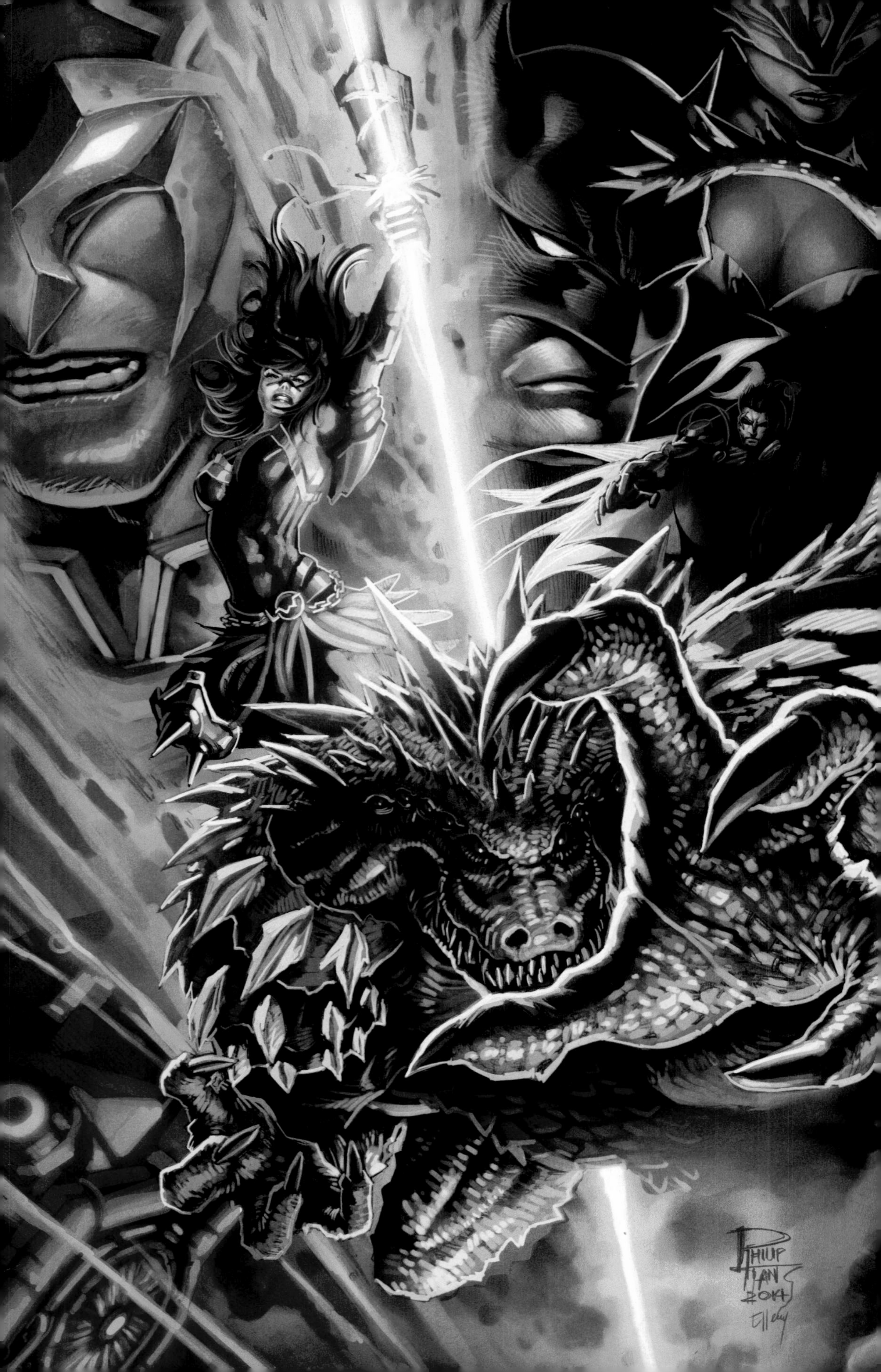

EARTH ENGINE

Eduardo Francisco **Christian Duce** Artists **Alejandro Sanchez** Colorist
Cover Art by **Philip Tan and Ellery Santos**

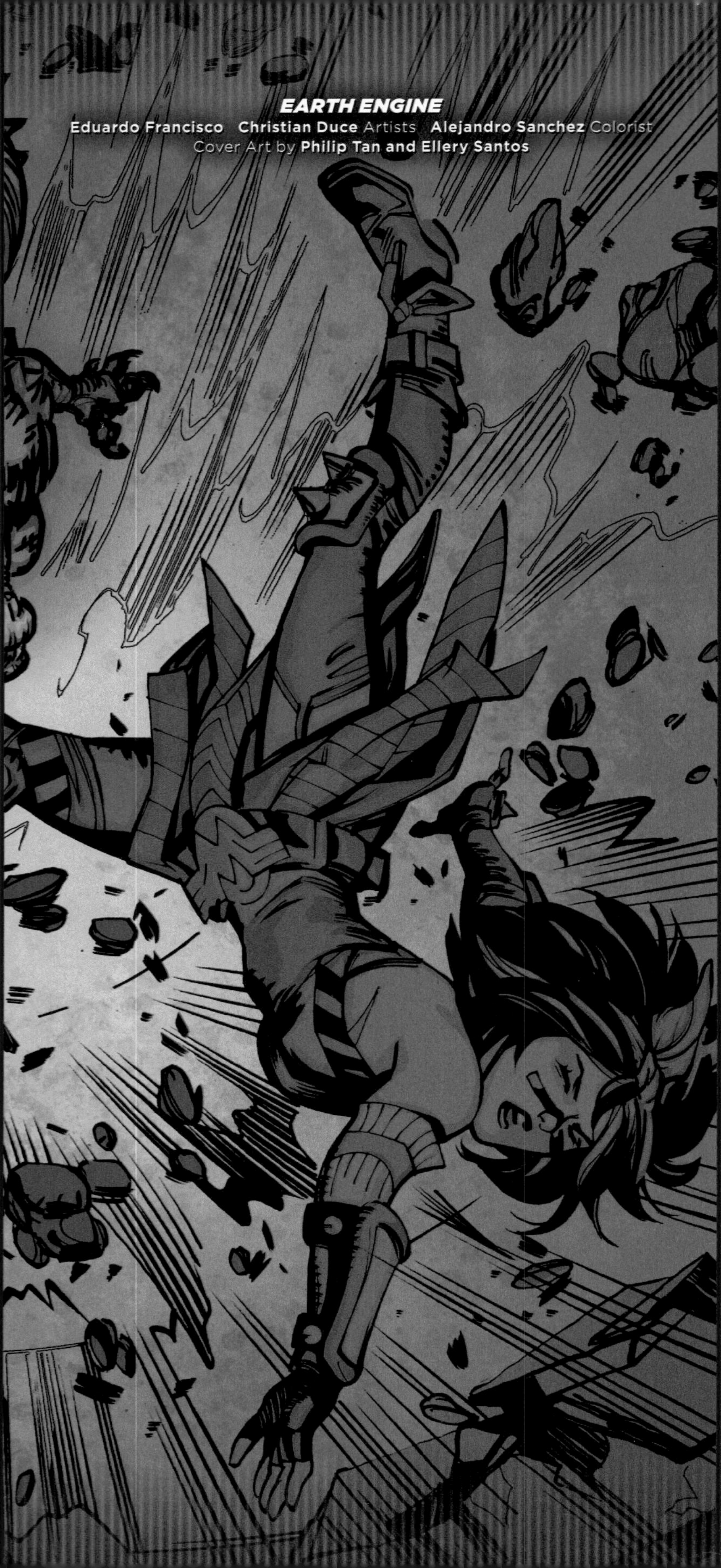

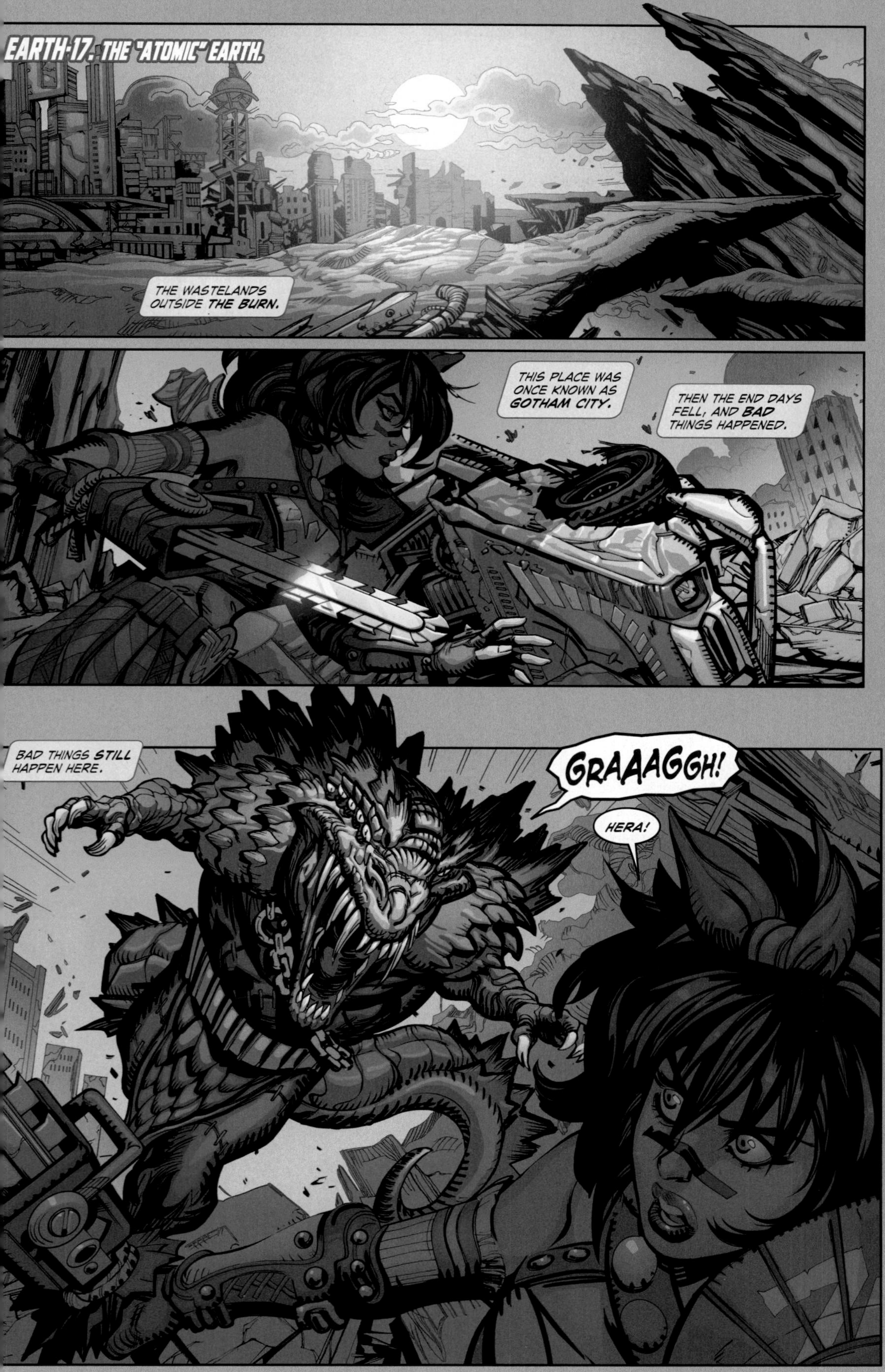

EARTH-17. THE "ATOMIC" EARTH.
THE WASTELANDS OUTSIDE THE BURN.
THIS PLACE WAS ONCE KNOWN AS GOTHAM CITY.
THEN THE END DAYS FELL, AND BAD THINGS HAPPENED.
BAD THINGS STILL HAPPEN HERE.
GRAAAGGH!
HERA!

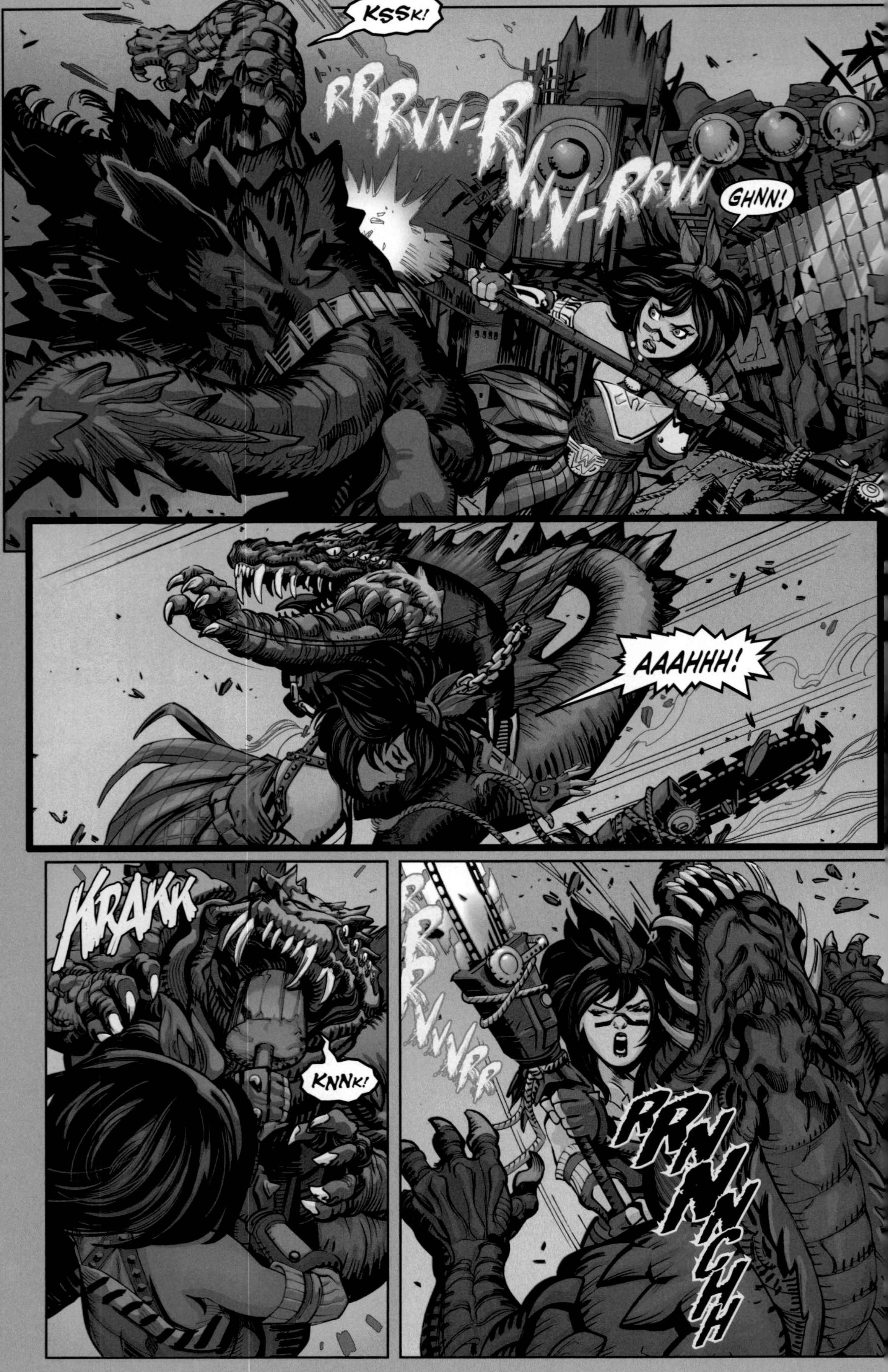
KSSK!
RRRVV-RVVV-RRVV
GHNN!
AAAHHH!
KRAKK
KNNK!
RRNNCH

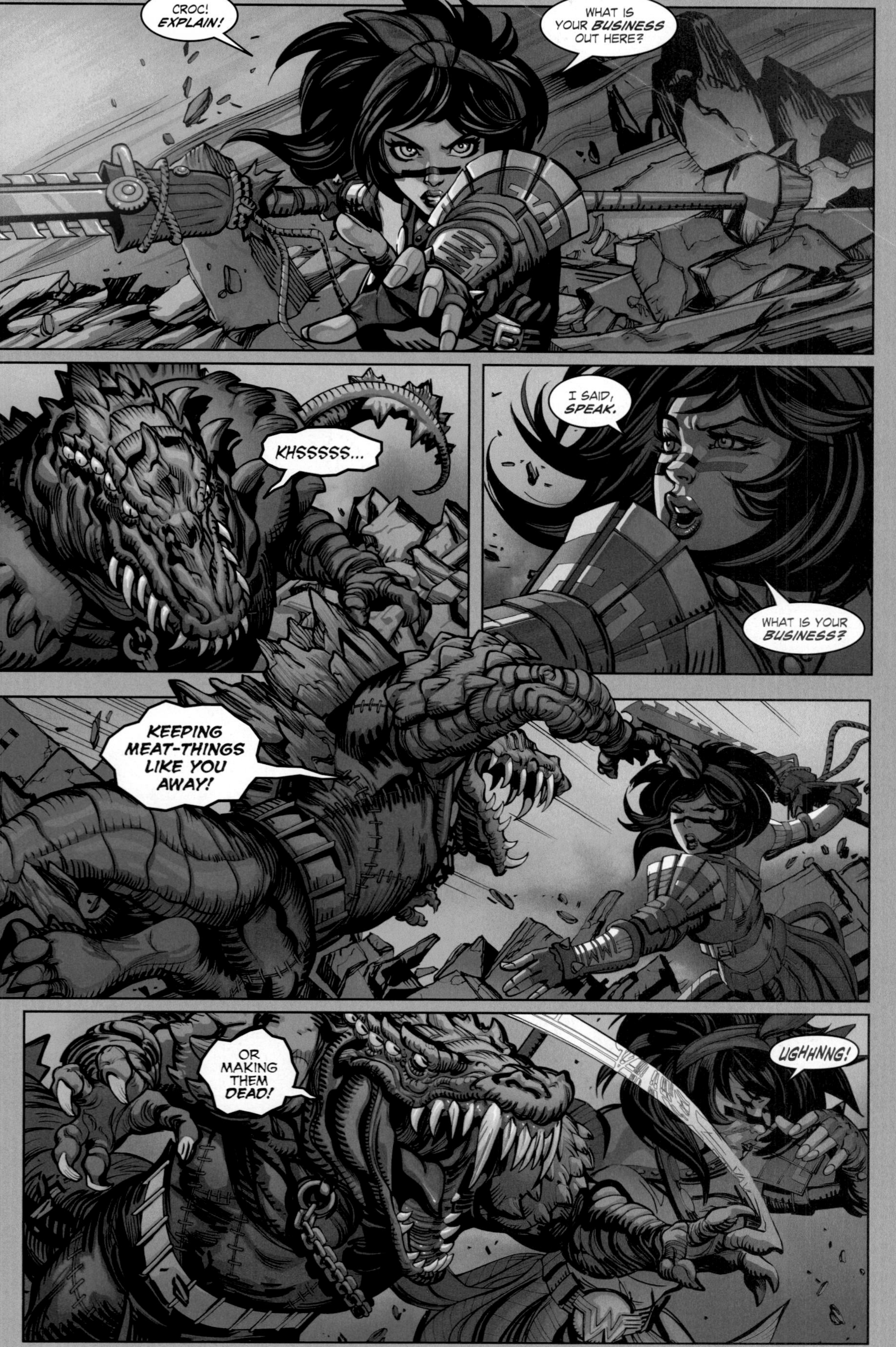
CROC! EXPLAIN!
WHAT IS YOUR BUSINESS OUT HERE?
KHSSSSS...
I SAID, SPEAK.
WHAT IS YOUR BUSINESS?
KEEPING MEAT-THINGS LIKE YOU AWAY!
OR MAKING THEM DEAD!
UGHHHNG!

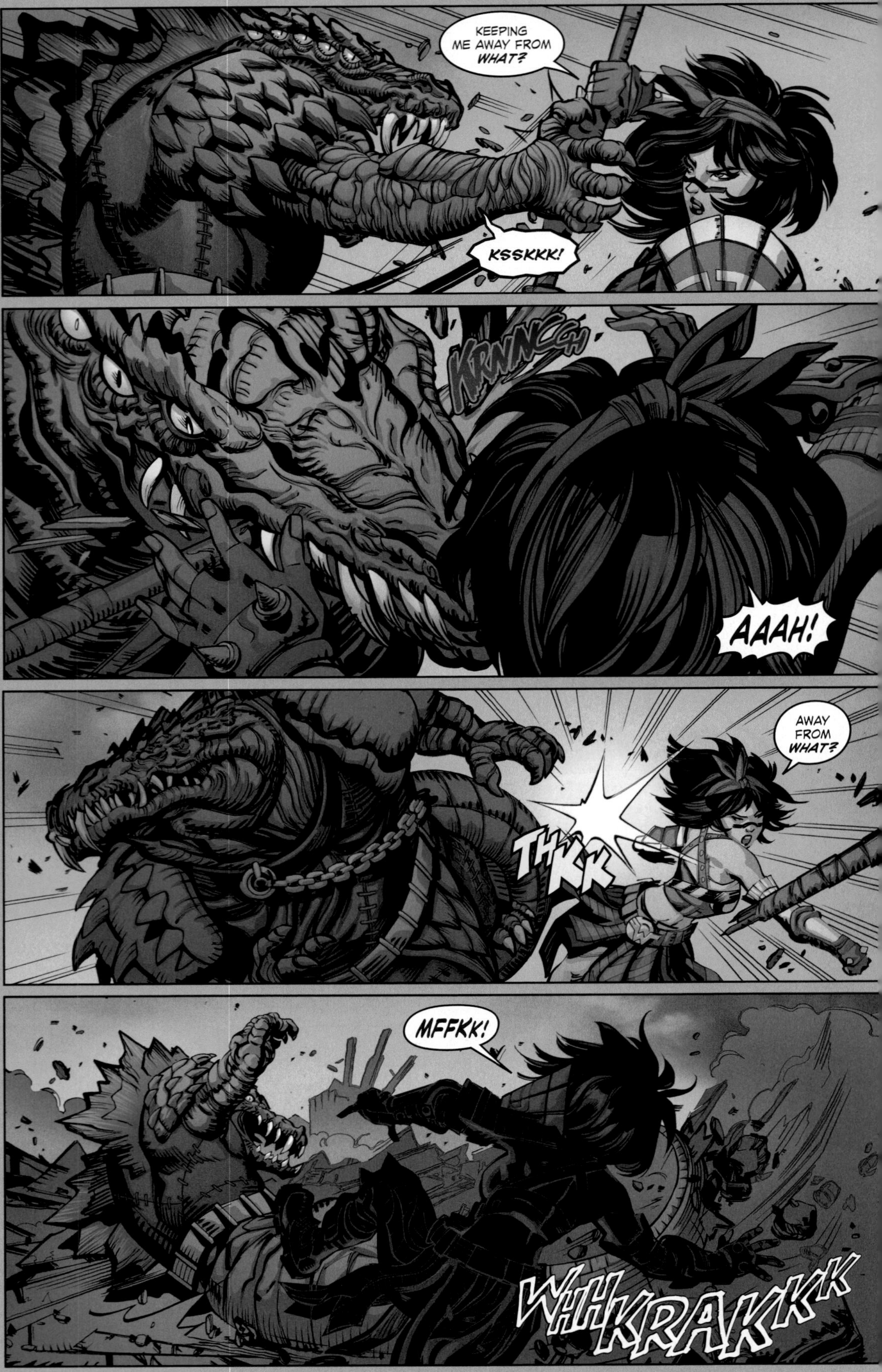
KEEPING ME AWAY FROM WHAT?
KSSKKK!
KRWNCCH
AAAH!
AWAY FROM WHAT?
THKK
MFFKK!
WHHKRAKKK

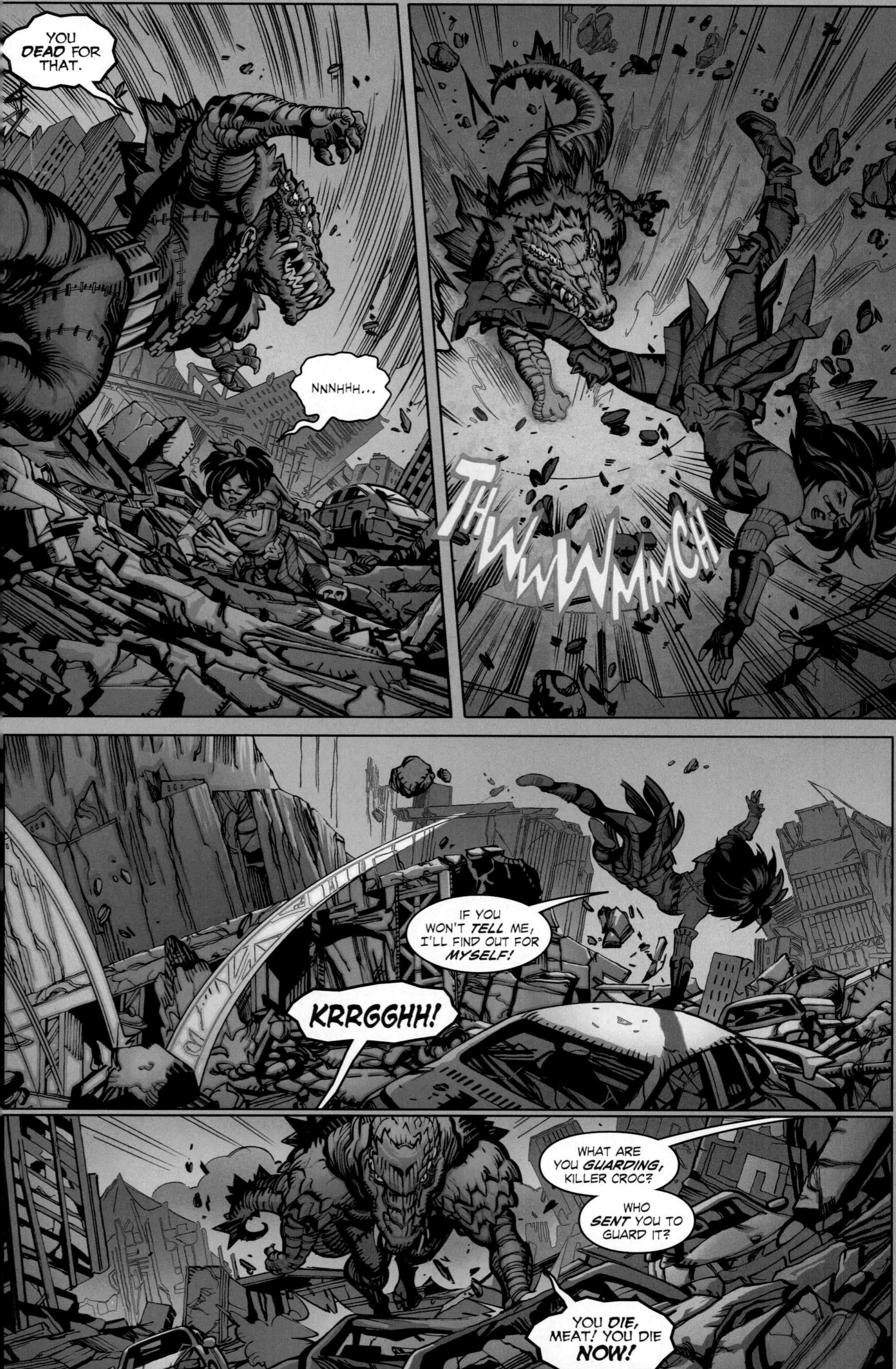
YOU DEAD FOR THAT.
NNNHHH...
THWWWWMMCH
IF YOU WON'T TELL ME, I'LL FIND OUT FOR MYSELF!
KRRGGHH!
WHAT ARE YOU GUARDING, KILLER CROC?
WHO SENT YOU TO GUARD IT?
YOU DIE, MEAT! YOU DIE NOW!

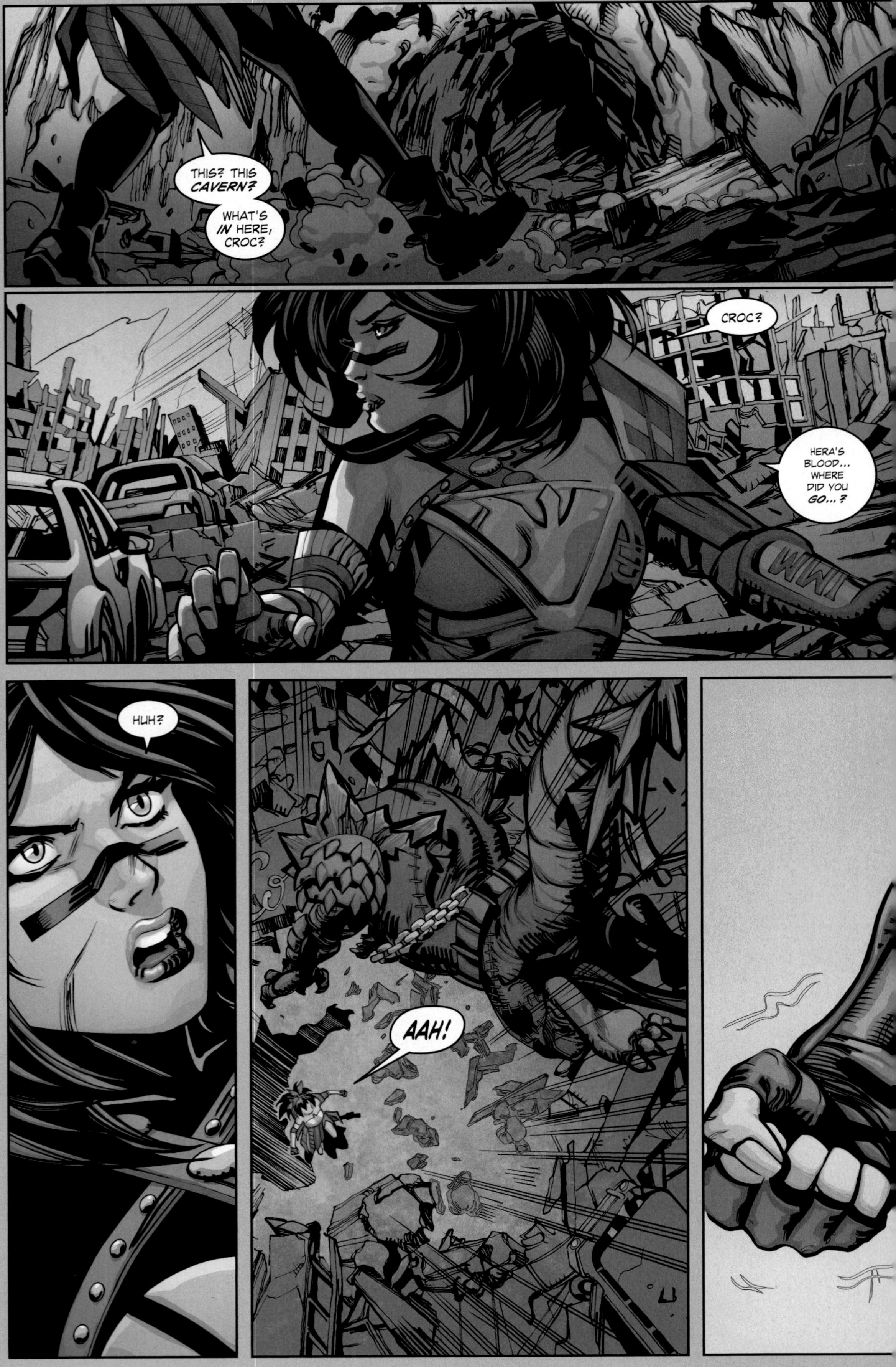
THIS? THIS CAVERN?
WHAT'S IN HERE, CROC?
CROC?
HERA'S BLOOD... WHERE DID YOU GO...?
HUH?
AAH!

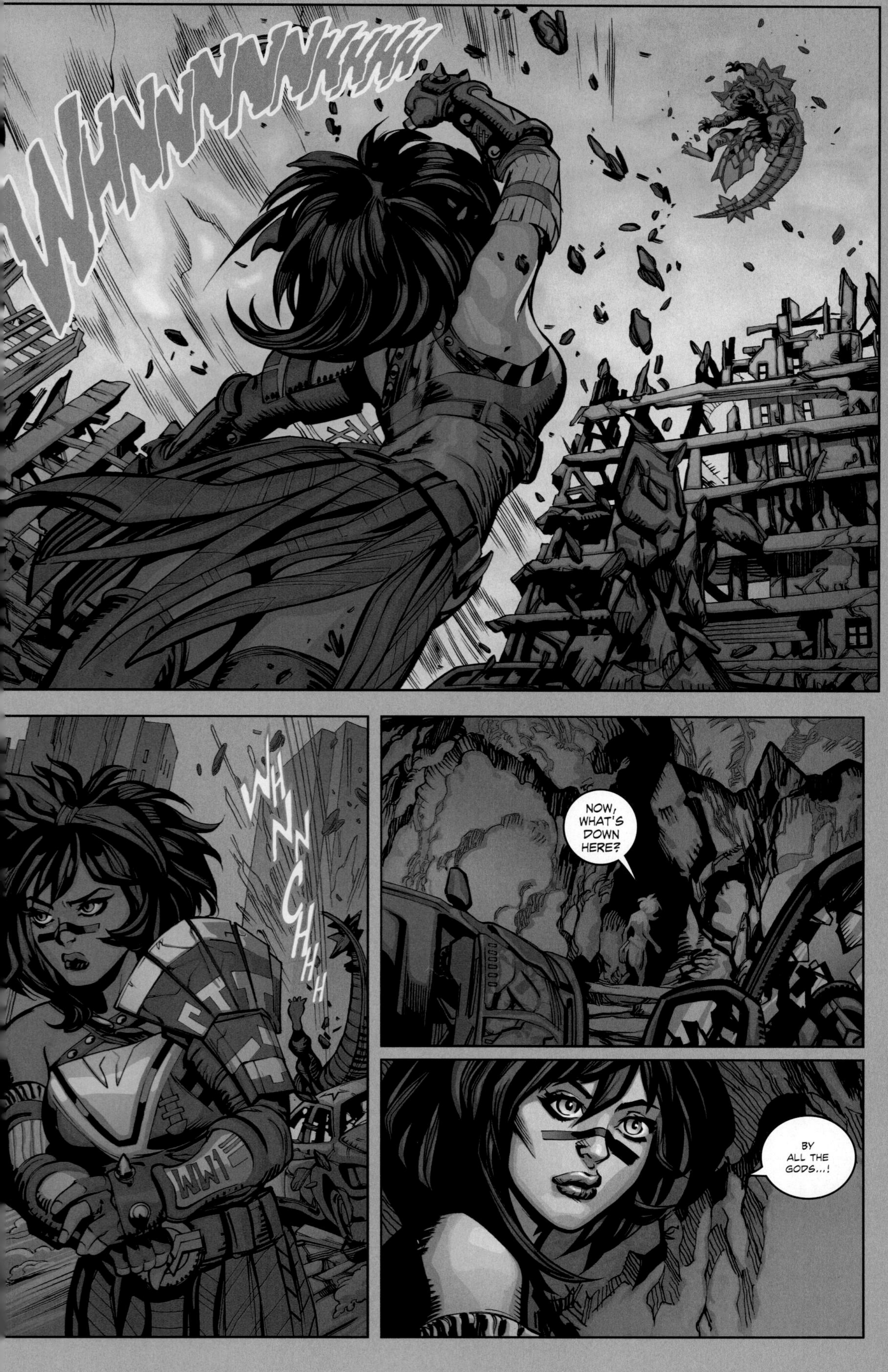
WHNNNNNKHHH!
WHNNCHHH
NOW, WHAT'S DOWN HERE?
BY ALL THE GODS...!

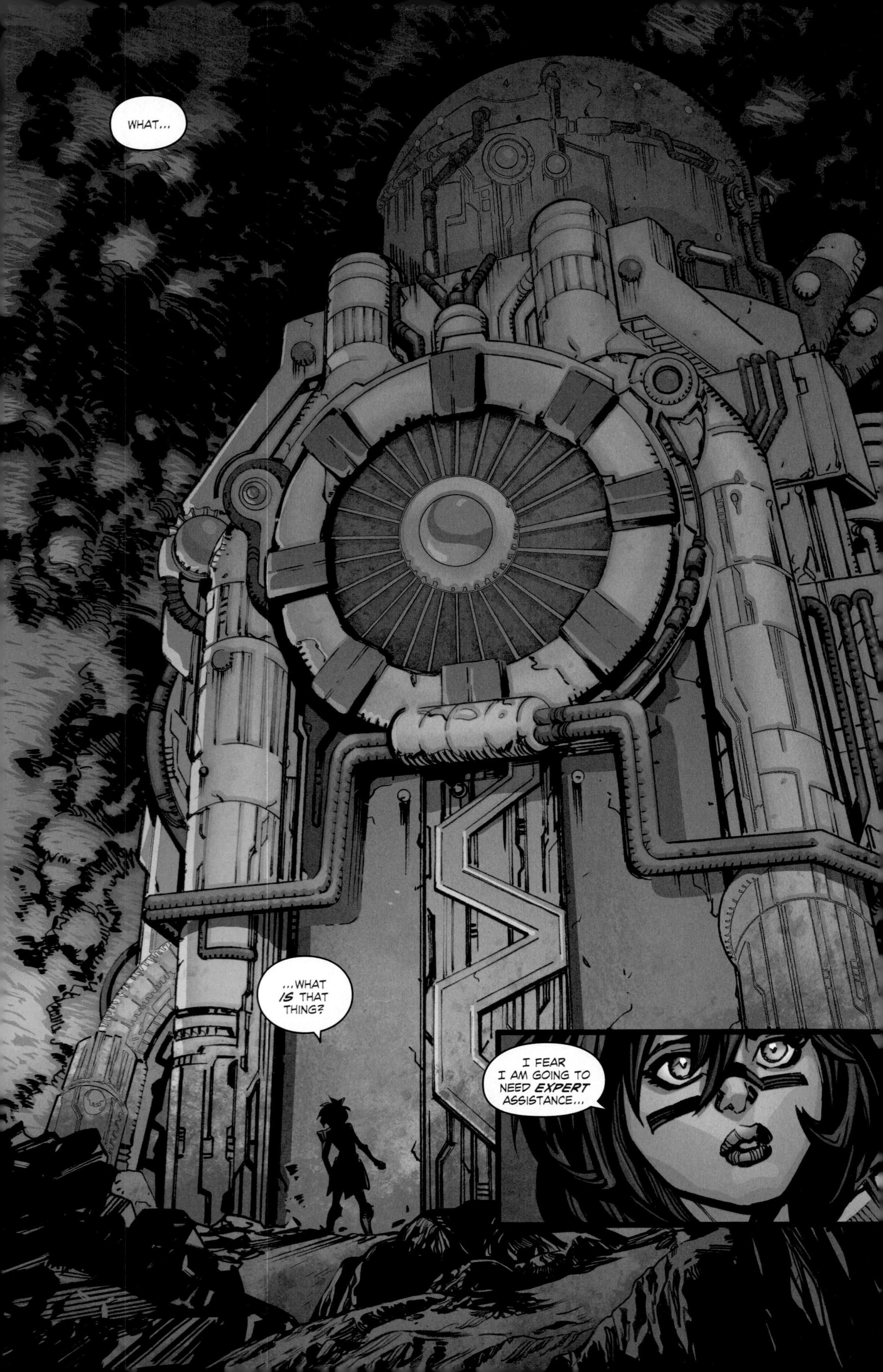
WHAT...
...WHAT *IS* THAT THING?
I FEAR I AM GOING TO NEED *EXPERT* ASSISTANCE...

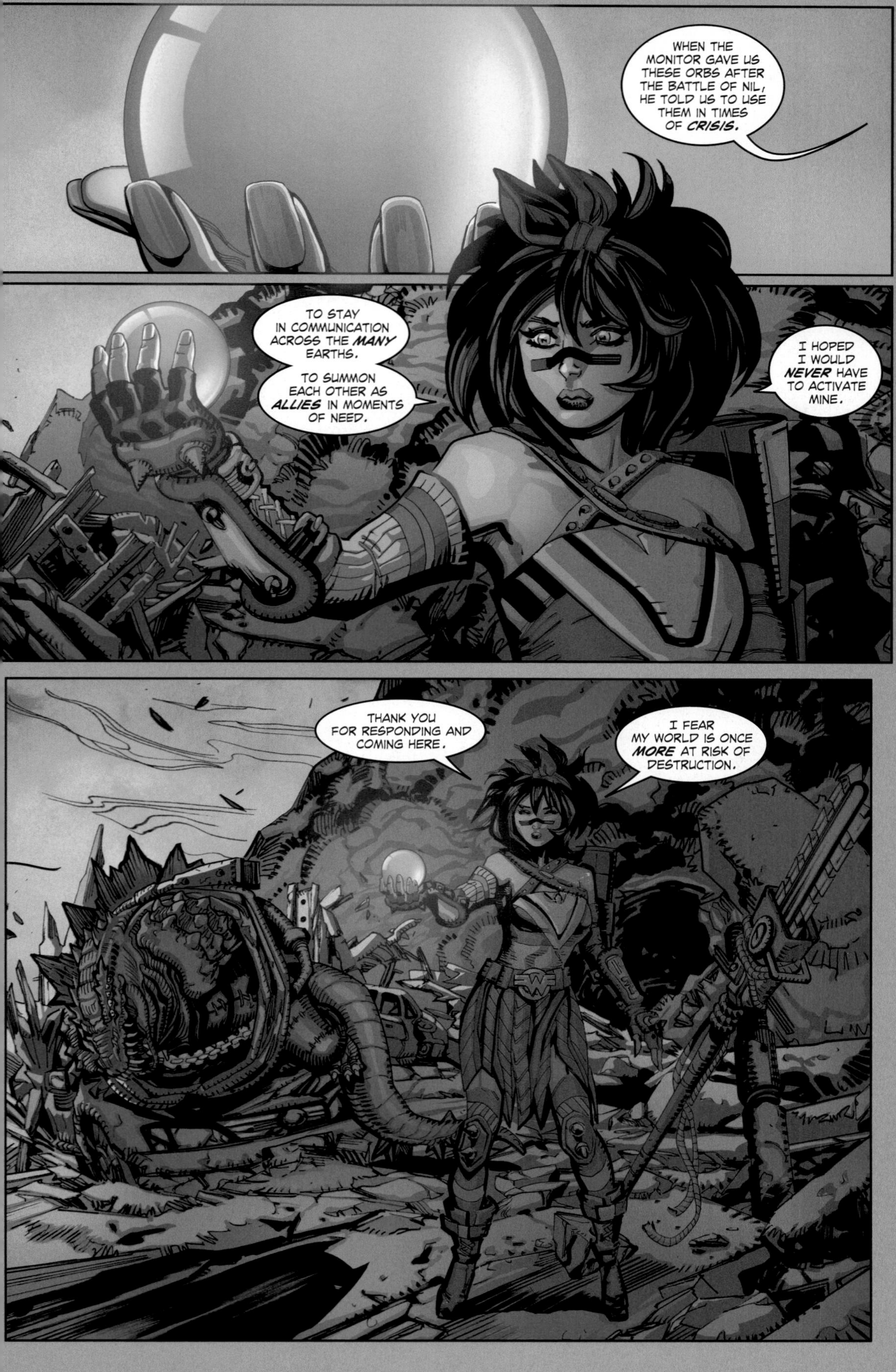
WHEN THE MONITOR GAVE US THESE ORBS AFTER THE BATTLE OF NIL, HE TOLD US TO USE THEM IN TIMES OF CRISIS.
TO STAY IN COMMUNICATION ACROSS THE MANY EARTHS.
TO SUMMON EACH OTHER AS ALLIES IN MOMENTS OF NEED.
I HOPED I WOULD NEVER HAVE TO ACTIVATE MINE.
THANK YOU FOR RESPONDING AND COMING HERE.
I FEAR MY WORLD IS ONCE MORE AT RISK OF DESTRUCTION.

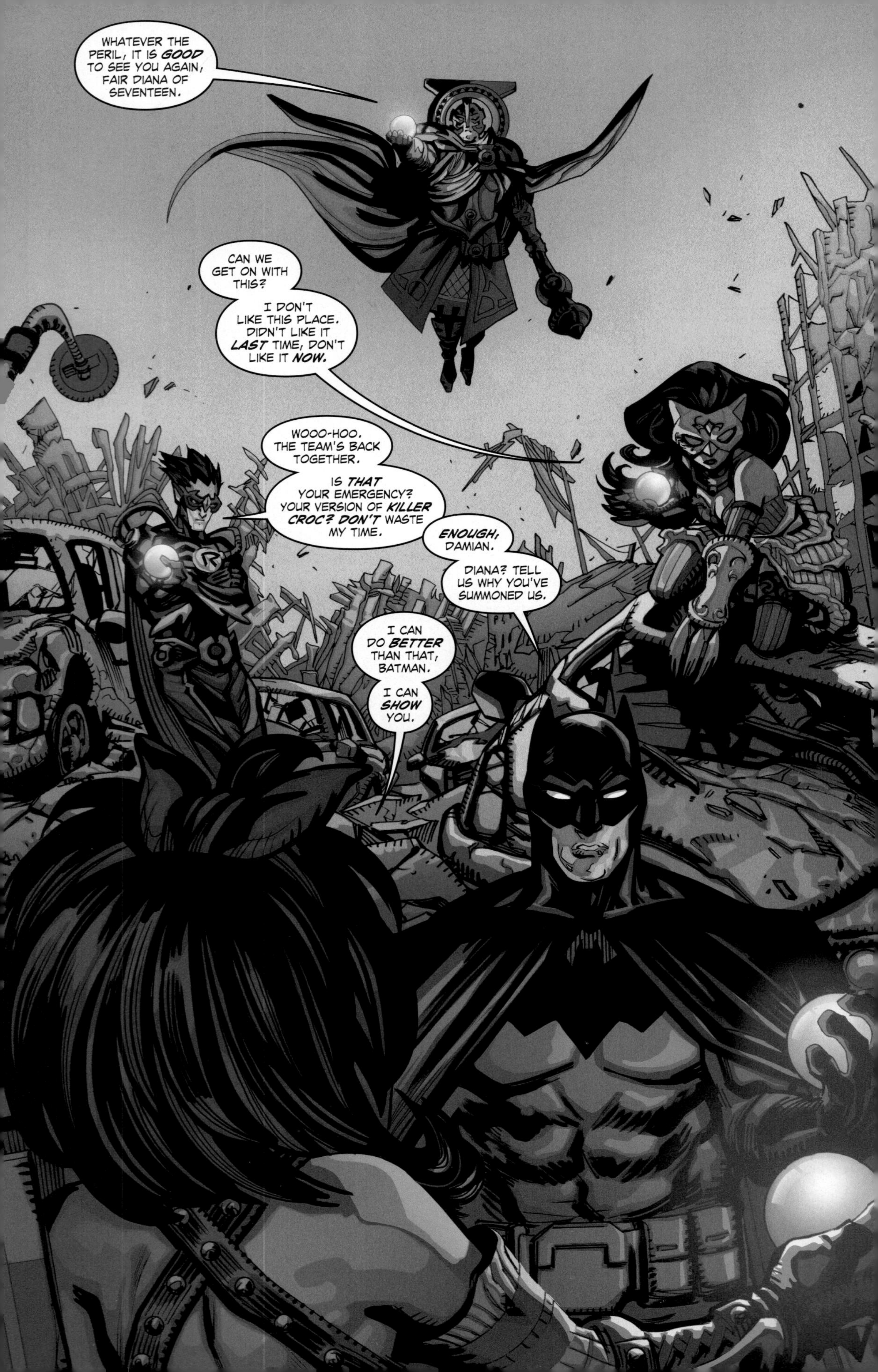
WHATEVER THE PERIL, IT IS GOOD TO SEE YOU AGAIN, FAIR DIANA OF SEVENTEEN.
CAN WE GET ON WITH THIS?
I DON'T LIKE THIS PLACE. DIDN'T LIKE IT LAST TIME, DON'T LIKE IT NOW.
WOOO-HOO. THE TEAM'S BACK TOGETHER.
IS THAT YOUR EMERGENCY? YOUR VERSION OF KILLER CROC? DON'T WASTE MY TIME.
ENOUGH, DAMIAN.
DIANA? TELL US WHY YOU'VE SUMMONED US.
I CAN DO BETTER THAN THAT, BATMAN.
I CAN SHOW YOU.

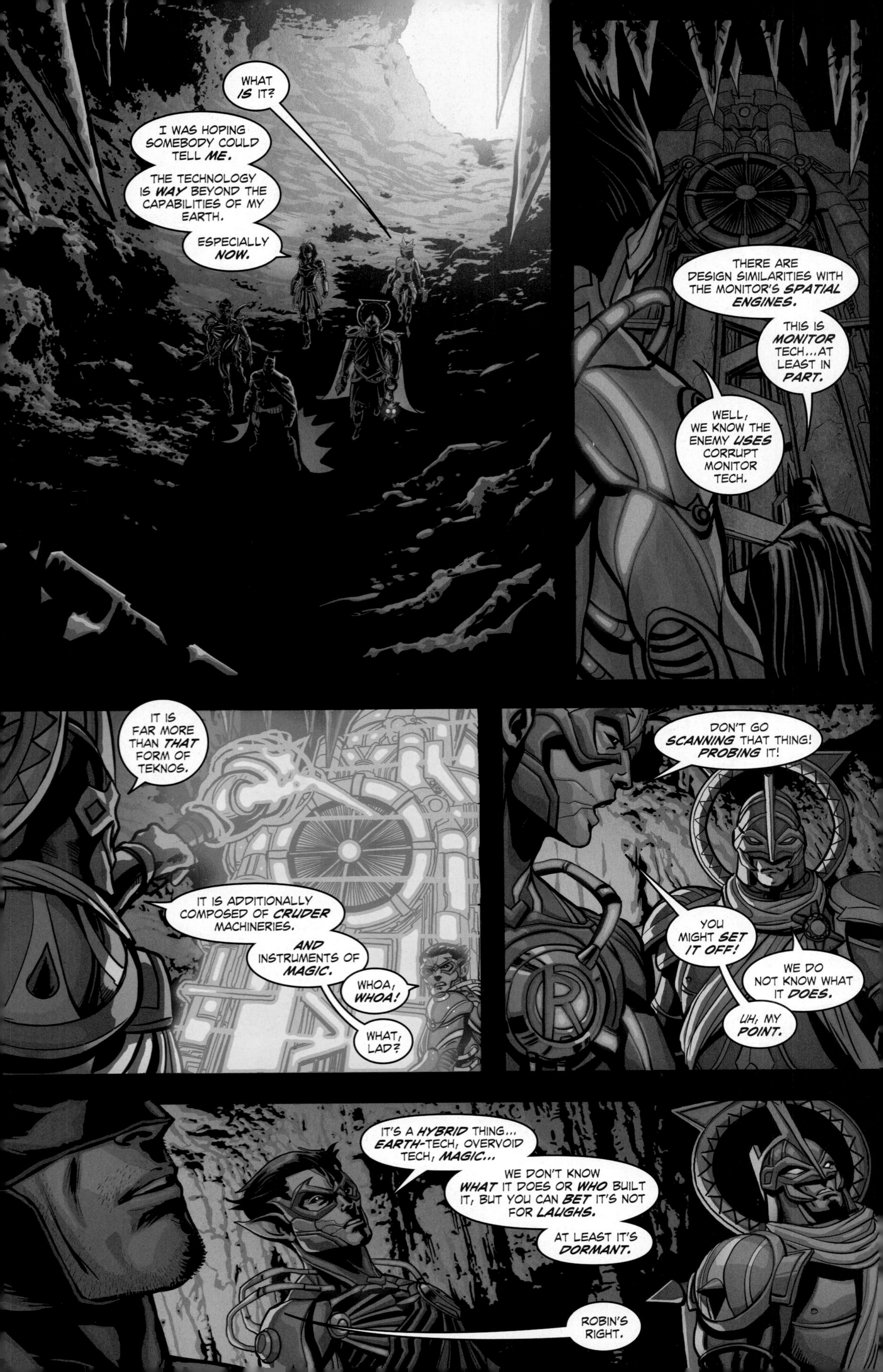

WHAT IS IT?
I WAS HOPING SOMEBODY COULD TELL ME.
THE TECHNOLOGY IS WAY BEYOND THE CAPABILITIES OF MY EARTH.
ESPECIALLY NOW.
THERE ARE DESIGN SIMILARITIES WITH THE MONITOR'S SPATIAL ENGINES.
THIS IS MONITOR TECH...AT LEAST IN PART.
WELL, WE KNOW THE ENEMY USES CORRUPT MONITOR TECH.
IT IS FAR MORE THAN THAT FORM OF TEKNOS.
IT IS ADDITIONALLY COMPOSED OF CRUDER MACHINERIES.
AND INSTRUMENTS OF MAGIC.
WHOA, WHOA!
WHAT, LAD?
DON'T GO SCANNING THAT THING! PROBING IT!
YOU MIGHT SET IT OFF!
WE DO NOT KNOW WHAT IT DOES.
UH, MY POINT.
IT'S A HYBRID THING... EARTH-TECH, OVERVOID TECH, MAGIC...
WE DON'T KNOW WHAT IT DOES OR WHO BUILT IT, BUT YOU CAN BET IT'S NOT FOR LAUGHS.
AT LEAST IT'S DORMANT.
ROBIN'S RIGHT.

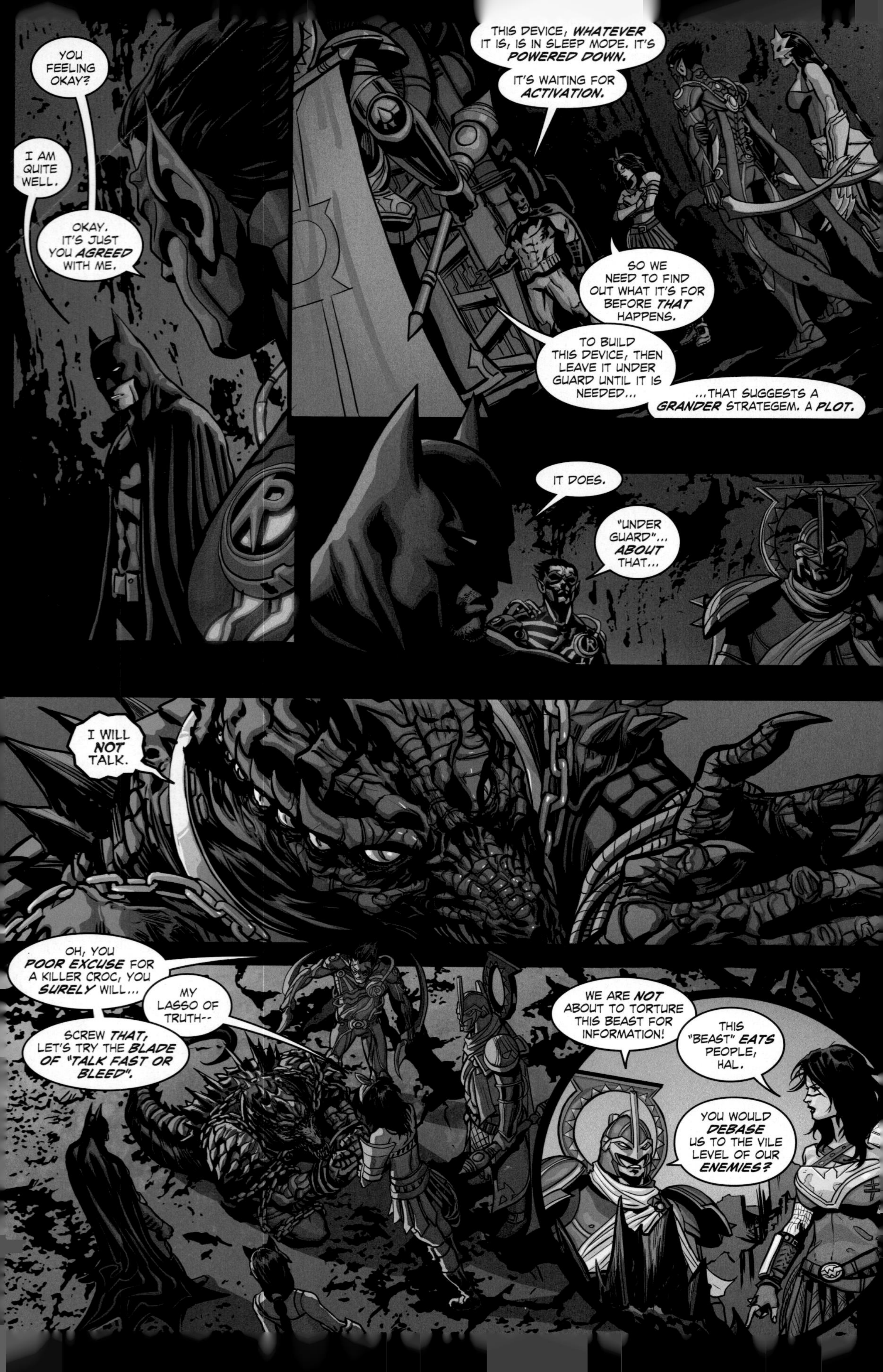
YOU FEELING OKAY?
I AM QUITE WELL.
OKAY. IT'S JUST YOU AGREED WITH ME.
THIS DEVICE, WHATEVER IT IS, IS IN SLEEP MODE. IT'S POWERED DOWN.
IT'S WAITING FOR ACTIVATION.
SO WE NEED TO FIND OUT WHAT IT'S FOR BEFORE THAT HAPPENS.
TO BUILD THIS DEVICE, THEN LEAVE IT UNDER GUARD UNTIL IT IS NEEDED...
...THAT SUGGESTS A GRANDER STRATEGEM. A PLOT.
IT DOES.
"UNDER GUARD"... ABOUT THAT...
I WILL NOT TALK.
OH, YOU POOR EXCUSE FOR A KILLER CROC, YOU SURELY WILL...
MY LASSO OF TRUTH--
SCREW THAT, LET'S TRY THE BLADE OF "TALK FAST OR BLEED".
WE ARE NOT ABOUT TO TORTURE THIS BEAST FOR INFORMATION!
THIS "BEAST" EATS PEOPLE, HAL.
YOU WOULD DEBASE US TO THE VILE LEVEL OF OUR ENEMIES?

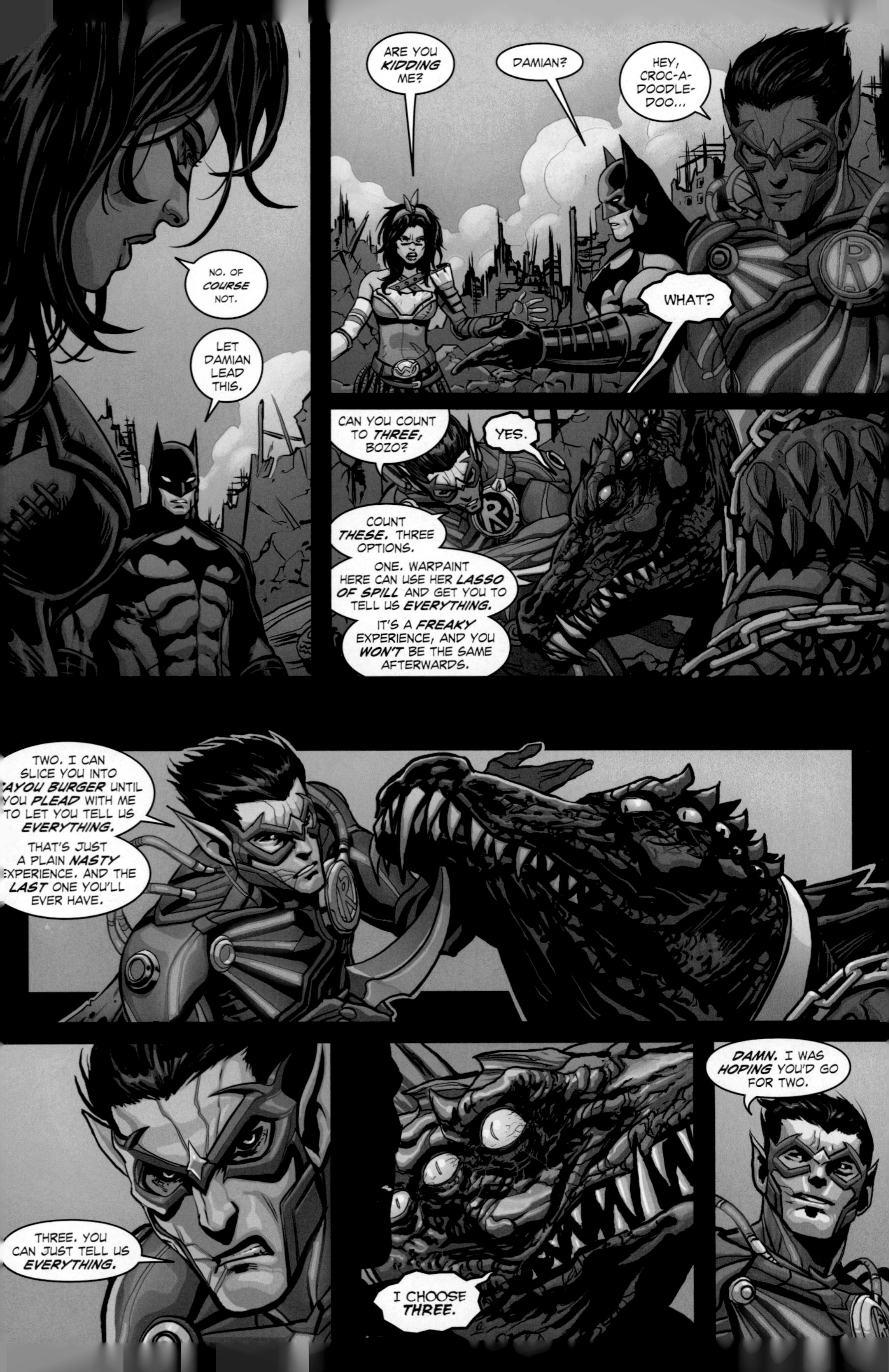
NO. OF *COURSE* NOT.
LET DAMIAN LEAD THIS.
ARE YOU *KIDDING* ME?
DAMIAN?
HEY, CROC-A-DOODLE-DOO...
WHAT?
CAN YOU COUNT TO *THREE,* BOZO?
YES.
COUNT *THESE.* THREE OPTIONS.
ONE. WARPAINT HERE CAN USE HER *LASSO OF SPILL* AND GET YOU TO TELL US *EVERYTHING.*
IT'S A *FREAKY* EXPERIENCE, AND YOU *WON'T* BE THE SAME AFTERWARDS.
TWO. I CAN SLICE YOU INTO *AYOU BURGER* UNTIL YOU *PLEAD* WITH ME TO LET YOU TELL US *EVERYTHING.*
THAT'S JUST A PLAIN *NASTY* XPERIENCE. AND THE *LAST* ONE YOU'LL EVER HAVE.
THREE. YOU CAN JUST TELL US *EVERYTHING.*
I CHOOSE *THREE.*
DAMN. I WAS *HOPING* YOU'D GO FOR TWO.

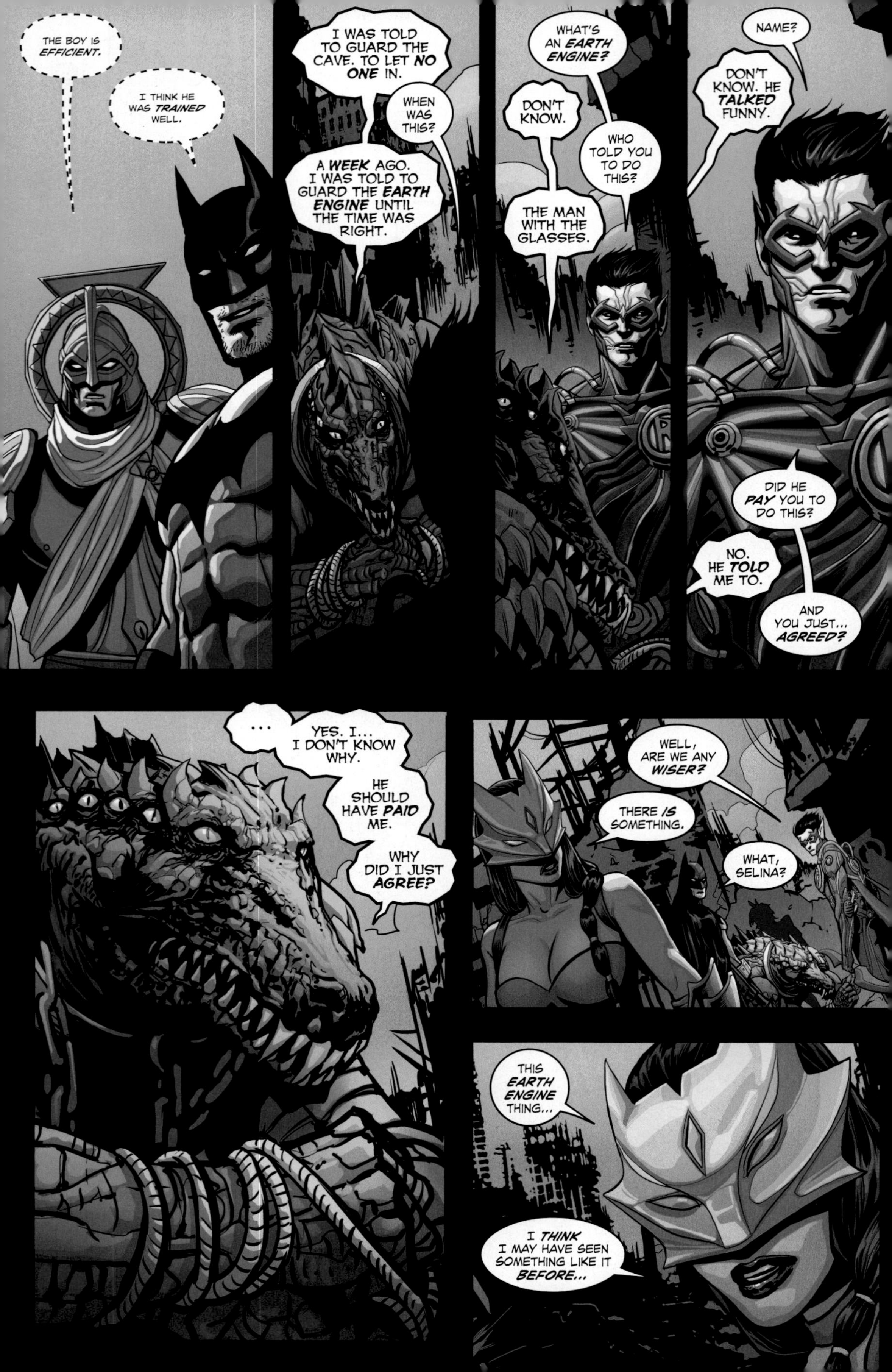

THE BOY IS EFFICIENT.
I THINK HE WAS TRAINED WELL.
I WAS TOLD TO GUARD THE CAVE. TO LET NO ONE IN.
WHEN WAS THIS?
A WEEK AGO. I WAS TOLD TO GUARD THE EARTH ENGINE UNTIL THE TIME WAS RIGHT.
WHAT'S AN EARTH ENGINE?
DON'T KNOW.
WHO TOLD YOU TO DO THIS?
THE MAN WITH THE GLASSES.
NAME?
DON'T KNOW. HE TALKED FUNNY.
DID HE PAY YOU TO DO THIS?
NO. HE TOLD ME TO.
AND YOU JUST... AGREED?
...
YES. I... I DON'T KNOW WHY.
HE SHOULD HAVE PAID ME.
WHY DID I JUST AGREE?
WELL, ARE WE ANY WISER?
THERE IS SOMETHING.
WHAT, SELINA?
THIS EARTH ENGINE THING...
I THINK I MAY HAVE SEEN SOMETHING LIKE IT BEFORE...

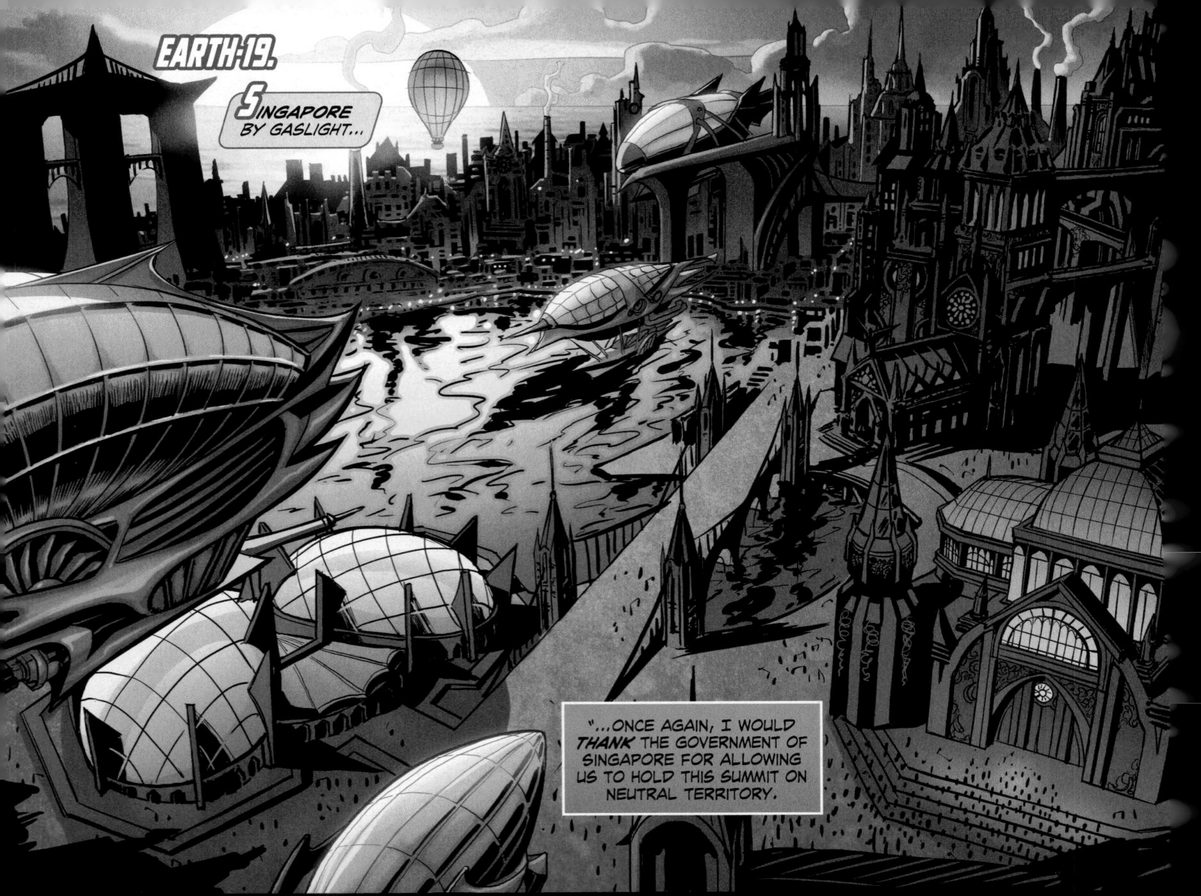
EARTH-19.
SINGAPORE BY GASLIGHT...
"...ONCE AGAIN, I WOULD THANK THE GOVERNMENT OF SINGAPORE FOR ALLOWING US TO HOLD THIS SUMMIT ON NEUTRAL TERRITORY.

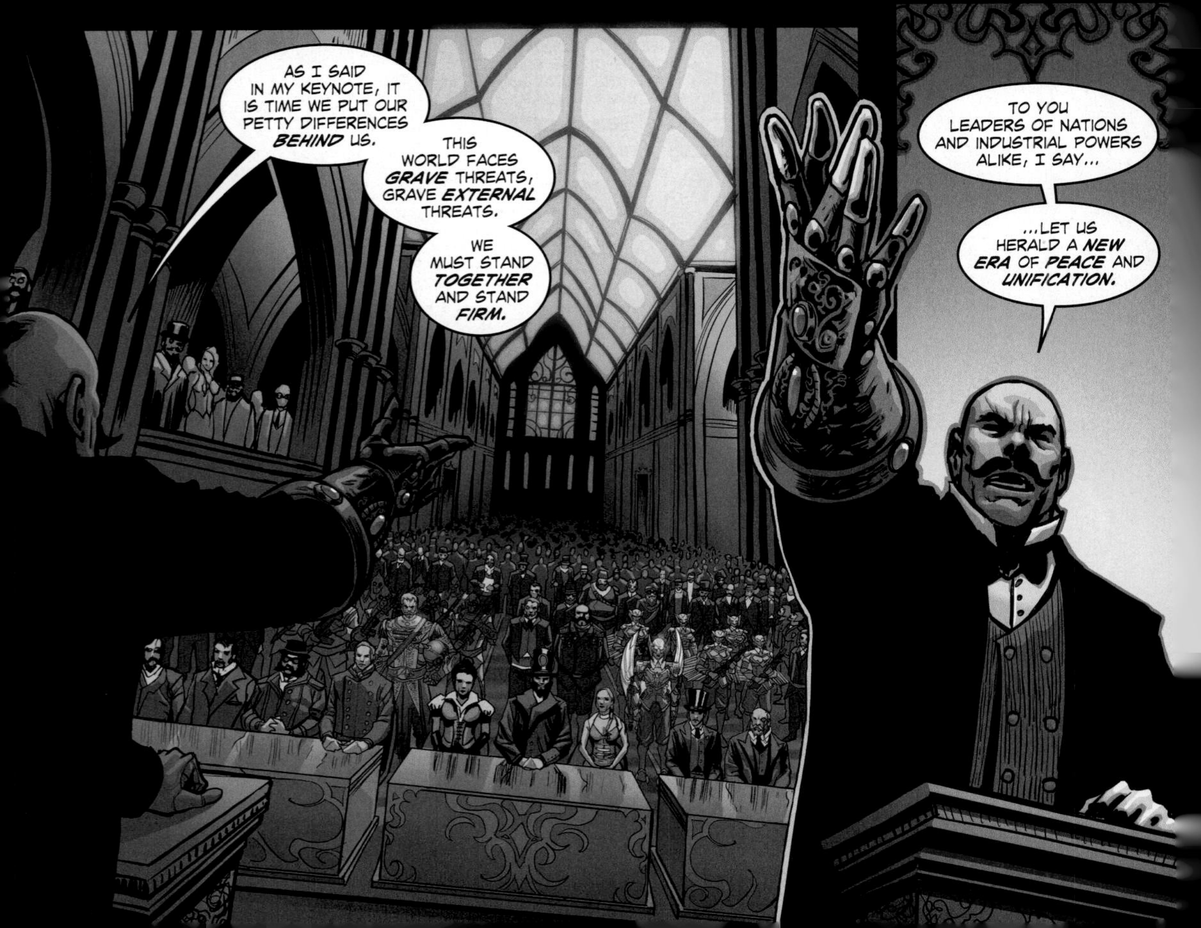
AS I SAID IN MY KEYNOTE, IT IS TIME WE PUT OUR PETTY DIFFERENCES BEHIND US.
THIS WORLD FACES GRAVE THREATS, GRAVE EXTERNAL THREATS.
WE MUST STAND TOGETHER AND STAND FIRM.
TO YOU LEADERS OF NATIONS AND INDUSTRIAL POWERS ALIKE, I SAY...
...LET US HERALD A NEW ERA OF PEACE AND UNIFICATION.

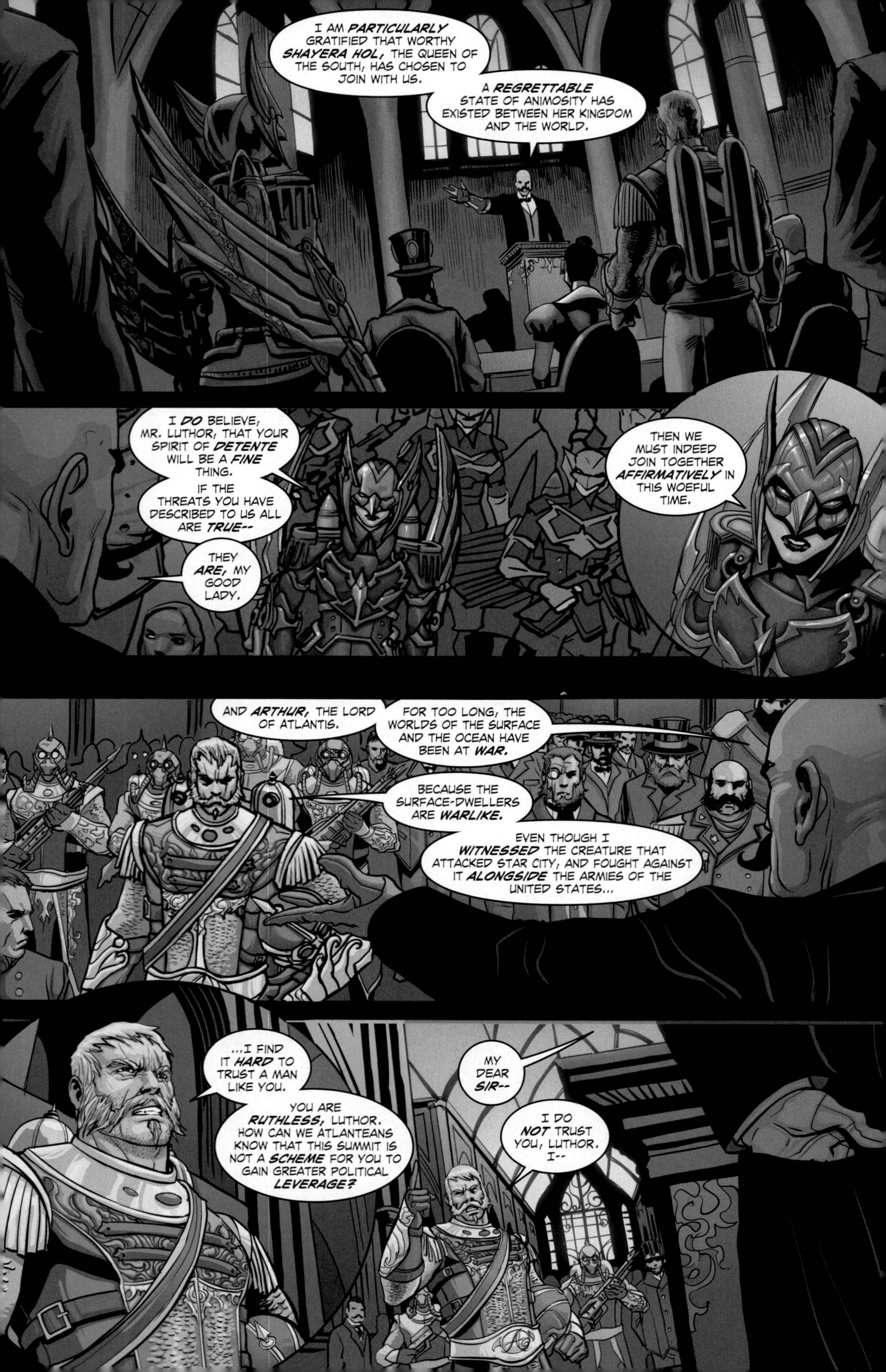

I AM PARTICULARLY GRATIFIED THAT WORTHY SHAYERA HOL, THE QUEEN OF THE SOUTH, HAS CHOSEN TO JOIN WITH US.
A REGRETTABLE STATE OF ANIMOSITY HAS EXISTED BETWEEN HER KINGDOM AND THE WORLD.
I DO BELIEVE, MR. LUTHOR, THAT YOUR SPIRIT OF DETENTE WILL BE A FINE THING.
IF THE THREATS YOU HAVE DESCRIBED TO US ALL ARE TRUE--
THEY ARE, MY GOOD LADY.
THEN WE MUST INDEED JOIN TOGETHER AFFIRMATIVELY IN THIS WOEFUL TIME.
AND ARTHUR, THE LORD OF ATLANTIS.
FOR TOO LONG, THE WORLDS OF THE SURFACE AND THE OCEAN HAVE BEEN AT WAR.
BECAUSE THE SURFACE-DWELLERS ARE WARLIKE.
EVEN THOUGH I WITNESSED THE CREATURE THAT ATTACKED STAR CITY, AND FOUGHT AGAINST IT ALONGSIDE THE ARMIES OF THE UNITED STATES...
...I FIND IT HARD TO TRUST A MAN LIKE YOU.
YOU ARE RUTHLESS, LUTHOR. HOW CAN WE ATLANTEANS KNOW THAT THIS SUMMIT IS NOT A SCHEME FOR YOU TO GAIN GREATER POLITICAL LEVERAGE?
MY DEAR SIR--
I DO NOT TRUST YOU, LUTHOR. I--

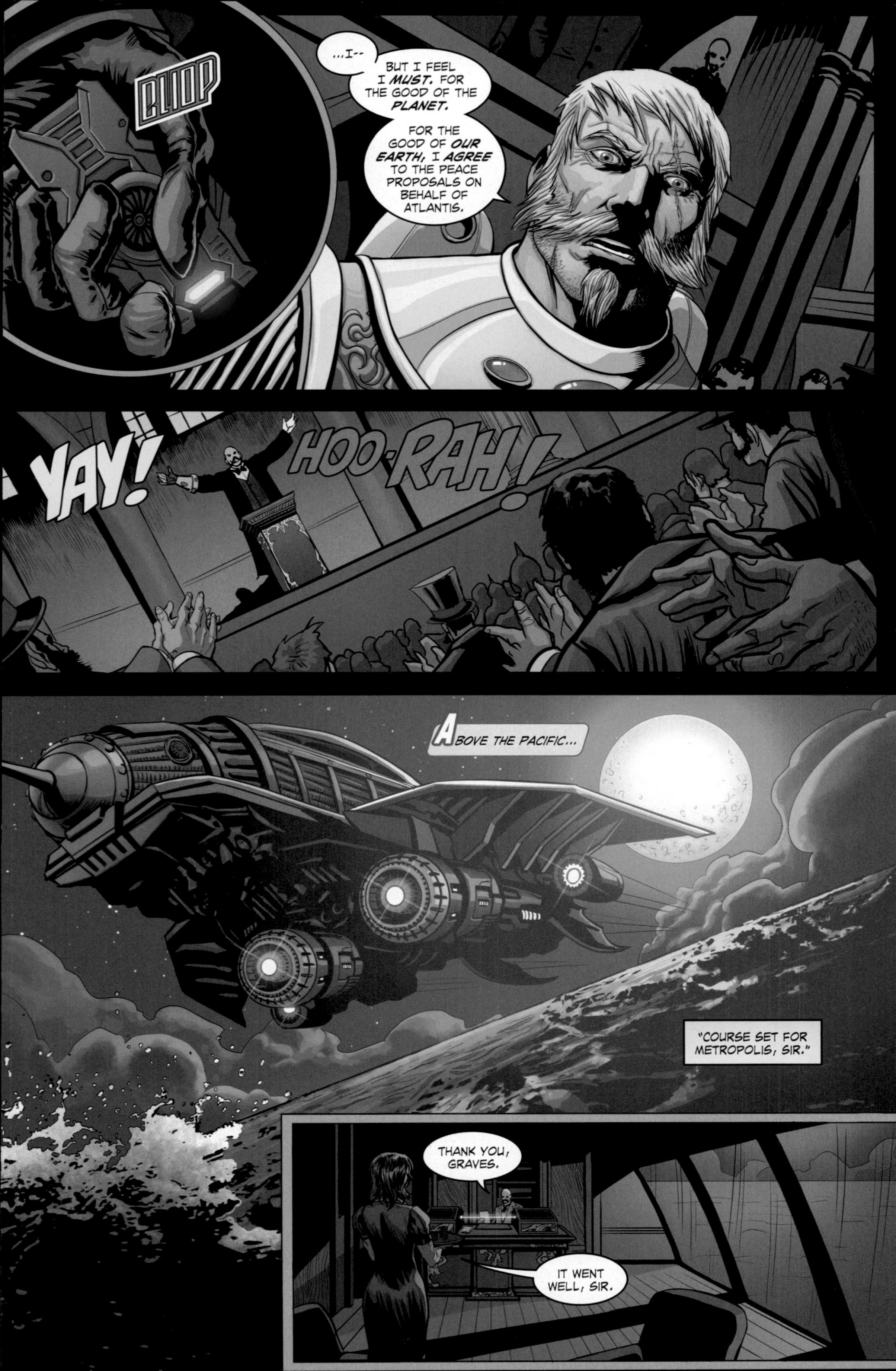

CLIQP
...I--
BUT I FEEL I *MUST.* FOR THE GOOD OF THE *PLANET.*
FOR THE GOOD OF *OUR EARTH,* I *AGREE* TO THE PEACE PROPOSALS ON BEHALF OF ATLANTIS.
YAY!
HOO-RAH!
ABOVE THE PACIFIC...
"COURSE SET FOR METROPOLIS, SIR."
THANK YOU, GRAVES.
IT WENT WELL, SIR.

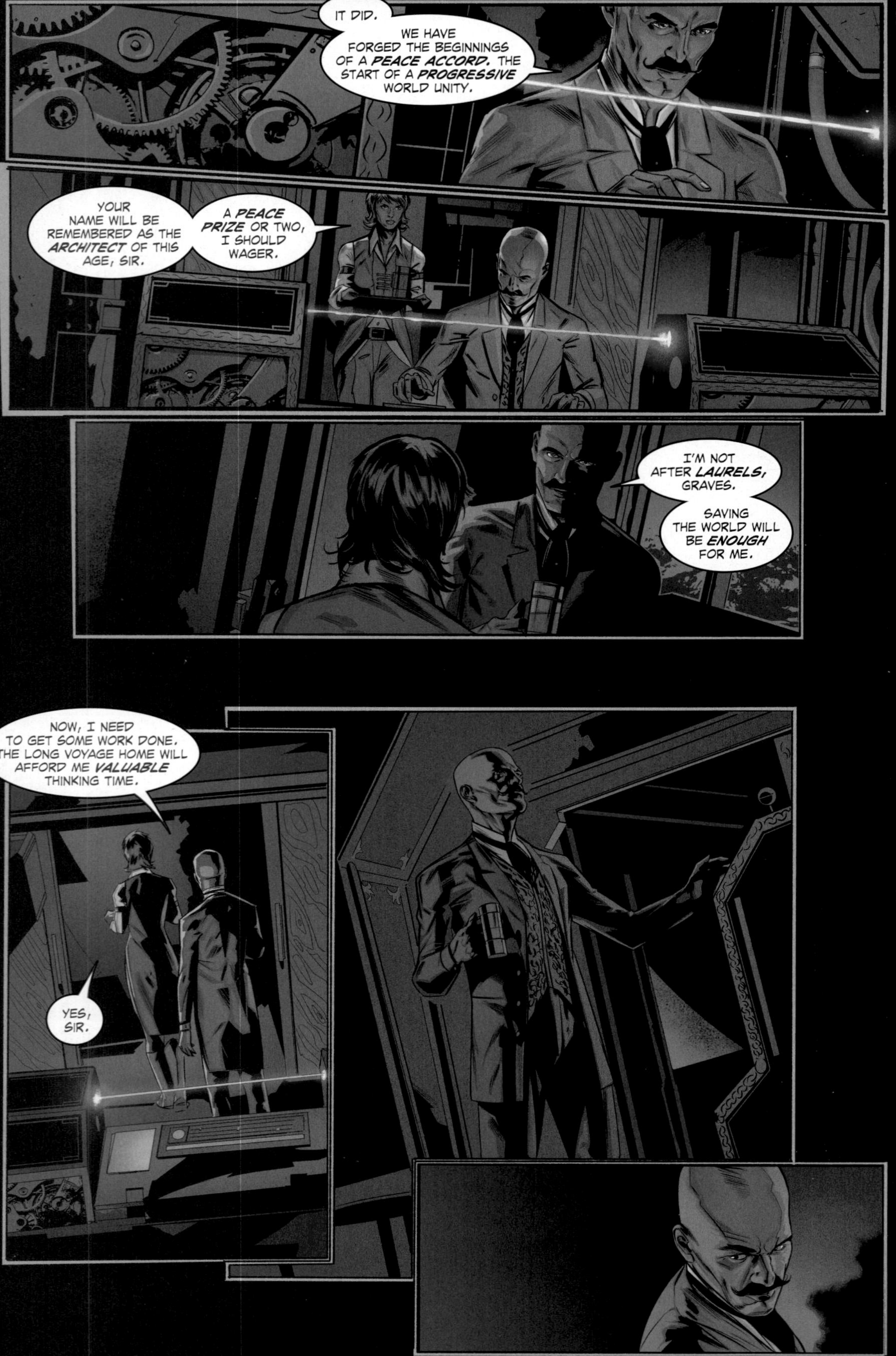
IT DID.
WE HAVE FORGED THE BEGINNINGS OF A PEACE ACCORD. THE START OF A PROGRESSIVE WORLD UNITY.
YOUR NAME WILL BE REMEMBERED AS THE ARCHITECT OF THIS AGE, SIR.
A PEACE PRIZE OR TWO, I SHOULD WAGER.
I'M NOT AFTER LAURELS, GRAVES.
SAVING THE WORLD WILL BE ENOUGH FOR ME.
NOW, I NEED TO GET SOME WORK DONE. THE LONG VOYAGE HOME WILL AFFORD ME VALUABLE THINKING TIME.
YES, SIR.

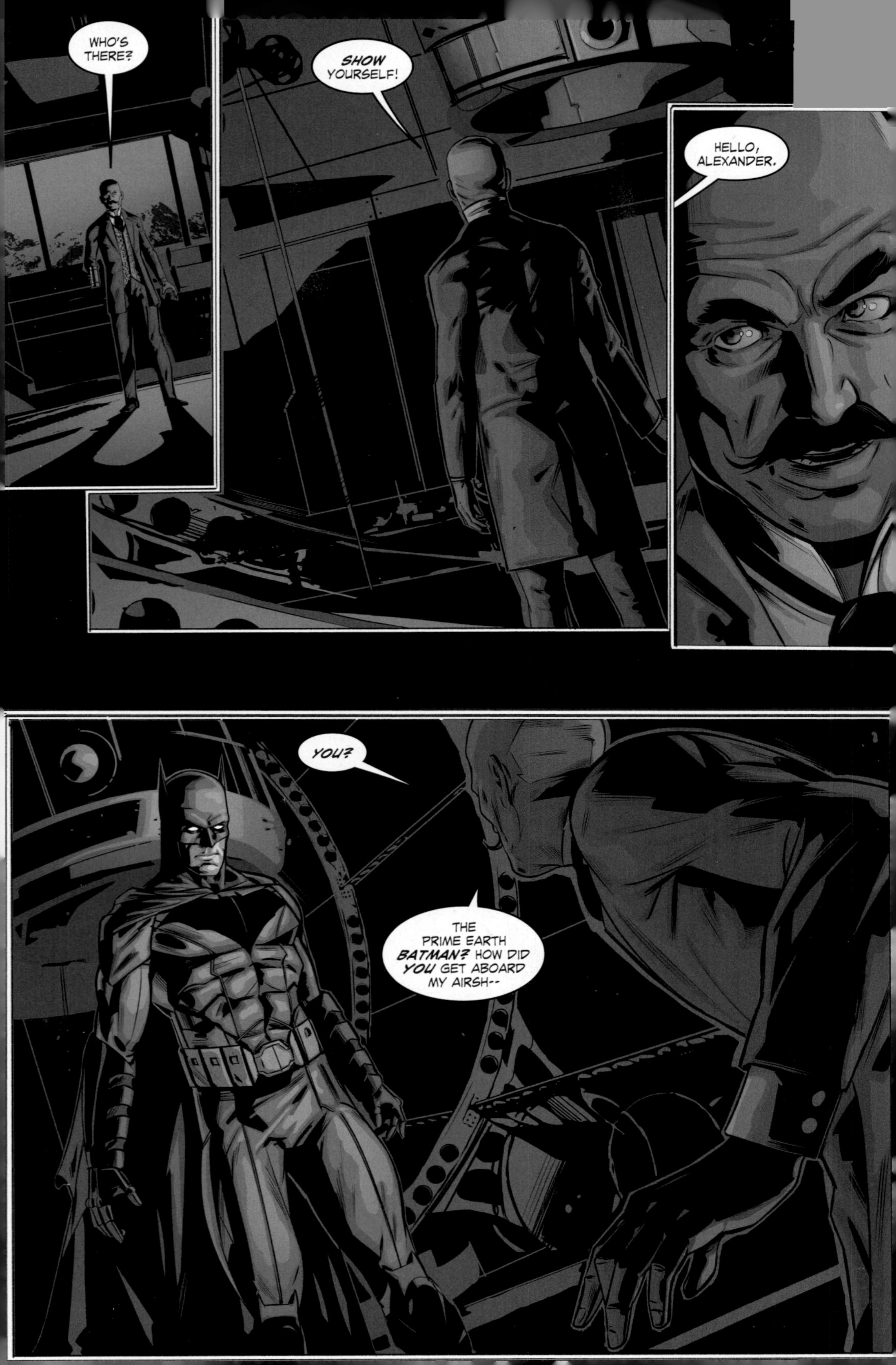
WHO'S THERE?
SHOW YOURSELF!
HELLO, ALEXANDER.
YOU?
THE PRIME EARTH BATMAN? HOW DID YOU GET ABOARD MY AIRSH--

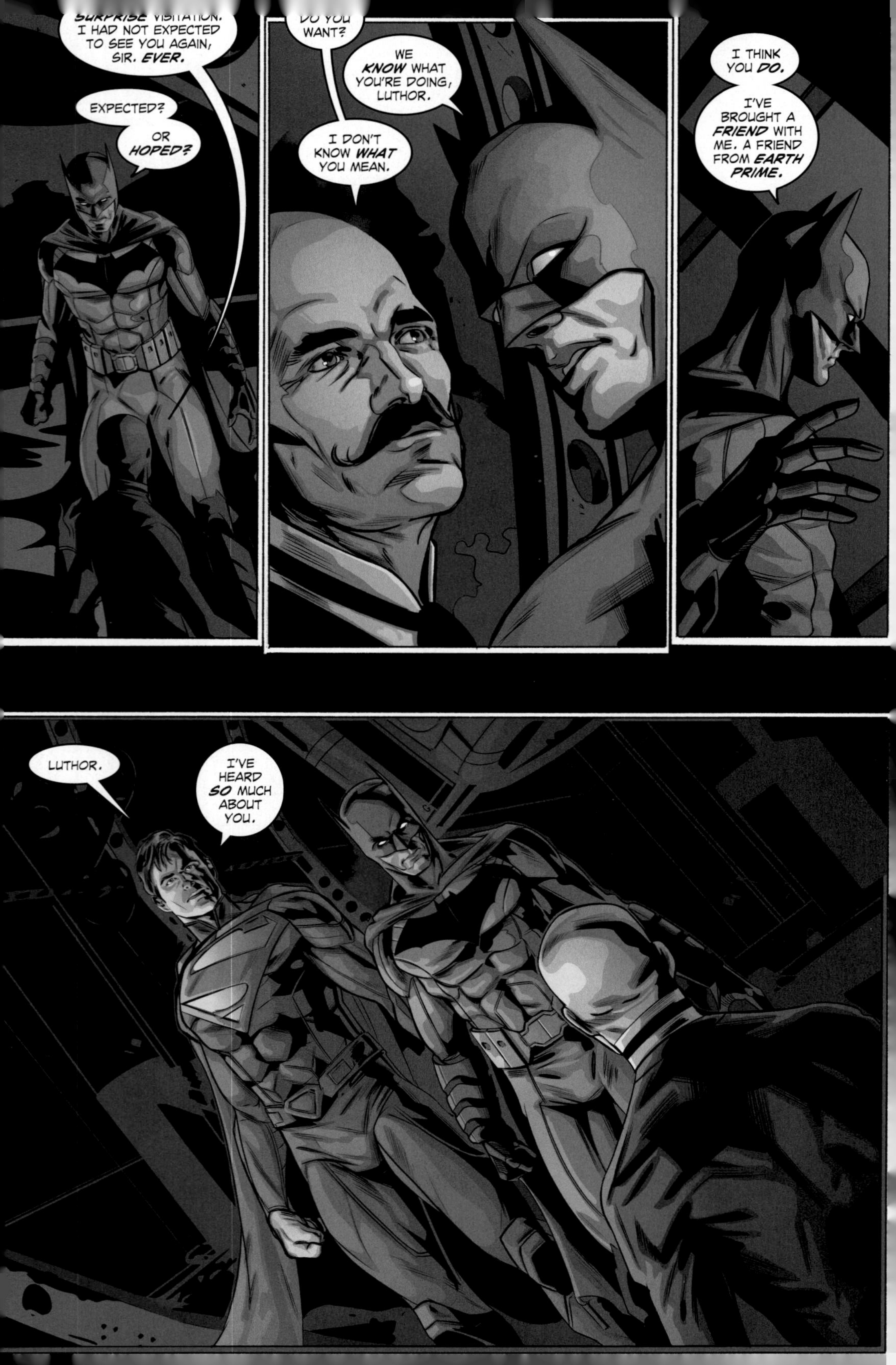
SURPRISE VISITATION. I HAD NOT EXPECTED TO SEE YOU AGAIN, SIR. EVER.
EXPECTED? OR HOPED?
DO YOU WANT?
WE KNOW WHAT YOU'RE DOING, LUTHOR.
I DON'T KNOW WHAT YOU MEAN.
I THINK YOU DO.
I'VE BROUGHT A FRIEND WITH ME. A FRIEND FROM EARTH PRIME.
LUTHOR.
I'VE HEARD SO MUCH ABOUT YOU.

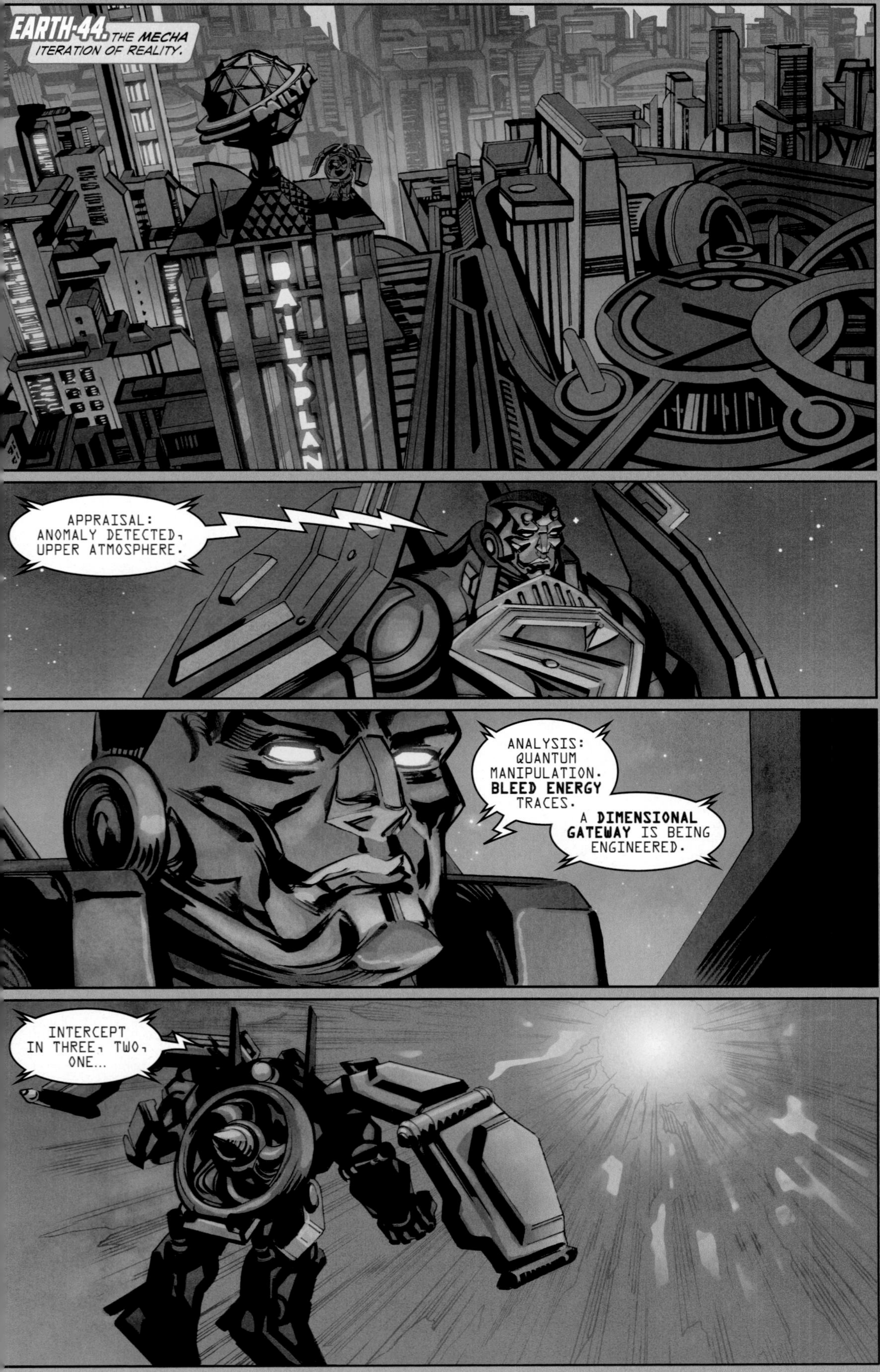
EARTH-44. THE MECHA ITERATION OF REALITY.
APPRAISAL: ANOMALY DETECTED, UPPER ATMOSPHERE.
ANALYSIS: QUANTUM MANIPULATION. BLEED ENERGY TRACES.
A DIMENSIONAL GATEWAY IS BEING ENGINEERED.
INTERCEPT IN THREE, TWO, ONE...

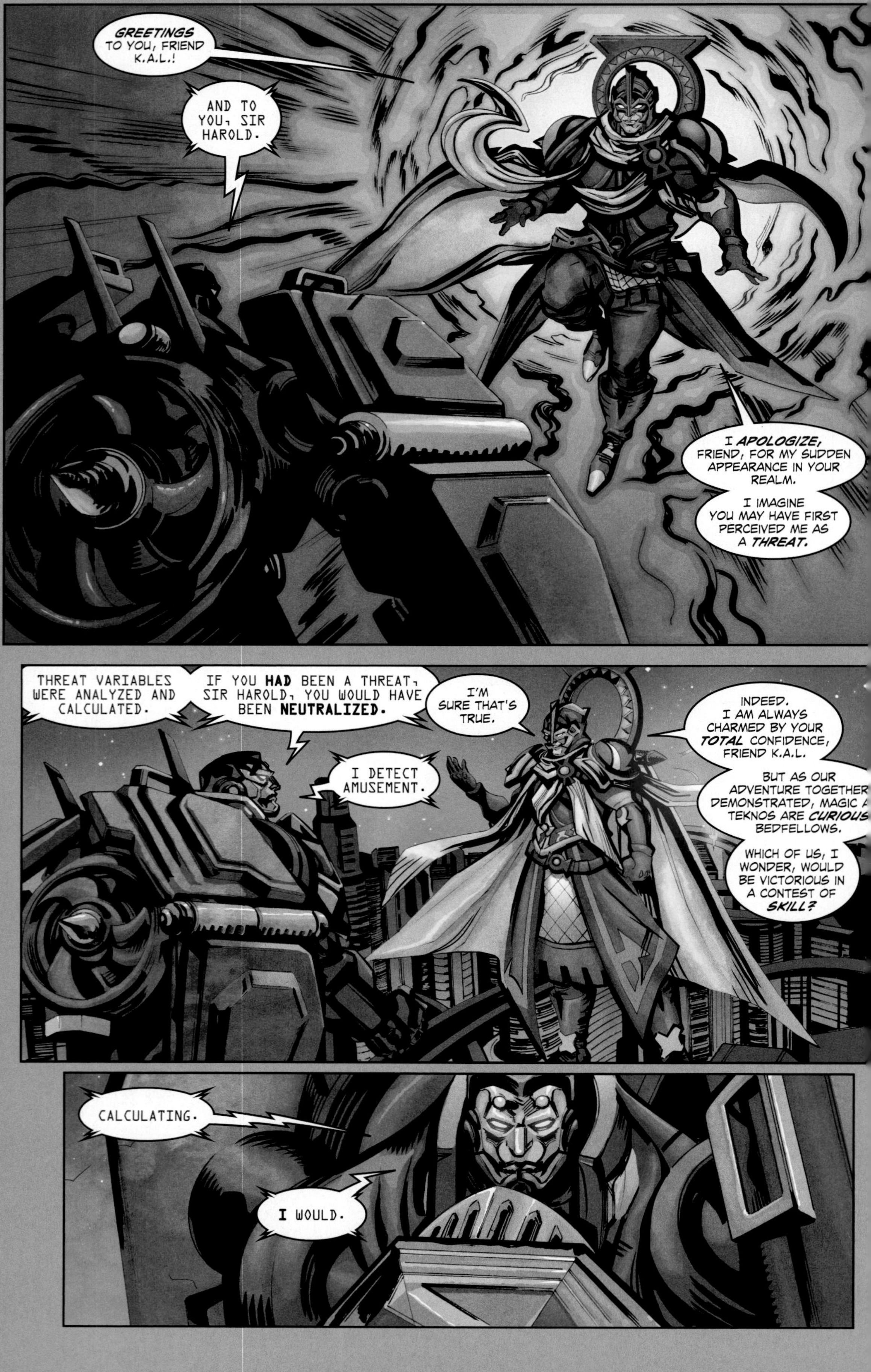
GREETINGS TO YOU, FRIEND K.A.L.!
AND TO YOU, SIR HAROLD.
I APOLOGIZE, FRIEND, FOR MY SUDDEN APPEARANCE IN YOUR REALM.
I IMAGINE YOU MAY HAVE FIRST PERCEIVED ME AS A THREAT.
THREAT VARIABLES WERE ANALYZED AND CALCULATED.
IF YOU HAD BEEN A THREAT, SIR HAROLD, YOU WOULD HAVE BEEN NEUTRALIZED.
I'M SURE THAT'S TRUE.
I DETECT AMUSEMENT.
INDEED. I AM ALWAYS CHARMED BY YOUR TOTAL CONFIDENCE, FRIEND K.A.L.
BUT AS OUR ADVENTURE TOGETHER DEMONSTRATED, MAGIC A TEKNOS ARE CURIOUS BEDFELLOWS.
WHICH OF US, I WONDER, WOULD BE VICTORIOUS IN A CONTEST OF SKILL?
CALCULATING.
I WOULD.

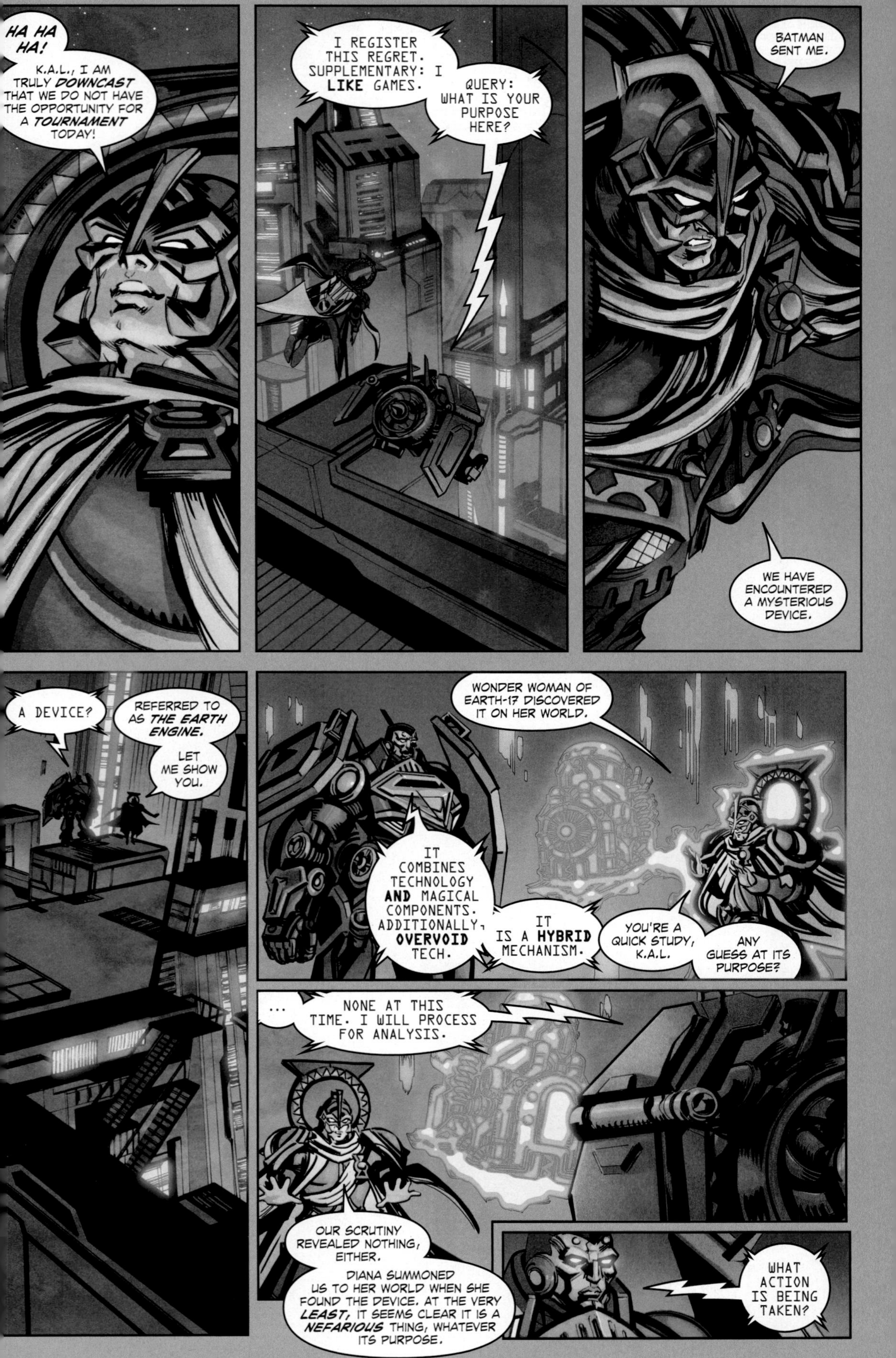
HA HA HA!
K.A.L., I AM TRULY DOWNCAST THAT WE DO NOT HAVE THE OPPORTUNITY FOR A TOURNAMENT TODAY!
I REGISTER THIS REGRET. SUPPLEMENTARY: I LIKE GAMES.
QUERY: WHAT IS YOUR PURPOSE HERE?
BATMAN SENT ME.
WE HAVE ENCOUNTERED A MYSTERIOUS DEVICE.
A DEVICE?
REFERRED TO AS THE EARTH ENGINE.
LET ME SHOW YOU.
WONDER WOMAN OF EARTH-17 DISCOVERED IT ON HER WORLD.
IT COMBINES TECHNOLOGY AND MAGICAL COMPONENTS. ADDITIONALLY, OVERVOID TECH.
IT IS A HYBRID MECHANISM.
YOU'RE A QUICK STUDY, K.A.L.
ANY GUESS AT ITS PURPOSE?
...
NONE AT THIS TIME. I WILL PROCESS FOR ANALYSIS.
OUR SCRUTINY REVEALED NOTHING, EITHER.
DIANA SUMMONED US TO HER WORLD WHEN SHE FOUND THE DEVICE. AT THE VERY LEAST, IT SEEMS CLEAR IT IS A NEFARIOUS THING, WHATEVER ITS PURPOSE.
WHAT ACTION IS BEING TAKEN?

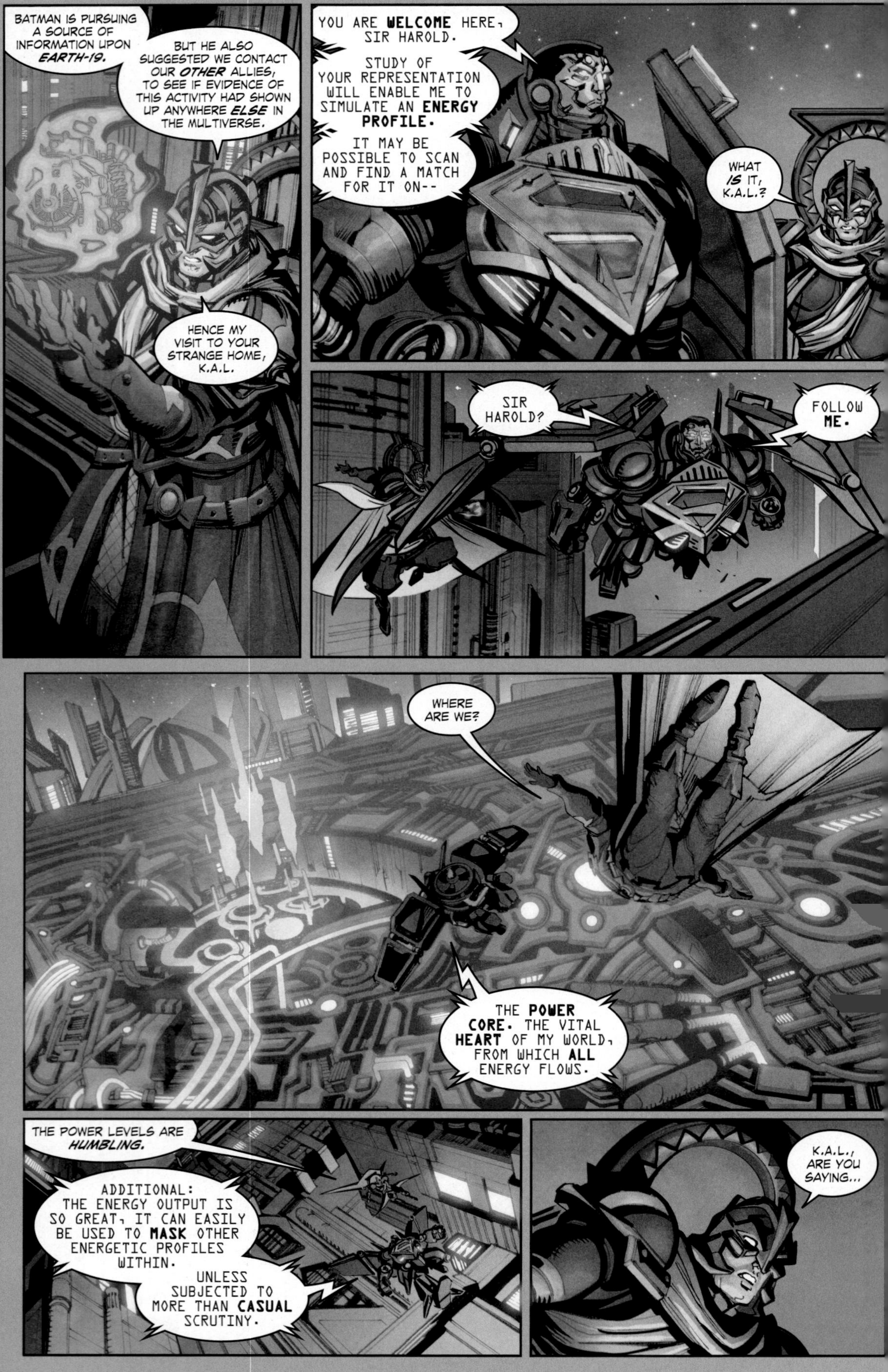
BATMAN IS PURSUING A SOURCE OF INFORMATION UPON EARTH-19.
BUT HE ALSO SUGGESTED WE CONTACT OUR OTHER ALLIES, TO SEE IF EVIDENCE OF THIS ACTIVITY HAD SHOWN UP ANYWHERE ELSE IN THE MULTIVERSE.
HENCE MY VISIT TO YOUR STRANGE HOME, K.A.L.
YOU ARE WELCOME HERE, SIR HAROLD.
STUDY OF YOUR REPRESENTATION WILL ENABLE ME TO SIMULATE AN ENERGY PROFILE.
IT MAY BE POSSIBLE TO SCAN AND FIND A MATCH FOR IT ON--
WHAT IS IT, K.A.L.?
SIR HAROLD?
FOLLOW ME.
WHERE ARE WE?
THE POWER CORE. THE VITAL HEART OF MY WORLD, FROM WHICH ALL ENERGY FLOWS.
THE POWER LEVELS ARE HUMBLING.
ADDITIONAL: THE ENERGY OUTPUT IS SO GREAT, IT CAN EASILY BE USED TO MASK OTHER ENERGETIC PROFILES WITHIN.
UNLESS SUBJECTED TO MORE THAN CASUAL SCRUTINY.
K.A.L., ARE YOU SAYING...

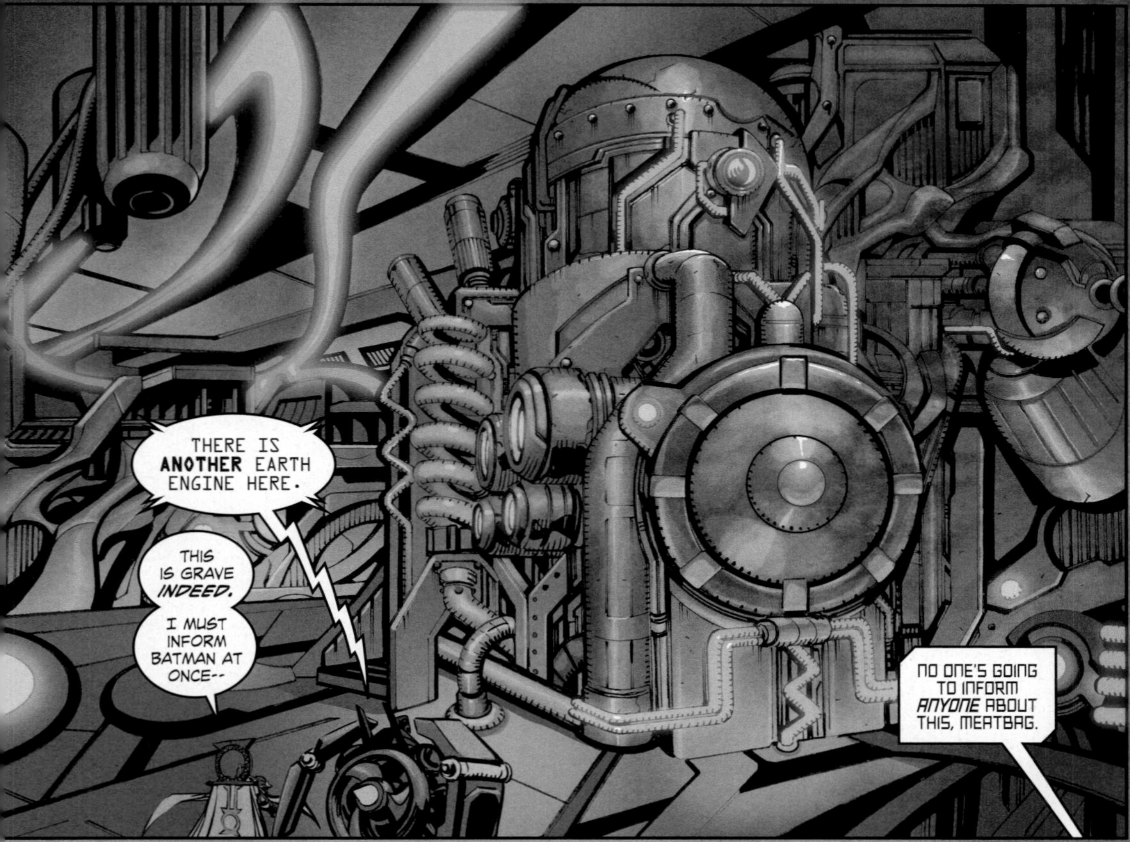
THERE IS ANOTHER EARTH ENGINE HERE.
THIS IS GRAVE INDEED.
I MUST INFORM BATMAN AT ONCE--
NO ONE'S GOING TO INFORM ANYONE ABOUT THIS, MEATBAG.

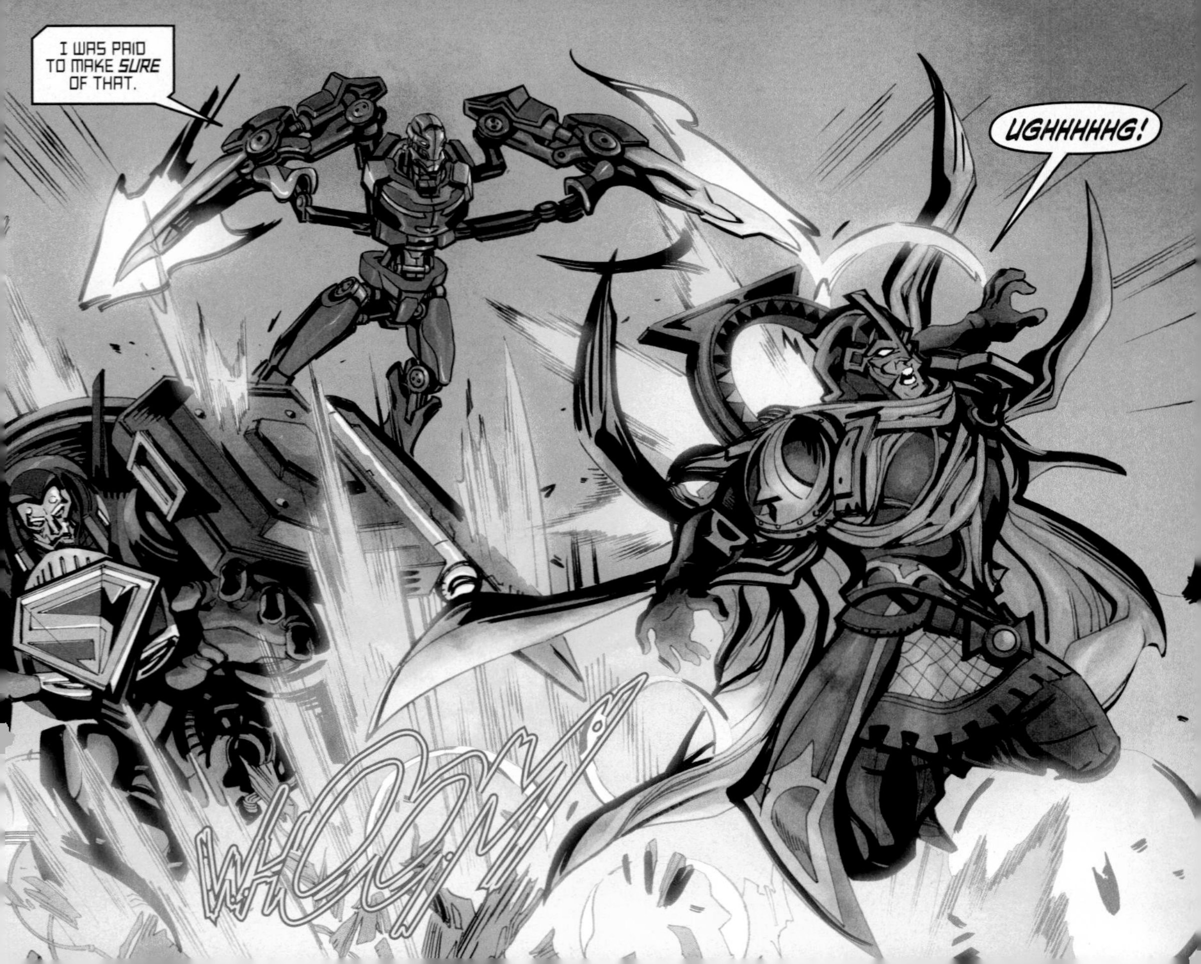
I WAS PAID TO MAKE SURE OF THAT.
UGHHHHHG!
WHOOM

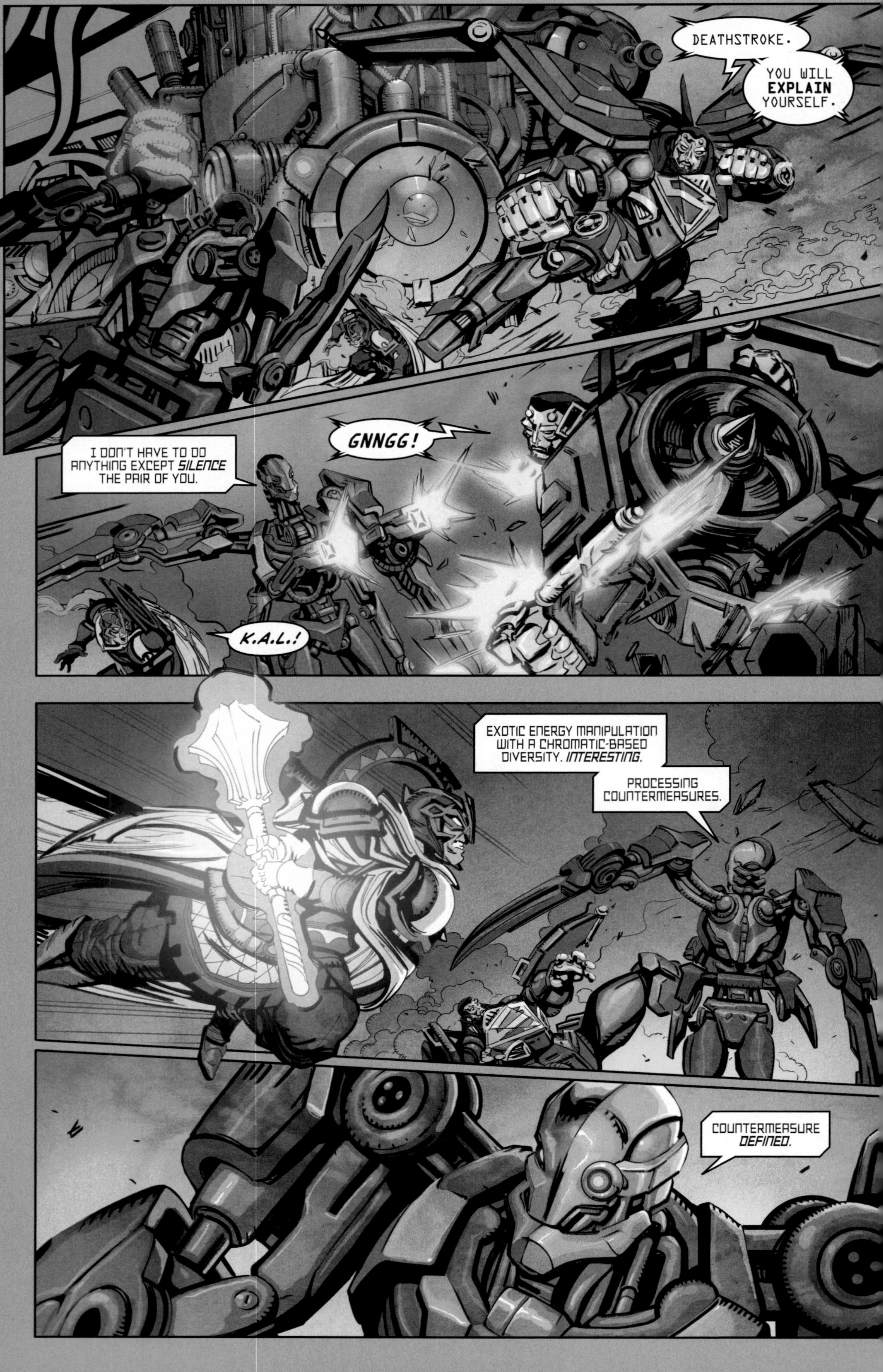
DEATHSTROKE.
YOU WILL **EXPLAIN** YOURSELF.
I DON'T HAVE TO DO ANYTHING EXCEPT *SILENCE* THE PAIR OF YOU.
GNNGG!
K.A.L.!
EXOTIC ENERGY MANIPULATION WITH A CHROMATIC-BASED DIVERSITY. *INTERESTING.*
PROCESSING COUNTERMEASURES.
COUNTERMEASURE *DEFINED.*

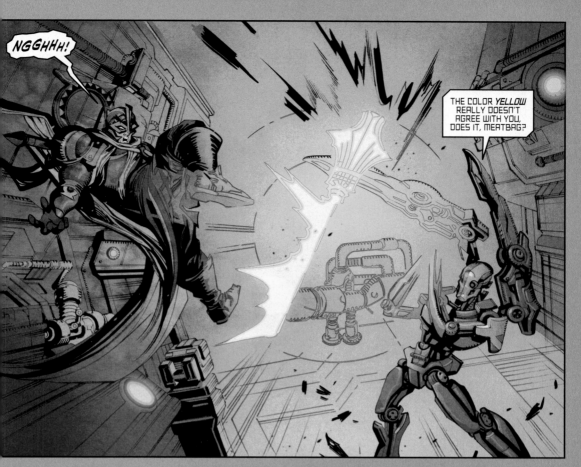

NGGHHH!

THE COLOR *YELLOW* REALLY DOESN'T AGREE WITH YOU, DOES IT, MEATBAG?

N-NO... I W-WILL *NOT* BE V-VANQUISHED...

ARGGGHH!!

PROBLEM *SOLVED.*

THE GASLIGHT WORLD.

"FASCINATING THOUGH IT IS TO MEET *ANOTHER* COLORFUL BEING FROM YOUR WORLD, BATMAN...

...YOUR ACCUSATIONS ARE *OUTRAGEOUS.*

WHAT IS THE EARTH ENGINE?

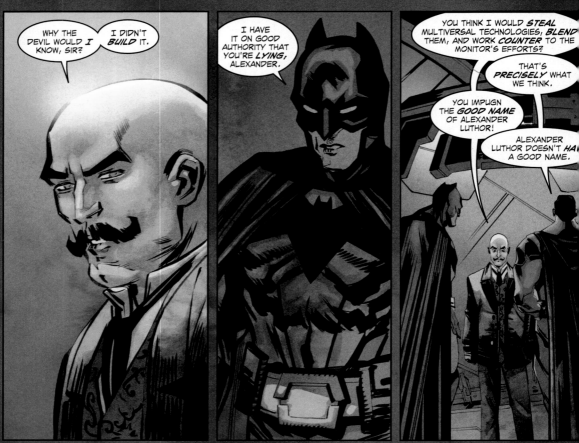

WHY THE DEVIL WOULD *I* KNOW, SIR?

I DIDN'T *BUILD* IT.

I HAVE IT ON GOOD AUTHORITY THAT YOU'RE *LYING,* ALEXANDER.

YOU THINK I WOULD *STEAL* MULTIVERSAL TECHNOLOGIES, *BLEND* THEM, AND WORK *COUNTER* TO THE MONITOR'S EFFORTS?

THAT'S *PRECISELY* WHAT WE THINK.

YOU IMPUGN THE *GOOD NAME* OF ALEXANDER LUTHOR!

ALEXANDER LUTHOR DOESN'T HA A GOOD NAME.

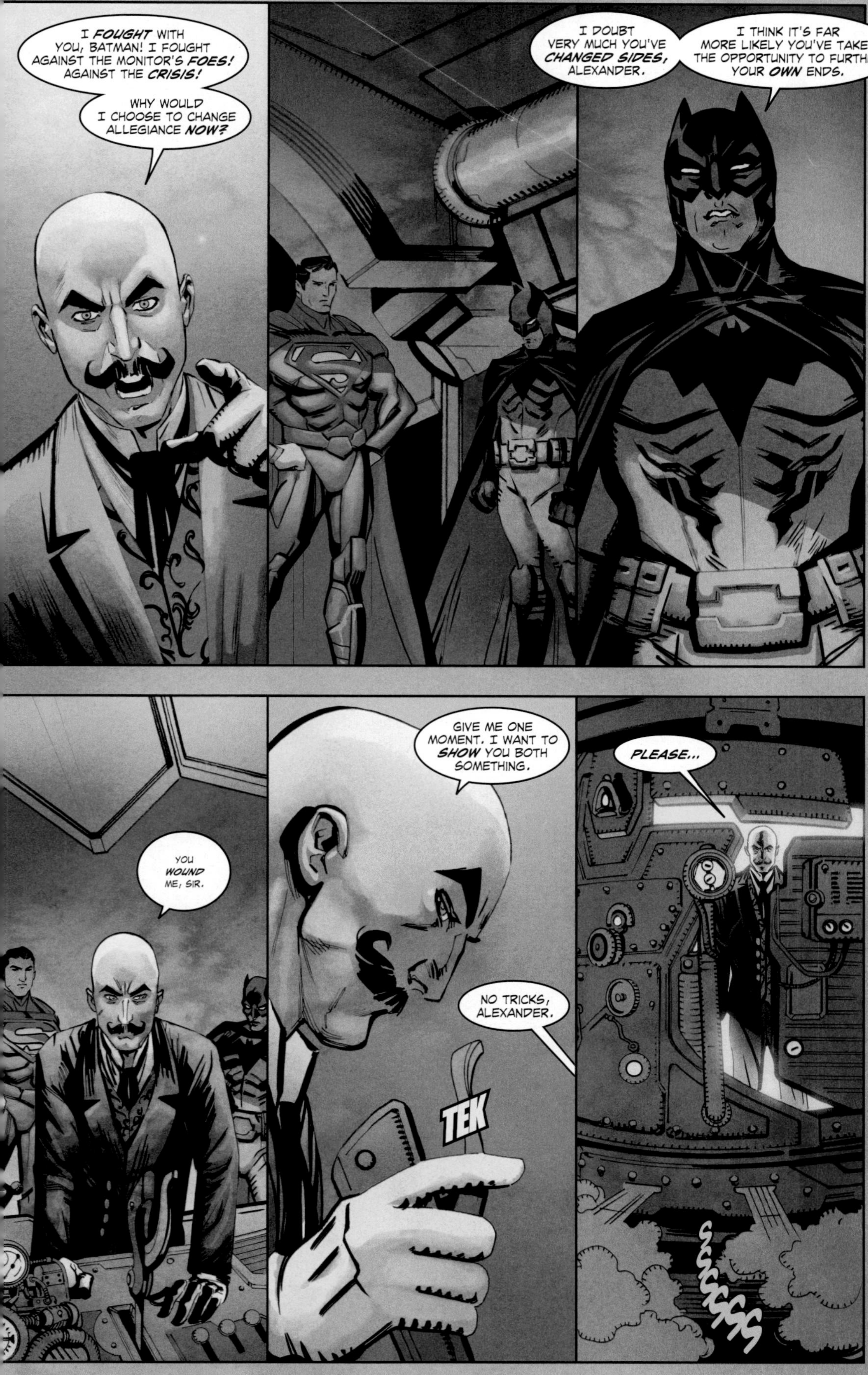
I FOUGHT WITH YOU, BATMAN! I FOUGHT AGAINST THE MONITOR'S FOES! AGAINST THE CRISIS!
WHY WOULD I CHOOSE TO CHANGE ALLEGIANCE NOW?
I DOUBT VERY MUCH YOU'VE CHANGED SIDES, ALEXANDER.
I THINK IT'S FAR MORE LIKELY YOU'VE TAKEN THE OPPORTUNITY TO FURTHER YOUR OWN ENDS.
YOU WOUND ME, SIR.
GIVE ME ONE MOMENT. I WANT TO SHOW YOU BOTH SOMETHING.
NO TRICKS, ALEXANDER.
TEK
PLEASE...
SSSSSSS

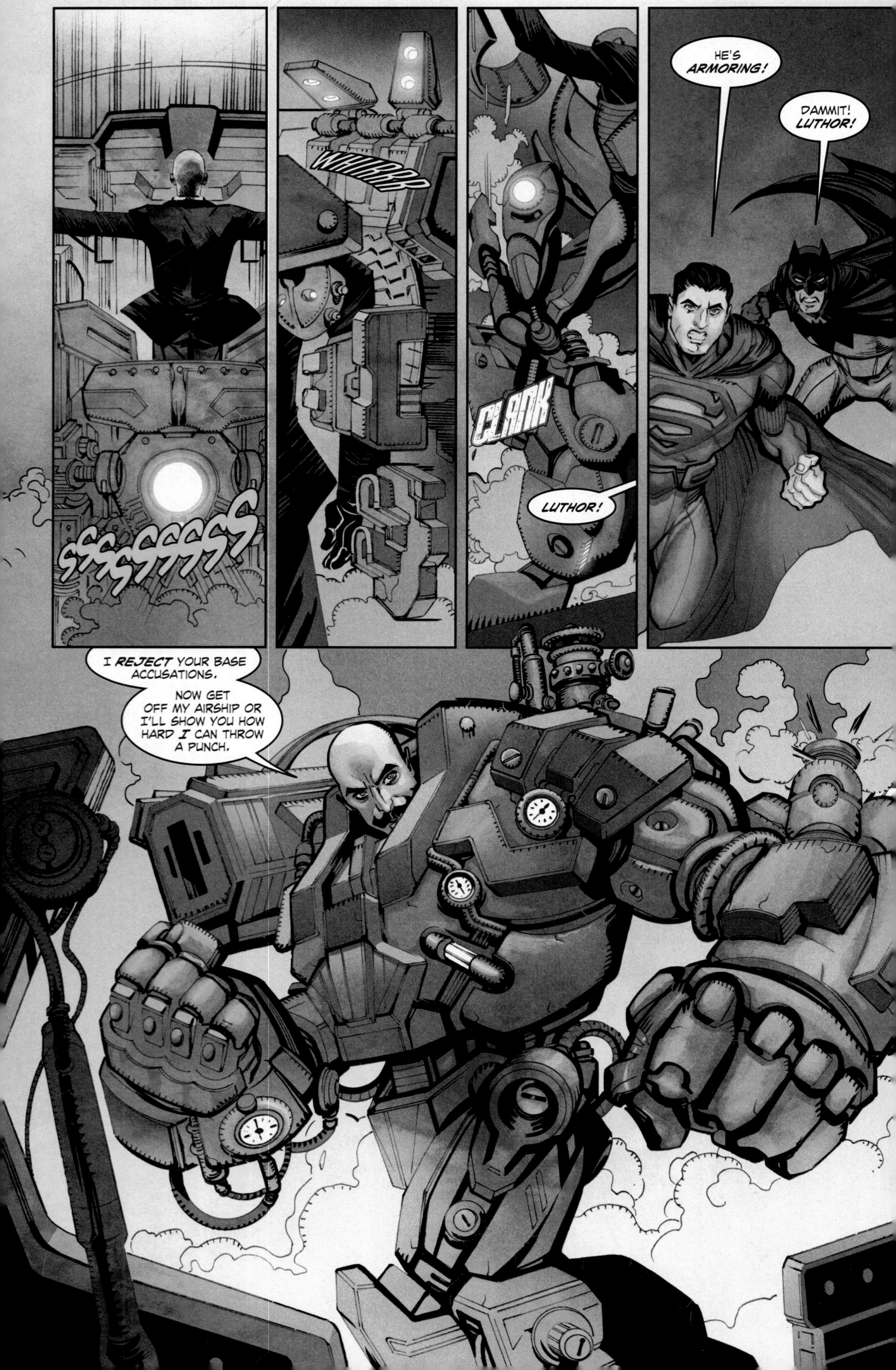
SSSSSSSSS
WHIRRR
CLANK
LUTHOR!
HE'S ARMORING!
DAMMIT! LUTHOR!
I REJECT YOUR BASE ACCUSATIONS.
NOW GET OFF MY AIRSHIP OR I'LL SHOW YOU HOW HARD I CAN THROW A PUNCH.

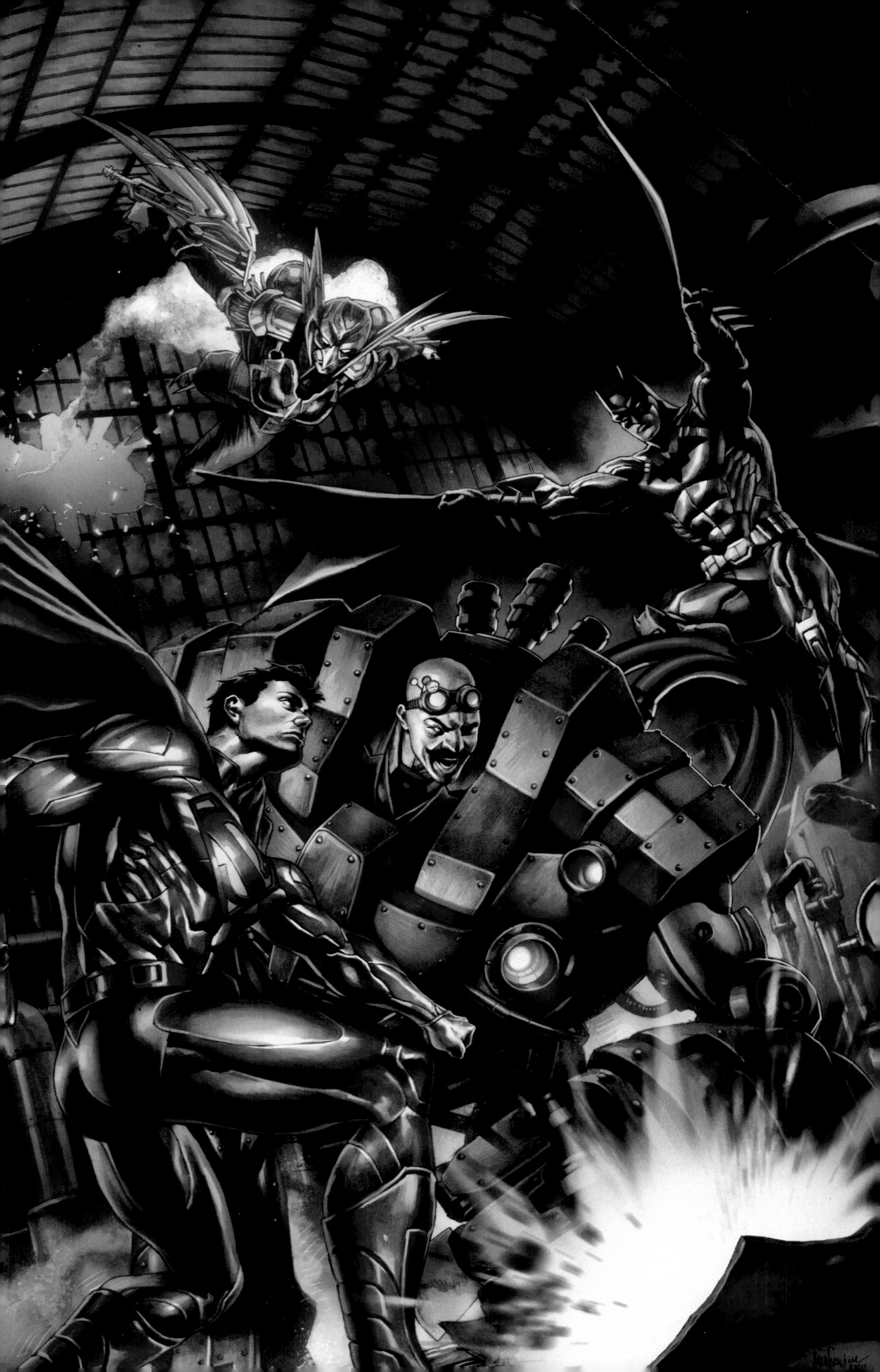

WORLDS' FINEST

Angel Hernandez Eduardo Francisco Artists **Alejandro Sanchez** Colorist
Cover Art by **Mico Suayan and Ellery Santos**

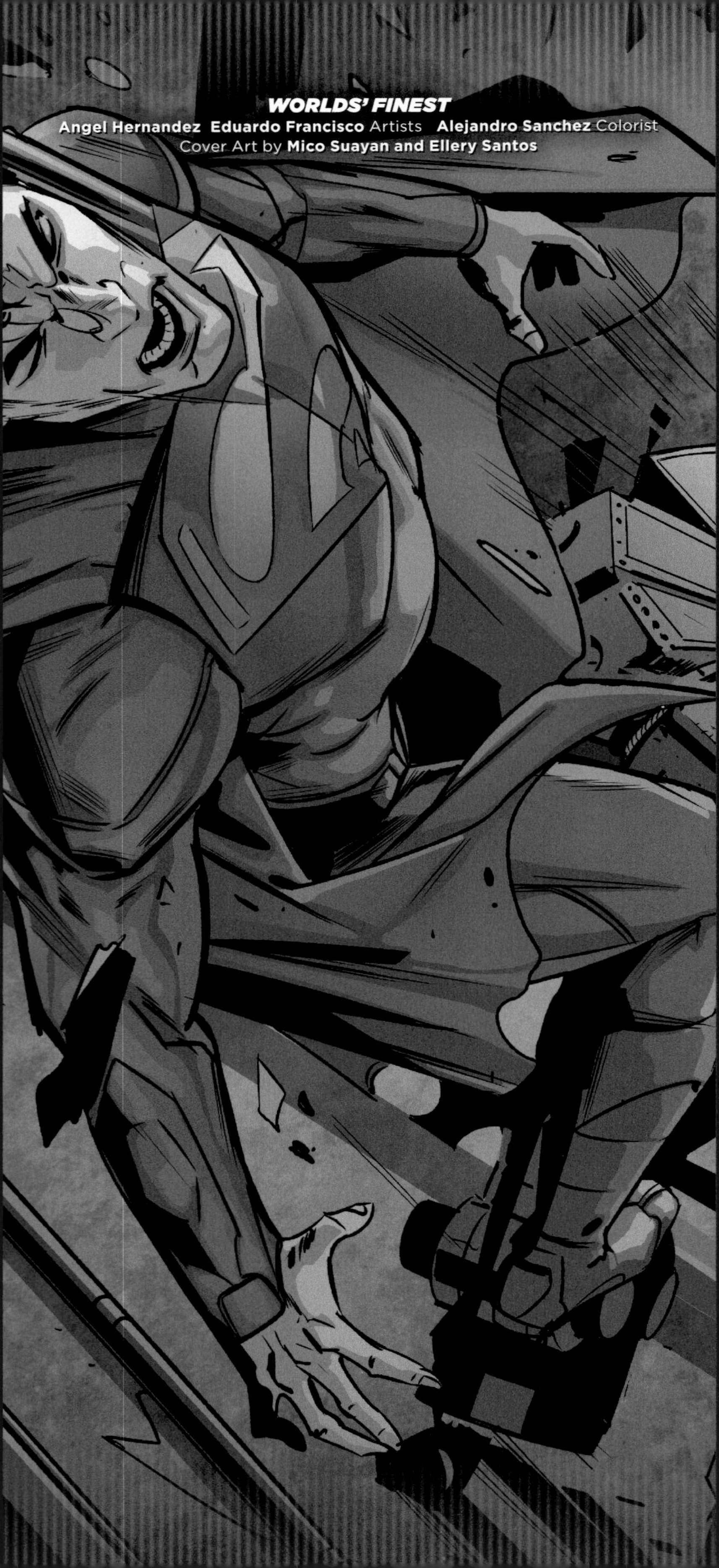

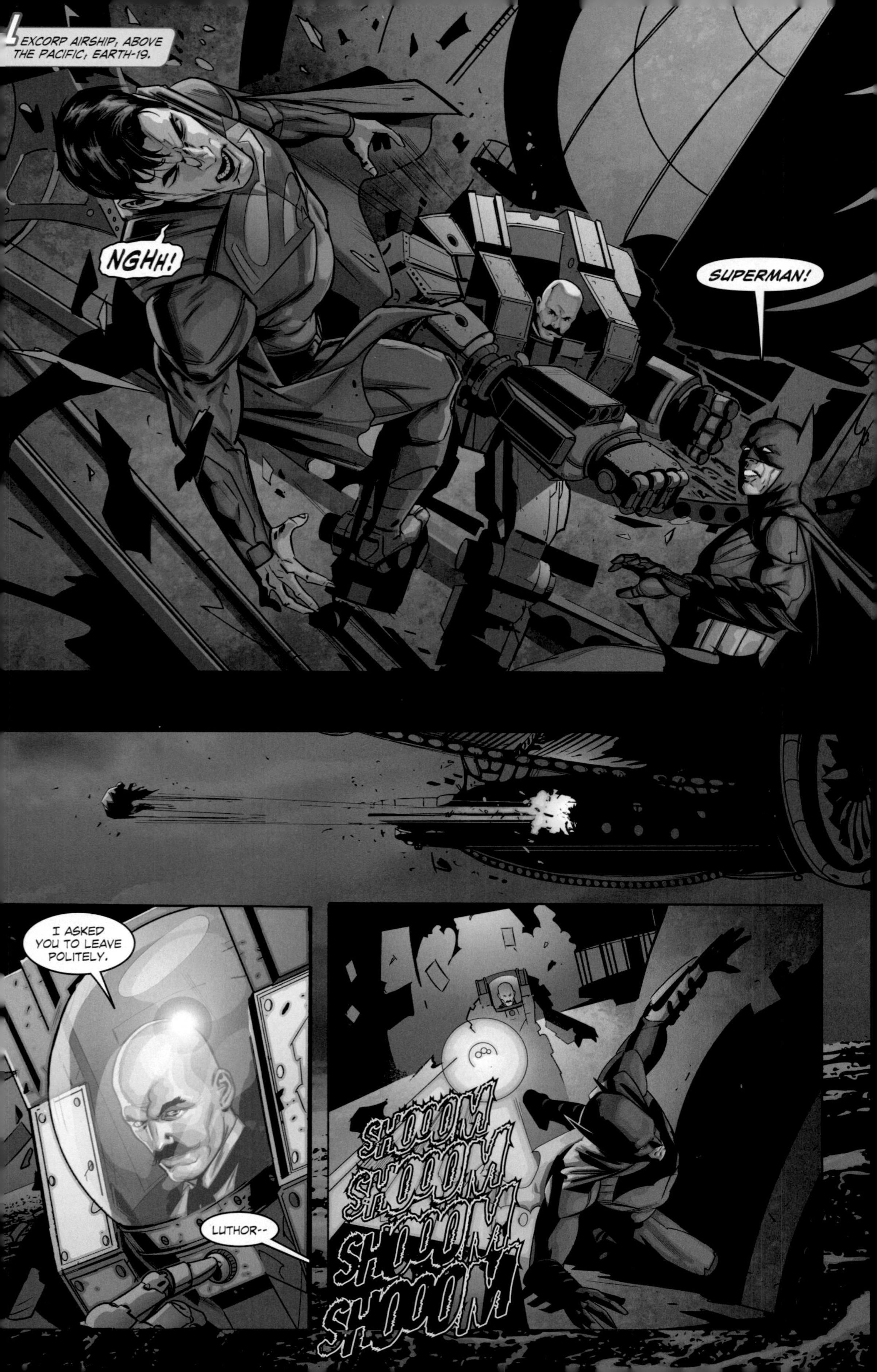
LEXCORP AIRSHIP, ABOVE THE PACIFIC, EARTH-19.
NGHH!
SUPERMAN!
I ASKED YOU TO LEAVE POLITELY.
LUTHOR--
SHOOOM SHOOOM SHOOOM SHOOOM SHOOOM

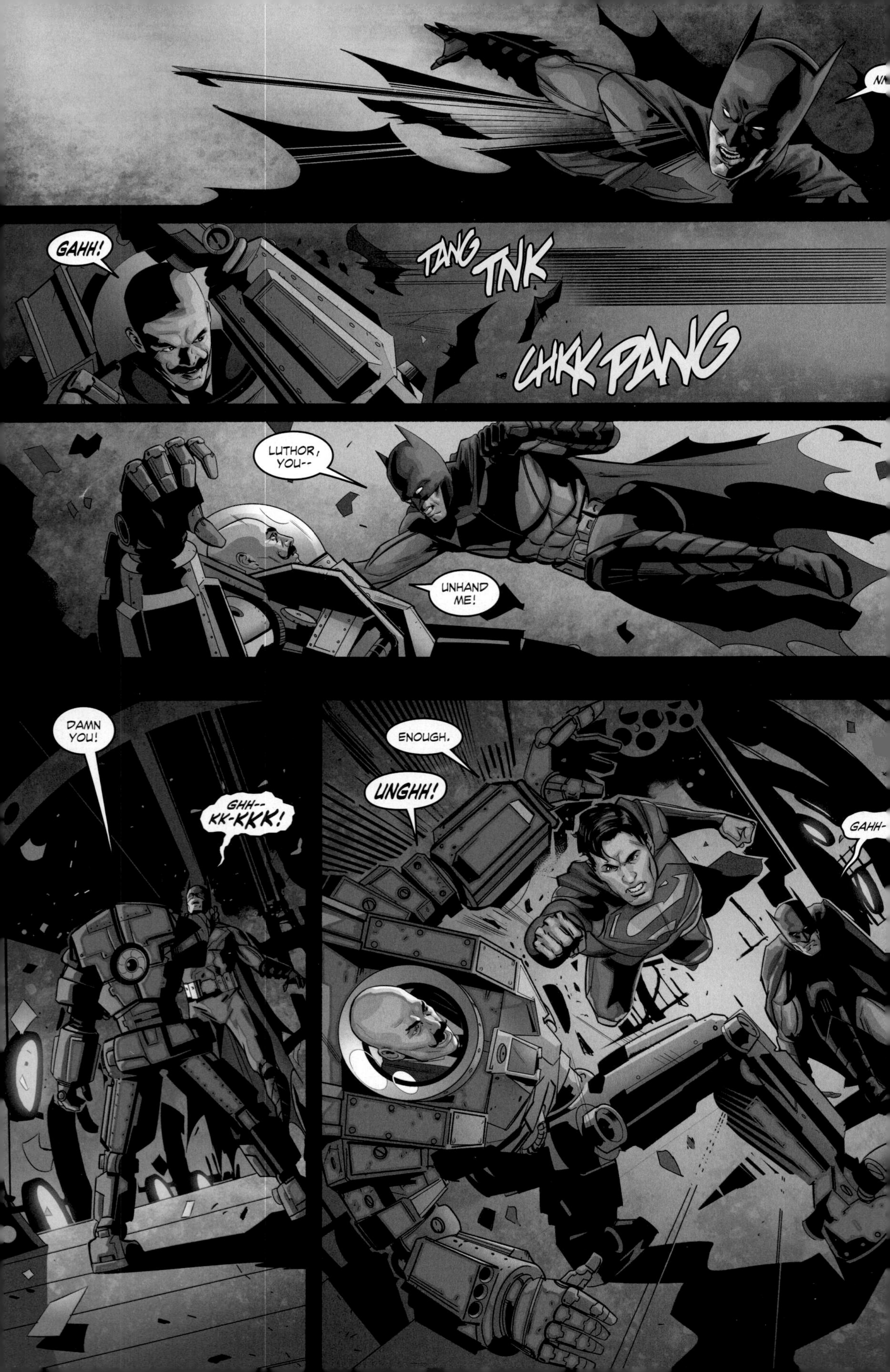
NN
GAHH!
TANG TNK
CHKK PANG
LUTHOR, YOU--
UNHAND ME!
DAMN YOU!
GHH-- KK-KKK!
ENOUGH.
UNGHH!
GAHH-

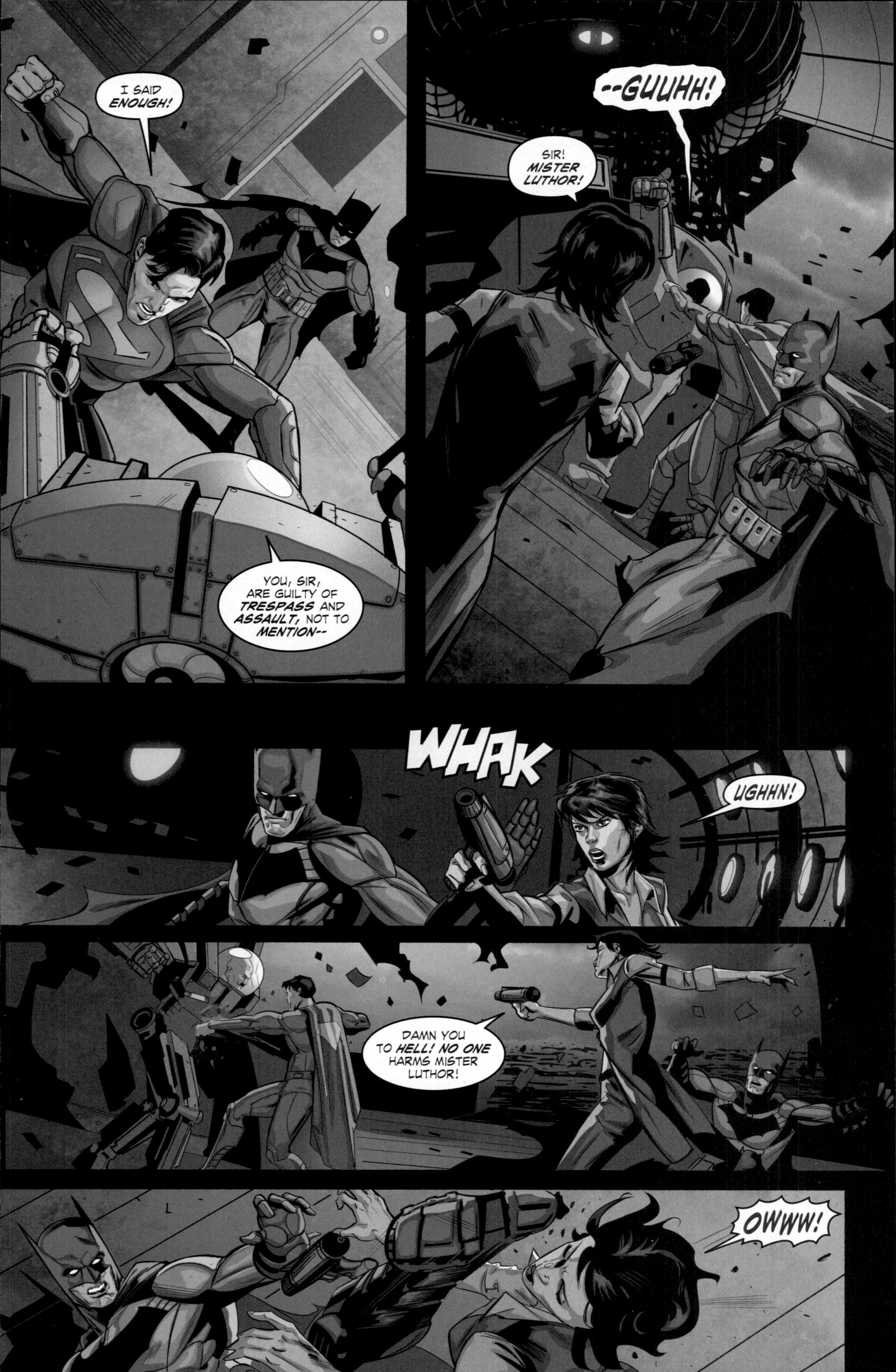
I SAID ENOUGH!
YOU, SIR, ARE GUILTY OF TRESPASS AND ASSAULT, NOT TO MENTION--
--GUUHH!
SIR! MISTER LUTHOR!
WHAK
UGHHN!
DAMN YOU TO HELL! NO ONE HARMS MISTER LUTHOR!
OWWW!

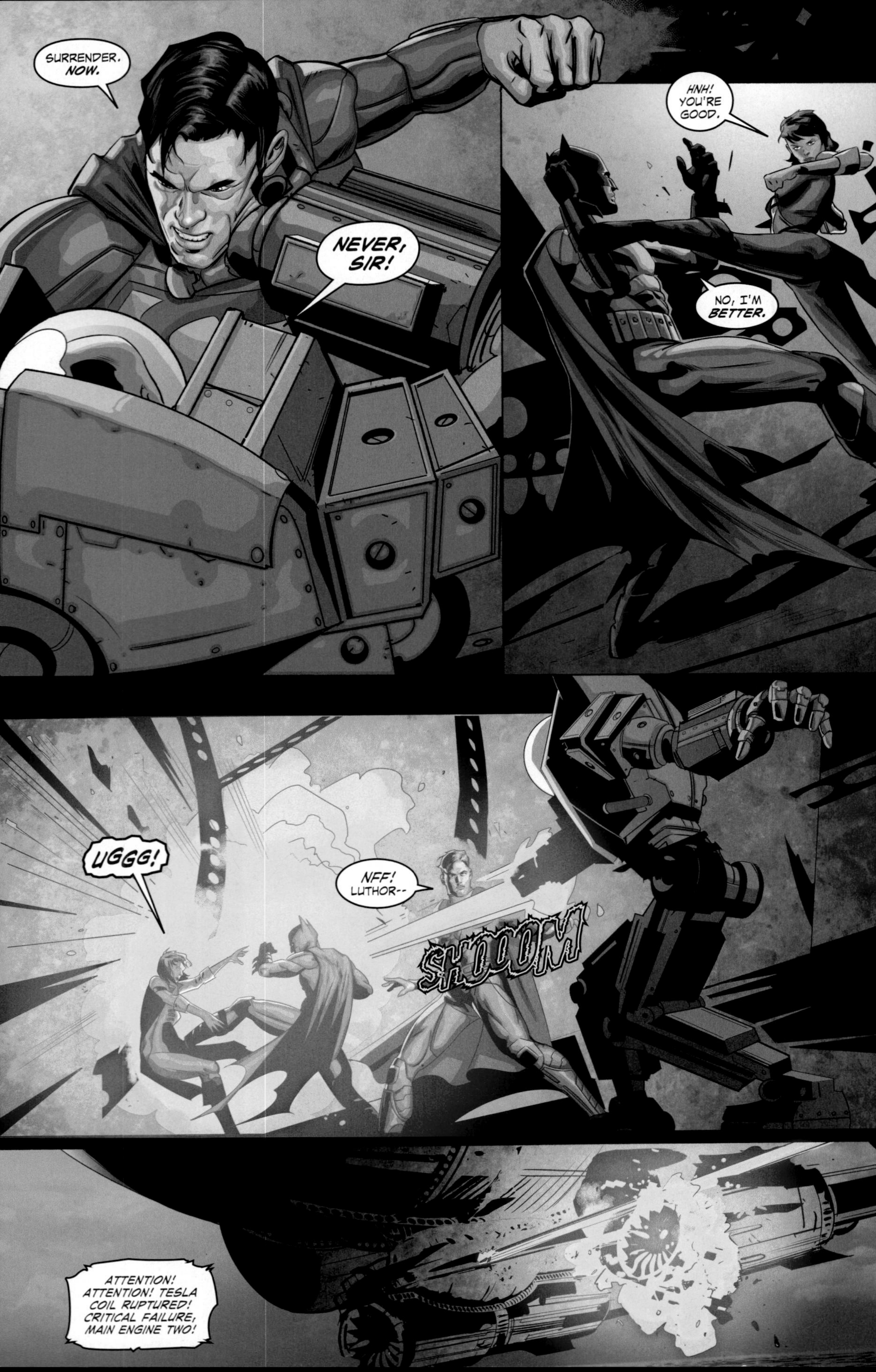
SURRENDER. NOW.
NEVER, SIR!
HNH! YOU'RE GOOD.
NO, I'M BETTER.
UGGG!
NFF! LUTHOR--
SHOOOM
ATTENTION! ATTENTION! TESLA COIL RUPTURED! CRITICAL FAILURE, MAIN ENGINE TWO!

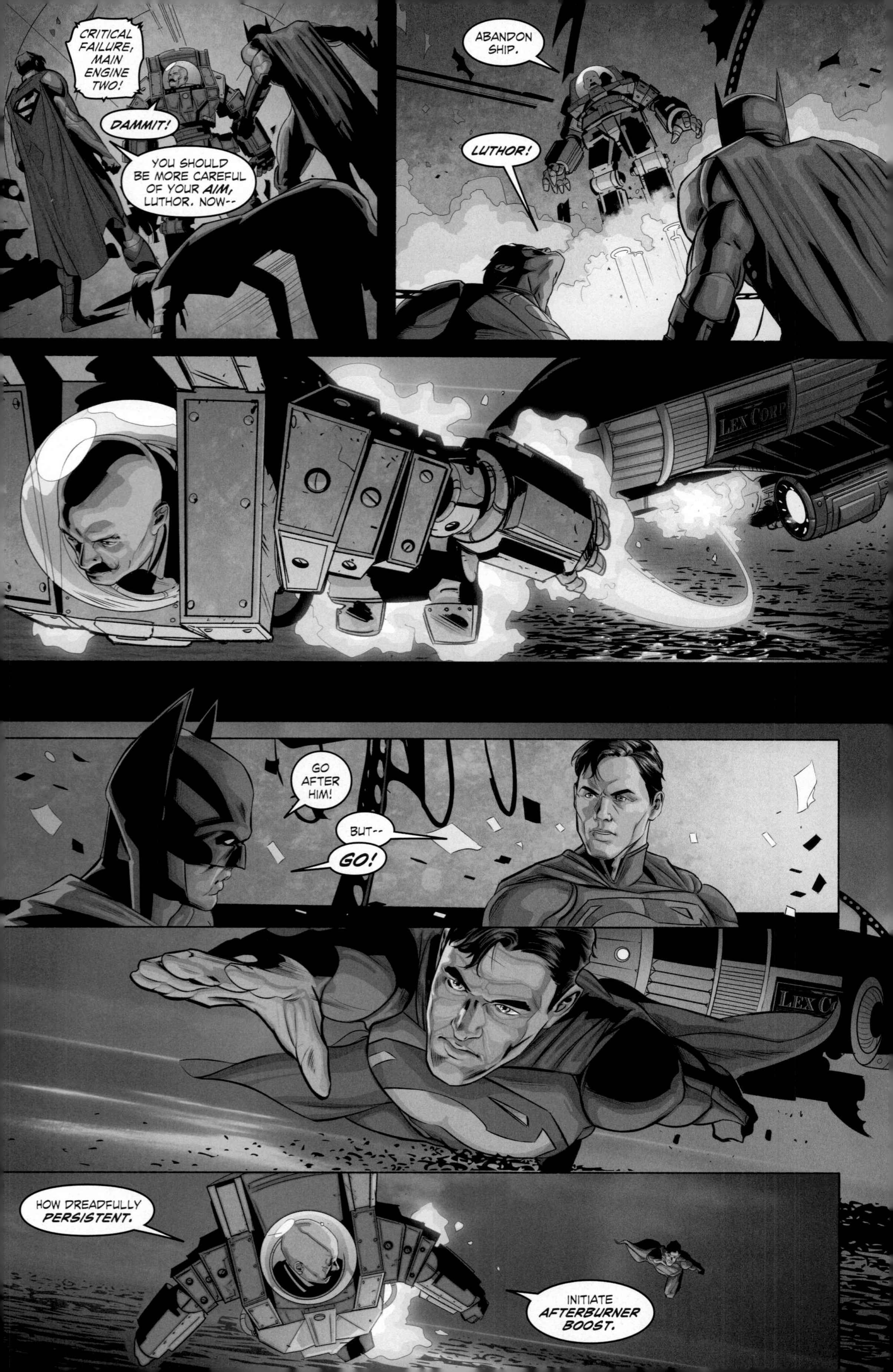
CRITICAL FAILURE, MAIN ENGINE TWO!
DAMMIT!
YOU SHOULD BE MORE CAREFUL OF YOUR AIM, LUTHOR. NOW--
ABANDON SHIP.
LUTHOR!
LEX CORP
GO AFTER HIM!
BUT--
GO!
LEX CO
HOW DREADFULLY PERSISTENT.
INITIATE AFTERBURNER BOOST.

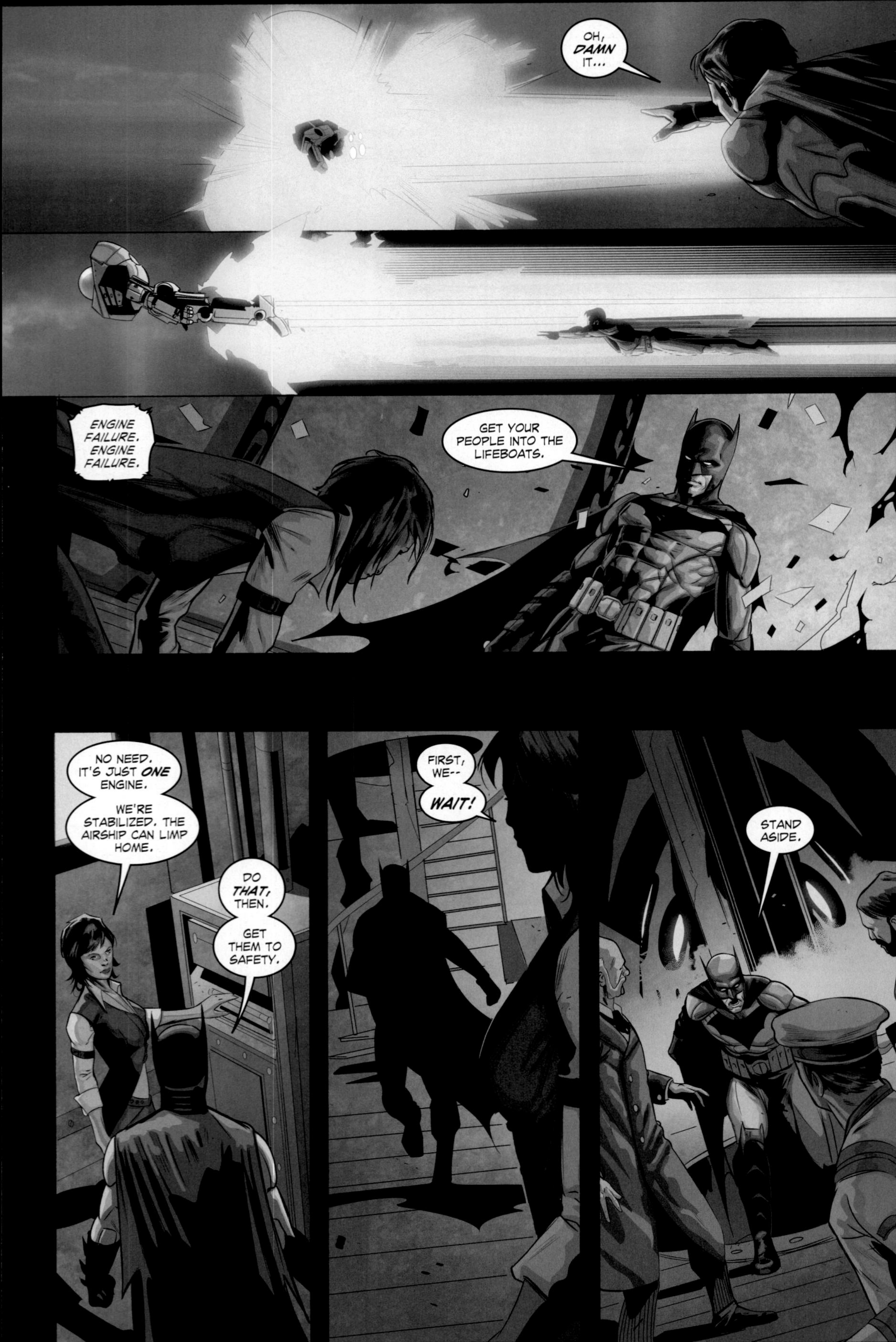
OH, DAMN IT...
ENGINE FAILURE. ENGINE FAILURE.
GET YOUR PEOPLE INTO THE LIFEBOATS.
NO NEED. IT'S JUST ONE ENGINE.
WE'RE STABILIZED. THE AIRSHIP CAN LIMP HOME.
DO THAT, THEN.
GET THEM TO SAFETY.
FIRST, WE--
WAIT!
STAND ASIDE.

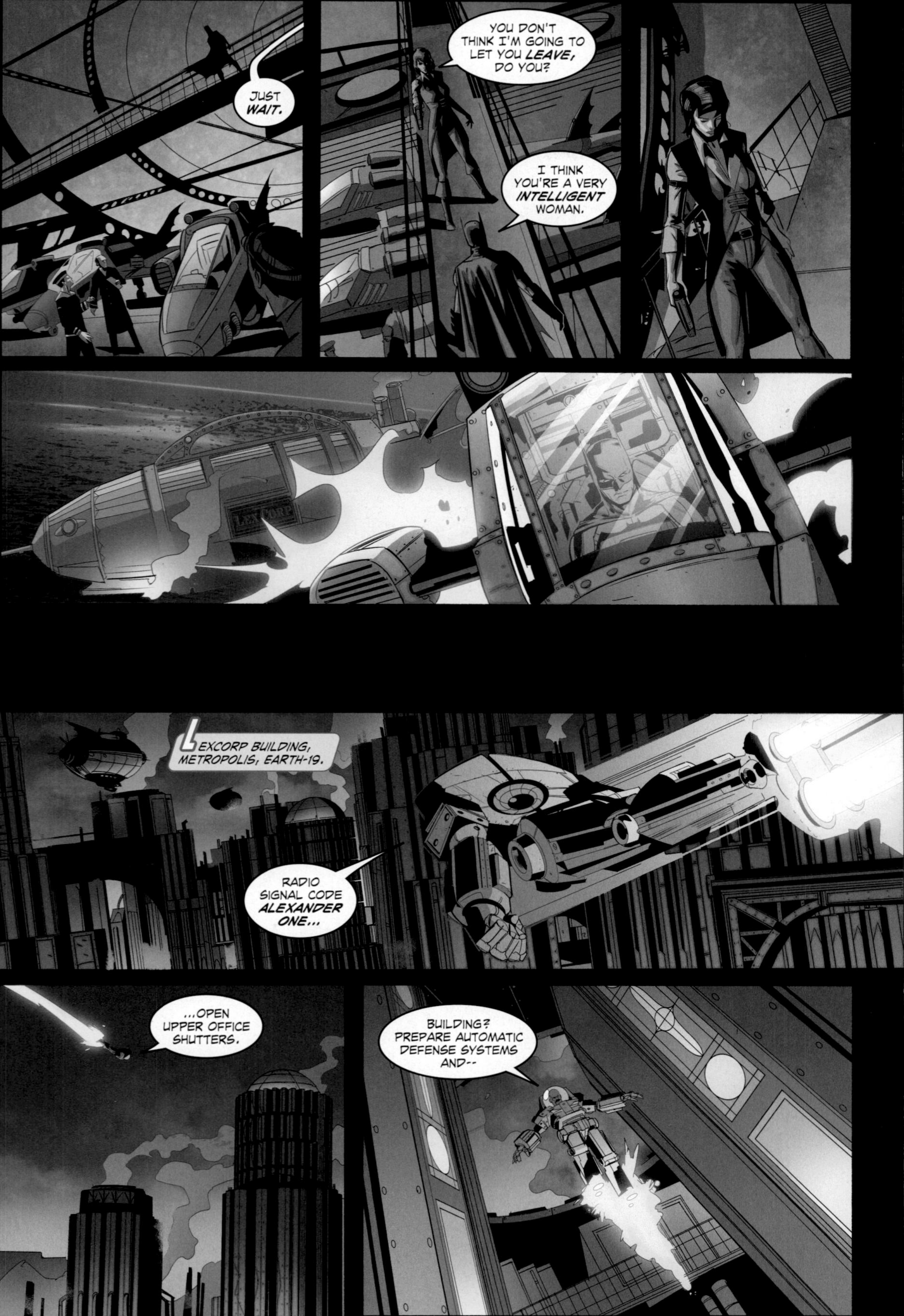

JUST WAIT.
YOU DON'T THINK I'M GOING TO LET YOU LEAVE, DO YOU?
I THINK YOU'RE A VERY INTELLIGENT WOMAN.
LEXCORP
LEXCORP BUILDING, METROPOLIS, EARTH-19.
RADIO SIGNAL CODE ALEXANDER ONE...
...OPEN UPPER OFFICE SHUTTERS.
BUILDING? PREPARE AUTOMATIC DEFENSE SYSTEMS AND--

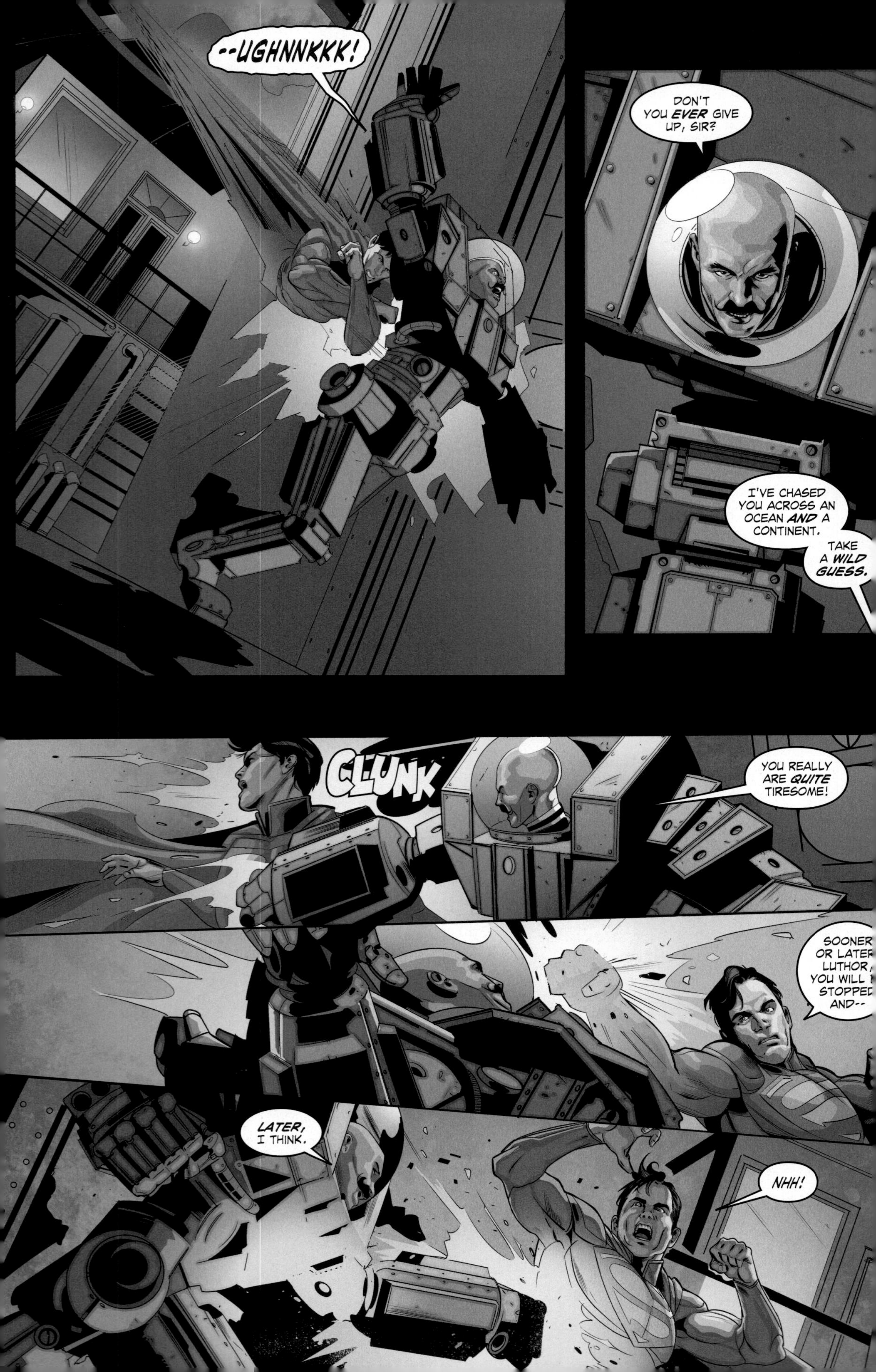
--UGHNNKKK!
DON'T YOU *EVER* GIVE UP, SIR?
I'VE CHASED YOU ACROSS AN OCEAN *AND* A CONTINENT.
TAKE A *WILD GUESS.*
CLUNK
YOU REALLY ARE *QUITE* TIRESOME!
SOONER OR LATER, LUTHOR, YOU WILL BE STOPPED AND--
LATER, I THINK.
NHH!

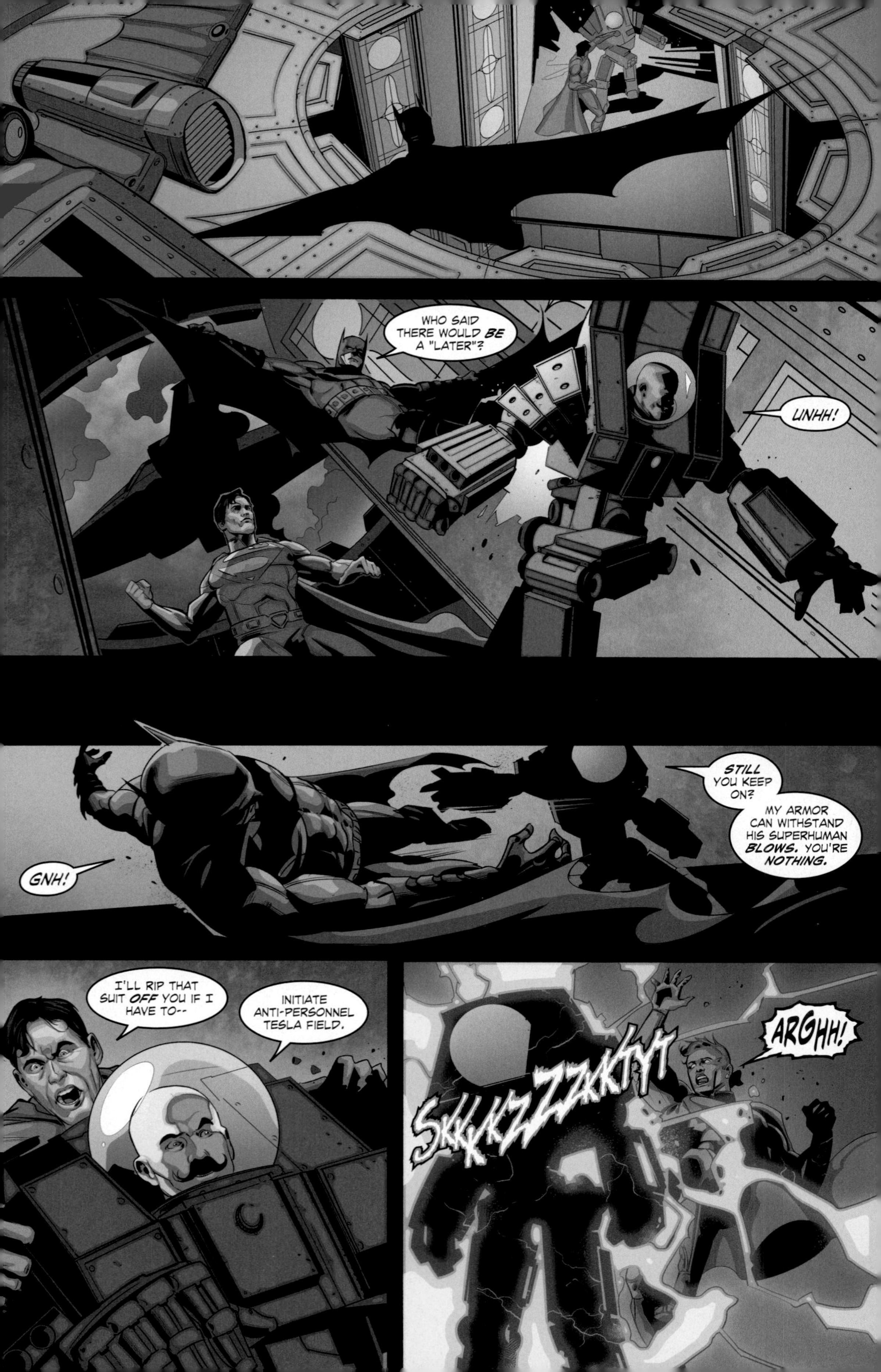
WHO SAID THERE WOULD BE A "LATER"?
UNHH!
STILL YOU KEEP ON?
MY ARMOR CAN WITHSTAND HIS SUPERHUMAN BLOWS. YOU'RE NOTHING.
GNH!
I'LL RIP THAT SUIT OFF YOU IF I HAVE TO--
INITIATE ANTI-PERSONNEL TESLA FIELD.
SKKKKZZZKKKTYT
ARGHH!

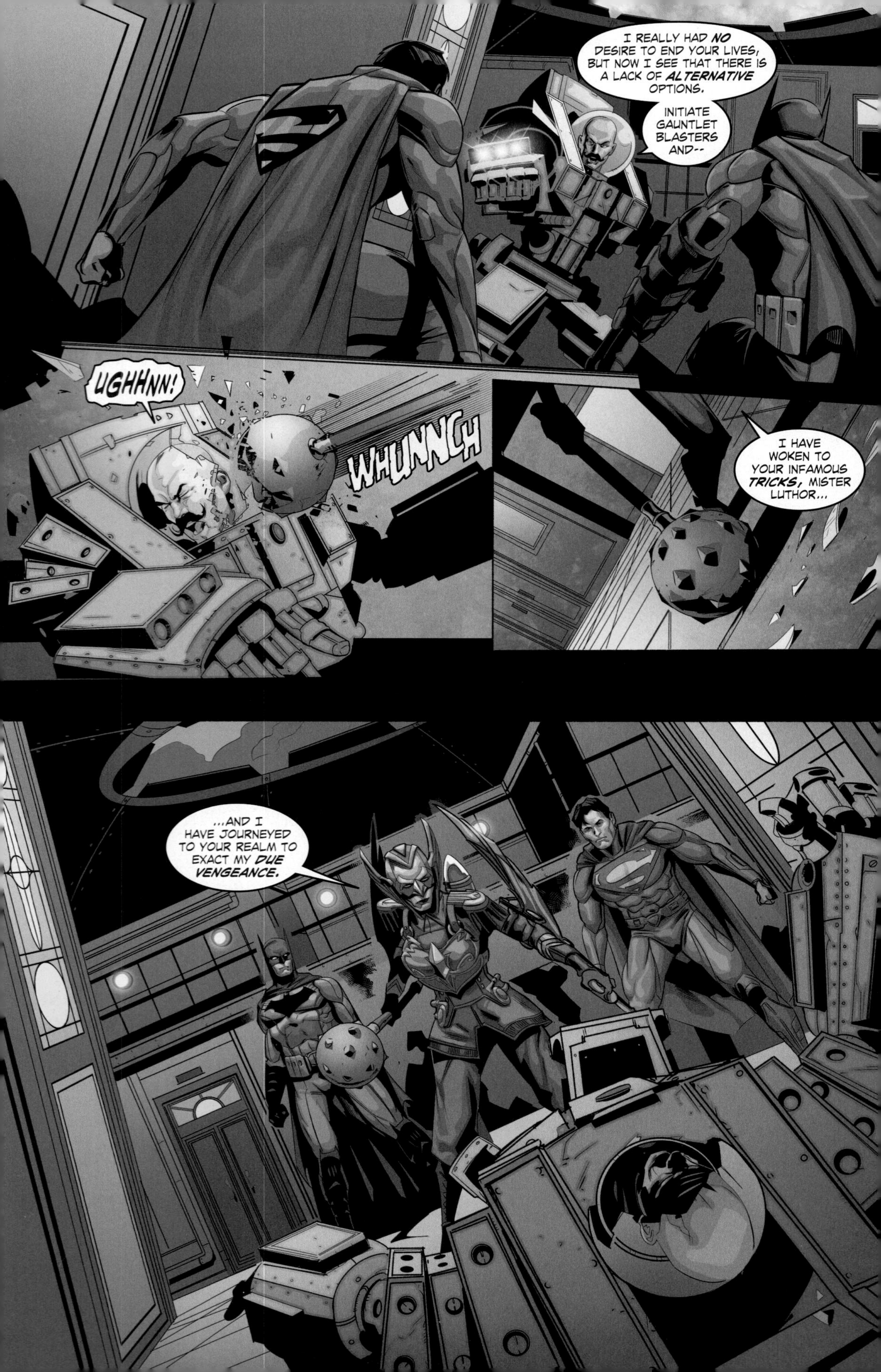
I REALLY HAD NO DESIRE TO END YOUR LIVES, BUT NOW I SEE THAT THERE IS A LACK OF ALTERNATIVE OPTIONS.
INITIATE GAUNTLET BLASTERS AND--
UGHHNN!
WHUNNCH
I HAVE WOKEN TO YOUR INFAMOUS TRICKS, MISTER LUTHOR...
...AND I HAVE JOURNEYED TO YOUR REALM TO EXACT MY DUE VENGEANCE.

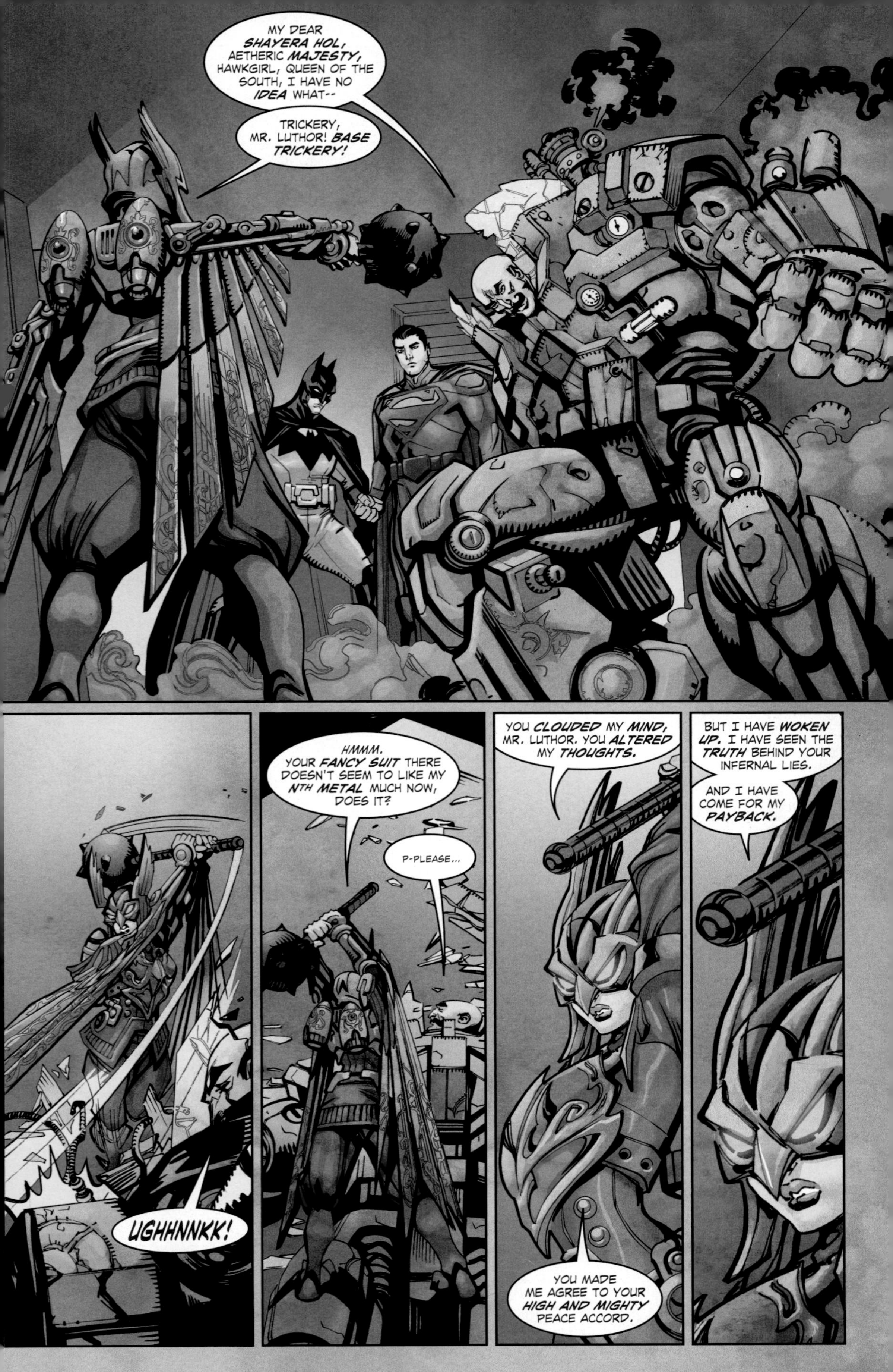
MY DEAR SHAYERA HOL, AETHERIC MAJESTY, HAWKGIRL, QUEEN OF THE SOUTH, I HAVE NO IDEA WHAT--
TRICKERY, MR. LUTHOR! BASE TRICKERY!
UGHHNNKK!
HMMM. YOUR FANCY SUIT THERE DOESN'T SEEM TO LIKE MY NTH METAL MUCH NOW, DOES IT?
P-PLEASE...
YOU CLOUDED MY MIND, MR. LUTHOR. YOU ALTERED MY THOUGHTS.
YOU MADE ME AGREE TO YOUR HIGH AND MIGHTY PEACE ACCORD.
BUT I HAVE WOKEN UP. I HAVE SEEN THE TRUTH BEHIND YOUR INFERNAL LIES.
AND I HAVE COME FOR MY PAYBACK.

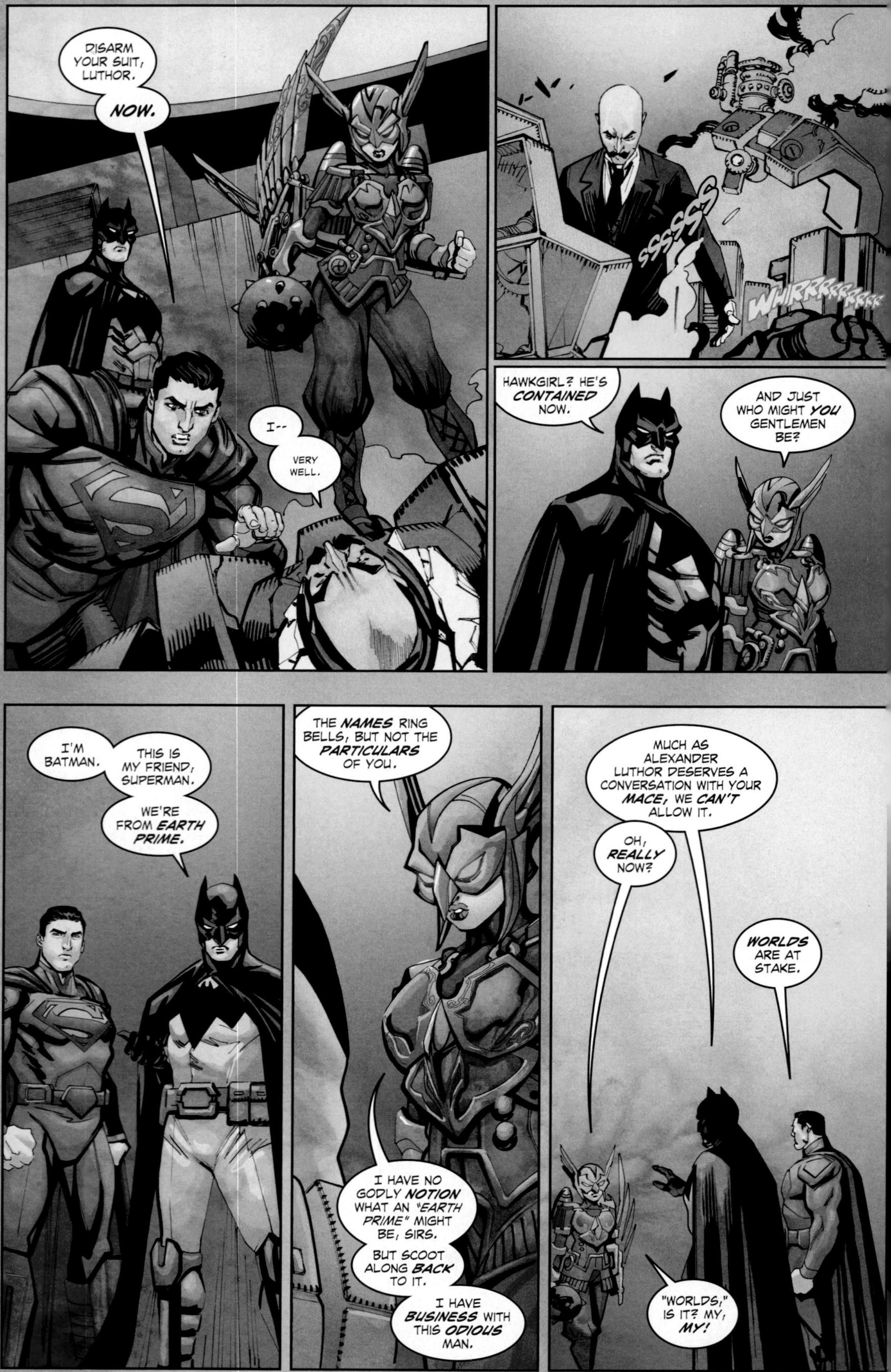
DISARM YOUR SUIT, LUTHOR.
NOW.
I--
VERY WELL.
SSSSSS
WHIRRRRRRRR
HAWKGIRL? HE'S CONTAINED NOW.
AND JUST WHO MIGHT YOU GENTLEMEN BE?
I'M BATMAN.
THIS IS MY FRIEND, SUPERMAN.
WE'RE FROM EARTH PRIME.
THE NAMES RING BELLS, BUT NOT THE PARTICULARS OF YOU.
I HAVE NO GODLY NOTION WHAT AN "EARTH PRIME" MIGHT BE, SIRS.
BUT SCOOT ALONG BACK TO IT.
I HAVE BUSINESS WITH THIS ODIOUS MAN.
MUCH AS ALEXANDER LUTHOR DESERVES A CONVERSATION WITH YOUR MACE, WE CAN'T ALLOW IT.
OH, REALLY NOW?
WORLDS ARE AT STAKE.
"WORLDS," IS IT? MY, MY!

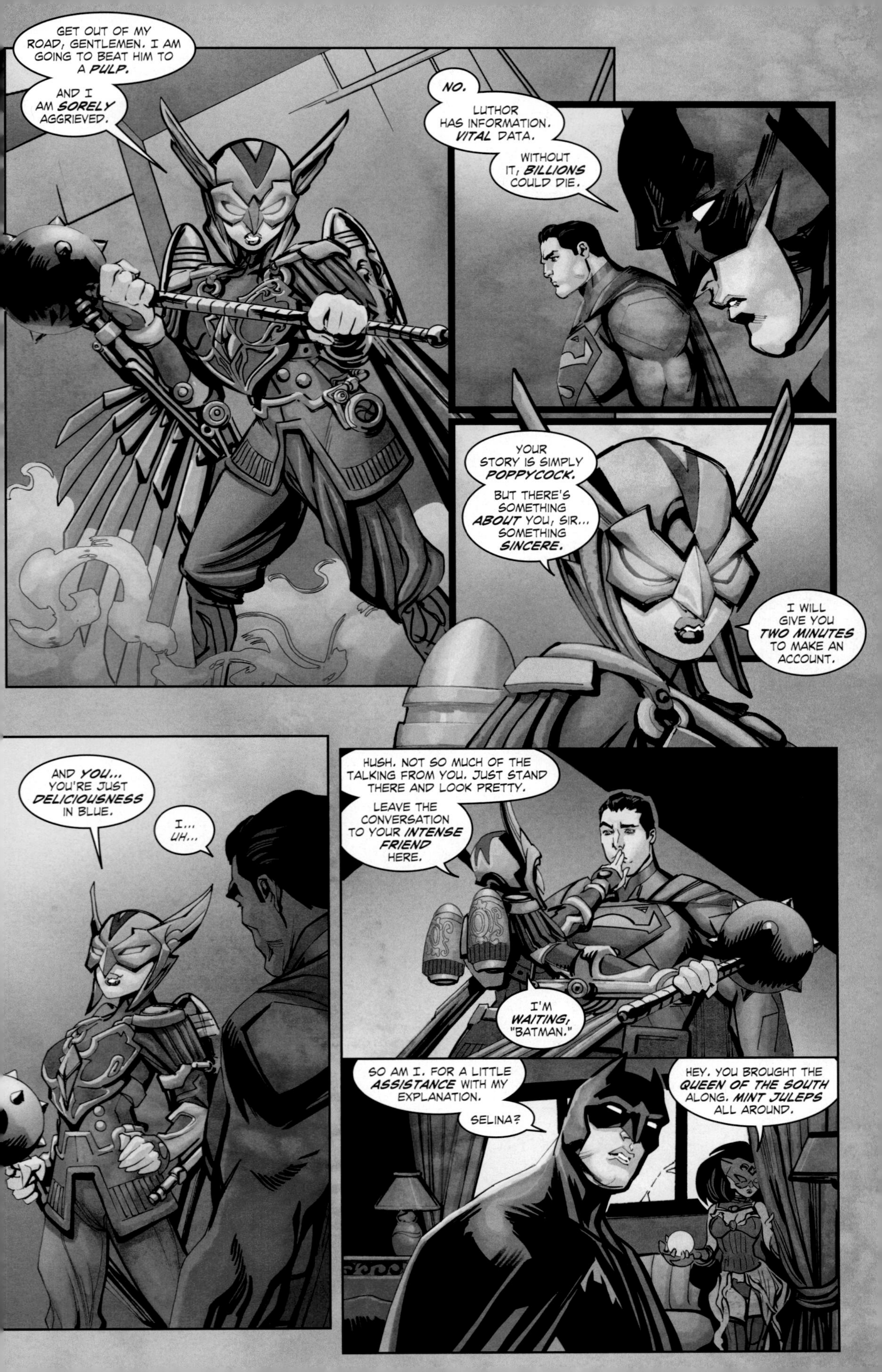

GET OUT OF MY ROAD, GENTLEMEN. I AM GOING TO BEAT HIM TO A *PULP.*
AND I AM *SORELY* AGGRIEVED.
NO.
LUTHOR HAS INFORMATION. *VITAL* DATA.
WITHOUT IT, *BILLIONS* COULD DIE.
YOUR STORY IS SIMPLY *POPPYCOCK.*
BUT THERE'S SOMETHING *ABOUT* YOU, SIR... SOMETHING *SINCERE.*
I WILL GIVE YOU *TWO MINUTES* TO MAKE AN ACCOUNT.
AND *YOU...* YOU'RE JUST *DELICIOUSNESS* IN BLUE.
I... UH...
HUSH. NOT SO MUCH OF THE TALKING FROM YOU. JUST STAND THERE AND LOOK PRETTY.
LEAVE THE CONVERSATION TO YOUR *INTENSE FRIEND* HERE.
I'M *WAITING,* "BATMAN."
SO AM I. FOR A LITTLE *ASSISTANCE* WITH MY EXPLANATION.
SELINA?
HEY. YOU BROUGHT THE *QUEEN OF THE SOUTH* ALONG. *MINT JULEPS* ALL AROUND.

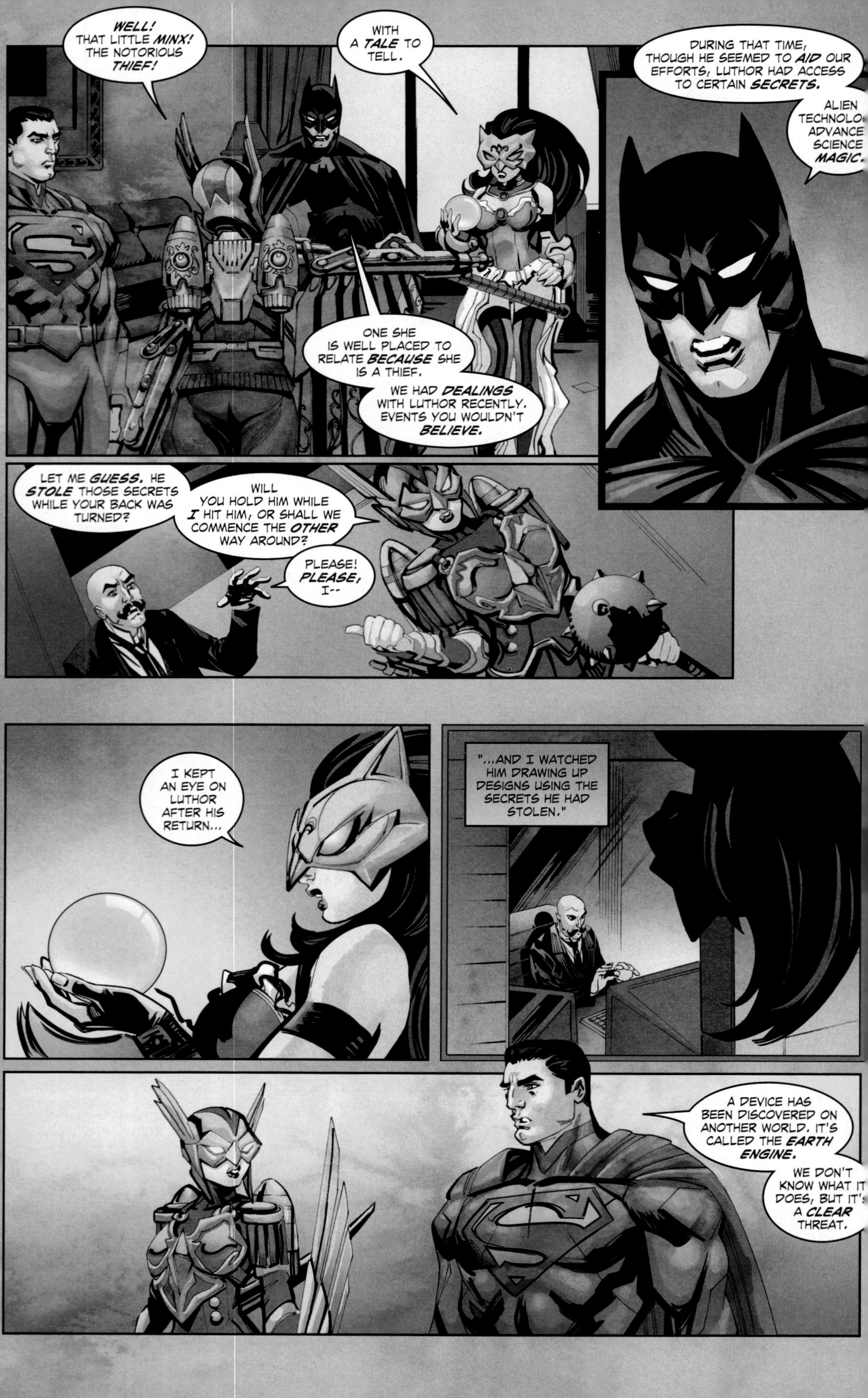

WELL! THAT LITTLE MINX! THE NOTORIOUS THIEF!
WITH A TALE TO TELL.
ONE SHE IS WELL PLACED TO RELATE BECAUSE SHE IS A THIEF.
WE HAD DEALINGS WITH LUTHOR RECENTLY. EVENTS YOU WOULDN'T BELIEVE.
DURING THAT TIME, THOUGH HE SEEMED TO AID OUR EFFORTS, LUTHOR HAD ACCESS TO CERTAIN SECRETS.
ALIEN TECHNOLO ADVANCE SCIENCE MAGIC.
LET ME GUESS. HE STOLE THOSE SECRETS WHILE YOUR BACK WAS TURNED?
WILL YOU HOLD HIM WHILE I HIT HIM, OR SHALL WE COMMENCE THE OTHER WAY AROUND?
PLEASE! PLEASE, I--
I KEPT AN EYE ON LUTHOR AFTER HIS RETURN...
"...AND I WATCHED HIM DRAWING UP DESIGNS USING THE SECRETS HE HAD STOLEN."
A DEVICE HAS BEEN DISCOVERED ON ANOTHER WORLD. IT'S CALLED THE EARTH ENGINE.
WE DON'T KNOW WHAT IT DOES, BUT IT' A CLEAR THREAT.

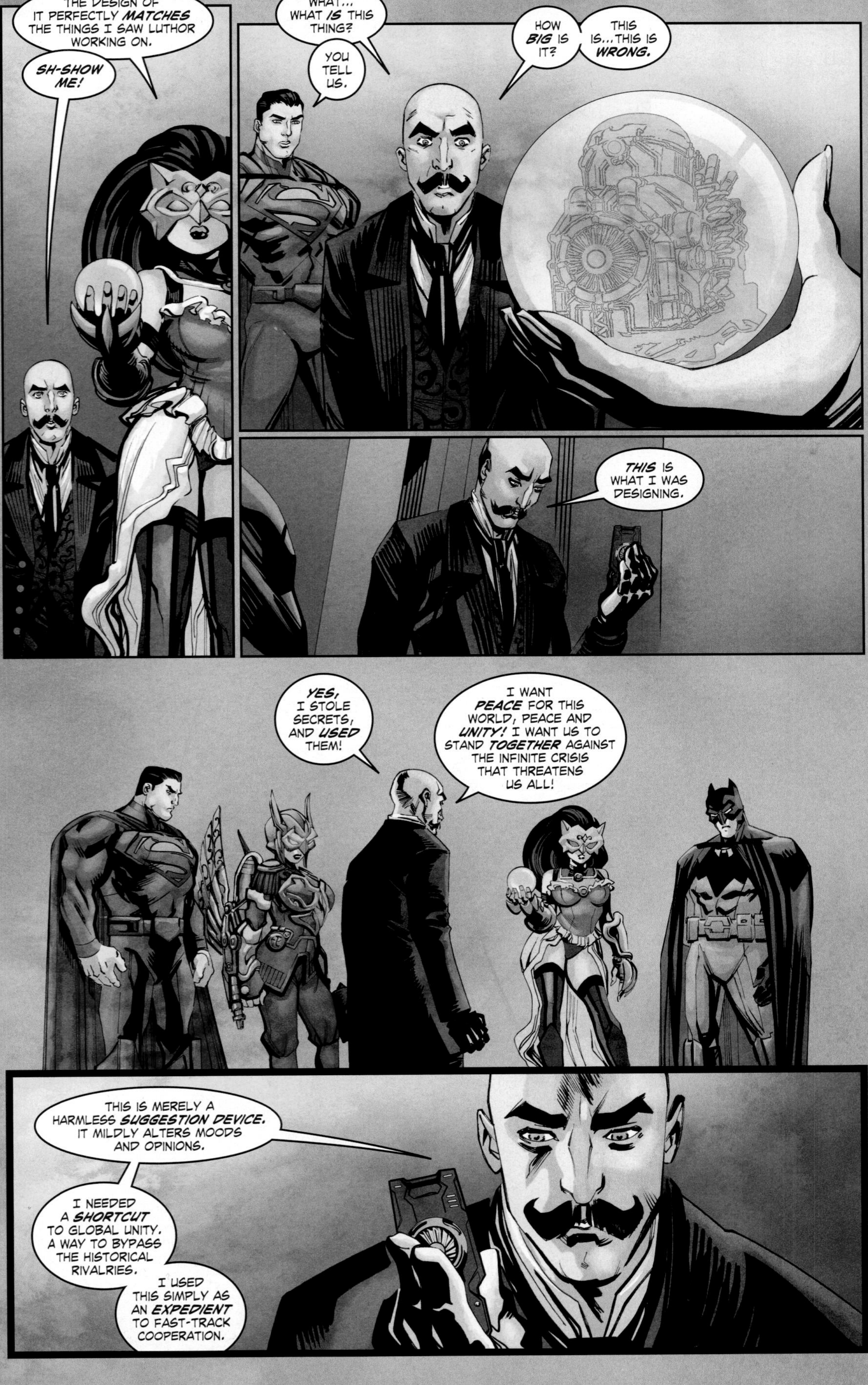
THE DESIGN OF IT PERFECTLY MATCHES THE THINGS I SAW LUTHOR WORKING ON.
SH-SHOW ME!
WHAT... WHAT IS THIS THING?
YOU TELL US.
HOW BIG IS IT?
THIS IS...THIS IS WRONG.
THIS IS WHAT I WAS DESIGNING.
YES, I STOLE SECRETS, AND USED THEM!
I WANT PEACE FOR THIS WORLD, PEACE AND UNITY! I WANT US TO STAND TOGETHER AGAINST THE INFINITE CRISIS THAT THREATENS US ALL!
THIS IS MERELY A HARMLESS SUGGESTION DEVICE. IT MILDLY ALTERS MOODS AND OPINIONS.
I NEEDED A SHORTCUT TO GLOBAL UNITY. A WAY TO BYPASS THE HISTORICAL RIVALRIES.
I USED THIS SIMPLY AS AN EXPEDIENT TO FAST-TRACK COOPERATION.

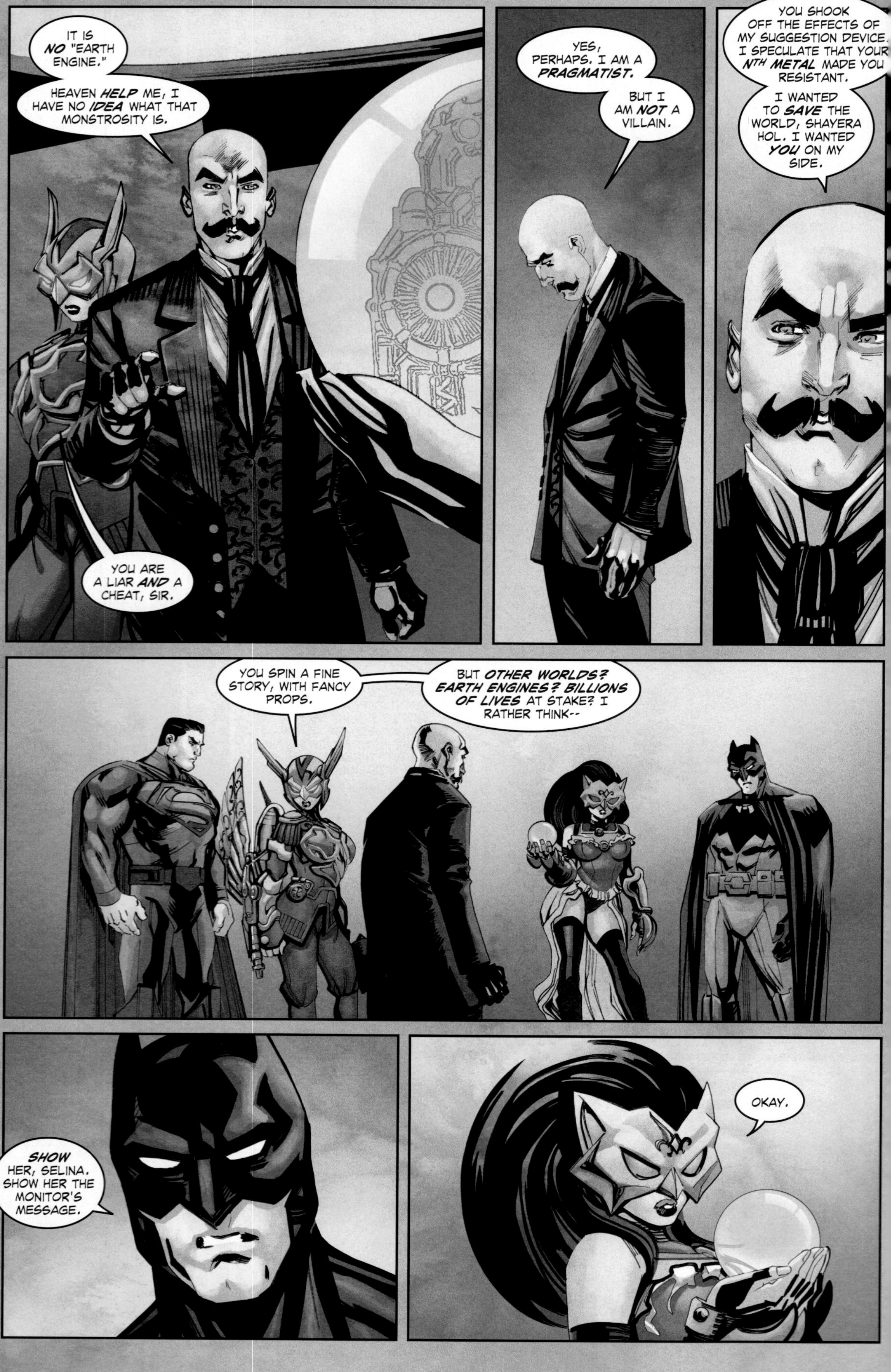
IT IS NO "EARTH ENGINE."
HEAVEN HELP ME, I HAVE NO IDEA WHAT THAT MONSTROSITY IS.
YOU ARE A LIAR AND A CHEAT, SIR.
YES, PERHAPS. I AM A PRAGMATIST.
BUT I AM NOT A VILLAIN.
YOU SHOOK OFF THE EFFECTS OF MY SUGGESTION DEVICE. I SPECULATE THAT YOUR NTH METAL MADE YOU RESISTANT.
I WANTED TO SAVE THE WORLD, SHAYERA HOL. I WANTED YOU ON MY SIDE.
YOU SPIN A FINE STORY, WITH FANCY PROPS.
BUT OTHER WORLDS? EARTH ENGINES? BILLIONS OF LIVES AT STAKE? I RATHER THINK--
SHOW HER, SELINA. SHOW HER THE MONITOR'S MESSAGE.
OKAY.

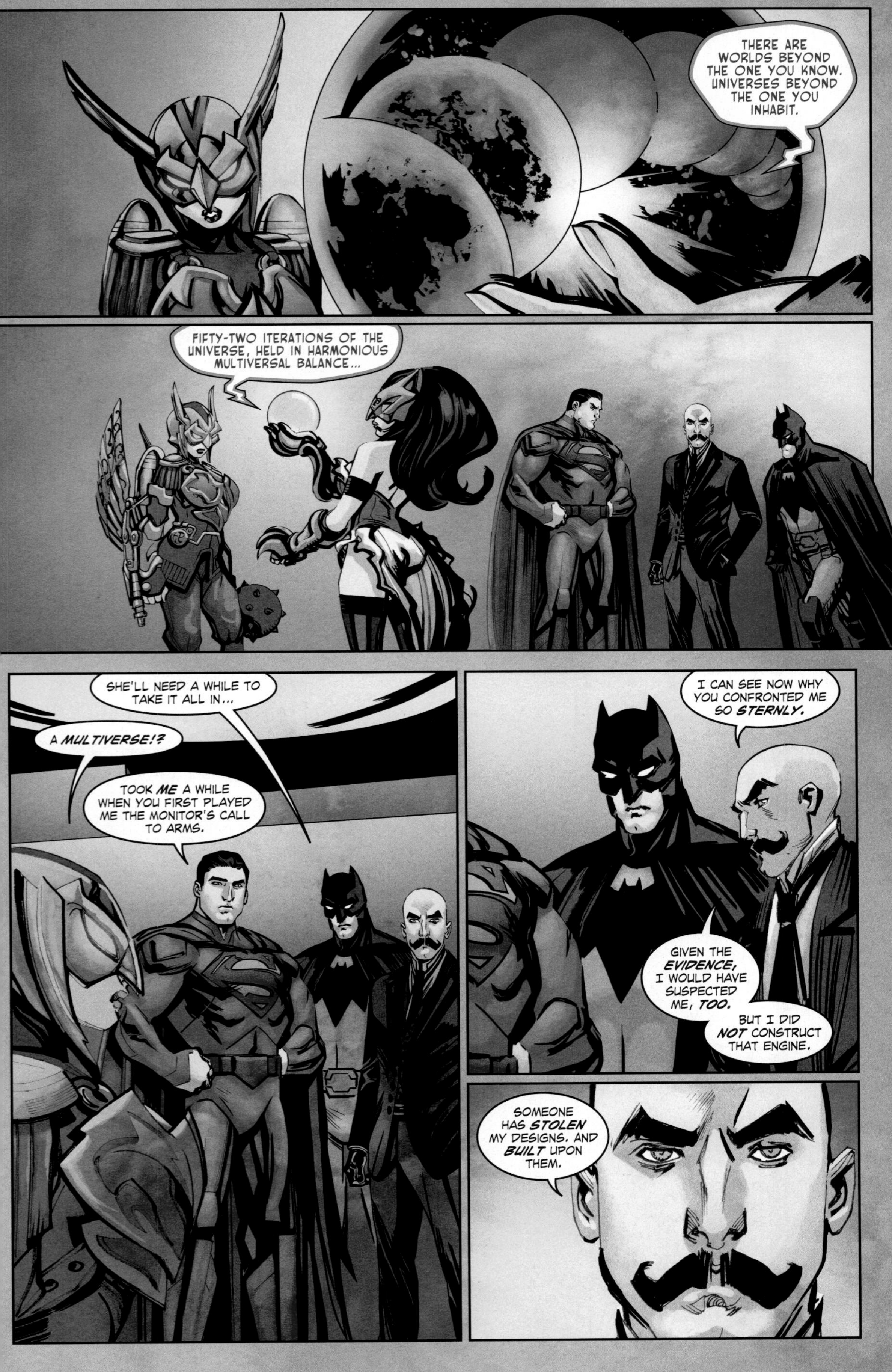
THERE ARE WORLDS BEYOND THE ONE YOU KNOW. UNIVERSES BEYOND THE ONE YOU INHABIT.
FIFTY-TWO ITERATIONS OF THE UNIVERSE, HELD IN HARMONIOUS MULTIVERSAL BALANCE...
SHE'LL NEED A WHILE TO TAKE IT ALL IN...
A MULTIVERSE!?
TOOK ME A WHILE WHEN YOU FIRST PLAYED ME THE MONITOR'S CALL TO ARMS.
I CAN SEE NOW WHY YOU CONFRONTED ME SO STERNLY.
GIVEN THE EVIDENCE, I WOULD HAVE SUSPECTED ME, TOO.
BUT I DID NOT CONSTRUCT THAT ENGINE.
SOMEONE HAS STOLEN MY DESIGNS. AND BUILT UPON THEM.

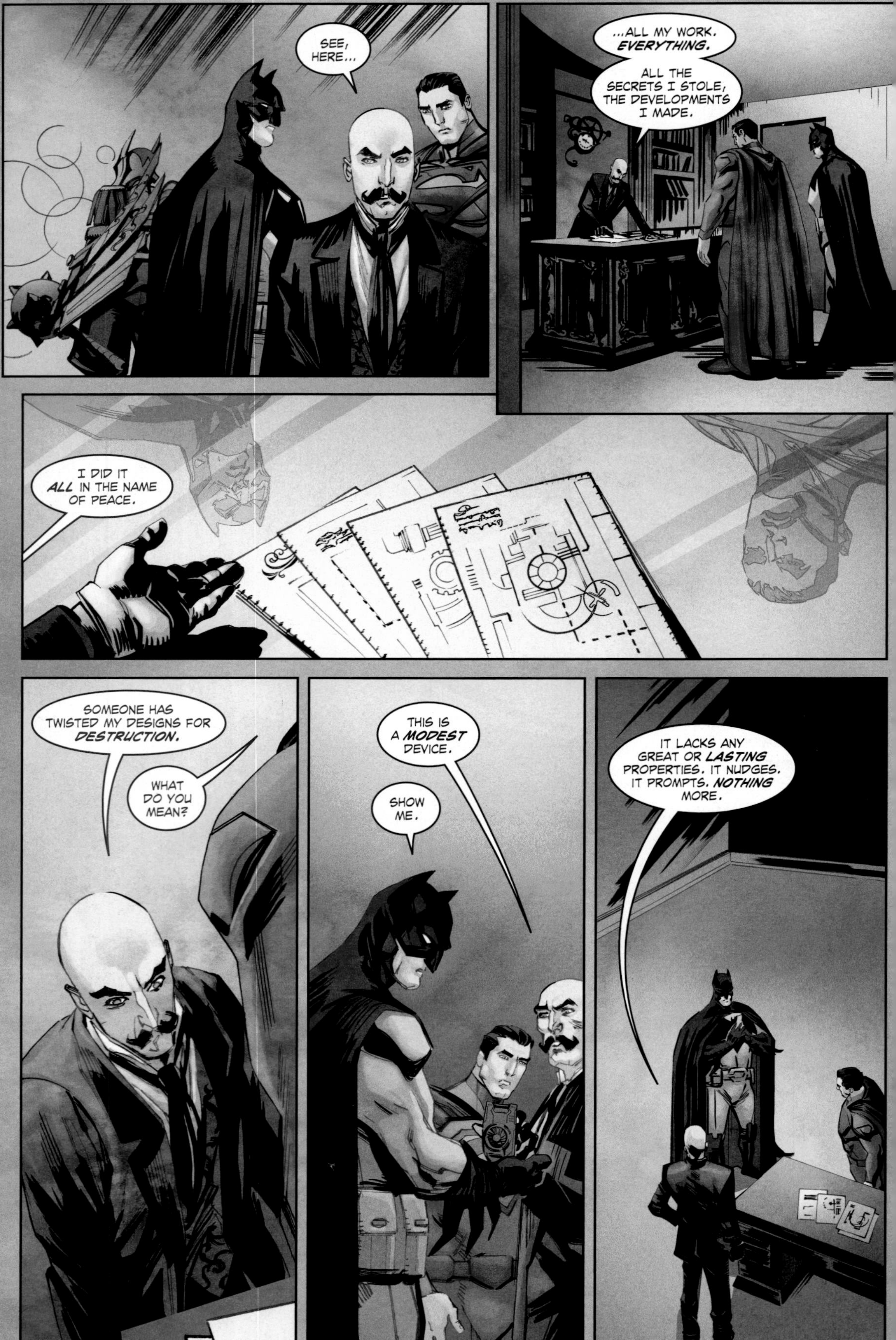
SEE, HERE...
...ALL MY WORK. EVERYTHING.
ALL THE SECRETS I STOLE, THE DEVELOPMENTS I MADE.
I DID IT ALL IN THE NAME OF PEACE.
SOMEONE HAS TWISTED MY DESIGNS FOR DESTRUCTION.
WHAT DO YOU MEAN?
THIS IS A MODEST DEVICE.
SHOW ME.
IT LACKS ANY GREAT OR LASTING PROPERTIES. IT NUDGES. IT PROMPTS. NOTHING MORE.

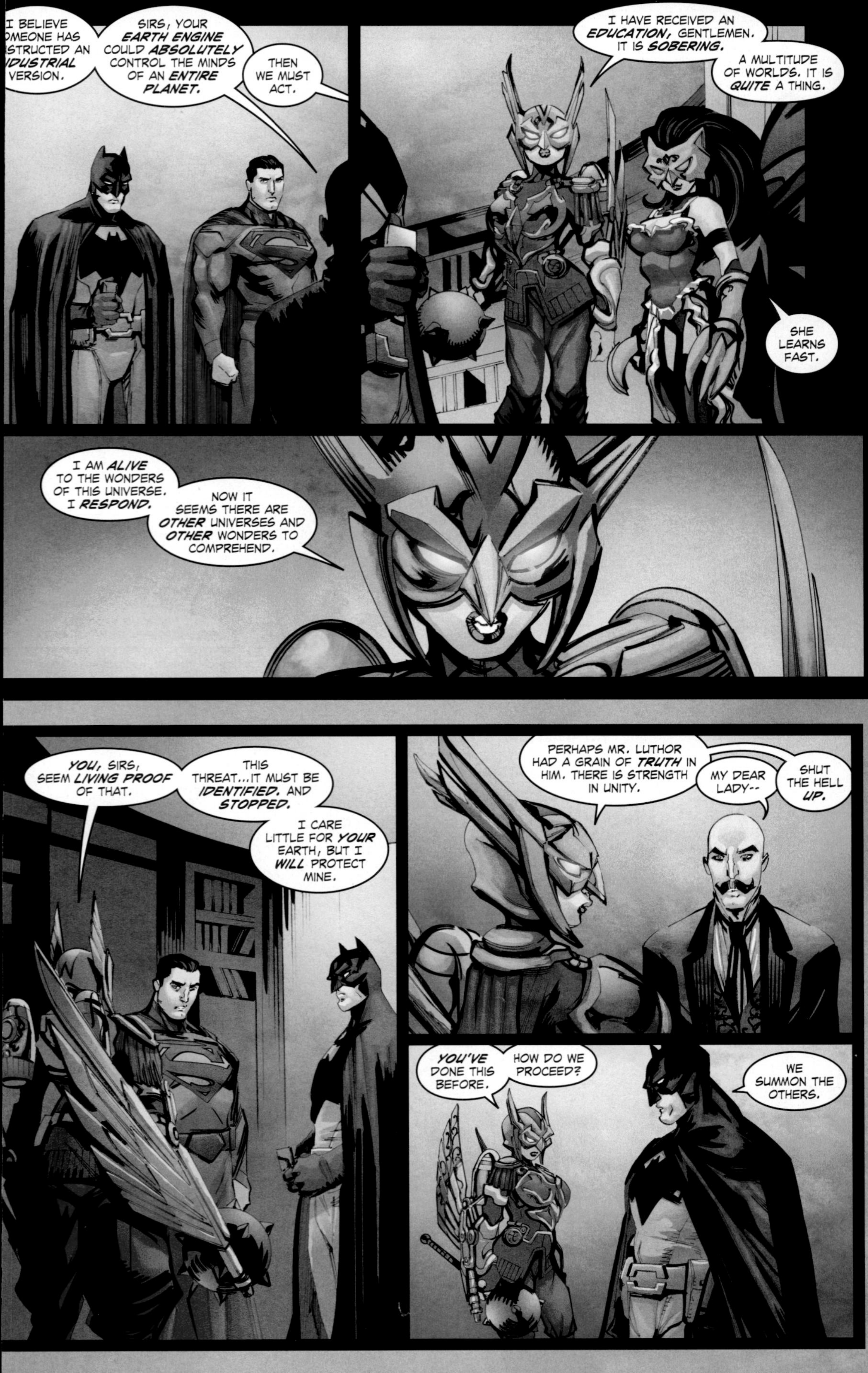
I BELIEVE
OMEONE HAS
STRUCTED AN
IDUSTRIAL
VERSION.
SIRS, YOUR EARTH ENGINE COULD ABSOLUTELY CONTROL THE MINDS OF AN ENTIRE PLANET.
THEN WE MUST ACT.
I HAVE RECEIVED AN EDUCATION, GENTLEMEN. IT IS SOBERING.
A MULTITUDE OF WORLDS. IT IS QUITE A THING.
SHE LEARNS FAST.
I AM ALIVE TO THE WONDERS OF THIS UNIVERSE. I RESPOND.
NOW IT SEEMS THERE ARE OTHER UNIVERSES AND OTHER WONDERS TO COMPREHEND.
YOU, SIRS, SEEM LIVING PROOF OF THAT.
THIS THREAT...IT MUST BE IDENTIFIED. AND STOPPED.
I CARE LITTLE FOR YOUR EARTH, BUT I WILL PROTECT MINE.
PERHAPS MR. LUTHOR HAD A GRAIN OF TRUTH IN HIM. THERE IS STRENGTH IN UNITY.
MY DEAR LADY--
SHUT THE HELL UP.
YOU'VE DONE THIS BEFORE.
HOW DO WE PROCEED?
WE SUMMON THE OTHERS.

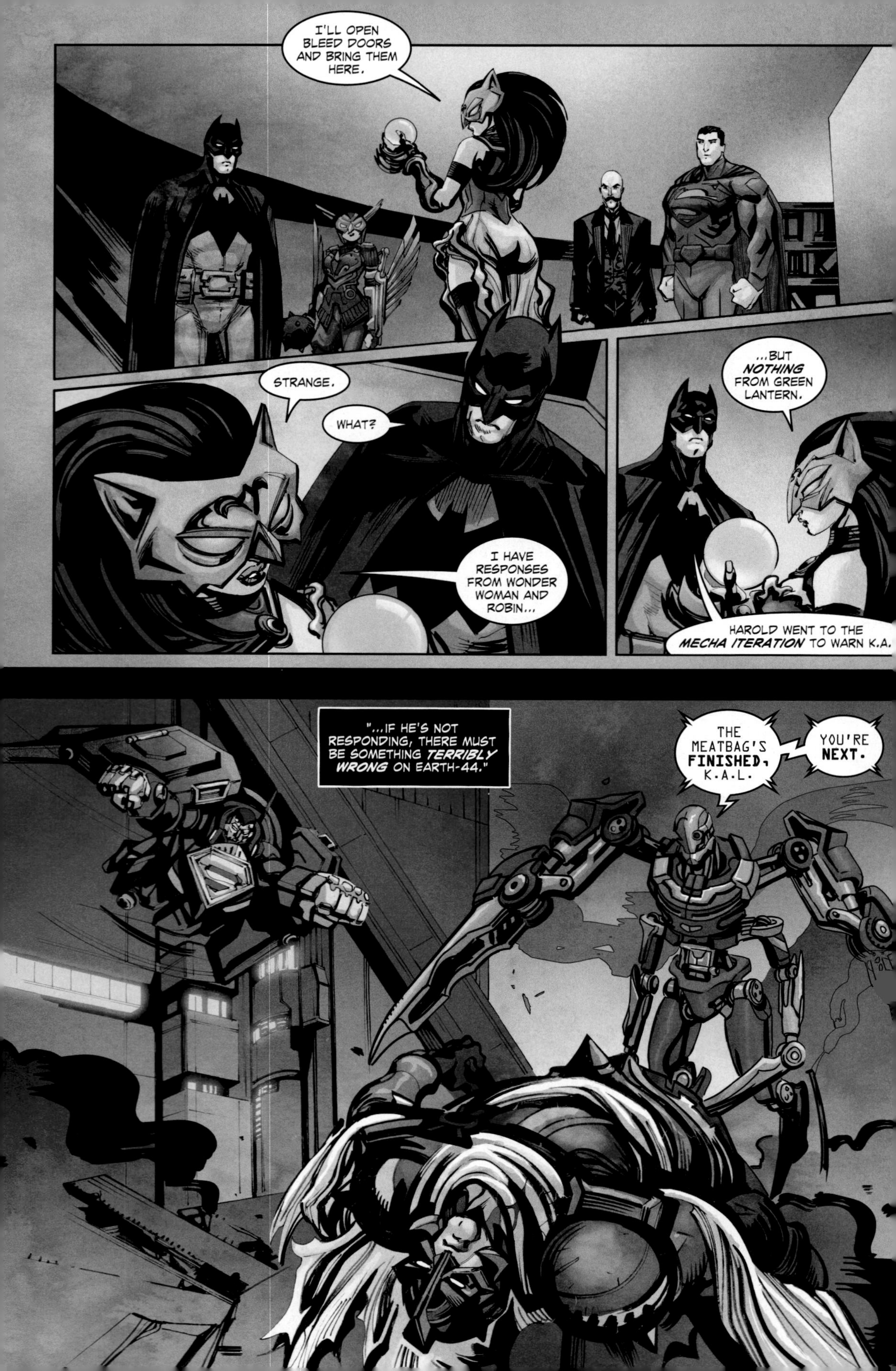
I'LL OPEN BLEED DOORS AND BRING THEM HERE.
STRANGE.
WHAT?
I HAVE RESPONSES FROM WONDER WOMAN AND ROBIN...
...BUT NOTHING FROM GREEN LANTERN.
HAROLD WENT TO THE MECHA ITERATION TO WARN K.A.L.
"...IF HE'S NOT RESPONDING, THERE MUST BE SOMETHING TERRIBLY WRONG ON EARTH-44."
THE MEATBAG'S FINISHED, K.A.L.
YOU'RE NEXT.

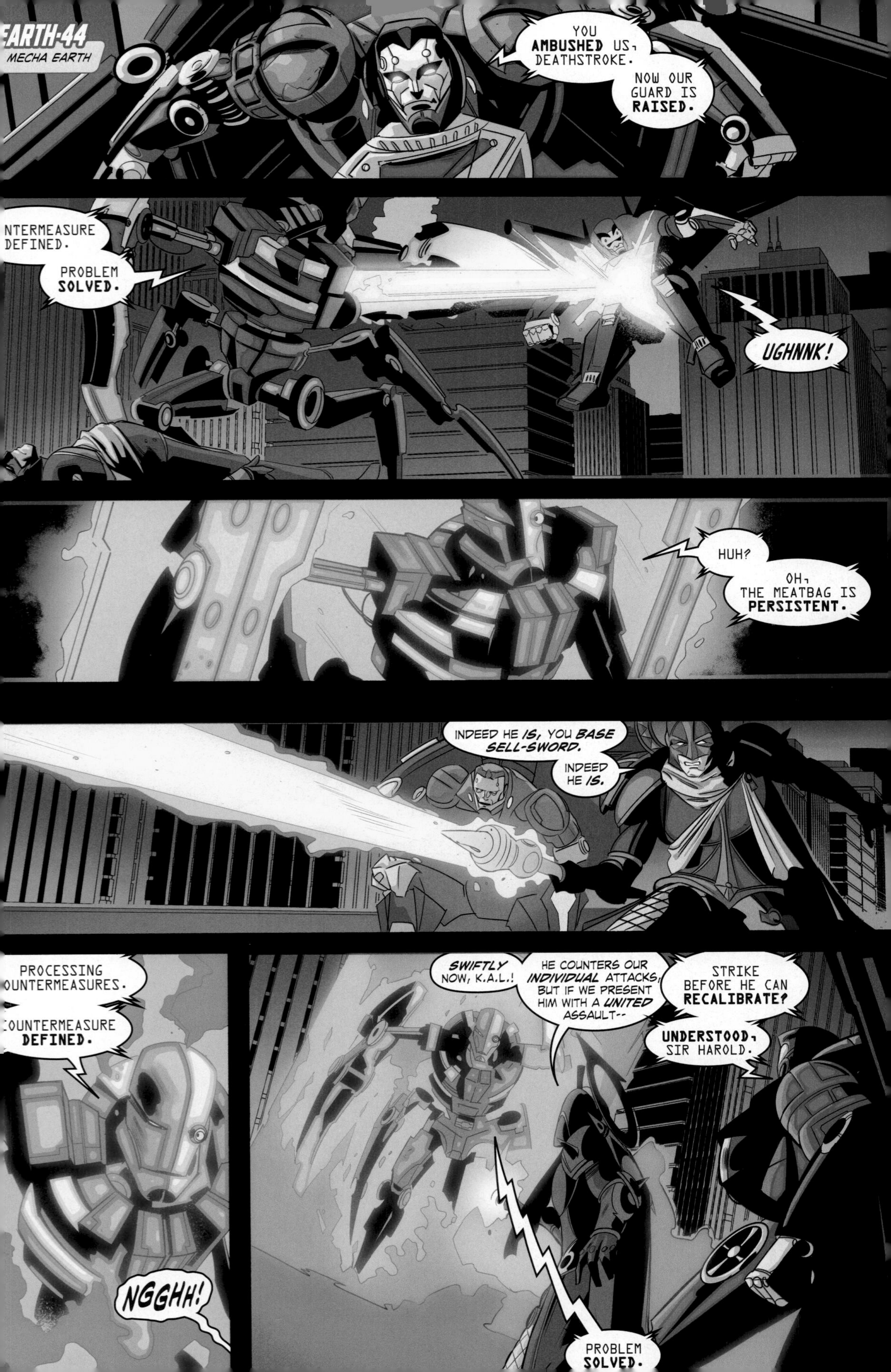
EARTH-44
MECHA EARTH
YOU AMBUSHED US, DEATHSTROKE.
NOW OUR GUARD IS RAISED.
NTERMEASURE DEFINED.
PROBLEM SOLVED.
UGHNNK!
HUH?
OH, THE MEATBAG IS PERSISTENT.
INDEED HE IS, YOU BASE SELL-SWORD.
INDEED HE IS.
PROCESSING OUNTERMEASURES.
COUNTERMEASURE DEFINED.
NGGHH!
SWIFTLY NOW, K.A.L.!
HE COUNTERS OUR INDIVIDUAL ATTACKS, BUT IF WE PRESENT HIM WITH A UNITED ASSAULT--
STRIKE BEFORE HE CAN RECALIBRATE?
UNDERSTOOD, SIR HAROLD.
PROBLEM SOLVED.

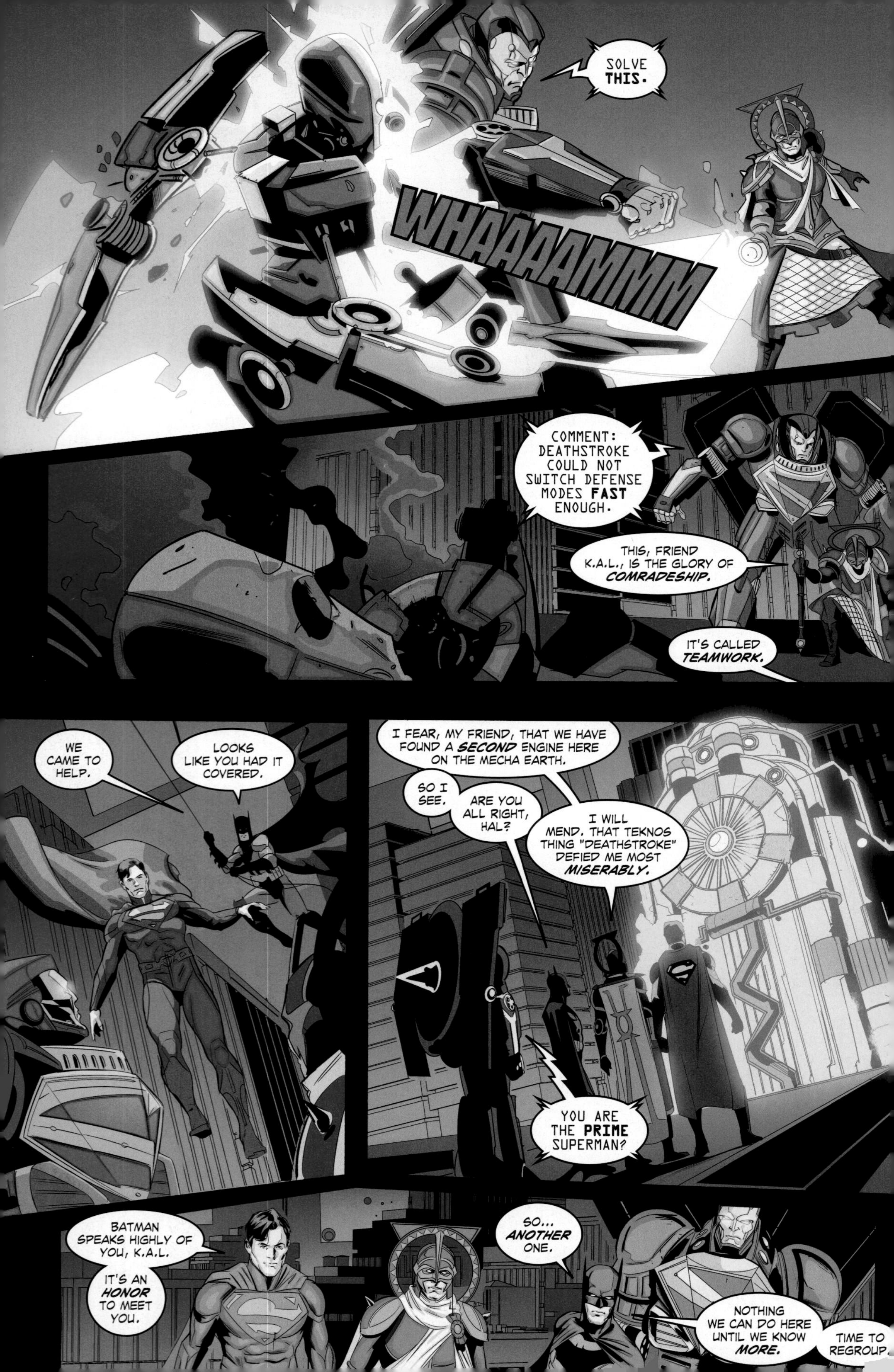

SOLVE THIS.
WHAAAAMMMM
COMMENT: DEATHSTROKE COULD NOT SWITCH DEFENSE MODES FAST ENOUGH.
THIS, FRIEND K.A.L., IS THE GLORY OF COMRADESHIP.
IT'S CALLED TEAMWORK.
WE CAME TO HELP.
LOOKS LIKE YOU HAD IT COVERED.
I FEAR, MY FRIEND, THAT WE HAVE FOUND A SECOND ENGINE HERE ON THE MECHA EARTH.
SO I SEE.
ARE YOU ALL RIGHT, HAL?
I WILL MEND. THAT TEKNOS THING "DEATHSTROKE" DEFIED ME MOST MISERABLY.
YOU ARE THE PRIME SUPERMAN?
BATMAN SPEAKS HIGHLY OF YOU, K.A.L.
IT'S AN HONOR TO MEET YOU.
SO... ANOTHER ONE.
NOTHING WE CAN DO HERE UNTIL WE KNOW MORE.
TIME TO REGROUP.

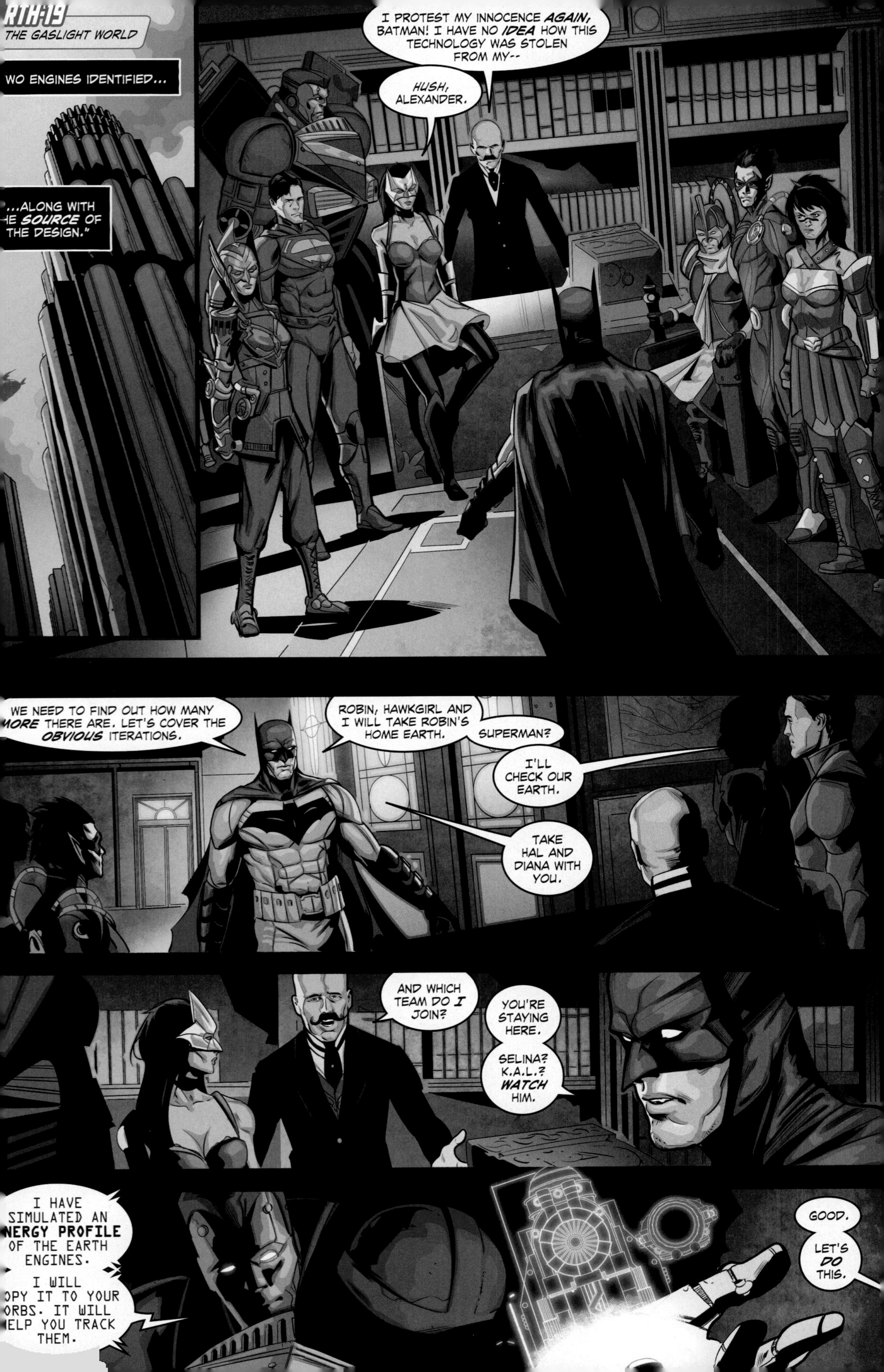

RTH:19
THE GASLIGHT WORLD
WO ENGINES IDENTIFIED...
...ALONG WITH
HE SOURCE OF
THE DESIGN."
I PROTEST MY INNOCENCE AGAIN, BATMAN! I HAVE NO IDEA HOW THIS TECHNOLOGY WAS STOLEN FROM MY--
HUSH, ALEXANDER.
WE NEED TO FIND OUT HOW MANY MORE THERE ARE. LET'S COVER THE OBVIOUS ITERATIONS.
ROBIN, HAWKGIRL AND I WILL TAKE ROBIN'S HOME EARTH.
SUPERMAN?
I'LL CHECK OUR EARTH.
TAKE HAL AND DIANA WITH YOU.
AND WHICH TEAM DO I JOIN?
YOU'RE STAYING HERE.
SELINA? K.A.L.? WATCH HIM.
I HAVE SIMULATED AN NERGY PROFILE OF THE EARTH ENGINES.
I WILL OPY IT TO YOUR ORBS. IT WILL ELP YOU TRACK THEM.
GOOD.
LET'S DO THIS.

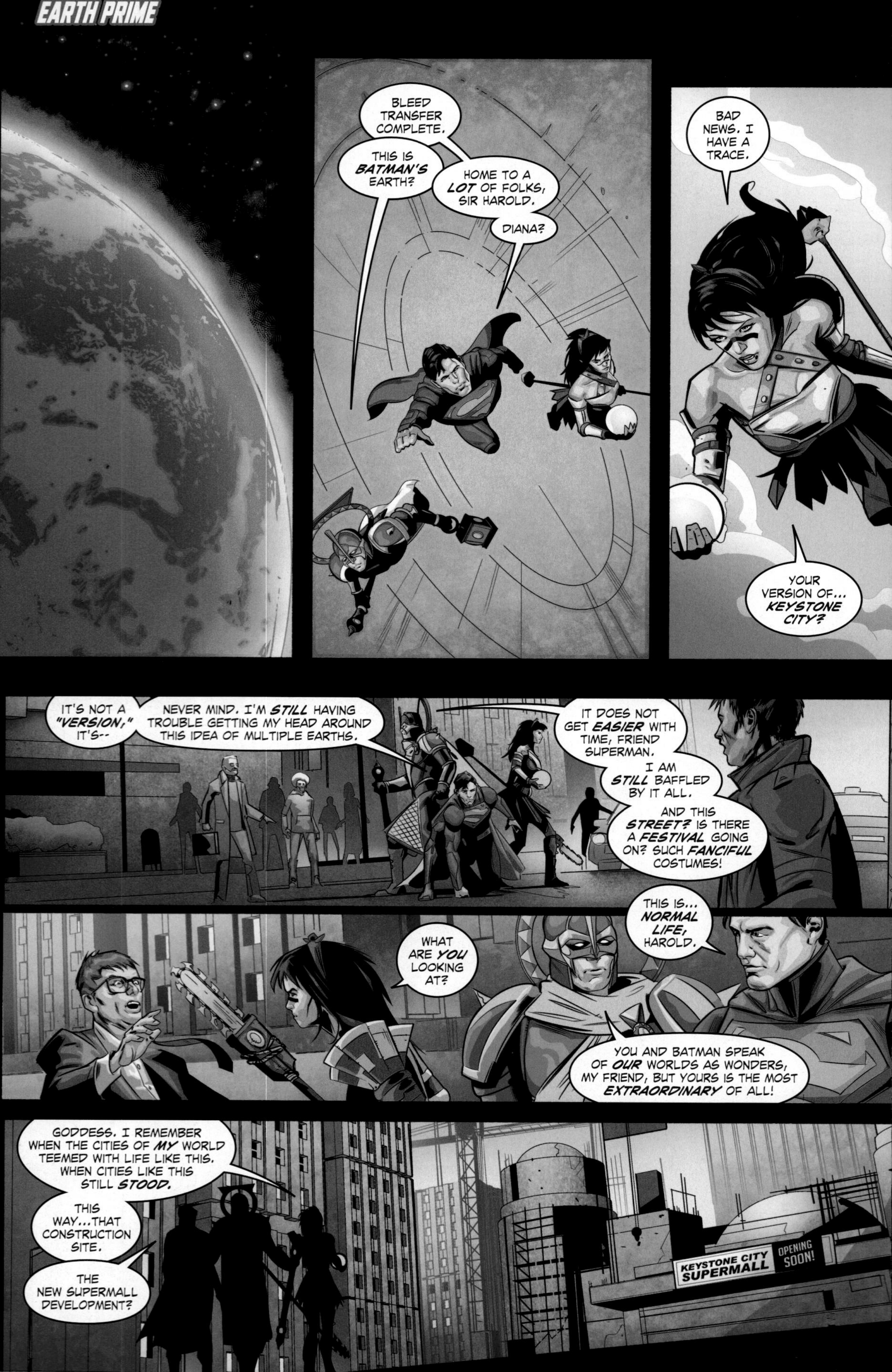
EARTH PRIME
BLEED TRANSFER COMPLETE.
THIS IS BATMAN'S EARTH?
HOME TO A LOT OF FOLKS, SIR HAROLD.
DIANA?
BAD NEWS. I HAVE A TRACE.
YOUR VERSION OF... KEYSTONE CITY?
IT'S NOT A "VERSION," IT'S--
NEVER MIND. I'M STILL HAVING TROUBLE GETTING MY HEAD AROUND THIS IDEA OF MULTIPLE EARTHS.
IT DOES NOT GET EASIER WITH TIME, FRIEND SUPERMAN.
I AM STILL BAFFLED BY IT ALL.
AND THIS STREET? IS THERE A FESTIVAL GOING ON? SUCH FANCIFUL COSTUMES!
WHAT ARE YOU LOOKING AT?
THIS IS... NORMAL LIFE, HAROLD.
YOU AND BATMAN SPEAK OF OUR WORLDS AS WONDERS, MY FRIEND, BUT YOURS IS THE MOST EXTRAORDINARY OF ALL!
GODDESS. I REMEMBER WHEN THE CITIES OF MY WORLD TEEMED WITH LIFE LIKE THIS. WHEN CITIES LIKE THIS STILL STOOD.
THIS WAY...THAT CONSTRUCTION SITE.
THE NEW SUPERMALL DEVELOPMENT?
KEYSTONE CITY SUPERMALL
OPENING SOON!

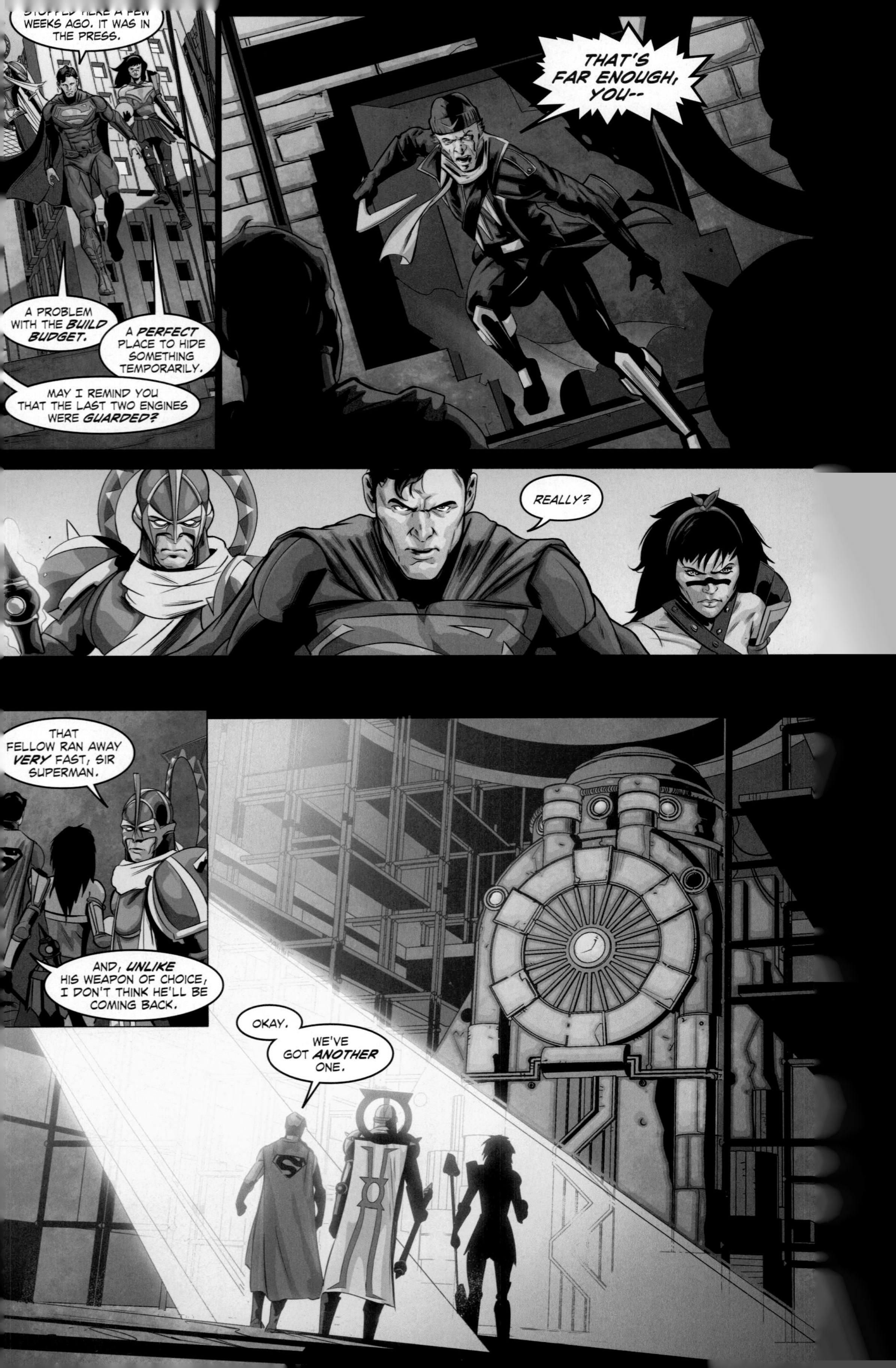
WEEKS AGO. IT WAS IN THE PRESS.
A PROBLEM WITH THE BUILD BUDGET.
A PERFECT PLACE TO HIDE SOMETHING TEMPORARILY.
MAY I REMIND YOU THAT THE LAST TWO ENGINES WERE GUARDED?
THAT'S FAR ENOUGH, YOU--
REALLY?
THAT FELLOW RAN AWAY VERY FAST, SIR SUPERMAN.
AND, UNLIKE HIS WEAPON OF CHOICE, I DON'T THINK HE'LL BE COMING BACK.
OKAY.
WE'VE GOT ANOTHER ONE.

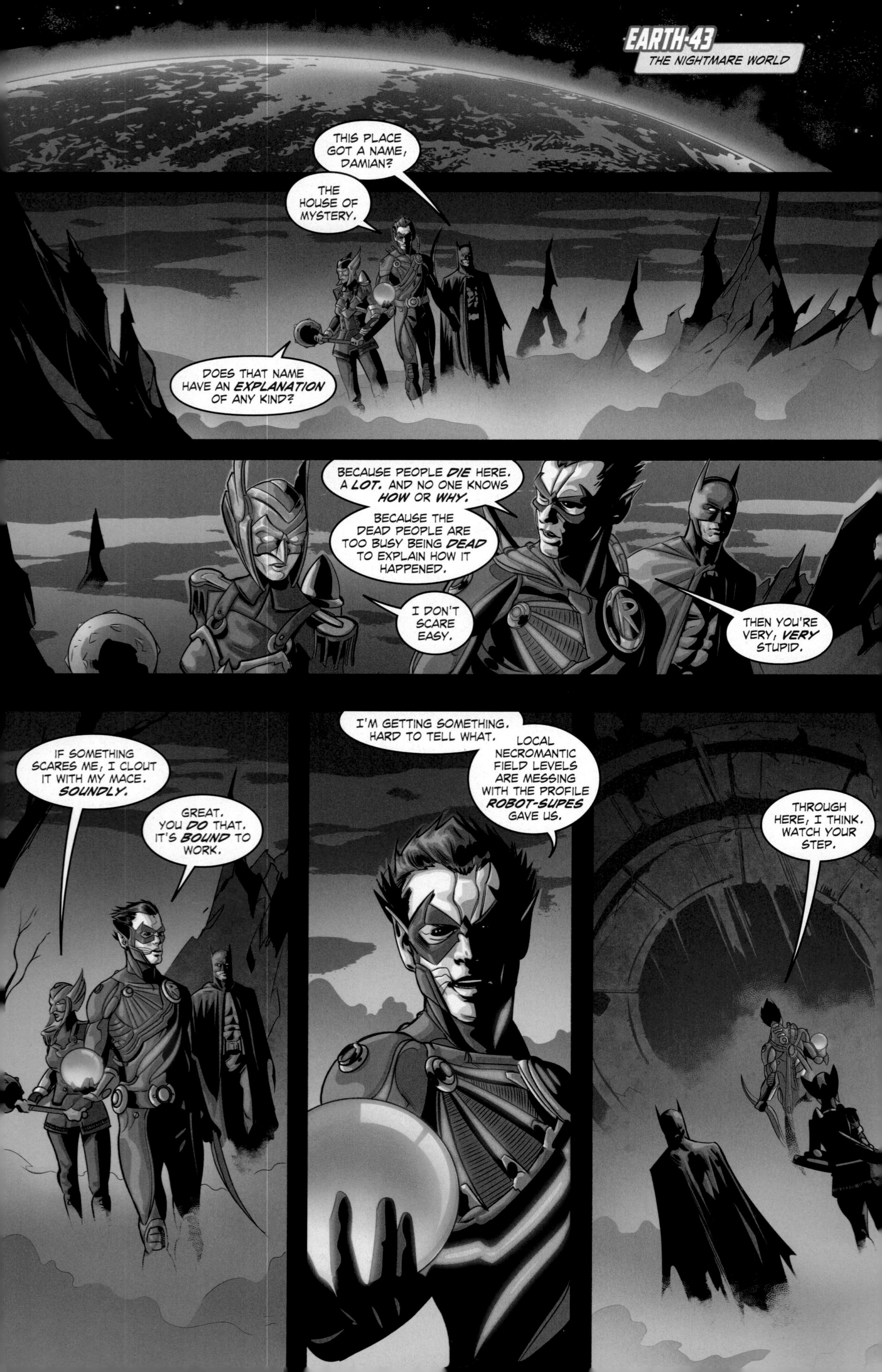
EARTH-43
THE NIGHTMARE WORLD
THIS PLACE GOT A NAME, DAMIAN?
THE HOUSE OF MYSTERY.
DOES THAT NAME HAVE AN EXPLANATION OF ANY KIND?
BECAUSE PEOPLE DIE HERE. A LOT. AND NO ONE KNOWS HOW OR WHY.
BECAUSE THE DEAD PEOPLE ARE TOO BUSY BEING DEAD TO EXPLAIN HOW IT HAPPENED.
I DON'T SCARE EASY.
THEN YOU'RE VERY, VERY STUPID.
IF SOMETHING SCARES ME, I CLOUT IT WITH MY MACE. SOUNDLY.
GREAT. YOU DO THAT. IT'S BOUND TO WORK.
I'M GETTING SOMETHING. HARD TO TELL WHAT.
LOCAL NECROMANTIC FIELD LEVELS ARE MESSING WITH THE PROFILE ROBOT-SUPES GAVE US.
THROUGH HERE, I THINK. WATCH YOUR STEP.

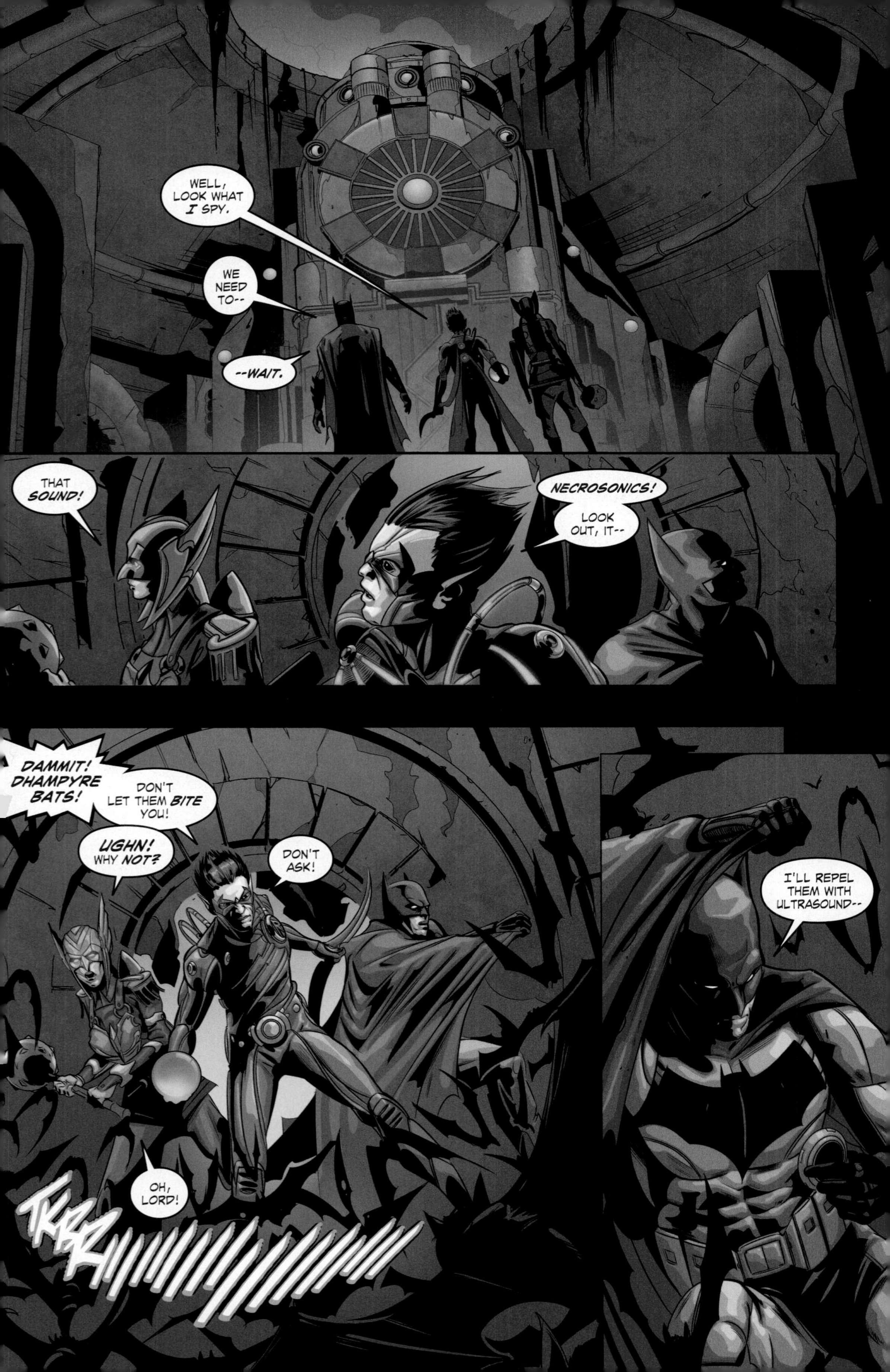
WELL, LOOK WHAT I SPY.
WE NEED TO--
--WAIT.
THAT SOUND!
NECROSONICS!
LOOK OUT, IT--
DAMMIT! DHAMPYRE BATS!
DON'T LET THEM BITE YOU!
UGHN! WHY NOT?
DON'T ASK!
OH, LORD!
TKRRIIIIIIIIIIIIIIIII
I'LL REPEL THEM WITH ULTRASOUND--

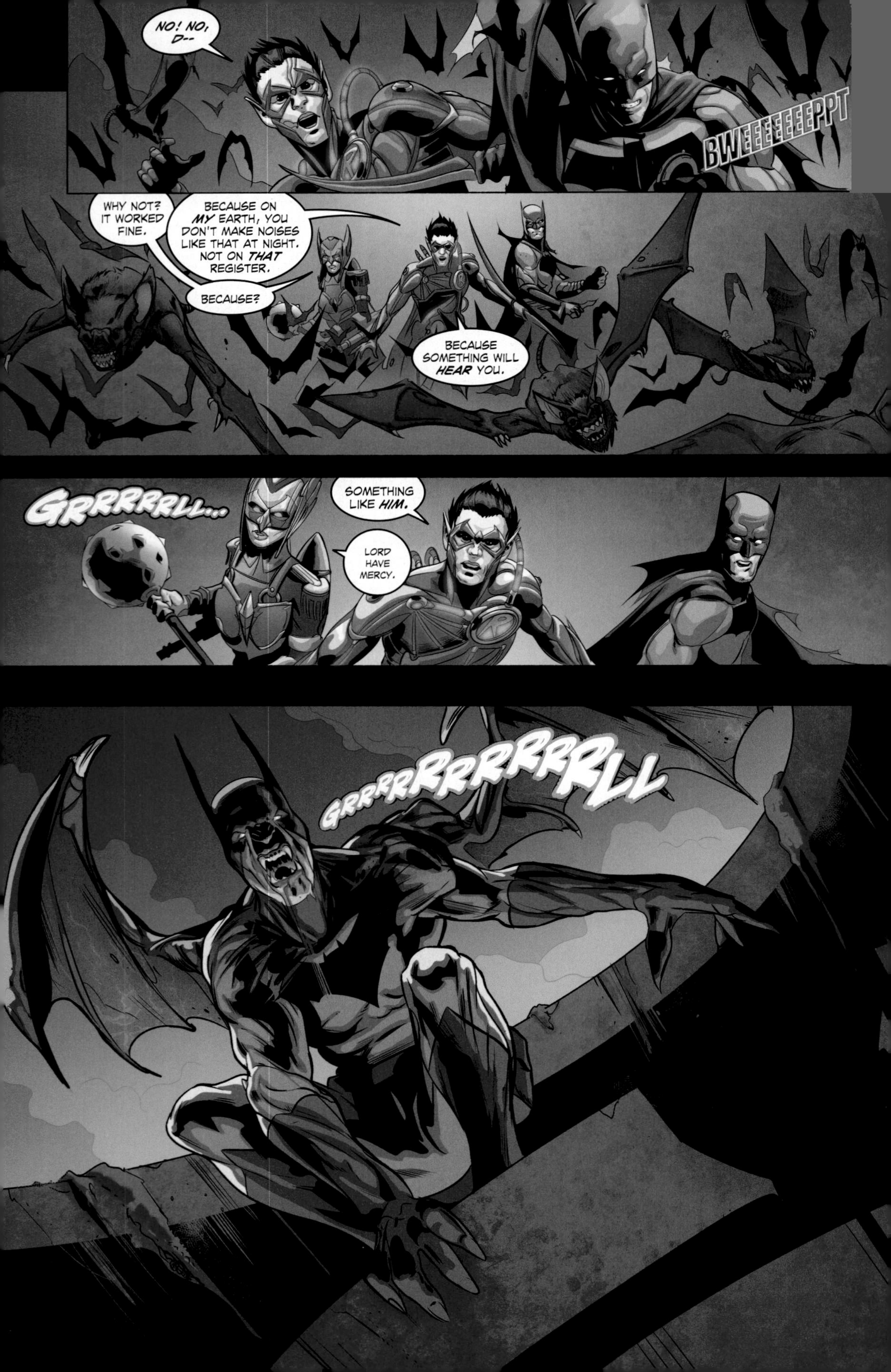
NO! NO; D--
BWEEEEEEEPPT
WHY NOT? IT WORKED FINE.
BECAUSE ON MY EARTH, YOU DON'T MAKE NOISES LIKE THAT AT NIGHT. NOT ON THAT REGISTER.
BECAUSE?
BECAUSE SOMETHING WILL HEAR YOU.
GRRRRRLL...
SOMETHING LIKE HIM.
LORD HAVE MERCY.
GRRRRRRRRRRLL

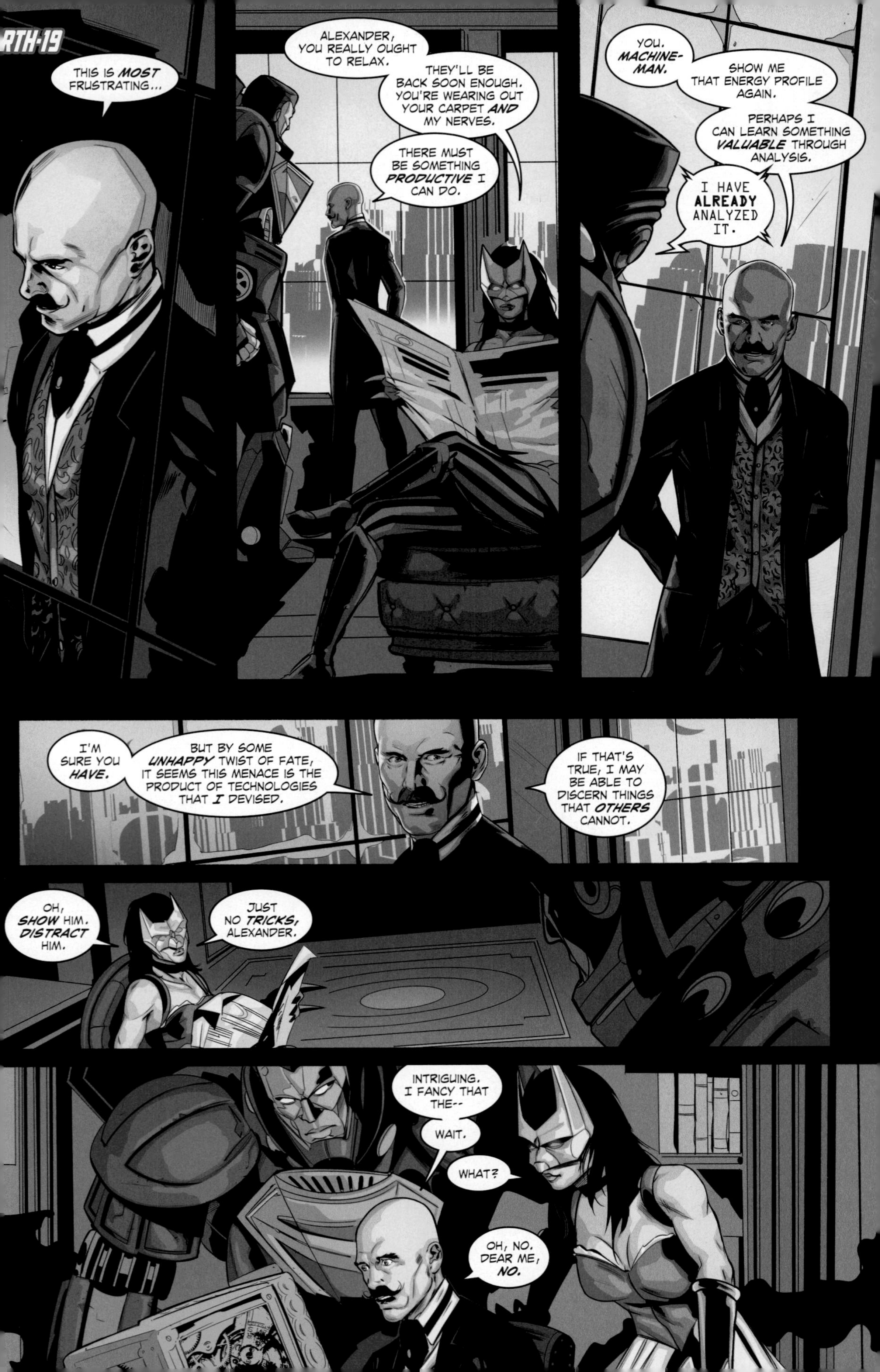
RTH-19
THIS IS MOST FRUSTRATING...
ALEXANDER, YOU REALLY OUGHT TO RELAX.
THEY'LL BE BACK SOON ENOUGH. YOU'RE WEARING OUT YOUR CARPET AND MY NERVES.
THERE MUST BE SOMETHING PRODUCTIVE I CAN DO.
YOU. MACHINE-MAN.
SHOW ME THAT ENERGY PROFILE AGAIN.
PERHAPS I CAN LEARN SOMETHING VALUABLE THROUGH ANALYSIS.
I HAVE ALREADY ANALYZED IT.
I'M SURE YOU HAVE.
BUT BY SOME UNHAPPY TWIST OF FATE, IT SEEMS THIS MENACE IS THE PRODUCT OF TECHNOLOGIES THAT I DEVISED.
IF THAT'S TRUE, I MAY BE ABLE TO DISCERN THINGS THAT OTHERS CANNOT.
OH, SHOW HIM. DISTRACT HIM.
JUST NO TRICKS, ALEXANDER.
INTRIGUING. I FANCY THAT THE--
WAIT.
WHAT?
OH, NO. DEAR ME, NO.

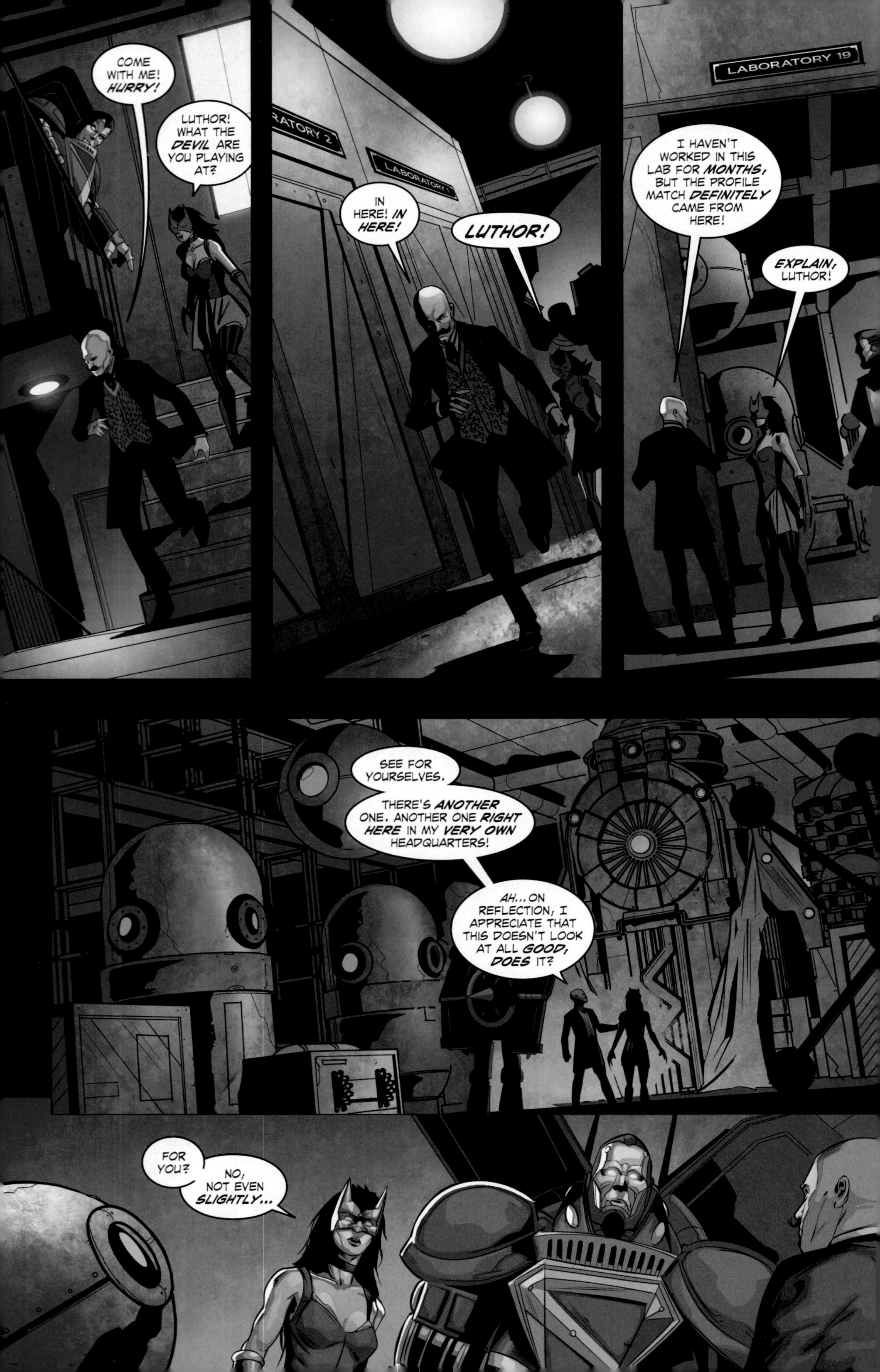
COME WITH ME! HURRY!
LUTHOR! WHAT THE DEVIL ARE YOU PLAYING AT?
RATORY 2
LABORATORY 1
IN HERE! IN HERE!
LUTHOR!
LABORATORY 19
I HAVEN'T WORKED IN THIS LAB FOR MONTHS, BUT THE PROFILE MATCH DEFINITELY CAME FROM HERE!
EXPLAIN, LUTHOR!
SEE FOR YOURSELVES.
THERE'S ANOTHER ONE. ANOTHER ONE RIGHT HERE IN MY VERY OWN HEADQUARTERS!
AH... ON REFLECTION, I APPRECIATE THAT THIS DOESN'T LOOK AT ALL GOOD, DOES IT?
FOR YOU?
NO, NOT EVEN SLIGHTLY...

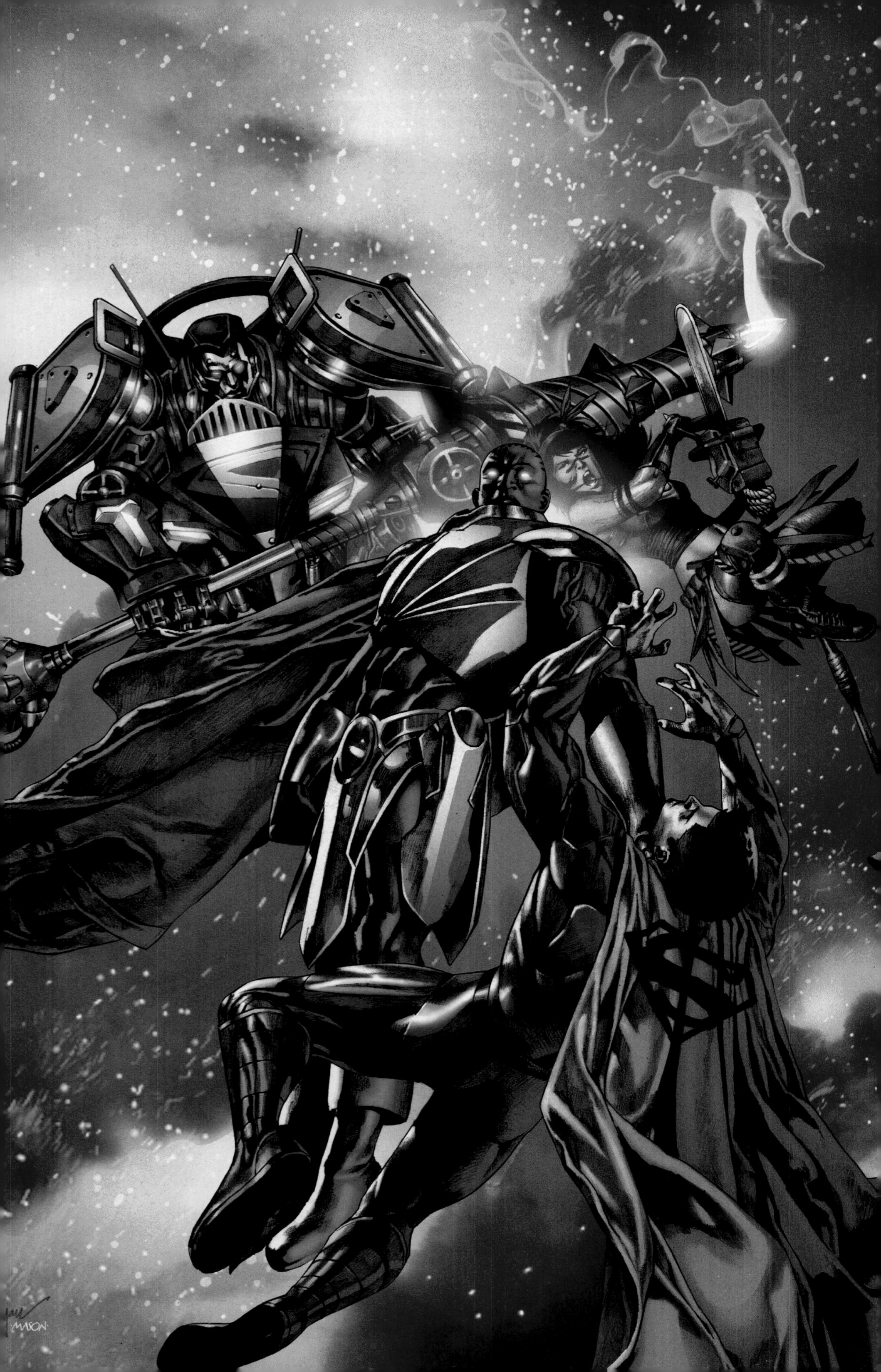
MASON

THE BRINK OF MADNESS

Angel Hernandez Eduardo Francisco Artists **Alejandro Sanchez** Colorist
Cover Art by **Mico Suayan and Thomas Mason**

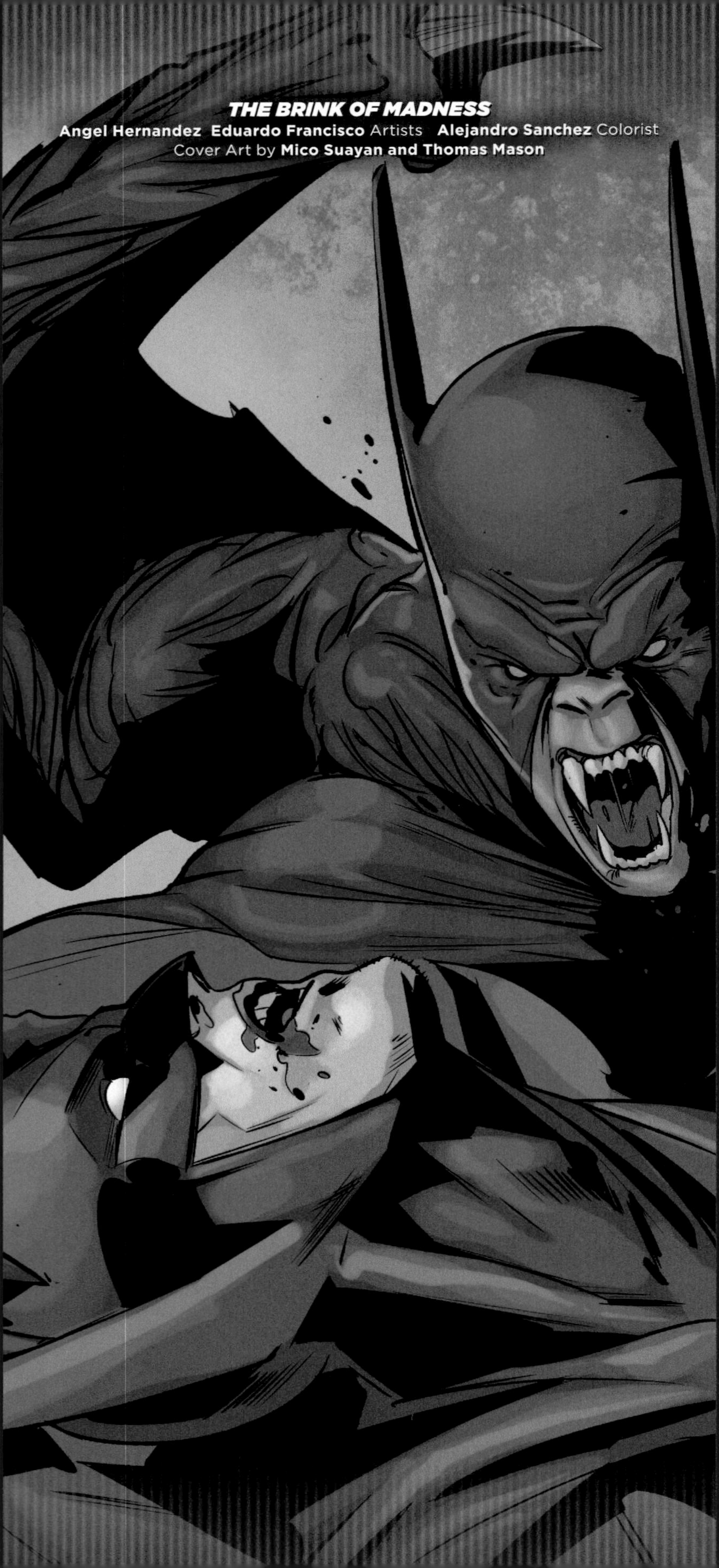

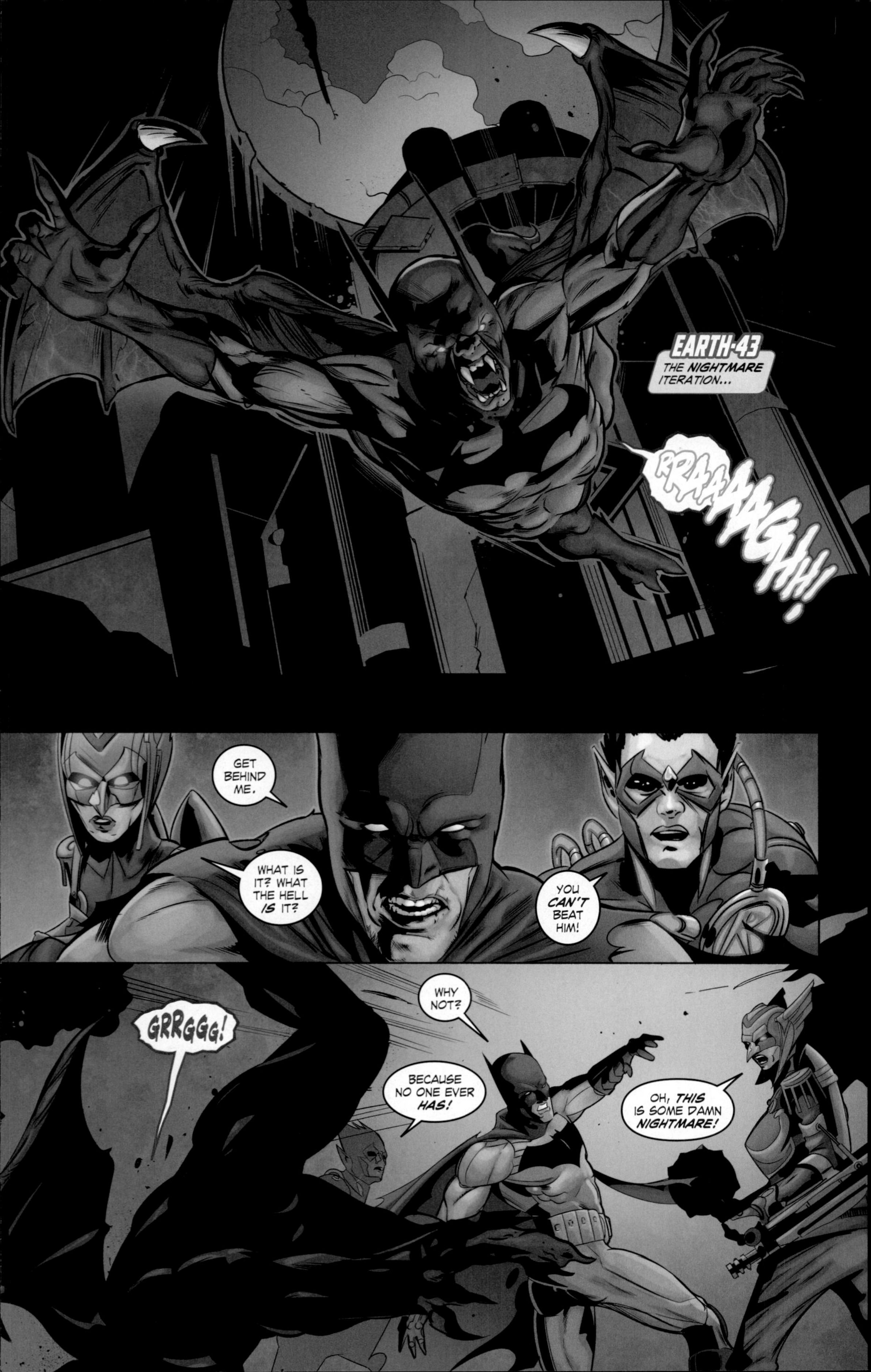
EARTH-43
THE NIGHTMARE ITERATION...
RRAAAAAGHH!
GET BEHIND ME.
WHAT IS IT? WHAT THE HELL IS IT?
YOU CAN'T BEAT HIM!
GRRGGG!
WHY NOT?
BECAUSE NO ONE EVER HAS!
OH, THIS IS SOME DAMN NIGHTMARE!

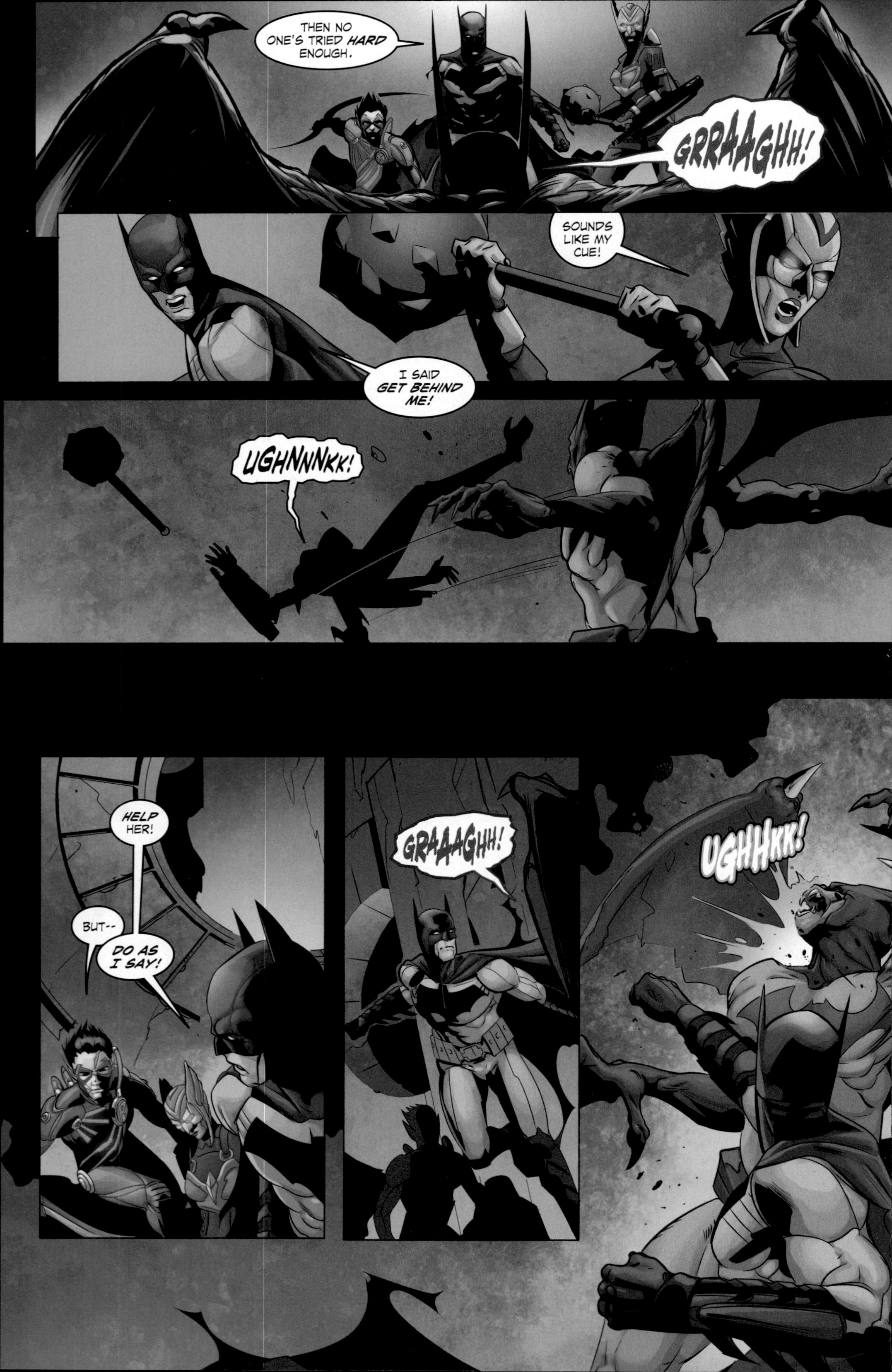
THEN NO ONE'S TRIED HARD ENOUGH.
GRRAAGHH!
SOUNDS LIKE MY CUE!
I SAID GET BEHIND ME!
UGHNNNKK!
HELP HER!
BUT--
DO AS I SAY!
GRAAAGHH!
UGHHKK!

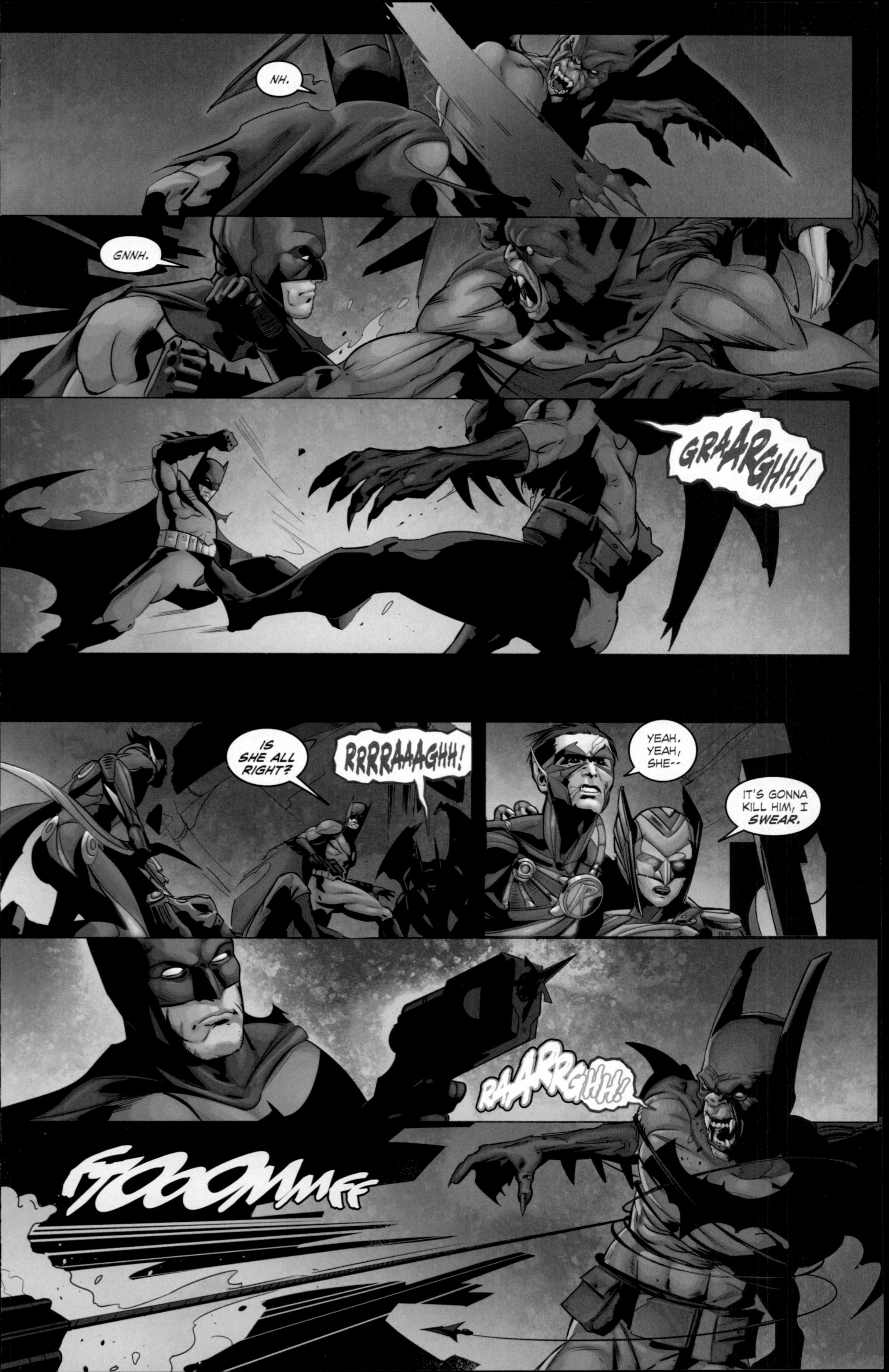
NH.
GNNH.
GRAARGHH!
IS SHE ALL RIGHT?
RRRRAAAGHH!
YEAH. YEAH, SHE--
IT'S GONNA KILL HIM, I SWEAR.
RAARRGHH!
FTOOOMMFF

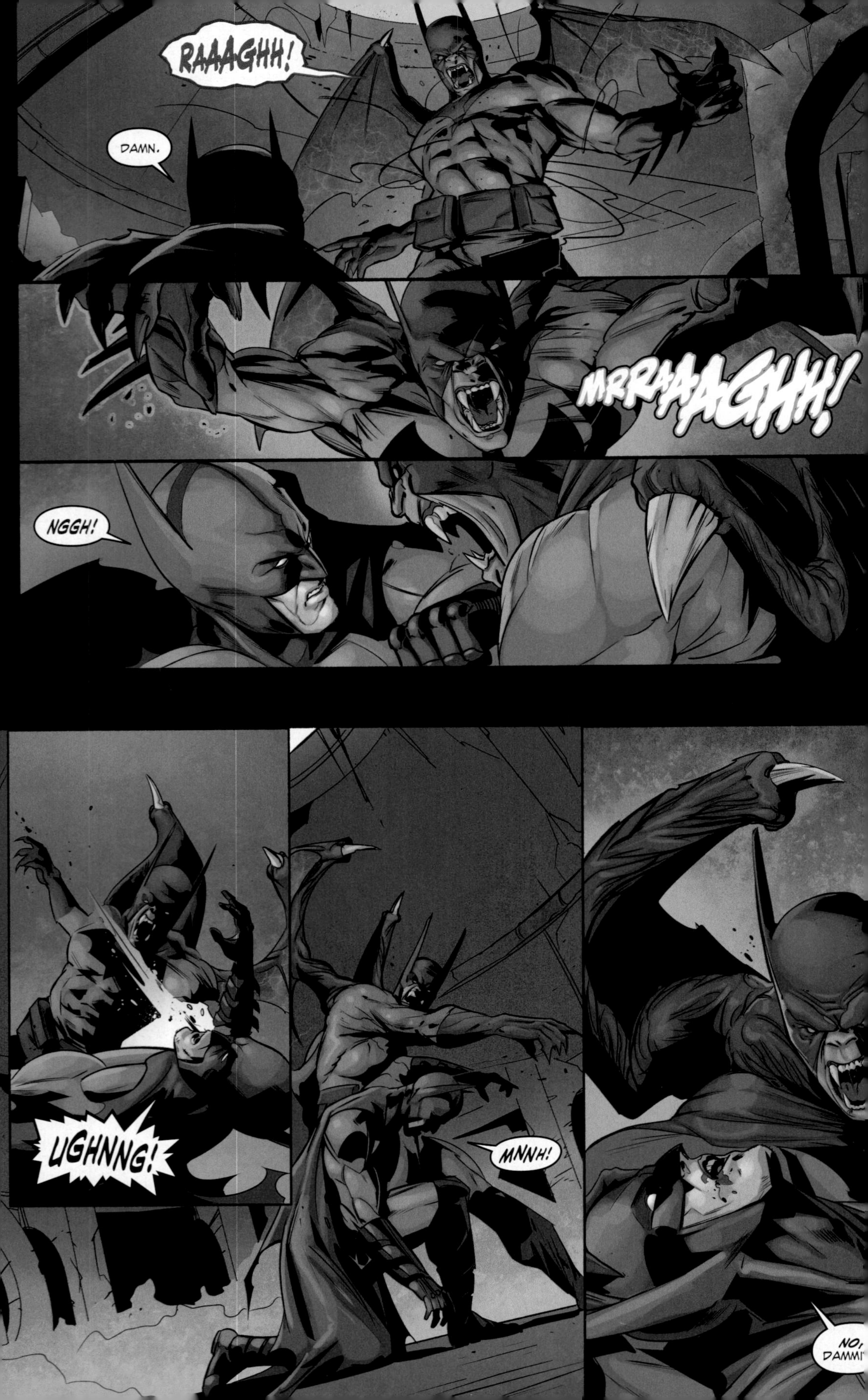
RAAAGHH!
DAMN.
MRRAAAGHH!
NGGH!
UGHNNG!
MNNH!
NO, DAMM

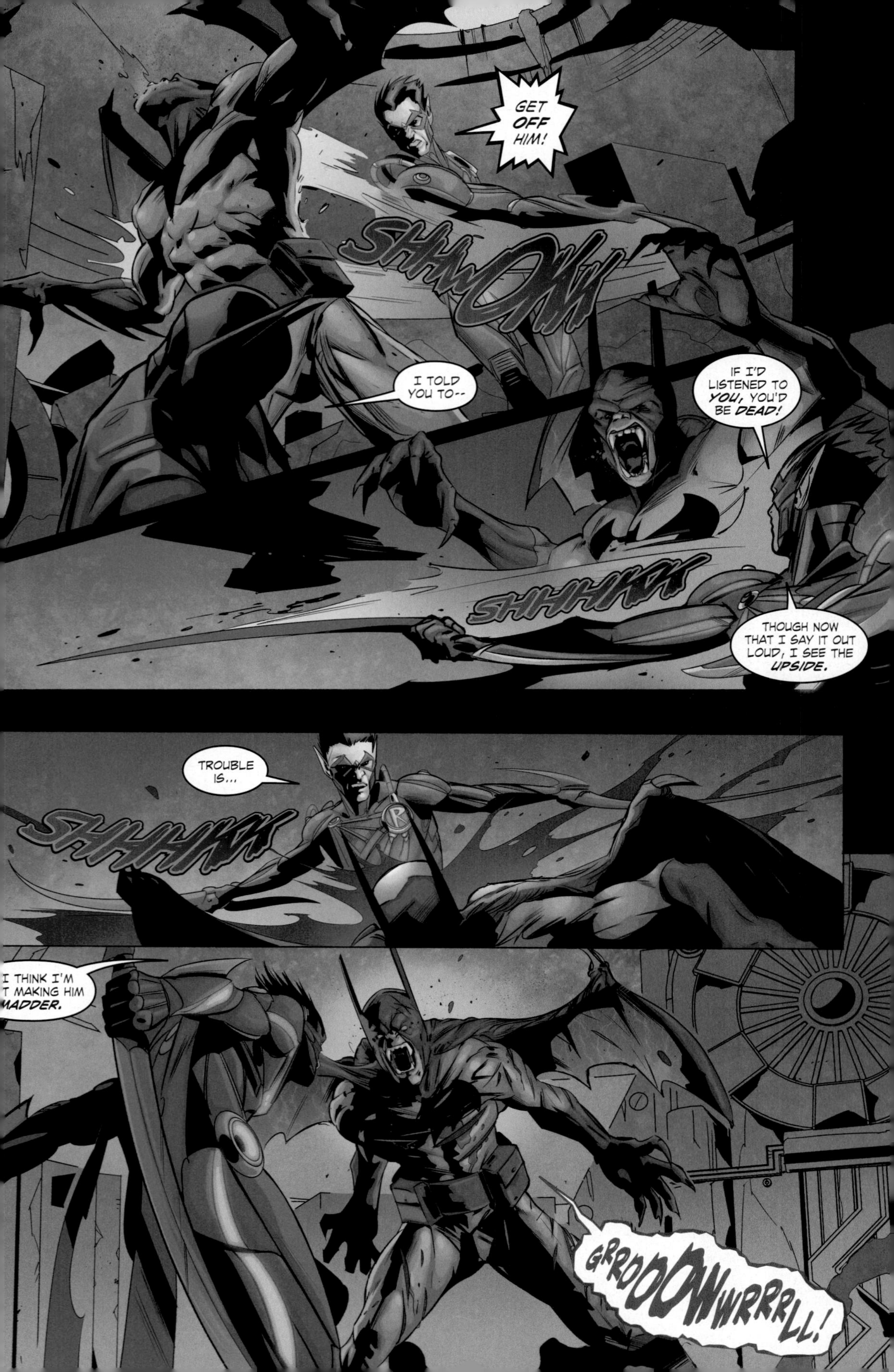
GET OFF HIM!
SHHWOMM
I TOLD YOU TO--
IF I'D LISTENED TO YOU, YOU'D BE DEAD!
SHHHKKK
THOUGH NOW THAT I SAY IT OUT LOUD, I SEE THE UPSIDE.
TROUBLE IS...
SHHHKKK
I THINK I'M MAKING HIM MADDER.
GRROOOWWRRRLL!

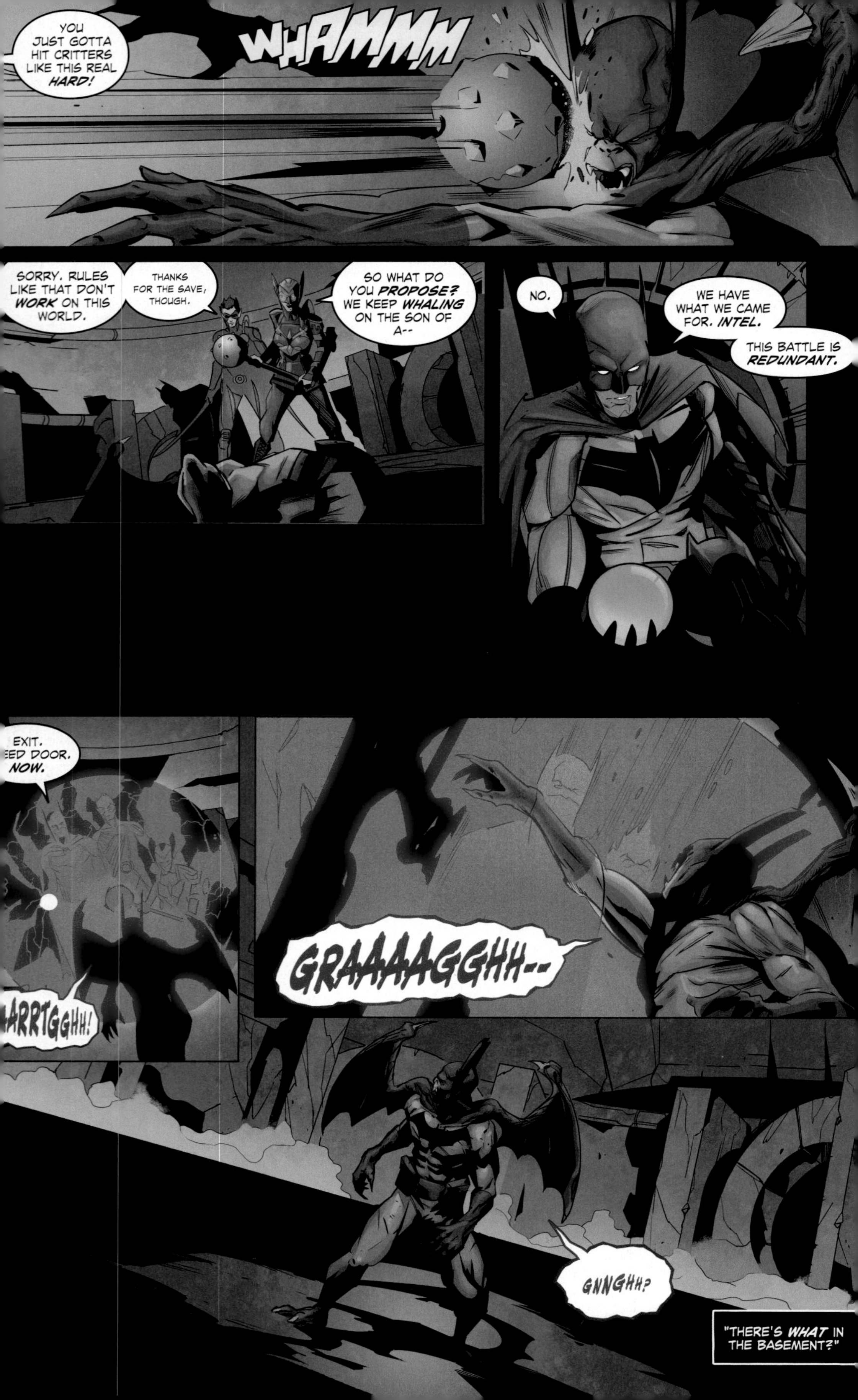
YOU JUST GOTTA HIT CRITTERS LIKE THIS REAL HARD!
WHAMMM
SORRY. RULES LIKE THAT DON'T WORK ON THIS WORLD.
THANKS FOR THE SAVE, THOUGH.
SO WHAT DO YOU PROPOSE? WE KEEP WHALING ON THE SON OF A--
NO.
WE HAVE WHAT WE CAME FOR. INTEL.
THIS BATTLE IS REDUNDANT.
EXIT.
EED DOOR.
NOW.
ARRTGGHH!
GRAAAAGGHH--
GNNGHH?
"THERE'S WHAT IN THE BASEMENT?"

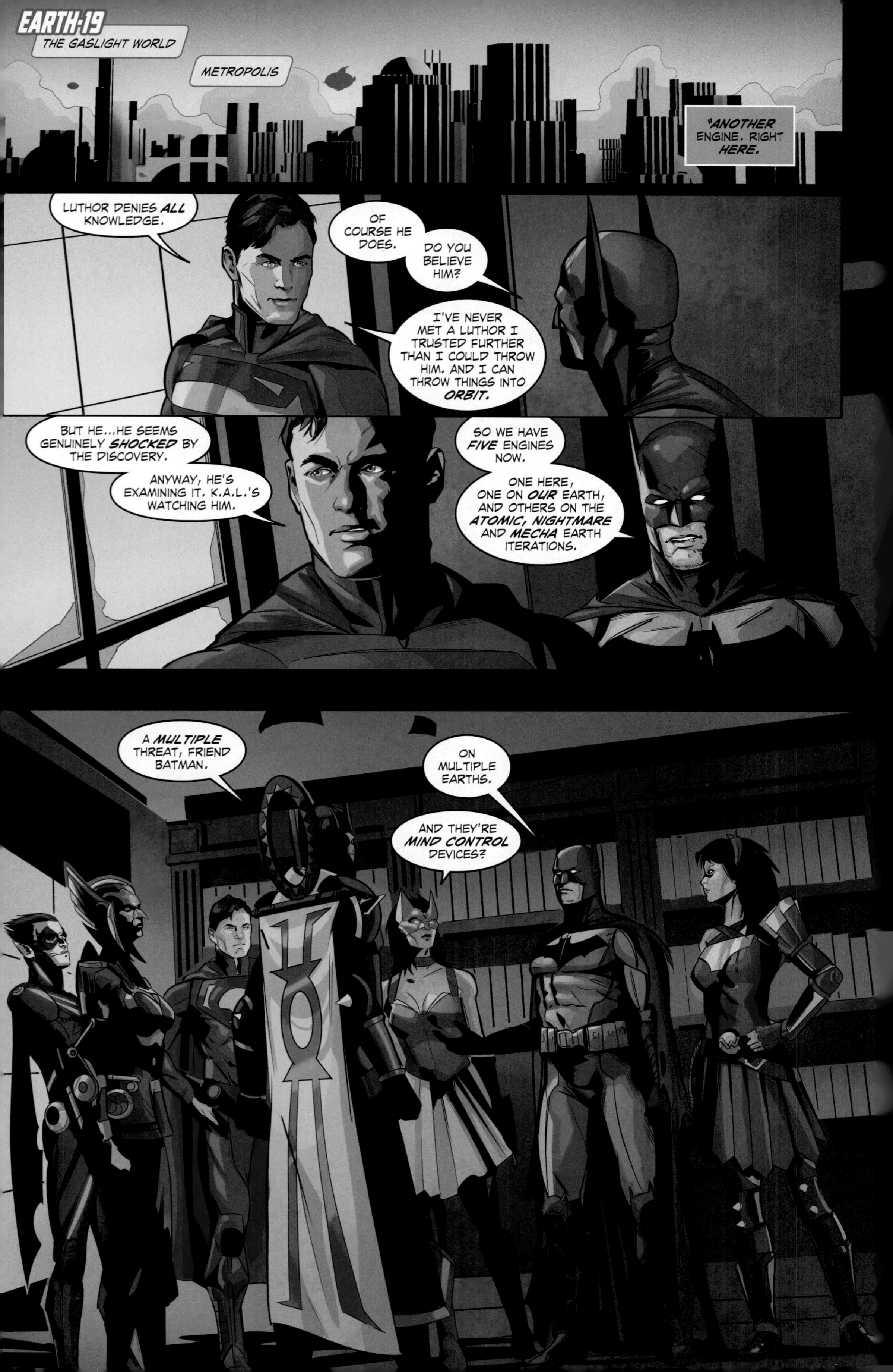
EARTH-19
THE GASLIGHT WORLD
METROPOLIS
"ANOTHER ENGINE. RIGHT HERE.
LUTHOR DENIES ALL KNOWLEDGE.
OF COURSE HE DOES.
DO YOU BELIEVE HIM?
I'VE NEVER MET A LUTHOR I TRUSTED FURTHER THAN I COULD THROW HIM. AND I CAN THROW THINGS INTO ORBIT.
BUT HE...HE SEEMS GENUINELY SHOCKED BY THE DISCOVERY.
ANYWAY, HE'S EXAMINING IT. K.A.L.'S WATCHING HIM.
SO WE HAVE FIVE ENGINES NOW.
ONE HERE, ONE ON OUR EARTH, AND OTHERS ON THE ATOMIC, NIGHTMARE AND MECHA EARTH ITERATIONS.
A MULTIPLE THREAT, FRIEND BATMAN.
ON MULTIPLE EARTHS.
AND THEY'RE MIND CONTROL DEVICES?

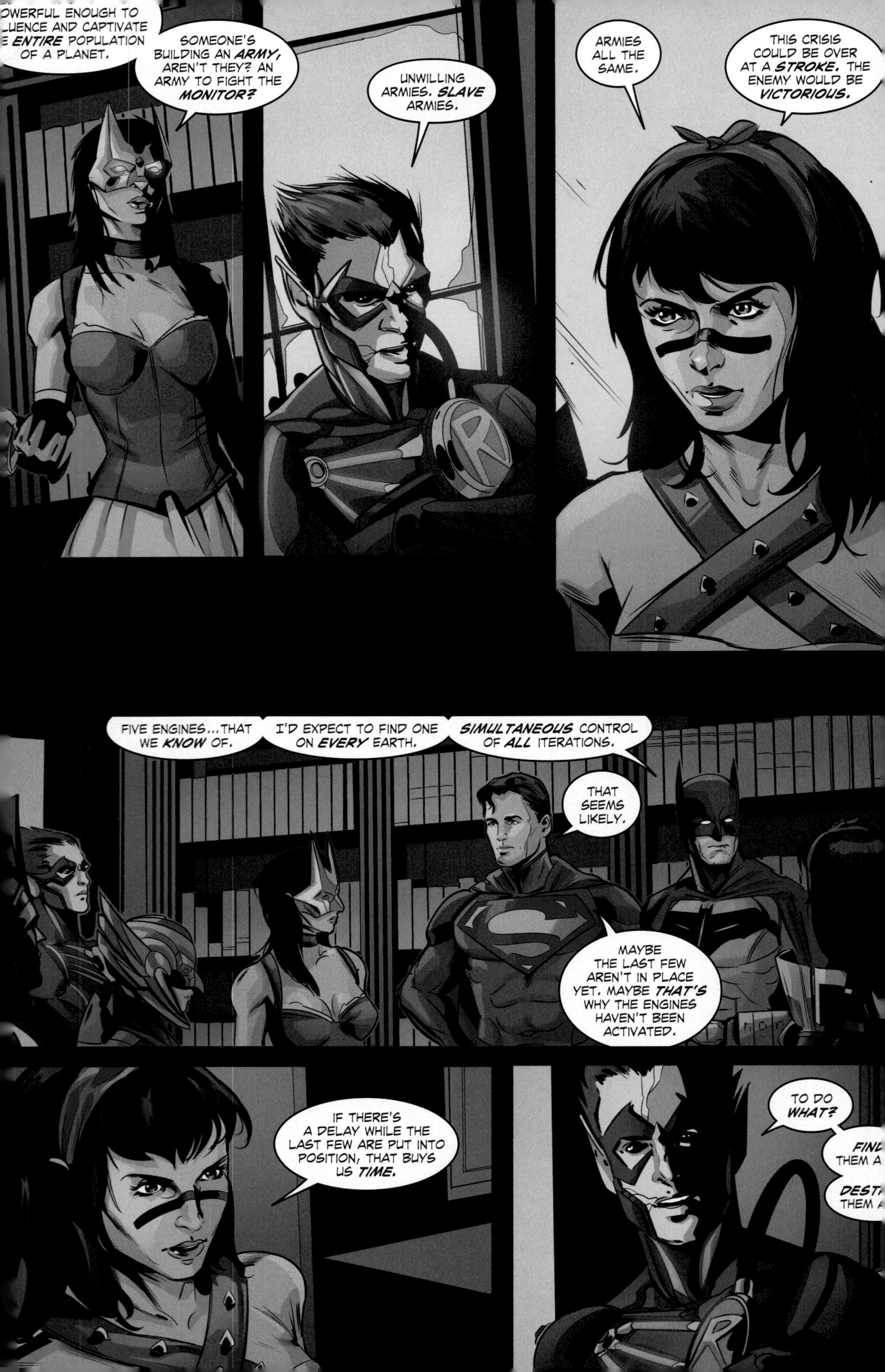

OWERFUL ENOUGH TO LUENCE AND CAPTIVATE E ENTIRE POPULATION OF A PLANET.
SOMEONE'S BUILDING AN ARMY, AREN'T THEY? AN ARMY TO FIGHT THE MONITOR?
UNWILLING ARMIES. SLAVE ARMIES.
ARMIES ALL THE SAME.
THIS CRISIS COULD BE OVER AT A STROKE. THE ENEMY WOULD BE VICTORIOUS.
FIVE ENGINES...THAT WE KNOW OF.
I'D EXPECT TO FIND ONE ON EVERY EARTH.
SIMULTANEOUS CONTROL OF ALL ITERATIONS.
THAT SEEMS LIKELY.
MAYBE THE LAST FEW AREN'T IN PLACE YET. MAYBE THAT'S WHY THE ENGINES HAVEN'T BEEN ACTIVATED.
IF THERE'S A DELAY WHILE THE LAST FEW ARE PUT INTO POSITION, THAT BUYS US TIME.
TO DO WHAT?

...WILL BE INFORMED, AT ANY RATE.

WE *NEED* HIS EXPERTISE. TEKNOS IS A STRANGE LORE TO ME AT *BEST,* BUT THIS TEKNOS DEFIES US ALL, EVEN BRAVE K.A.L. AND THE GIFTED ALEXANDER.

HAL. BEYOND OUR SCOPE NOW. NONE OF US HAS THE *COSMIC* OVERSIGHT.

SUMMON HIM, DIANA.

SUMMON THE MONITOR HERE, RIGHT *NOW.*

MONITOR, IT IS DIANA. WE NEED YOU ON EARTH-19 AS A MATTER OF *URGENCY...*

I WANT TO TAKE A LOOK AT THE ENGINE HERE...

I WANT WHAT [END] ER IS

THE WORKMANSHIP IS QUITE SIMPLY *EXTRAORDINARY.*

SOME OF THE DESIGN ELEMENTS ARE GENIUS. JUST *GENIUS.*

OF COURSE, WITHOUT *MY* BASIC DEVELOPMENT WORK IN THE FIRST PLACE, IT WOULD BE *NOTHING.*

THAT *TROUBLES* YOU, DOESN'T IT, MY FRIEND?

STATEMENT: *YOU* TROUBLE ME.

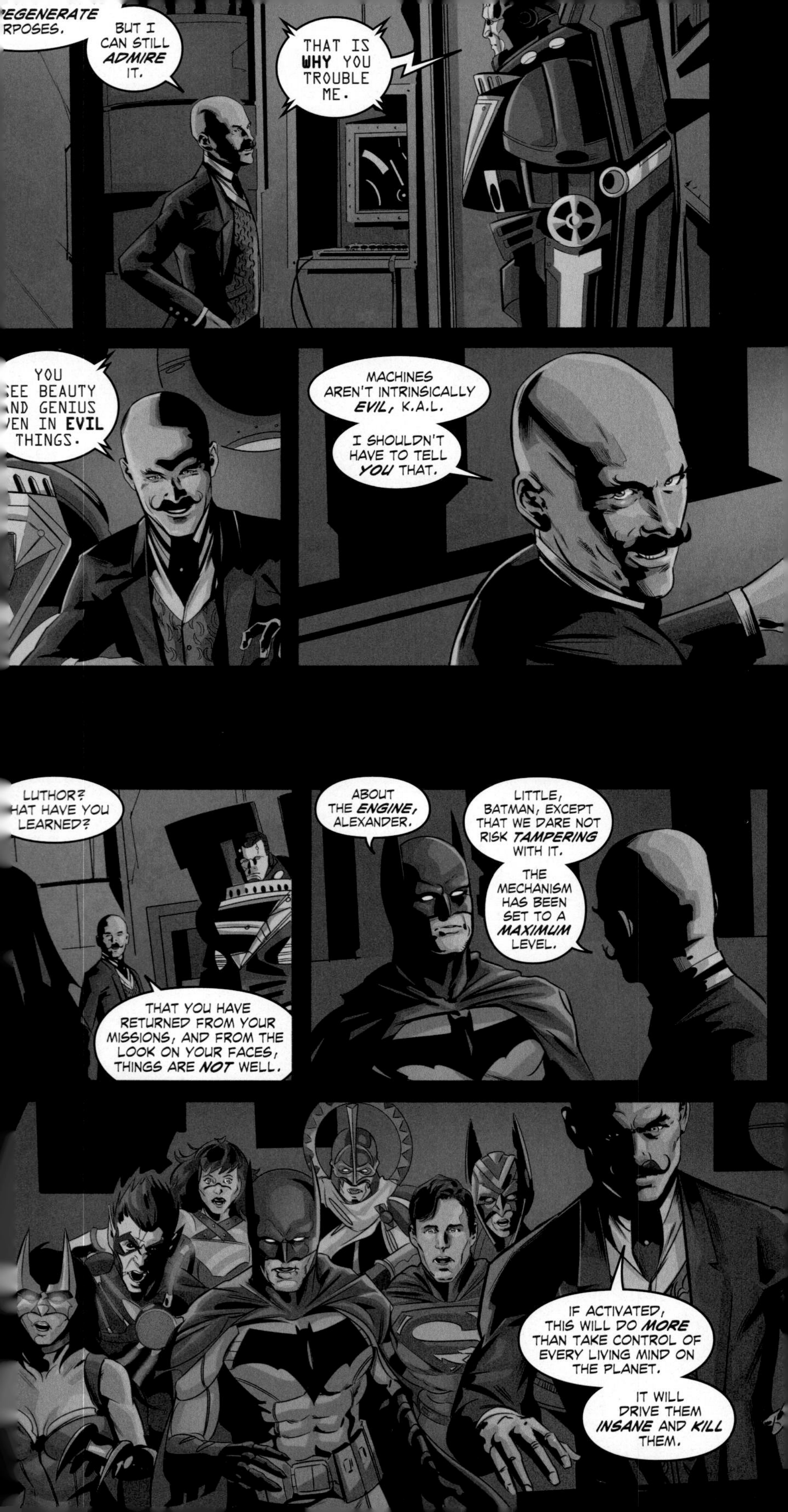
EGENERATE
RPOSES.
BUT I CAN STILL ***ADMIRE*** IT.
THAT IS **WHY** YOU TROUBLE ME.
YOU EE BEAUTY ND GENIUS VEN IN **EVIL** THINGS.
MACHINES AREN'T INTRINSICALLY ***EVIL,*** K.A.L.
I SHOULDN'T HAVE TO TELL ***YOU*** THAT.
LUTHOR? HAT HAVE YOU LEARNED?
THAT YOU HAVE RETURNED FROM YOUR MISSIONS, AND FROM THE LOOK ON YOUR FACES, THINGS ARE ***NOT*** WELL.
ABOUT THE ***ENGINE,*** ALEXANDER.
LITTLE, BATMAN, EXCEPT THAT WE DARE NOT RISK ***TAMPERING*** WITH IT.
THE MECHANISM HAS BEEN SET TO A ***MAXIMUM*** LEVEL.
IF ACTIVATED, THIS WILL DO ***MORE*** THAN TAKE CONTROL OF EVERY LIVING MIND ON THE PLANET.
IT WILL DRIVE THEM ***INSANE*** AND ***KILL*** THEM.

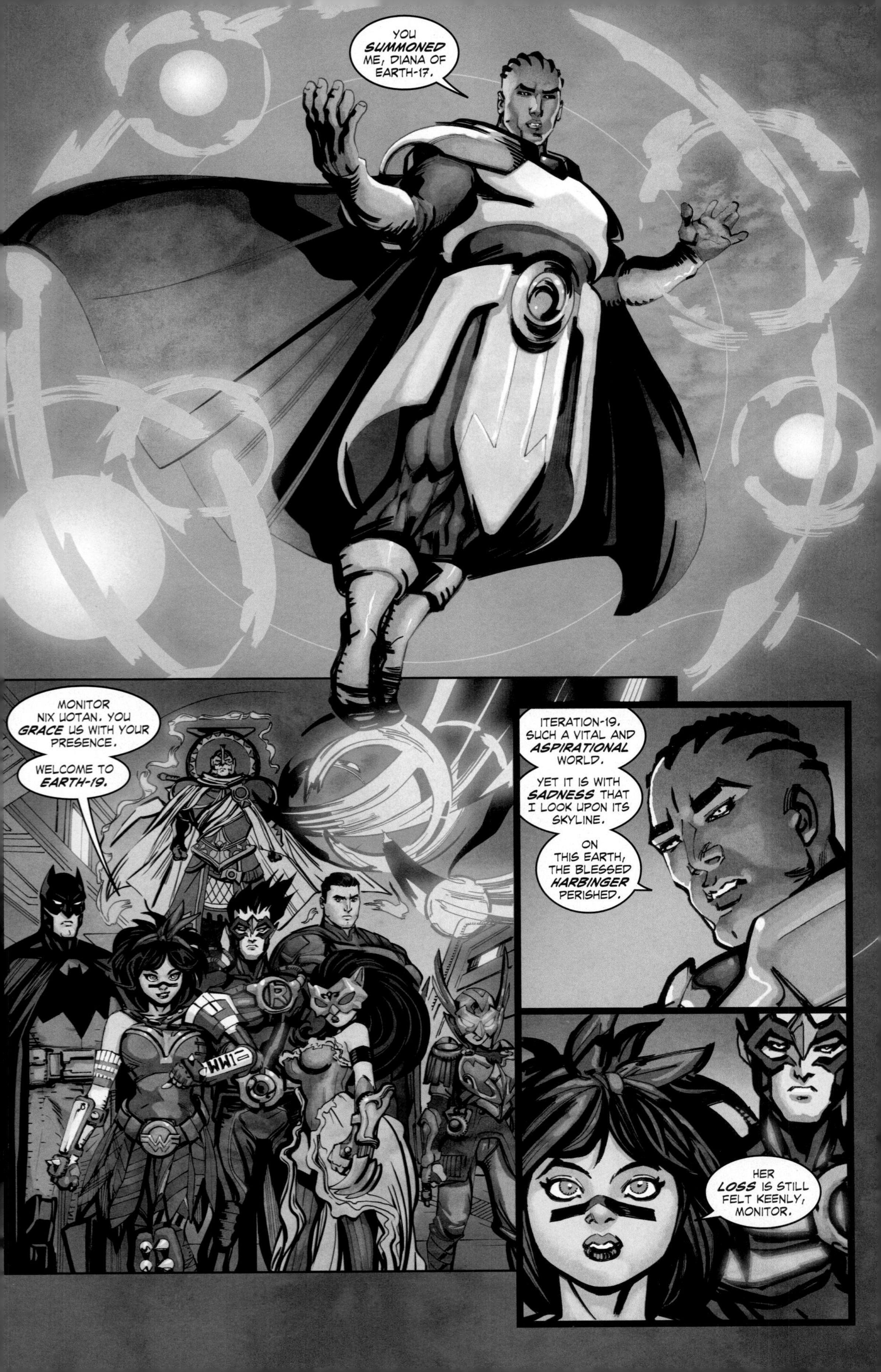
YOU SUMMONED ME, DIANA OF EARTH-17.
MONITOR NIX UOTAN. YOU GRACE US WITH YOUR PRESENCE.
WELCOME TO EARTH-19.
ITERATION-19. SUCH A VITAL AND ASPIRATIONAL WORLD.
YET IT IS WITH SADNESS THAT I LOOK UPON ITS SKYLINE.
ON THIS EARTH, THE BLESSED HARBINGER PERISHED.
HER LOSS IS STILL FELT KEENLY, MONITOR.

YOU HAVE DRAWN TOGETHER THE CHAMPIONS WHO STOOD WITH YOU BEFORE, I SEE.

YES, MONITOR. THE INFINITE CRISIS IS *STILL* UPON US.

AND NEW CHAMPIONS, TOO.

TWO INDIVIDUALS OF *GREAT PROMISE.* INDIVIDUALS WHOSE LIVES I HAVE WATCHED OVER THE YEARS WITH *MUCH* INTEREST.

YOU'VE... *WATCHED* US?

WITHOUT US KNOWING? THAT'S *UNGENTLEMANLY.*

I AM NO *VOYEUR.*

I AM THE GUARDIAN OF THE *MULTIVERSE.* IT IS MY *DUTY* TO OBSERVE AND--

SHAYERA HOL MEANT NOTHING BY IT, MONITOR.

PLEASE. THERE IS SOMETHING YOU MUST SEE.

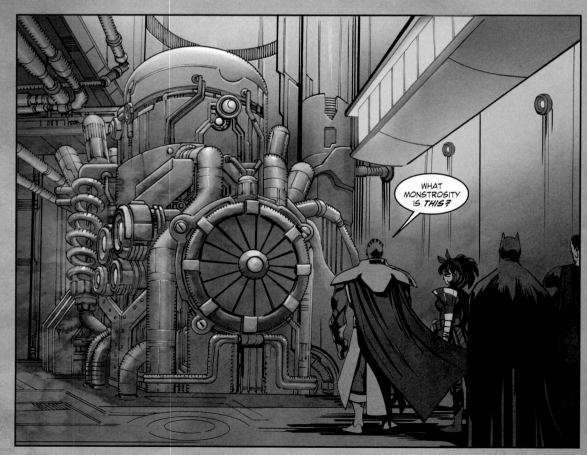

WHAT MONSTROSITY IS *THIS?*

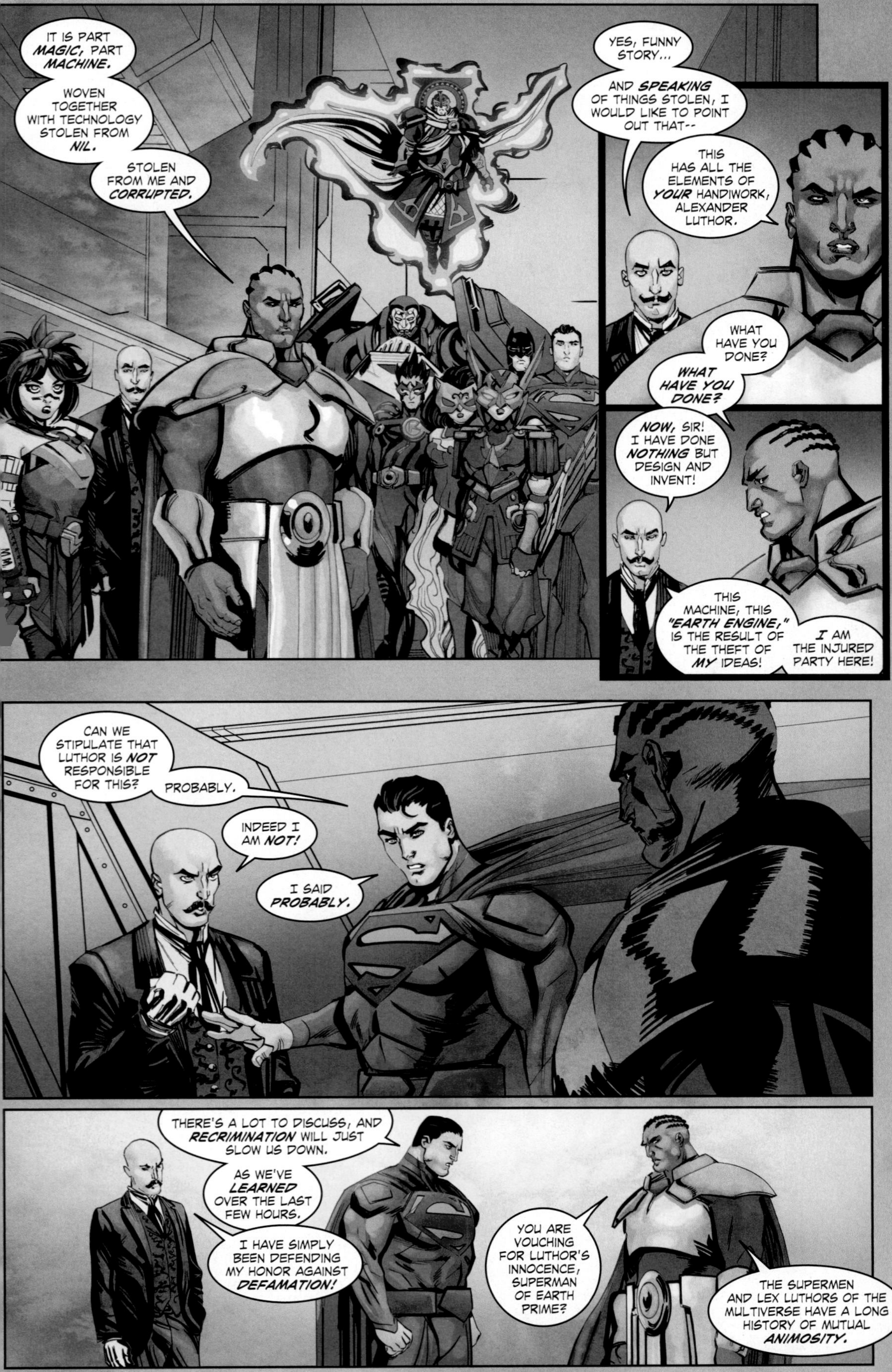
IT IS PART *MAGIC*, PART *MACHINE.*
WOVEN TOGETHER WITH TECHNOLOGY STOLEN FROM *NIL.*
STOLEN FROM ME AND *CORRUPTED.*
YES, FUNNY STORY...
AND *SPEAKING* OF THINGS STOLEN, I WOULD LIKE TO POINT OUT THAT--
THIS HAS ALL THE ELEMENTS OF *YOUR* HANDIWORK, ALEXANDER LUTHOR.
WHAT HAVE YOU DONE?
WHAT HAVE YOU DONE?
NOW, SIR! I HAVE DONE *NOTHING* BUT DESIGN AND INVENT!
THIS MACHINE, THIS *"EARTH ENGINE,"* IS THE RESULT OF THE THEFT OF *MY* IDEAS!
I AM THE INJURED PARTY HERE!
CAN WE STIPULATE THAT LUTHOR IS *NOT* RESPONSIBLE FOR THIS?
PROBABLY.
INDEED I AM *NOT!*
I SAID *PROBABLY.*
THERE'S A LOT TO DISCUSS, AND *RECRIMINATION* WILL JUST SLOW US DOWN.
AS WE'VE *LEARNED* OVER THE LAST FEW HOURS.
I HAVE SIMPLY BEEN DEFENDING MY HONOR AGAINST *DEFAMATION!*
YOU ARE VOUCHING FOR LUTHOR'S INNOCENCE, SUPERMAN OF EARTH PRIME?
THE SUPERMEN AND LEX LUTHORS OF THE MULTIVERSE HAVE A LONG HISTORY OF MUTUAL *ANIMOSITY.*

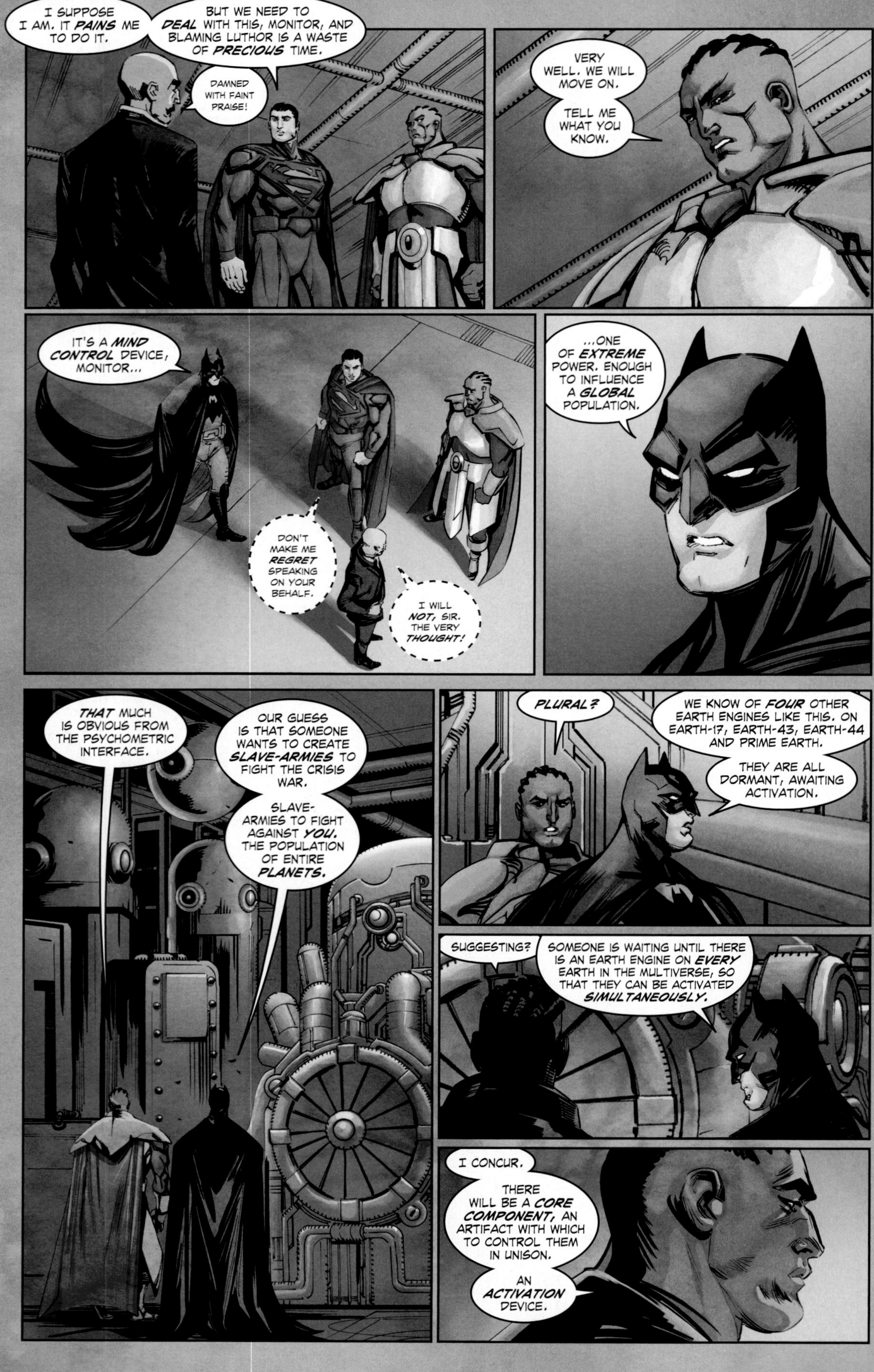
I SUPPOSE I AM. IT *PAINS* ME TO DO IT.
BUT WE NEED TO *DEAL* WITH THIS, MONITOR, AND BLAMING LUTHOR IS A WASTE OF *PRECIOUS* TIME.
DAMNED WITH FAINT PRAISE!
VERY WELL. WE WILL MOVE ON.
TELL ME WHAT YOU KNOW.
IT'S A *MIND CONTROL* DEVICE, MONITOR...
DON'T MAKE ME *REGRET* SPEAKING ON YOUR BEHALF.
I WILL *NOT*, SIR. THE VERY *THOUGHT!*
...ONE OF *EXTREME* POWER. ENOUGH TO INFLUENCE A *GLOBAL* POPULATION.
THAT MUCH IS OBVIOUS FROM THE PSYCHOMETRIC INTERFACE.
OUR GUESS IS THAT SOMEONE WANTS TO CREATE *SLAVE-ARMIES* TO FIGHT THE CRISIS WAR.
SLAVE-ARMIES TO FIGHT AGAINST *YOU.* THE POPULATION OF ENTIRE *PLANETS.*
PLURAL?
WE KNOW OF *FOUR* OTHER EARTH ENGINES LIKE THIS. ON EARTH-17, EARTH-43, EARTH-44 AND PRIME EARTH.
THEY ARE ALL DORMANT, AWAITING ACTIVATION.
SUGGESTING?
SOMEONE IS WAITING UNTIL THERE IS AN EARTH ENGINE ON *EVERY* EARTH IN THE MULTIVERSE, SO THAT THEY CAN BE ACTIVATED *SIMULTANEOUSLY.*
I CONCUR.
THERE WILL BE A *CORE COMPONENT,* AN ARTIFACT WITH WHICH TO CONTROL THEM IN UNISON.
AN *ACTIVATION* DEVICE.

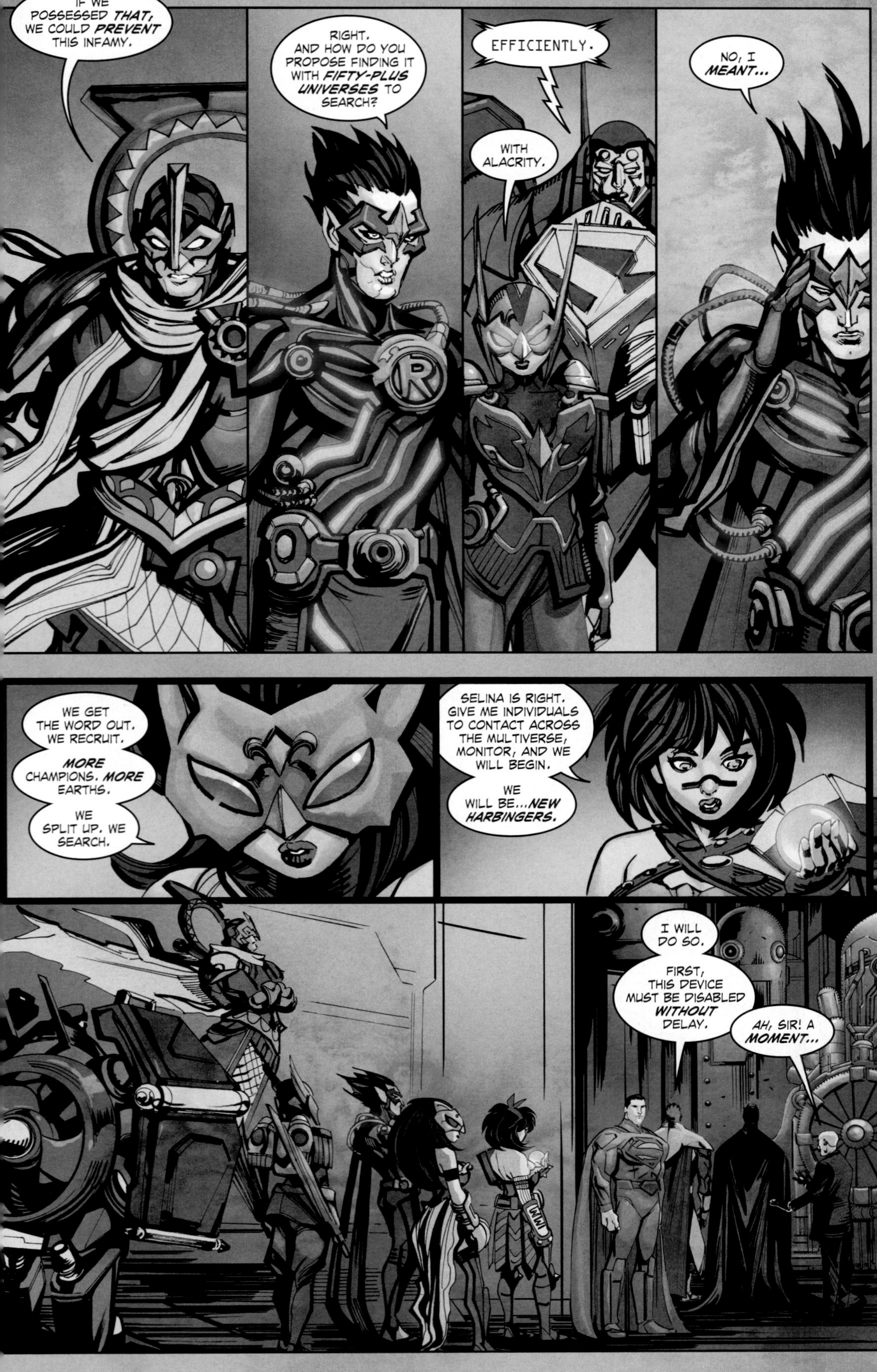
IF WE POSSESSED THAT, WE COULD PREVENT THIS INFAMY.
RIGHT. AND HOW DO YOU PROPOSE FINDING IT WITH FIFTY-PLUS UNIVERSES TO SEARCH?
EFFICIENTLY.
WITH ALACRITY.
NO, I MEANT...
WE GET THE WORD OUT. WE RECRUIT.
MORE CHAMPIONS. MORE EARTHS.
WE SPLIT UP. WE SEARCH.
SELINA IS RIGHT. GIVE ME INDIVIDUALS TO CONTACT ACROSS THE MULTIVERSE, MONITOR, AND WE WILL BEGIN.
WE WILL BE...NEW HARBINGERS.
I WILL DO SO.
FIRST, THIS DEVICE MUST BE DISABLED WITHOUT DELAY.
AH, SIR! A MOMENT...

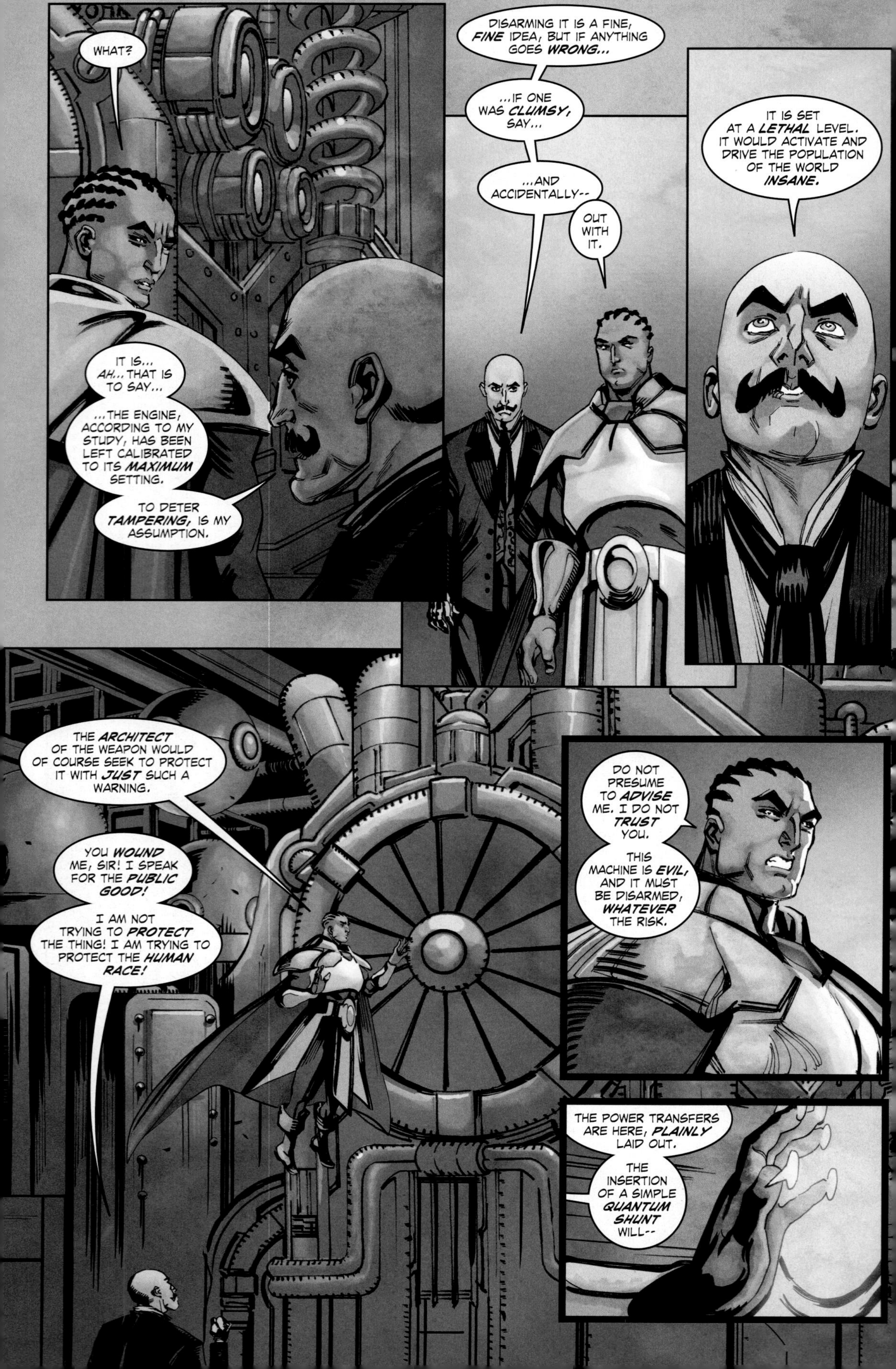
WHAT?
IT IS... AH... THAT IS TO SAY...
...THE ENGINE, ACCORDING TO MY STUDY, HAS BEEN LEFT CALIBRATED TO ITS MAXIMUM SETTING.
TO DETER TAMPERING, IS MY ASSUMPTION.
DISARMING IT IS A FINE, FINE IDEA, BUT IF ANYTHING GOES WRONG...
...IF ONE WAS CLUMSY, SAY...
...AND ACCIDENTALLY--
OUT WITH IT.
IT IS SET AT A LETHAL LEVEL. IT WOULD ACTIVATE AND DRIVE THE POPULATION OF THE WORLD INSANE.
THE ARCHITECT OF THE WEAPON WOULD OF COURSE SEEK TO PROTECT IT WITH JUST SUCH A WARNING.
YOU WOUND ME, SIR! I SPEAK FOR THE PUBLIC GOOD!
I AM NOT TRYING TO PROTECT THE THING! I AM TRYING TO PROTECT THE HUMAN RACE!
DO NOT PRESUME TO ADVISE ME. I DO NOT TRUST YOU.
THIS MACHINE IS EVIL, AND IT MUST BE DISARMED, WHATEVER THE RISK.
THE POWER TRANSFERS ARE HERE, PLAINLY LAID OUT.
THE INSERTION OF A SIMPLE QUANTUM SHUNT WILL--

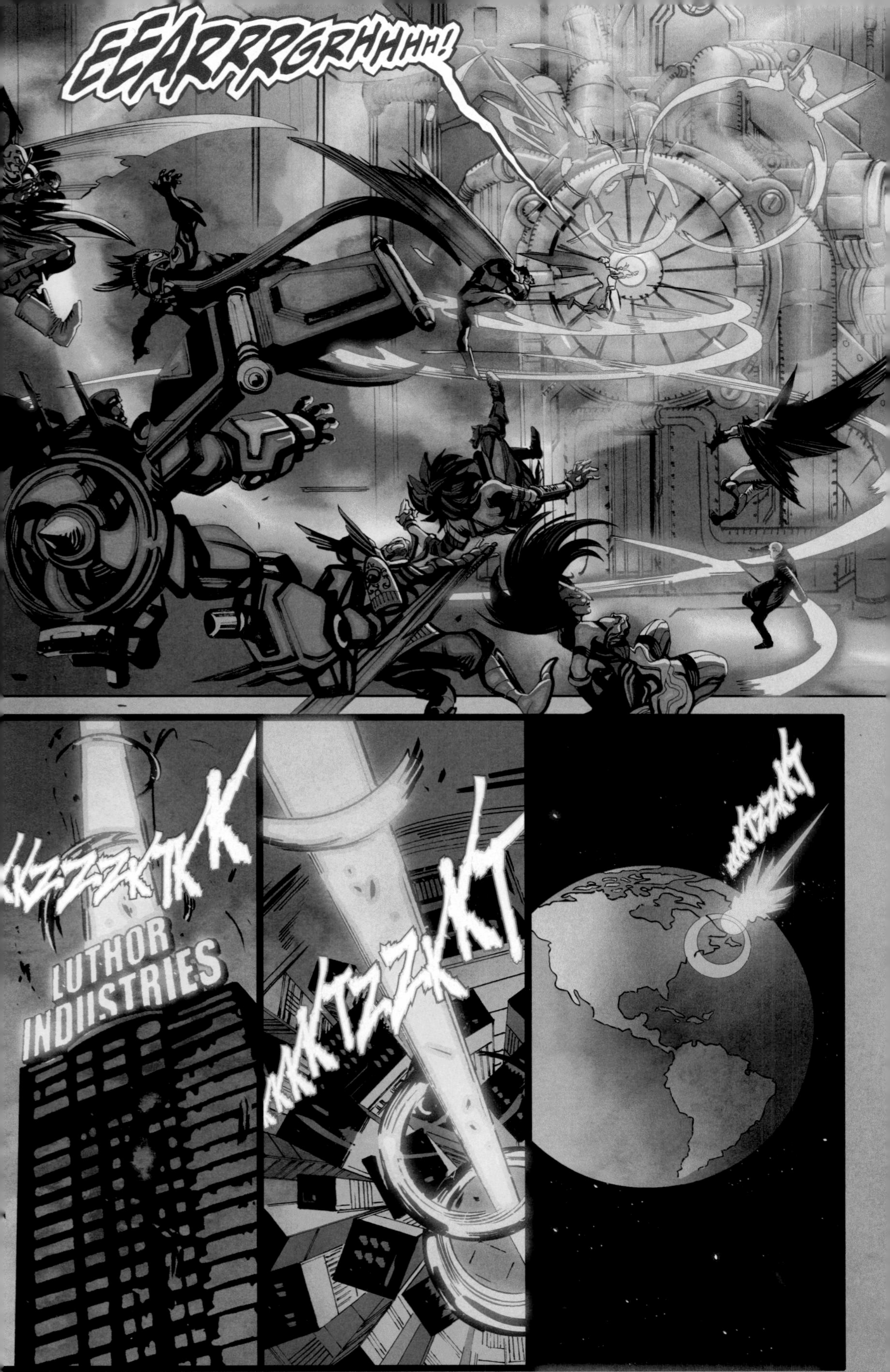
EEARRRGRHHHH!
LUTHOR INDUSTRIES

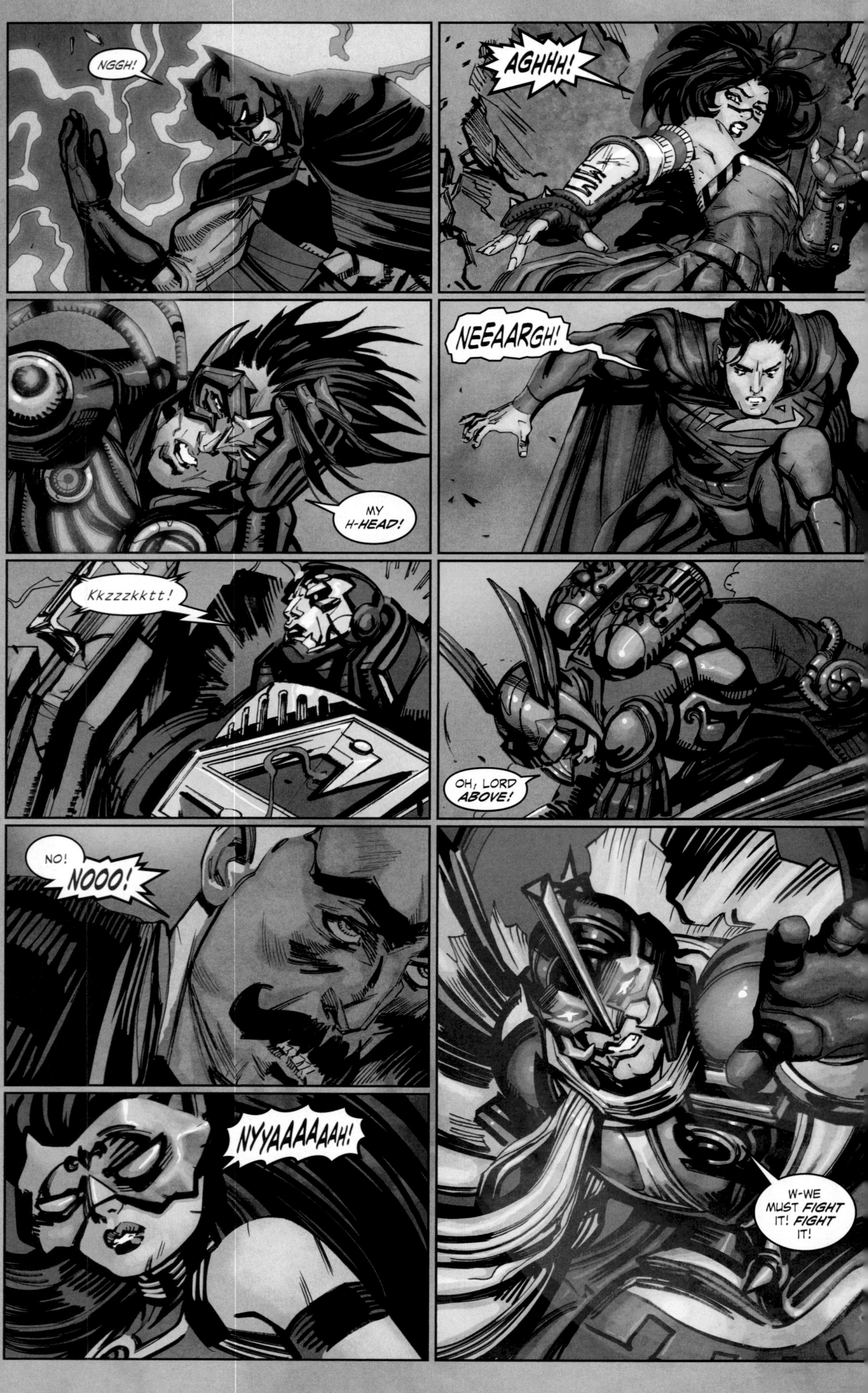
NGGH!
AGHHH!
MY H-HEAD!
NEEAARGH!
Kkzzzkktt!
OH, LORD ABOVE!
NO! NOOO!
NYYAAAAAAH!
W-WE MUST FIGHT IT! FIGHT IT!

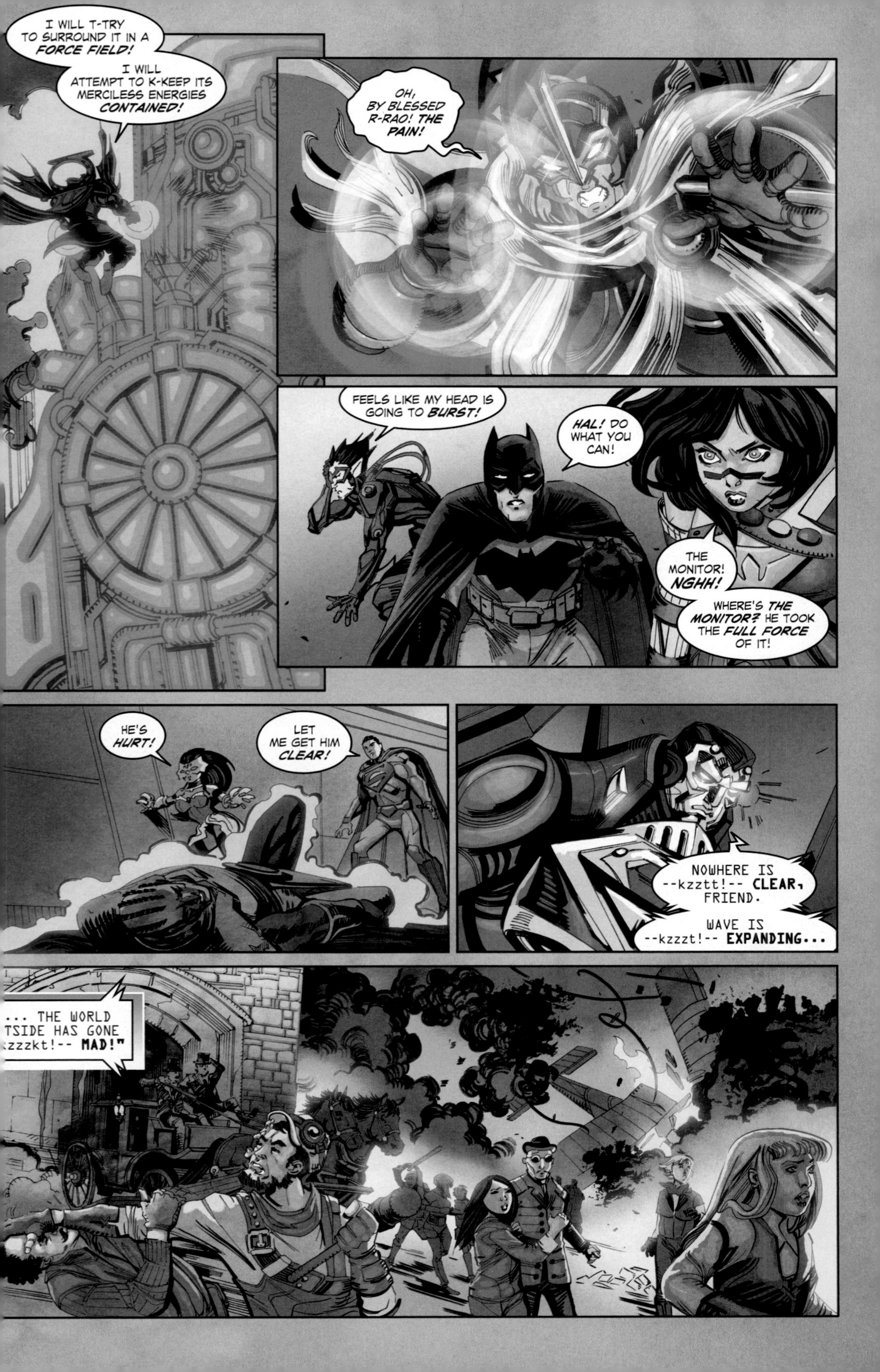

I WILL T-TRY TO SURROUND IT IN A *FORCE FIELD!*
I WILL ATTEMPT TO K-KEEP ITS MERCILESS ENERGIES *CONTAINED!*
OH, BY BLESSED R-RAO! *THE PAIN!*
FEELS LIKE MY HEAD IS GOING TO *BURST!*
HAL! DO WHAT YOU CAN!
THE MONITOR! *NGHH!*
WHERE'S *THE MONITOR?* HE TOOK THE *FULL FORCE* OF IT!
HE'S *HURT!*
LET ME GET HIM *CLEAR!*
NOWHERE IS --kzztt!-- **CLEAR,** FRIEND.
WAVE IS --kzzzt!-- **EXPANDING...**
... THE WORLD TSIDE HAS GONE kzzzkt!-- **MAD!"**

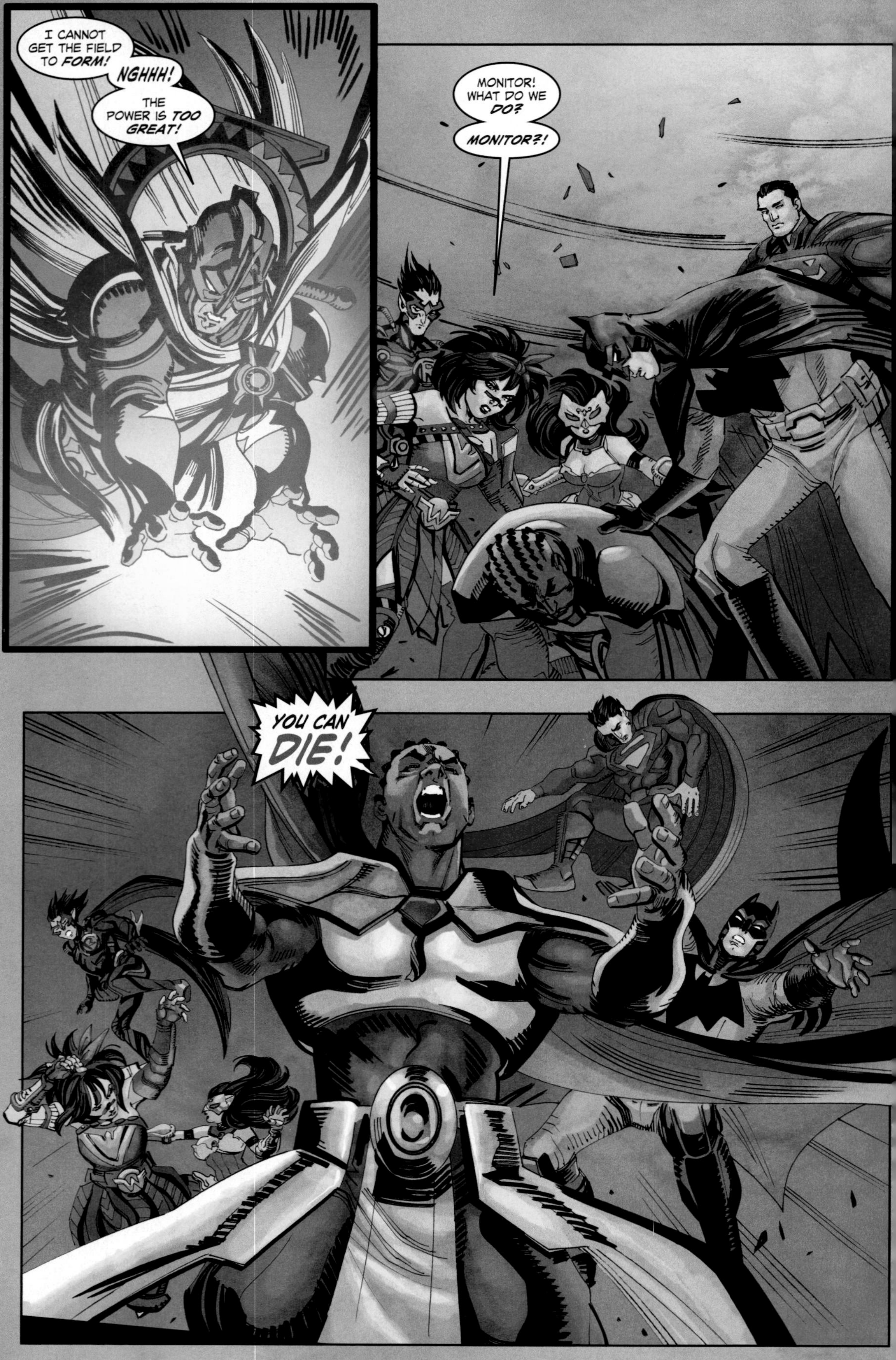
I CANNOT GET THE FIELD TO FORM!
NGHHH!
THE POWER IS TOO GREAT!
MONITOR! WHAT DO WE DO?
MONITOR?!
YOU CAN DIE!

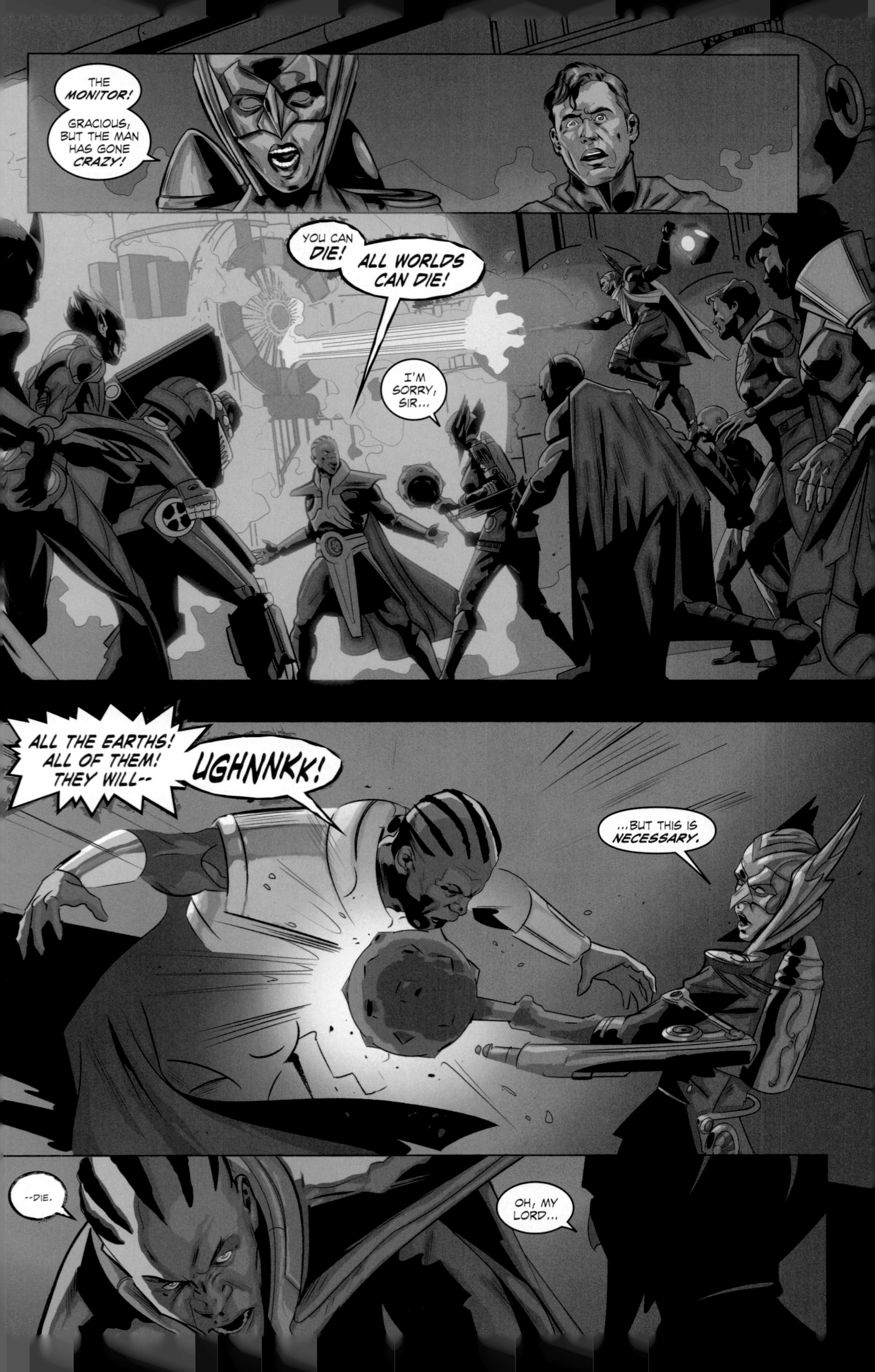
THE MONITOR!
GRACIOUS, BUT THE MAN HAS GONE CRAZY!
YOU CAN DIE!
ALL WORLDS CAN DIE!
I'M SORRY, SIR...
ALL THE EARTHS! ALL OF THEM! THEY WILL--
UGHNNKK!
...BUT THIS IS NECESSARY.
--DIE.
OH, MY LORD...

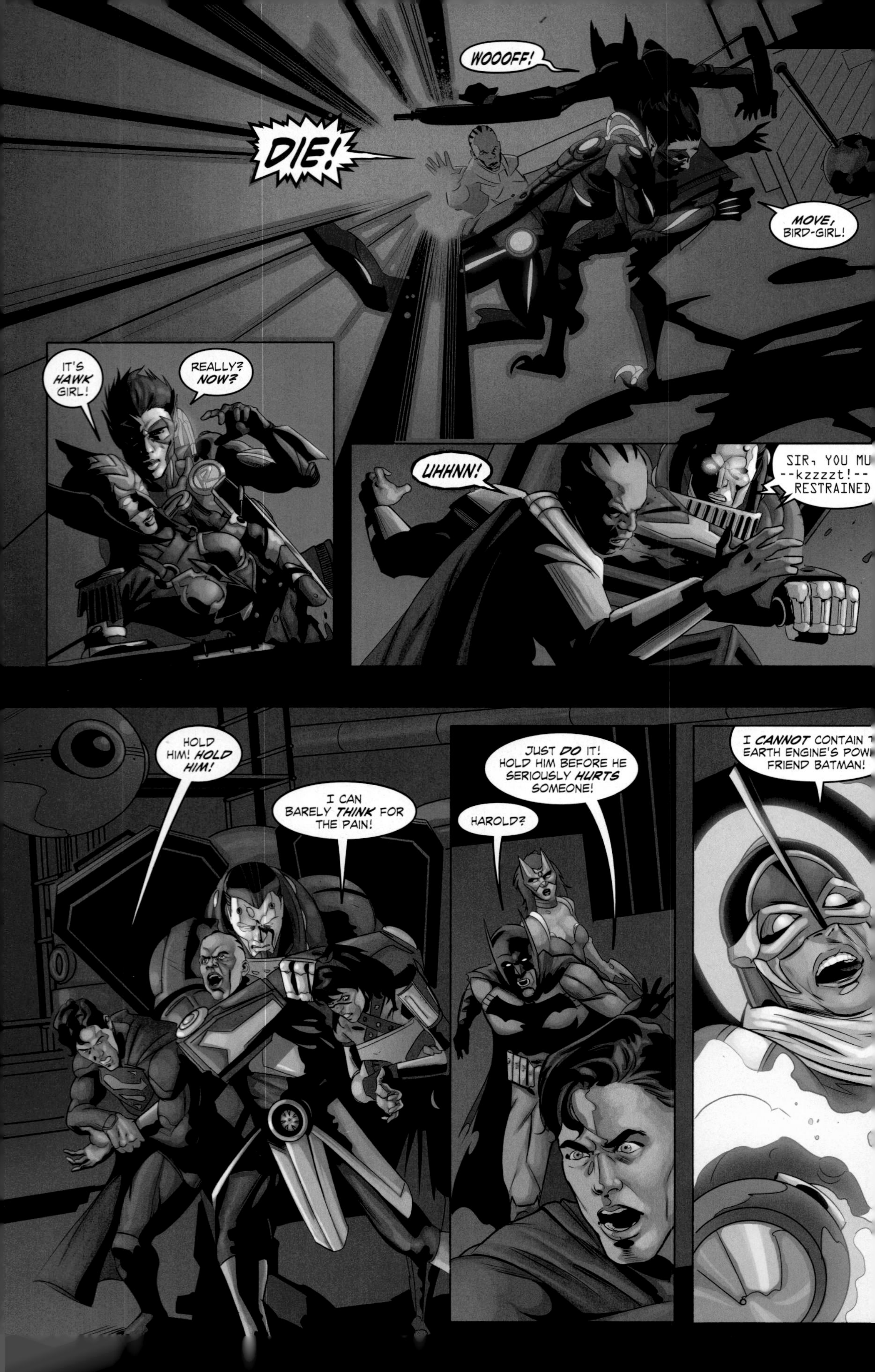
WOOOFF!
DIE!
MOVE, BIRD-GIRL!
IT'S HAWK GIRL!
REALLY? NOW?
UHHNN!
SIR, YOU MU
--kzzzzt!--
RESTRAINED
HOLD HIM! HOLD HIM!
I CAN BARELY THINK FOR THE PAIN!
JUST DO IT! HOLD HIM BEFORE HE SERIOUSLY HURTS SOMEONE!
HAROLD?
I CANNOT CONTAIN
EARTH ENGINE'S POW
FRIEND BATMAN!

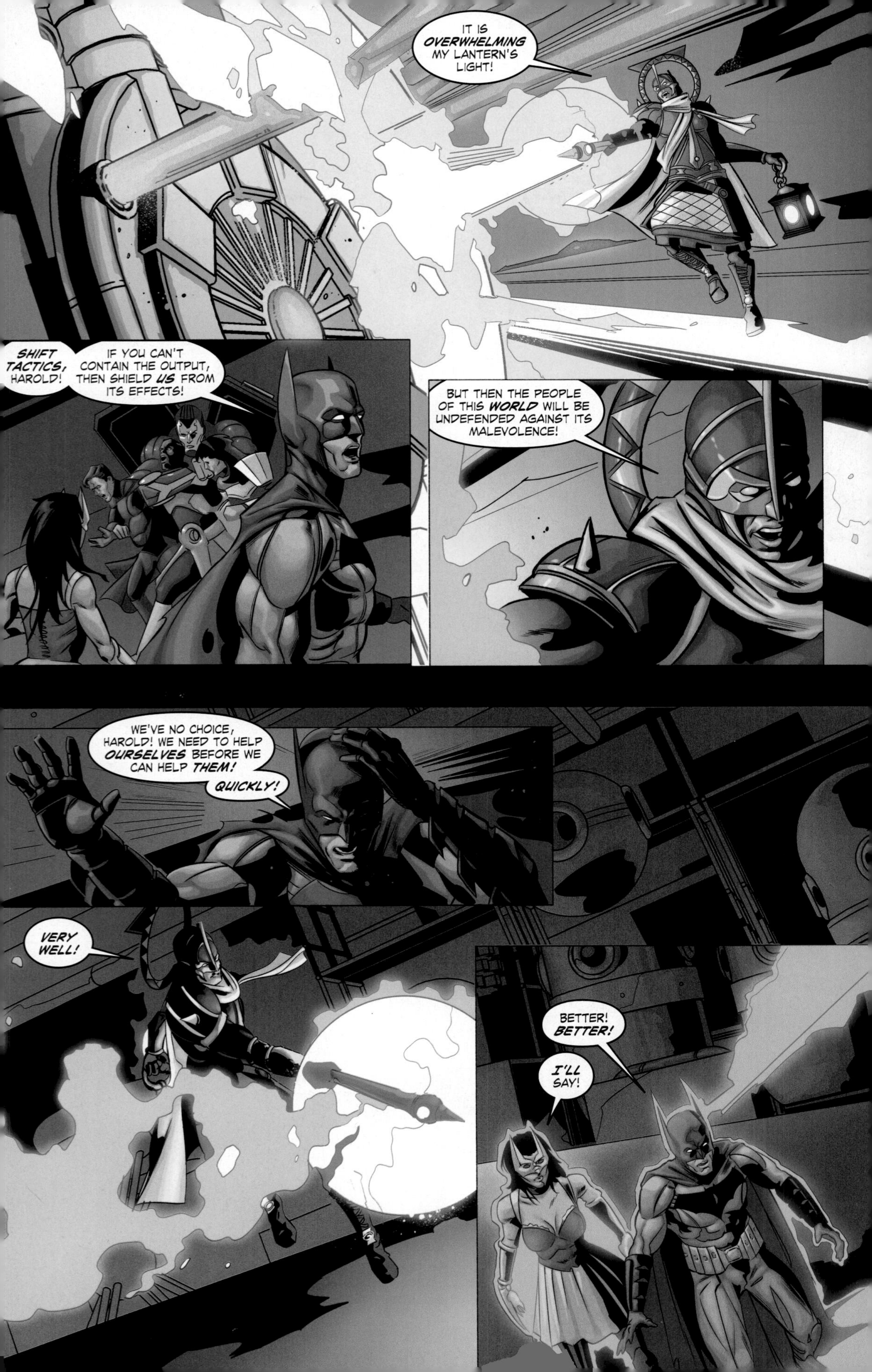
IT IS OVERWHELMING MY LANTERN'S LIGHT!
SHIFT TACTICS, HAROLD!
IF YOU CAN'T CONTAIN THE OUTPUT, THEN SHIELD US FROM ITS EFFECTS!
BUT THEN THE PEOPLE OF THIS WORLD WILL BE UNDEFENDED AGAINST ITS MALEVOLENCE!
WE'VE NO CHOICE, HAROLD! WE NEED TO HELP OURSELVES BEFORE WE CAN HELP THEM!
QUICKLY!
VERY WELL!
BETTER! BETTER!
I'LL SAY!

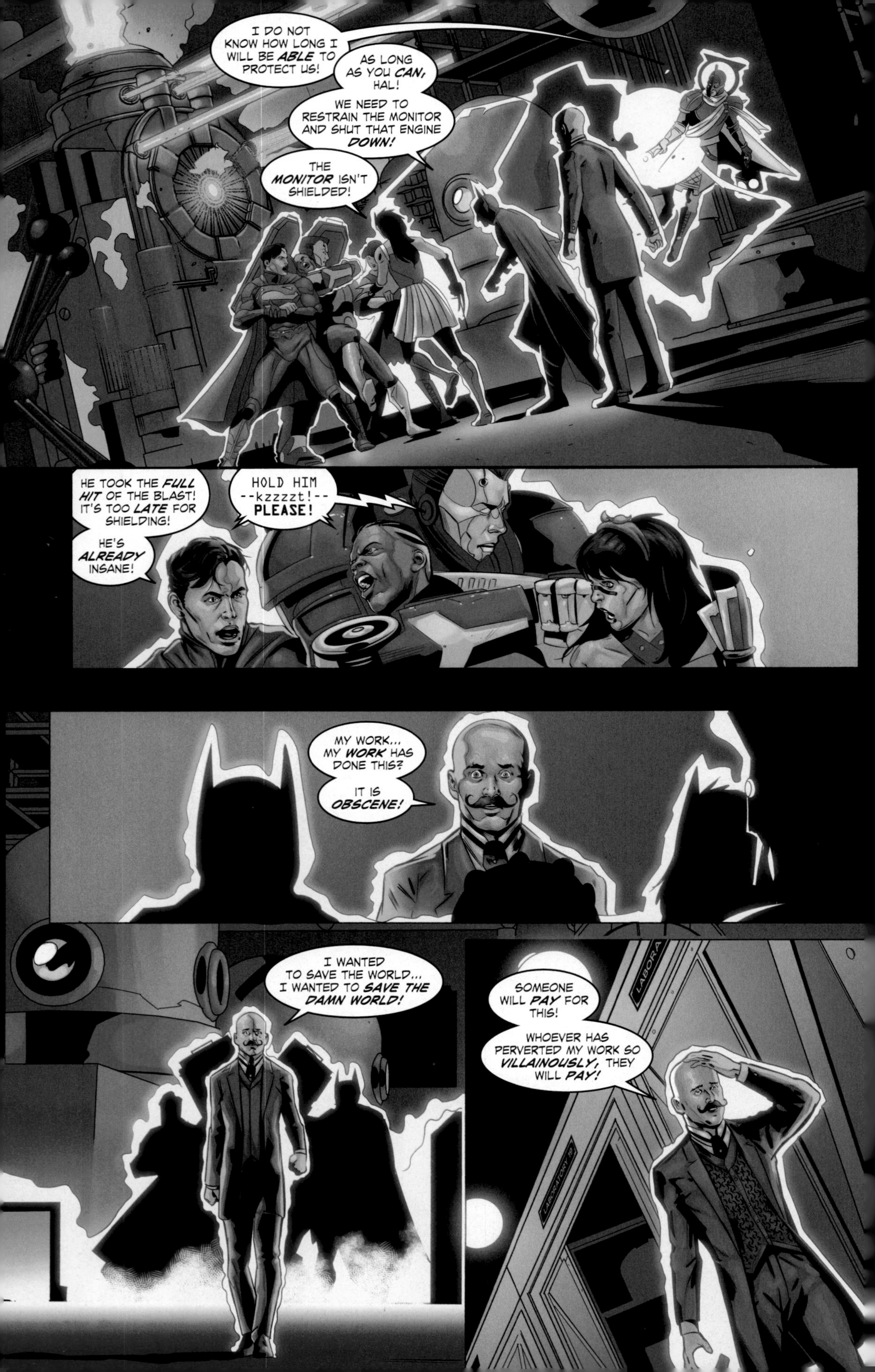
I DO NOT KNOW HOW LONG I WILL BE *ABLE* TO PROTECT US!
AS LONG AS YOU *CAN,* HAL!
WE NEED TO RESTRAIN THE MONITOR AND SHUT THAT ENGINE *DOWN!*
THE *MONITOR* ISN'T SHIELDED!
HE TOOK THE *FULL HIT* OF THE BLAST! IT'S TOO *LATE* FOR SHIELDING!
HOLD HIM --kzzzzt!-- PLEASE!
HE'S *ALREADY* INSANE!
MY WORK... MY *WORK* HAS DONE THIS?
IT IS *OBSCENE!*
I WANTED TO SAVE THE WORLD... I WANTED TO *SAVE THE DAMN WORLD!*
SOMEONE WILL *PAY* FOR THIS!
WHOEVER HAS PERVERTED MY WORK SO *VILLAINOUSLY,* THEY WILL *PAY!*
LABORA

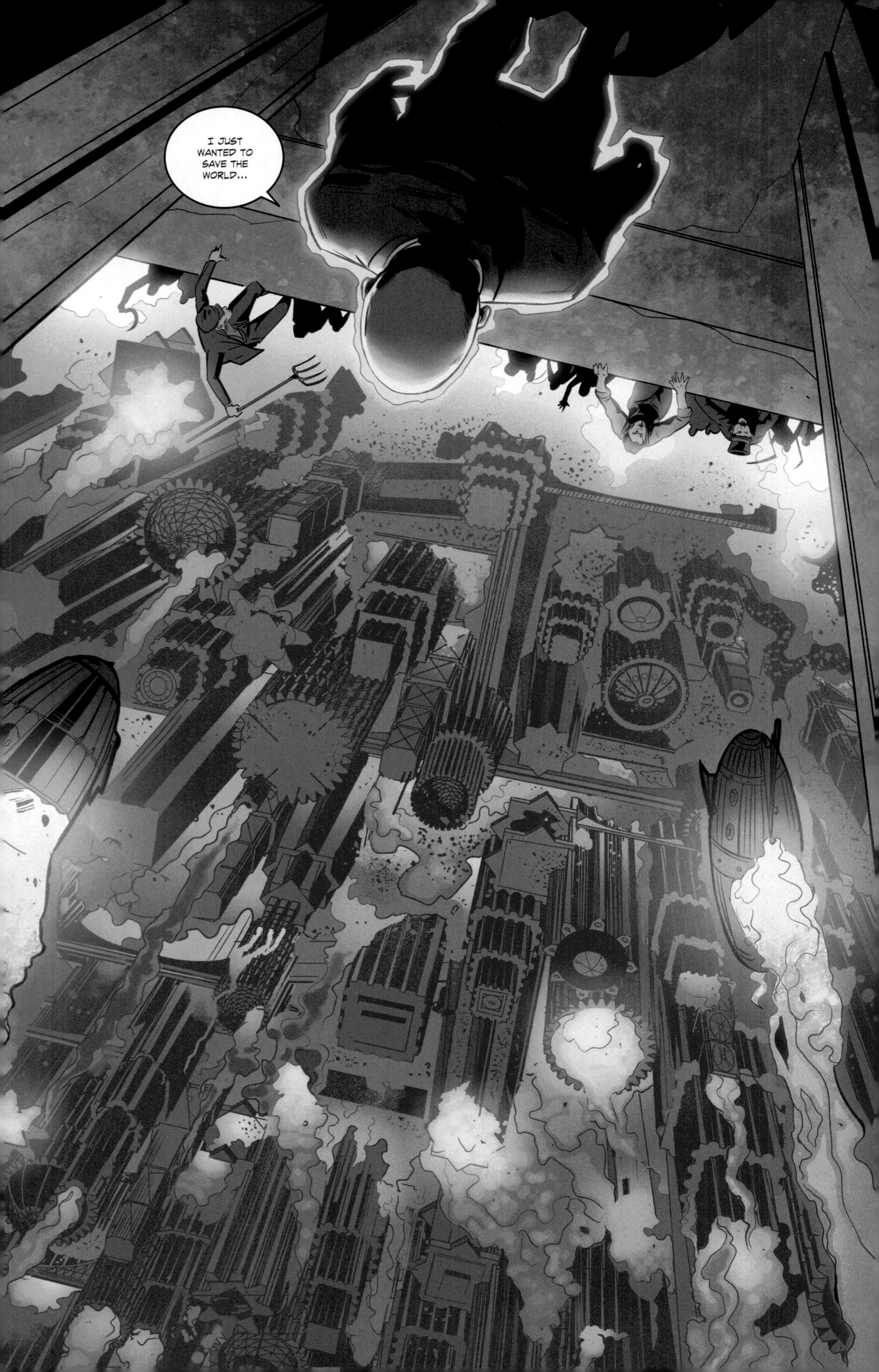
I JUST WANTED TO SAVE THE WORLD...

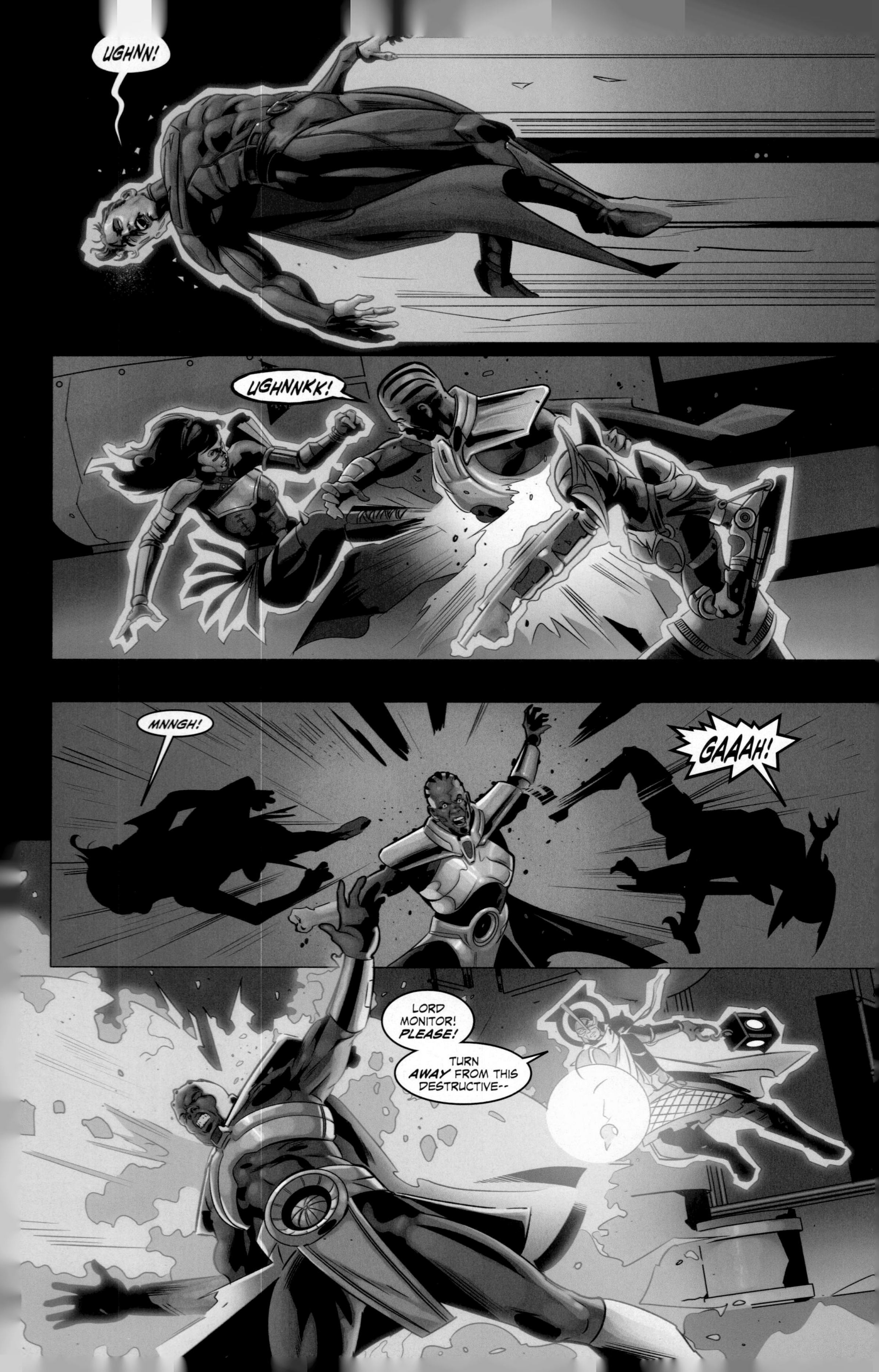
UGHNN!
UGHNNKK!
MNNGH!
GAAAH!
LORD MONITOR! PLEASE!
TURN AWAY FROM THIS DESTRUCTIVE--

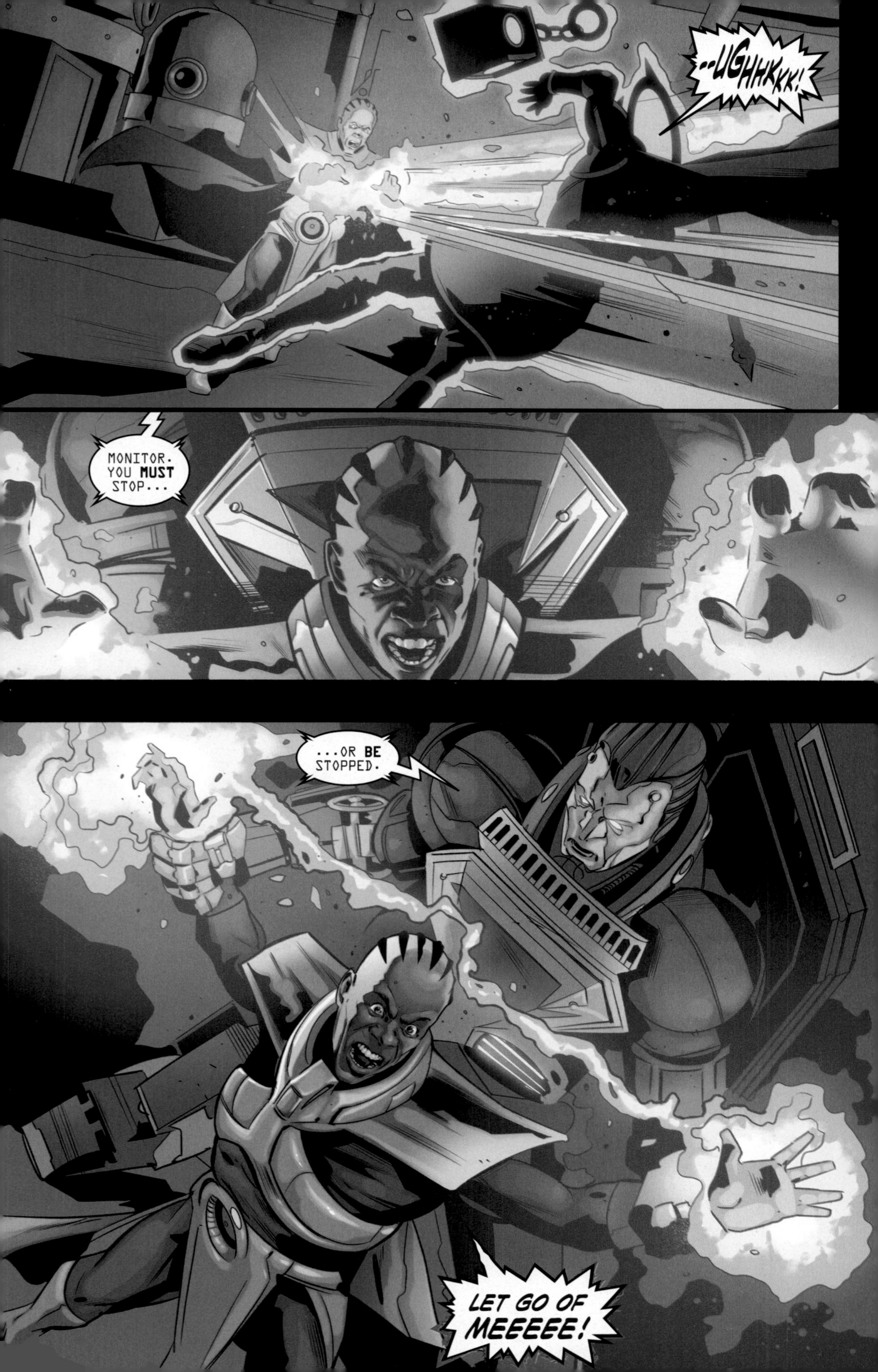
--UGHHKKK!
MONITOR. YOU MUST STOP...
...OR BE STOPPED.
LET GO OF MEEEEE!

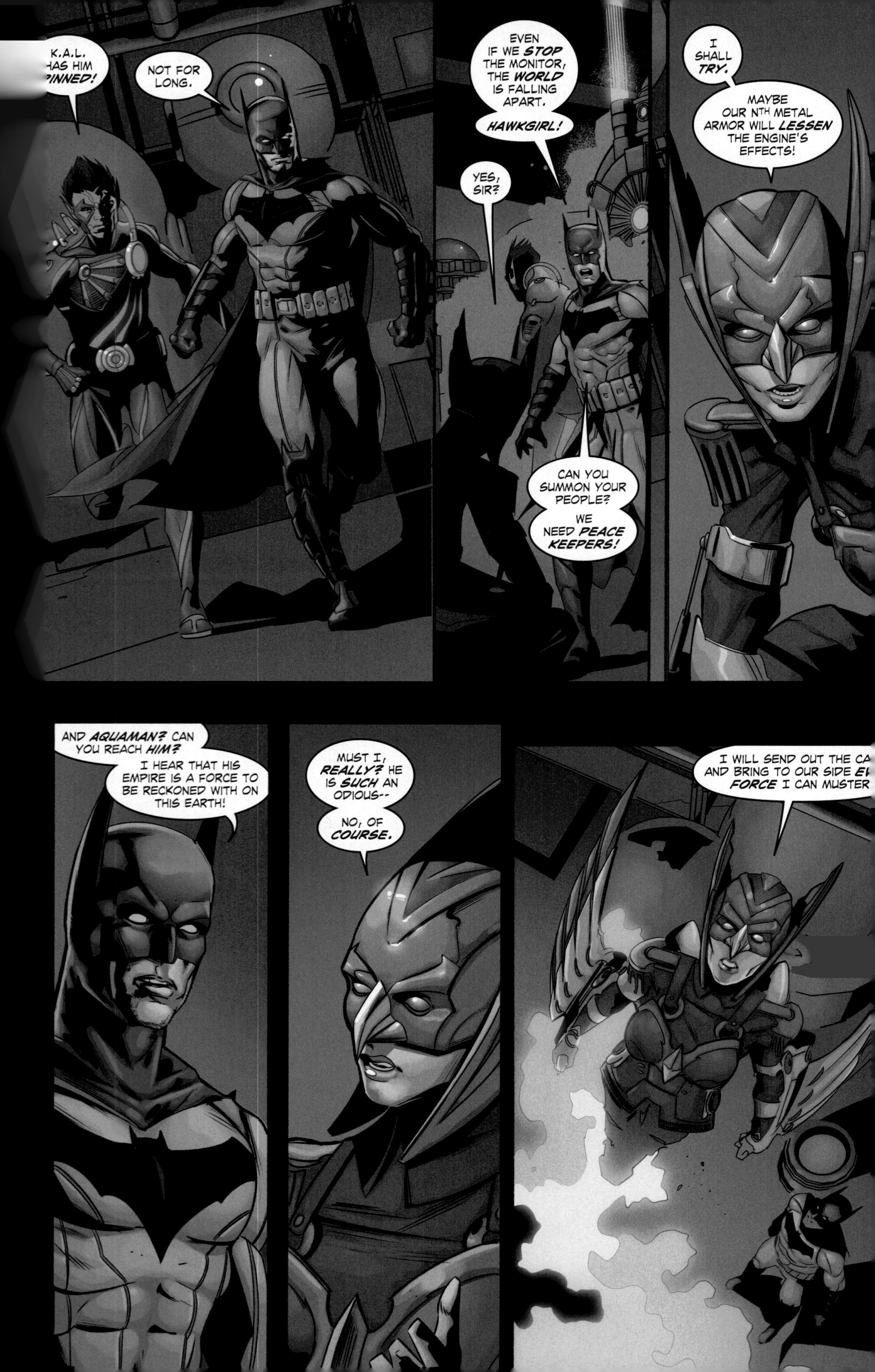
K.A.L. HAS HIM PINNED!
NOT FOR LONG.
EVEN IF WE STOP THE MONITOR, THE WORLD IS FALLING APART.
HAWKGIRL!
YES, SIR?
CAN YOU SUMMON YOUR PEOPLE?
WE NEED PEACE KEEPERS!
I SHALL TRY.
MAYBE OUR NTH METAL ARMOR WILL LESSEN THE ENGINE'S EFFECTS!
AND AQUAMAN? CAN YOU REACH HIM?
I HEAR THAT HIS EMPIRE IS A FORCE TO BE RECKONED WITH ON THIS EARTH!
MUST I, REALLY? HE IS SUCH AN ODIOUS--
NO, OF COURSE.
I WILL SEND OUT THE CA AND BRING TO OUR SIDE EV FORCE I CAN MUSTER

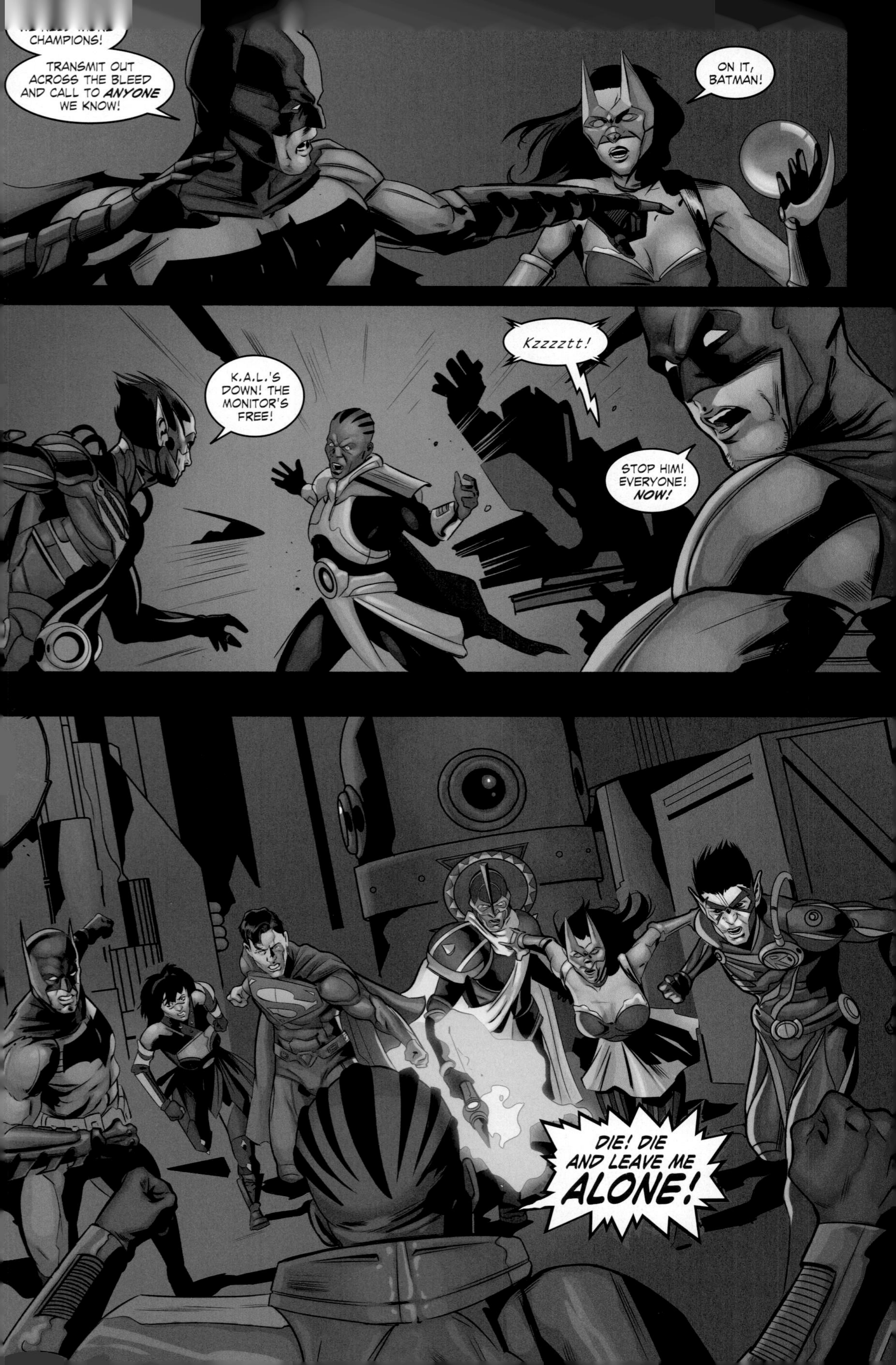
CHAMPIONS!
TRANSMIT OUT ACROSS THE BLEED AND CALL TO *ANYONE* WE KNOW!
ON IT, BATMAN!
K.A.L.'S DOWN! THE MONITOR'S FREE!
Kzzzzzt!
STOP HIM! EVERYONE! *NOW!*
DIE! DIE AND LEAVE ME ALONE!

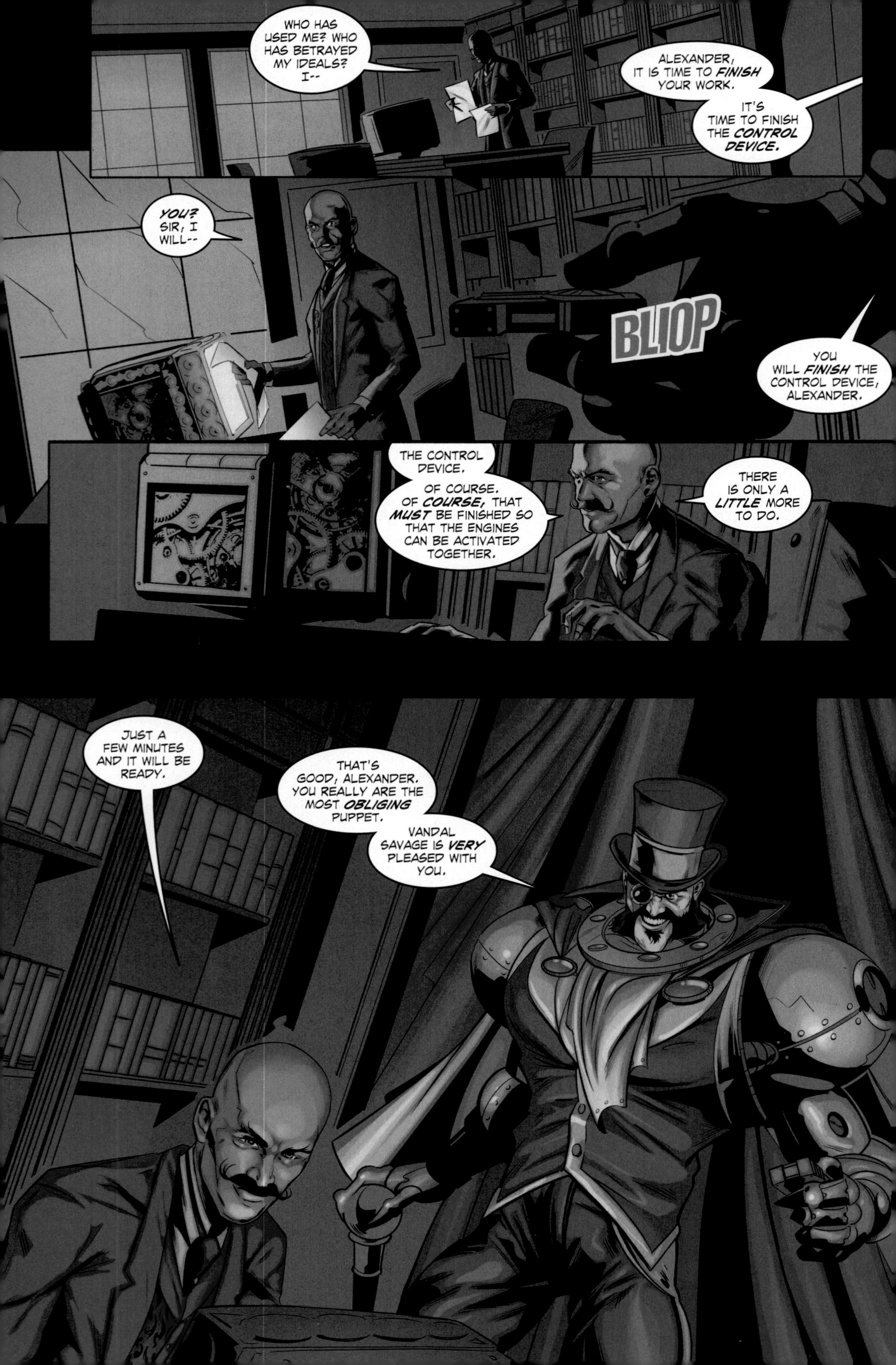
WHO HAS USED ME? WHO HAS BETRAYED MY IDEALS? I--
ALEXANDER, IT IS TIME TO FINISH YOUR WORK.
IT'S TIME TO FINISH THE CONTROL DEVICE.
YOU? SIR, I WILL--
BLIOP
YOU WILL FINISH THE CONTROL DEVICE, ALEXANDER.
THE CONTROL DEVICE.
OF COURSE. OF COURSE, THAT MUST BE FINISHED SO THAT THE ENGINES CAN BE ACTIVATED TOGETHER.
THERE IS ONLY A LITTLE MORE TO DO.
JUST A FEW MINUTES AND IT WILL BE READY.
THAT'S GOOD, ALEXANDER. YOU REALLY ARE THE MOST OBLIGING PUPPET.
VANDAL SAVAGE IS VERY PLEASED WITH YOU.

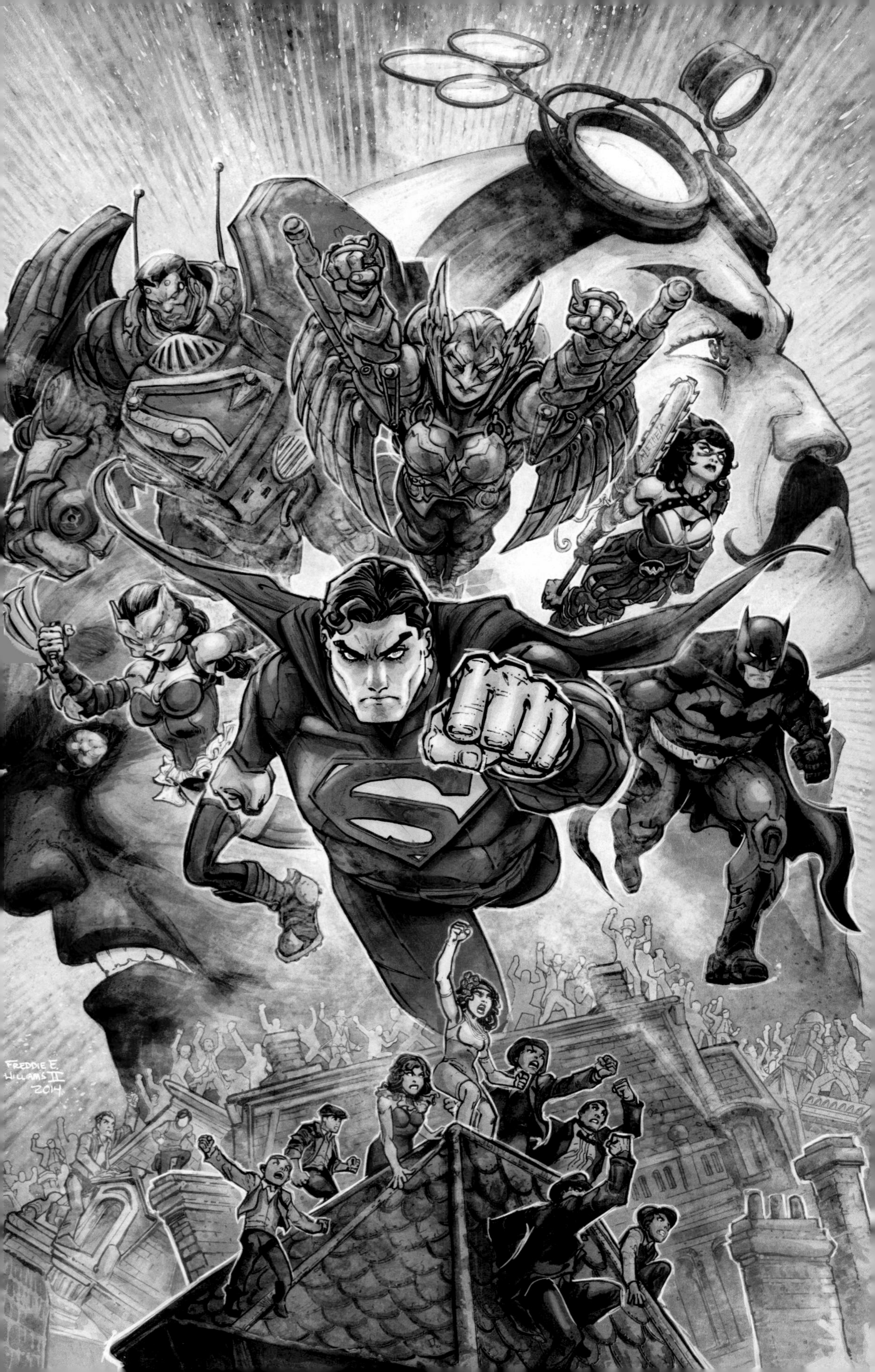
FREDDIE E. WILLIAMS II 2014

THE END OF ALL EARTHS

Angel Hernandez **Tom Derenick** Artists **Alejandro Sanchez** Colorist
Cover Art by **Freddie E. Williams II**

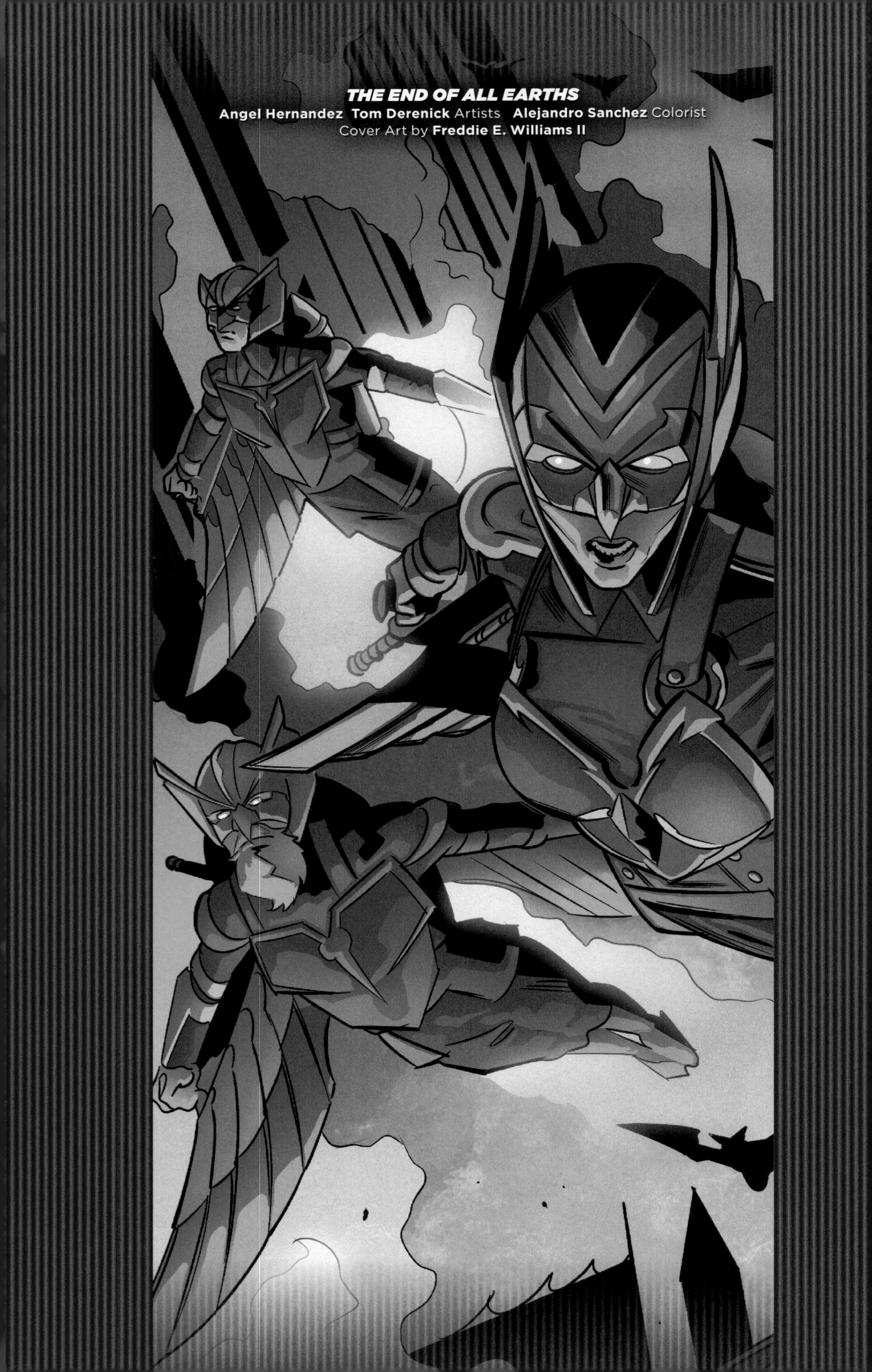

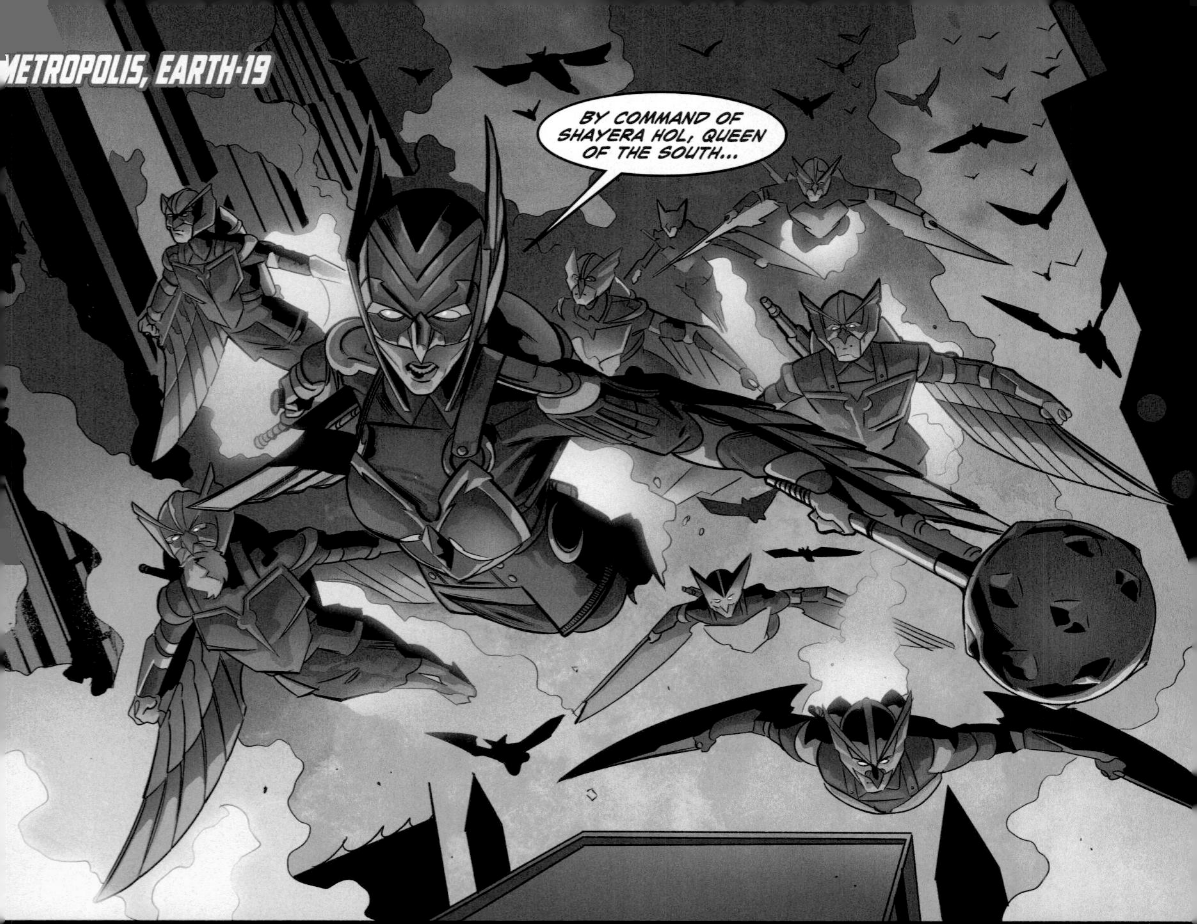
METROPOLIS, EARTH-19
BY COMMAND OF SHAYERA HOL, QUEEN OF THE SOUTH...

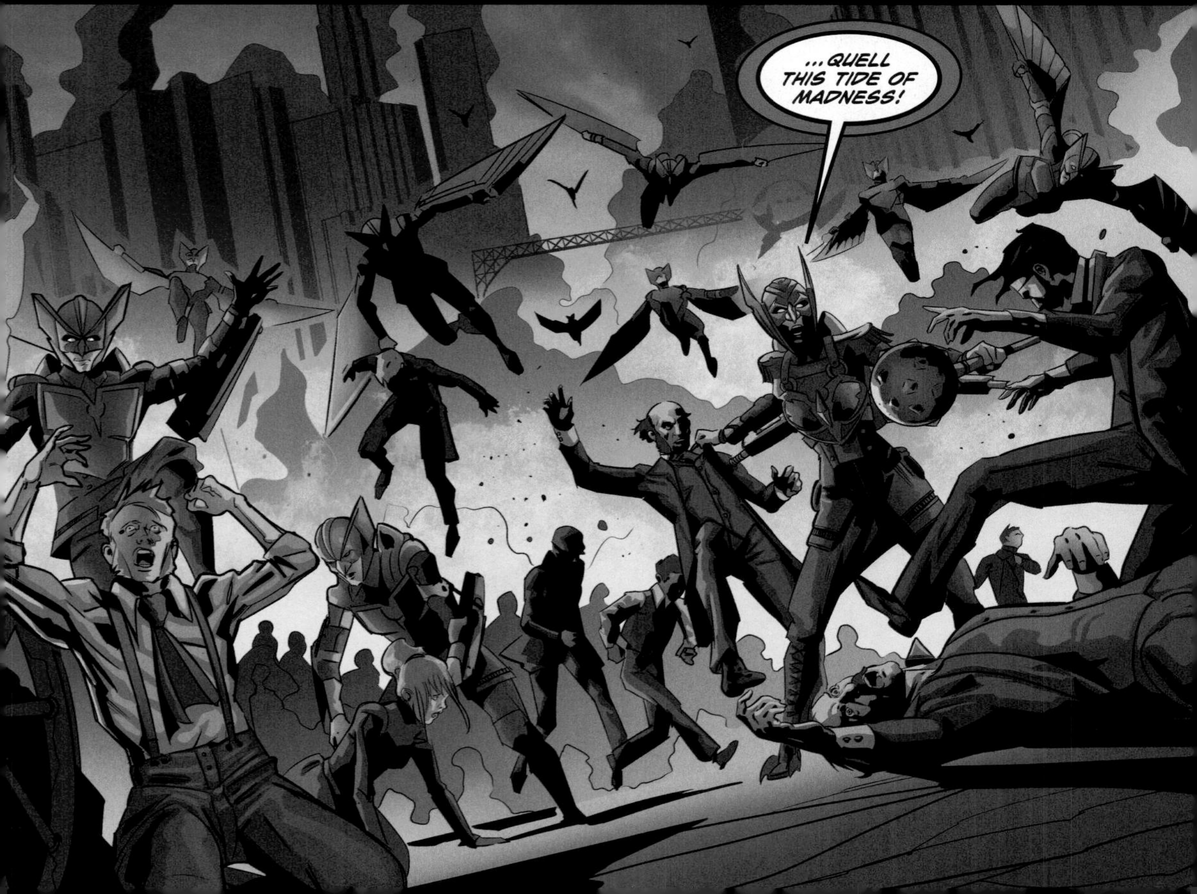
...QUELL THIS TIDE OF MADNESS!

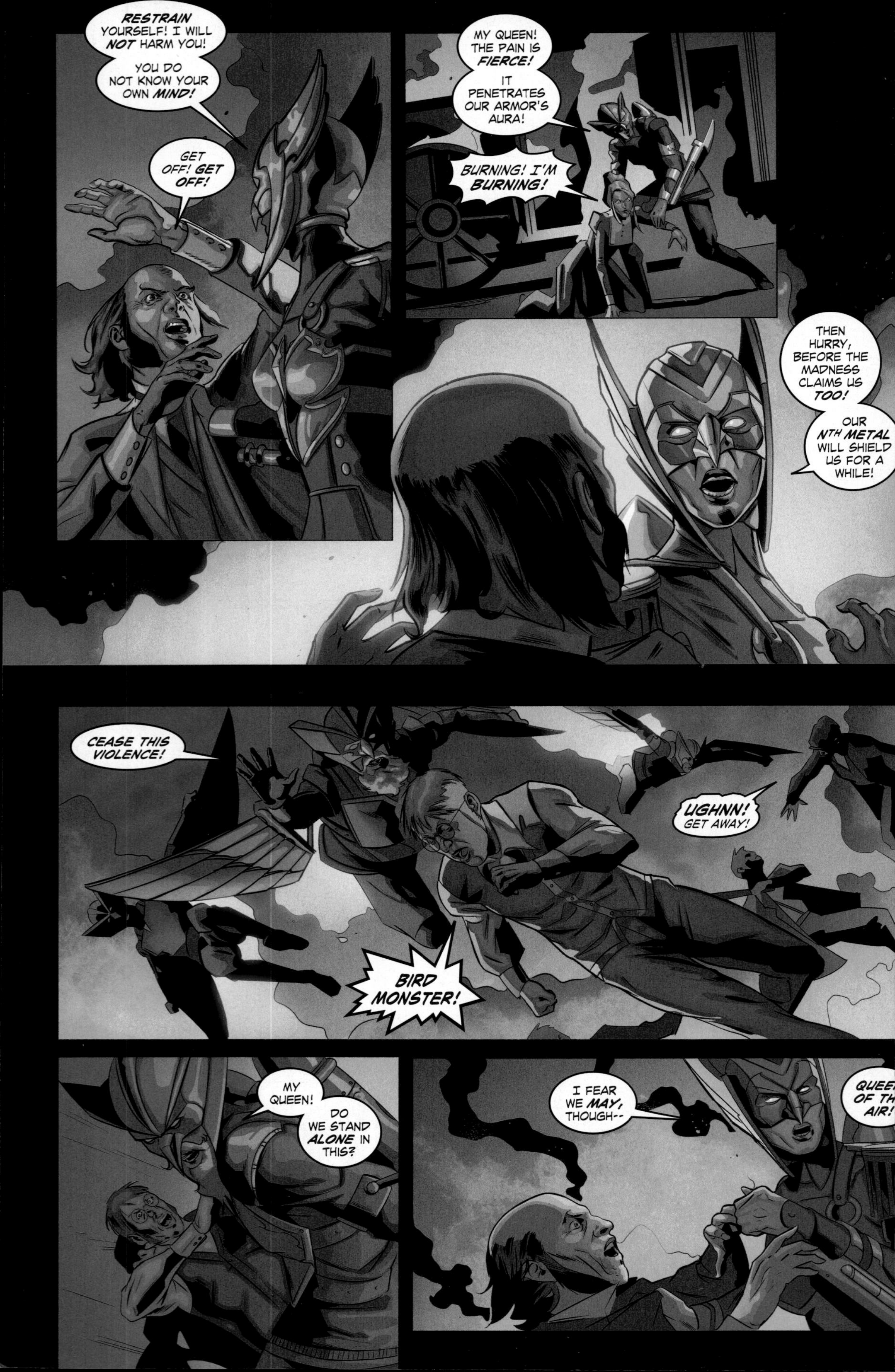

RESTRAIN YOURSELF! I WILL NOT HARM YOU!
YOU DO NOT KNOW YOUR OWN MIND!
GET OFF! GET OFF!
MY QUEEN! THE PAIN IS FIERCE!
IT PENETRATES OUR ARMOR'S AURA!
BURNING! I'M BURNING!
THEN HURRY, BEFORE THE MADNESS CLAIMS US TOO!
OUR NTH METAL WILL SHIELD US FOR A WHILE!
CEASE THIS VIOLENCE!
UGHNN! GET AWAY!
BIRD MONSTER!
MY QUEEN!
DO WE STAND ALONE IN THIS?
I FEAR WE MAY, THOUGH--

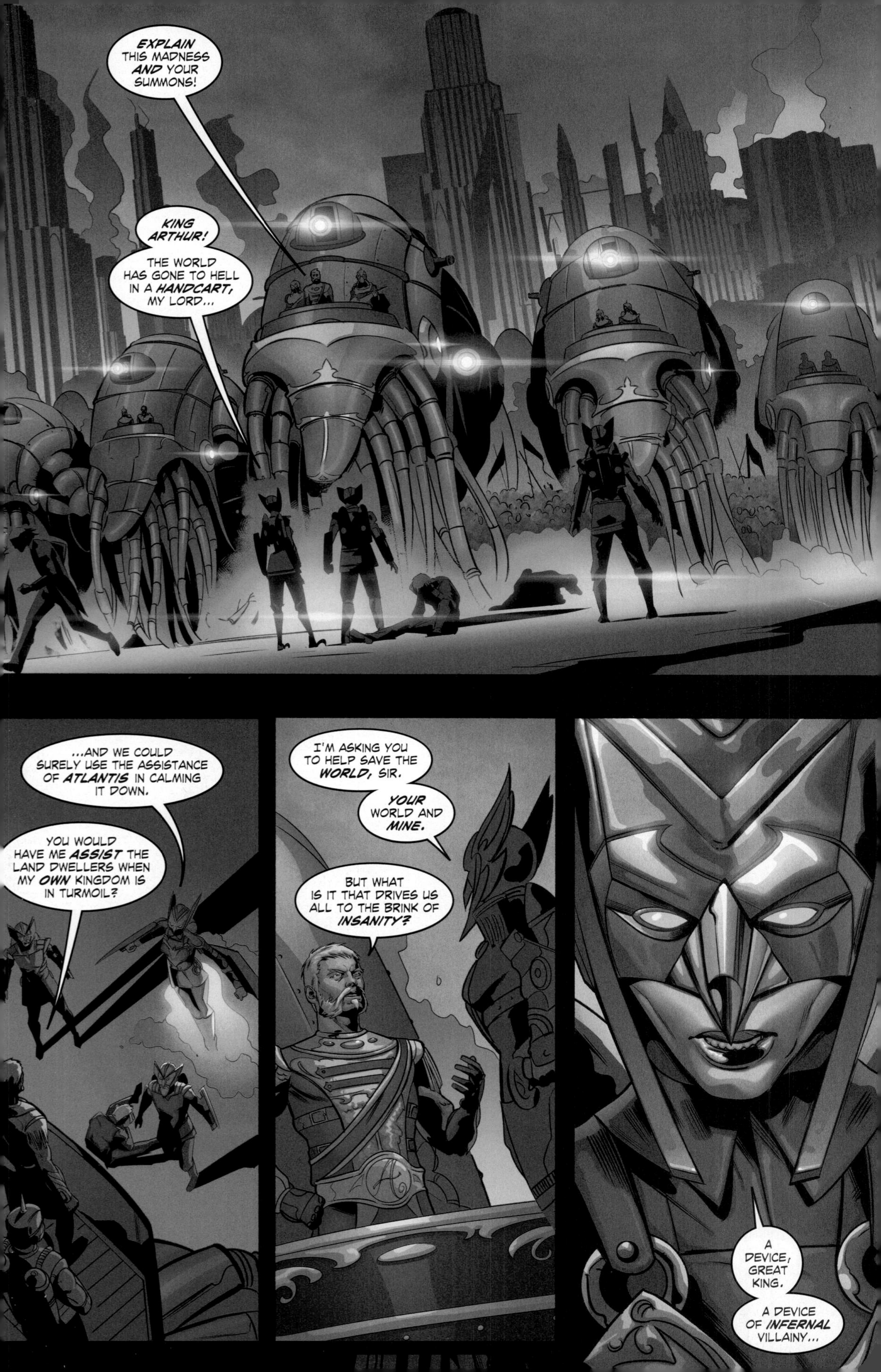
EXPLAIN THIS MADNESS AND YOUR SUMMONS!
KING ARTHUR!
THE WORLD HAS GONE TO HELL IN A HANDCART, MY LORD...
...AND WE COULD SURELY USE THE ASSISTANCE OF ATLANTIS IN CALMING IT DOWN.
YOU WOULD HAVE ME ASSIST THE LAND DWELLERS WHEN MY OWN KINGDOM IS IN TURMOIL?
I'M ASKING YOU TO HELP SAVE THE WORLD, SIR.
YOUR WORLD AND MINE.
BUT WHAT IS IT THAT DRIVES US ALL TO THE BRINK OF INSANITY?
A DEVICE, GREAT KING.
A DEVICE OF INFERNAL VILLAINY...

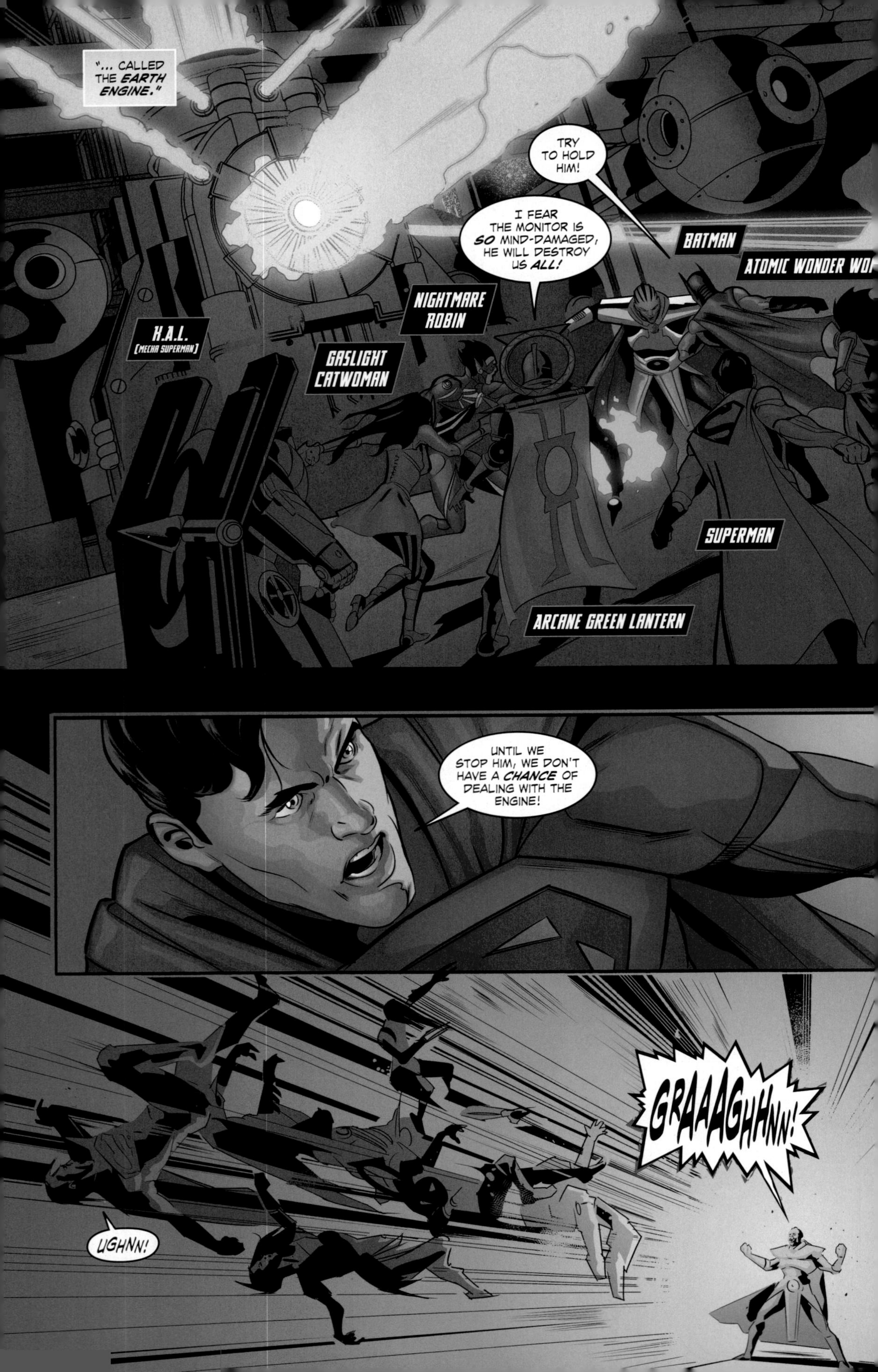
"... CALLED THE *EARTH ENGINE.*"
TRY TO HOLD HIM!
I FEAR THE MONITOR IS *SO* MIND-DAMAGED, HE WILL DESTROY US *ALL!*
BATMAN
ATOMIC WONDER WO
NIGHTMARE ROBIN
H.A.L. [MECHA SUPERMAN]
GASLIGHT CATWOMAN
SUPERMAN
ARCANE GREEN LANTERN
UNTIL WE STOP HIM, WE DON'T HAVE A *CHANCE* OF DEALING WITH THE ENGINE!
GRAAAGHHNN!
UGHNN!

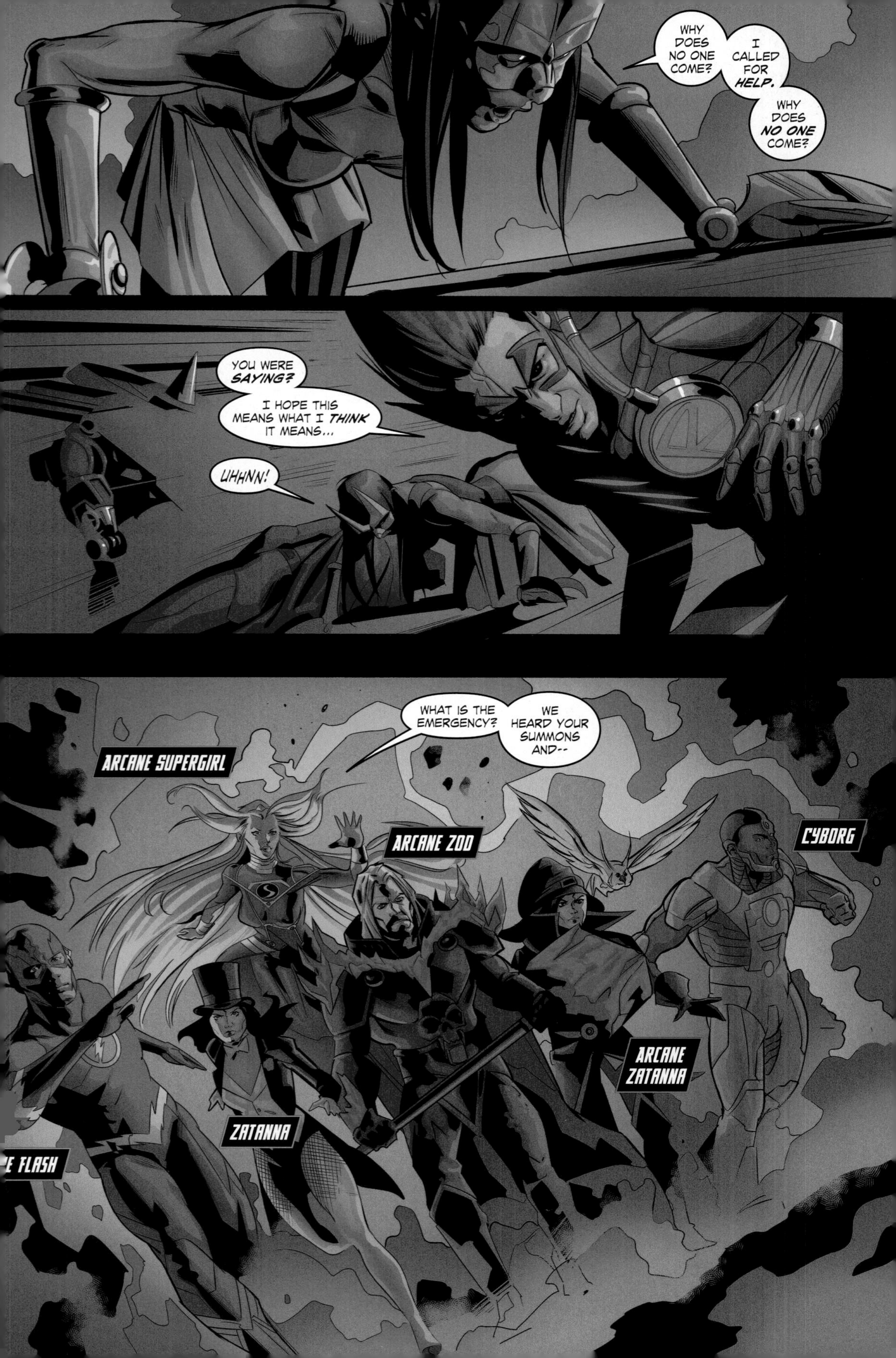
WHY DOES NO ONE COME?
I CALLED FOR HELP.
WHY DOES NO ONE COME?
YOU WERE SAYING?
I HOPE THIS MEANS WHAT I THINK IT MEANS...
UHHNN!
WHAT IS THE EMERGENCY?
WE HEARD YOUR SUMMONS AND--
ARCANE SUPERGIRL
ARCANE ZOD
CYBORG
ARCANE ZATANNA
ZATANNA
E FLASH

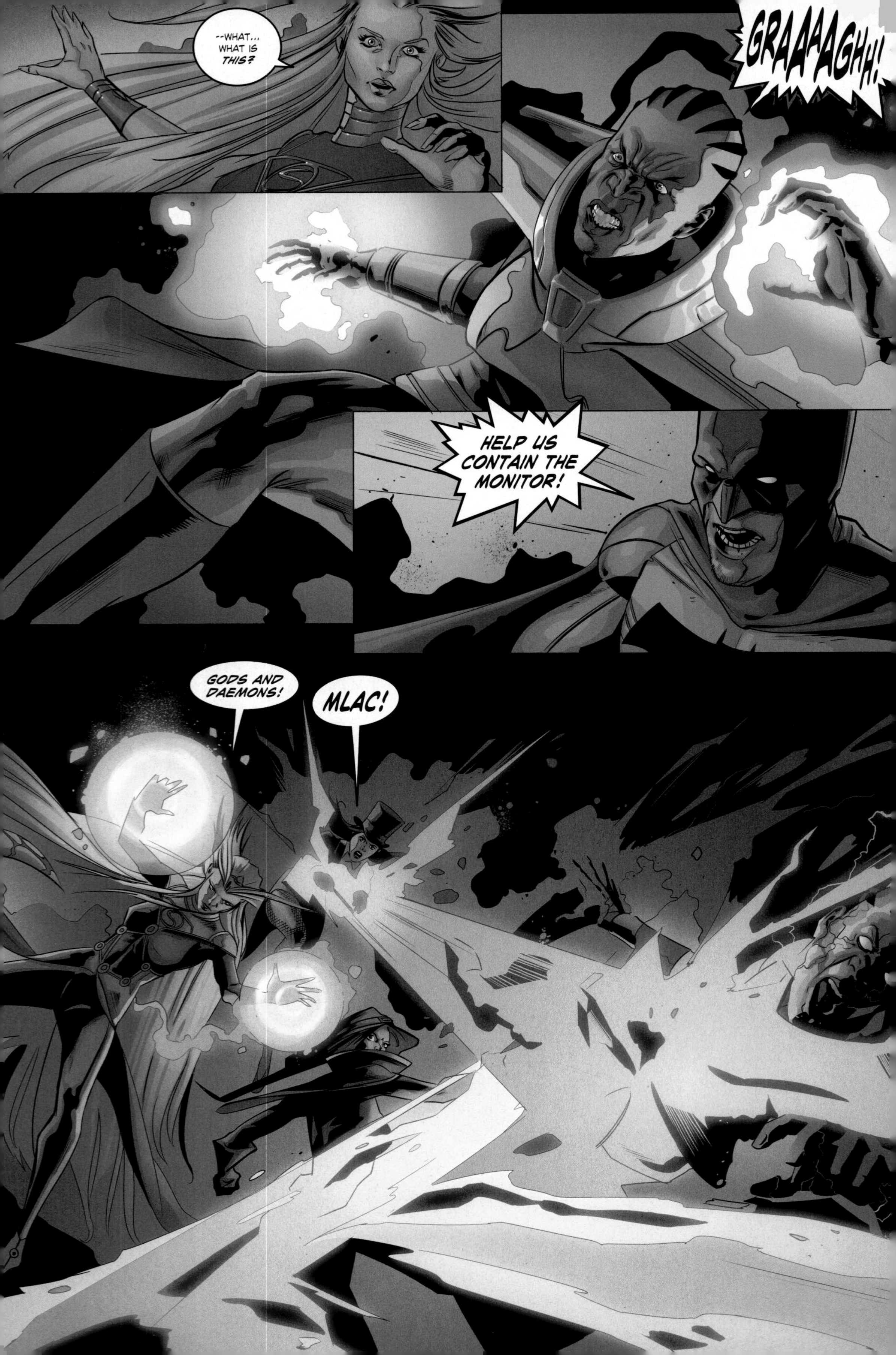
--WHAT... WHAT IS THIS?
GRAAAAAGHH!
HELP US CONTAIN THE MONITOR!
GODS AND DAEMONS!
MLAC!

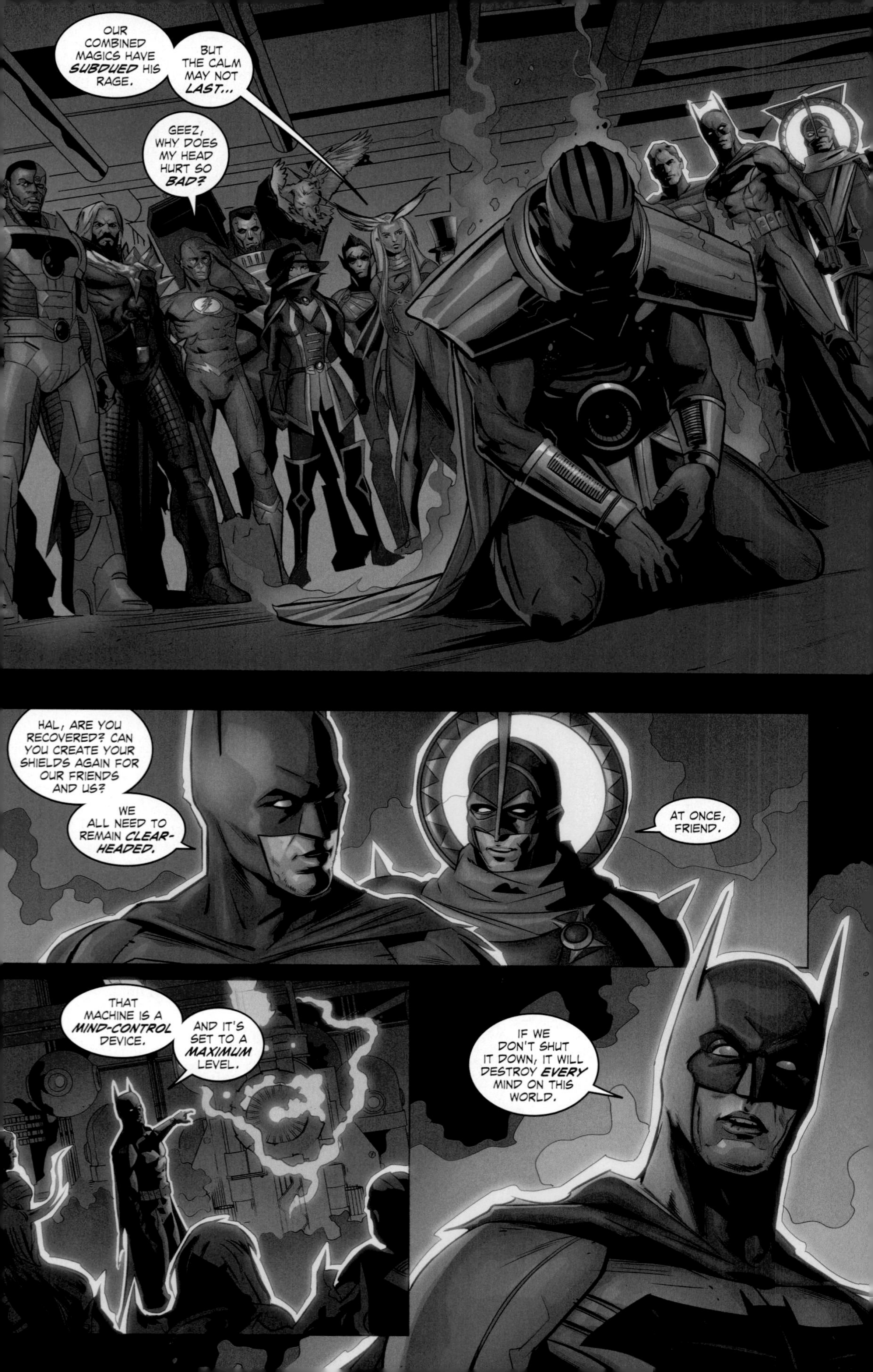
OUR COMBINED MAGICS HAVE SUBDUED HIS RAGE.
BUT THE CALM MAY NOT LAST...
GEEZ, WHY DOES MY HEAD HURT SO BAD?
HAL, ARE YOU RECOVERED? CAN YOU CREATE YOUR SHIELDS AGAIN FOR OUR FRIENDS AND US?
WE ALL NEED TO REMAIN CLEAR-HEADED.
AT ONCE, FRIEND.
THAT MACHINE IS A MIND-CONTROL DEVICE.
AND IT'S SET TO A MAXIMUM LEVEL.
IF WE DON'T SHUT IT DOWN, IT WILL DESTROY EVERY MIND ON THIS WORLD.

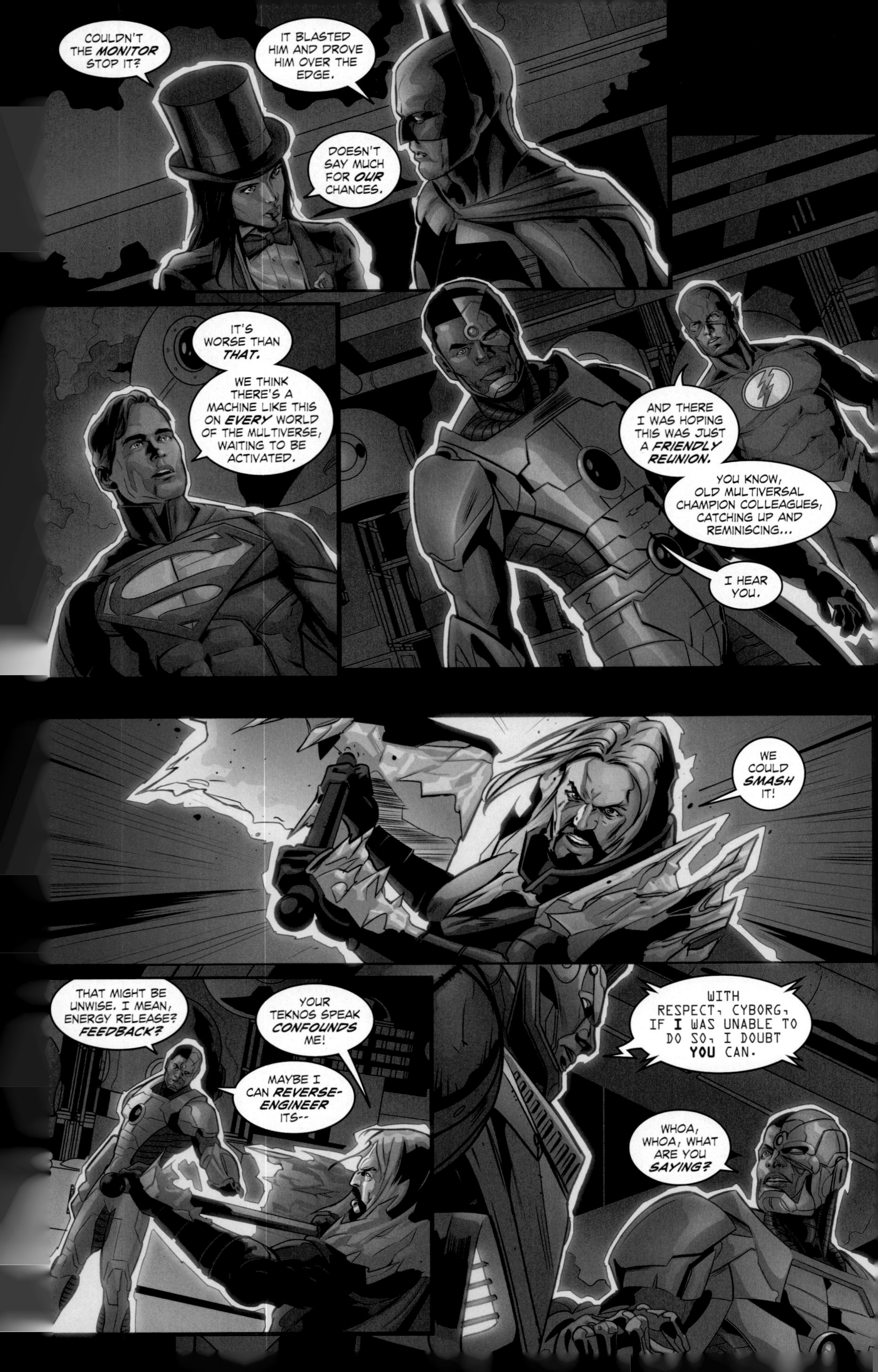
COULDN'T THE MONITOR STOP IT?
IT BLASTED HIM AND DROVE HIM OVER THE EDGE.
DOESN'T SAY MUCH FOR OUR CHANCES.
IT'S WORSE THAN THAT.
WE THINK THERE'S A MACHINE LIKE THIS ON EVERY WORLD OF THE MULTIVERSE, WAITING TO BE ACTIVATED.
AND THERE I WAS HOPING THIS WAS JUST A FRIENDLY REUNION.
YOU KNOW, OLD MULTIVERSAL CHAMPION COLLEAGUES, CATCHING UP AND REMINISCING...
I HEAR YOU.
WE COULD SMASH IT!
THAT MIGHT BE UNWISE. I MEAN, ENERGY RELEASE? FEEDBACK?
YOUR TEKNOS SPEAK CONFOUNDS ME!
MAYBE I CAN REVERSE-ENGINEER ITS--
WITH RESPECT, CYBORG, IF I WAS UNABLE TO DO SO, I DOUBT YOU CAN.
WHOA, WHOA, WHAT ARE YOU SAYING?

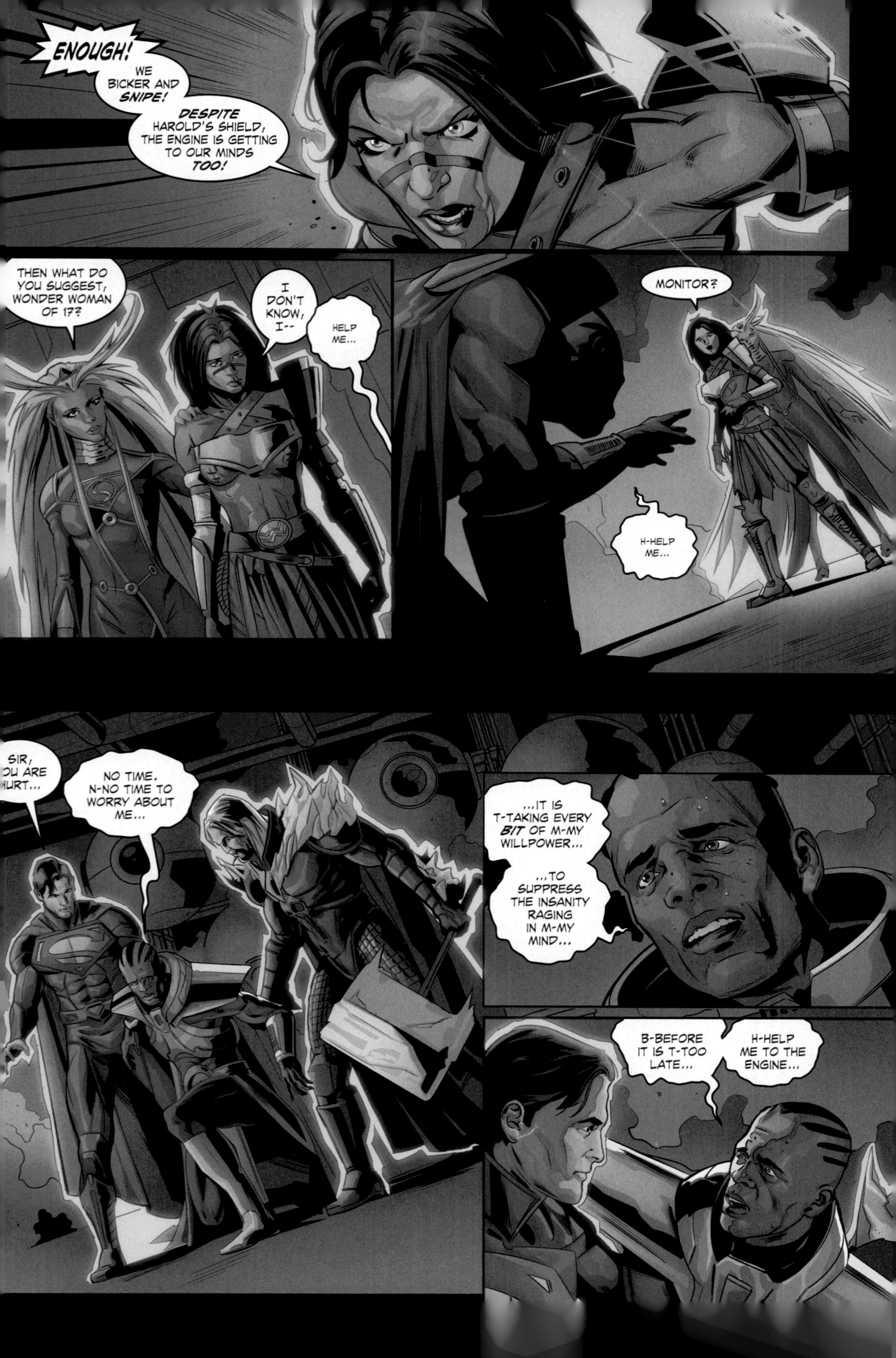
ENOUGH!
WE BICKER AND SNIPE!
DESPITE HAROLD'S SHIELD, THE ENGINE IS GETTING TO OUR MINDS TOO!
THEN WHAT DO YOU SUGGEST, WONDER WOMAN OF 17?
I DON'T KNOW, I--
HELP ME...
MONITOR?
H-HELP ME...
SIR, YOU ARE HURT...
NO TIME. N-NO TIME TO WORRY ABOUT ME...
...IT IS T-TAKING EVERY BIT OF M-MY WILLPOWER...
...TO SUPPRESS THE INSANITY RAGING IN M-MY MIND...
B-BEFORE IT IS T-TOO LATE...
H-HELP ME TO THE ENGINE...

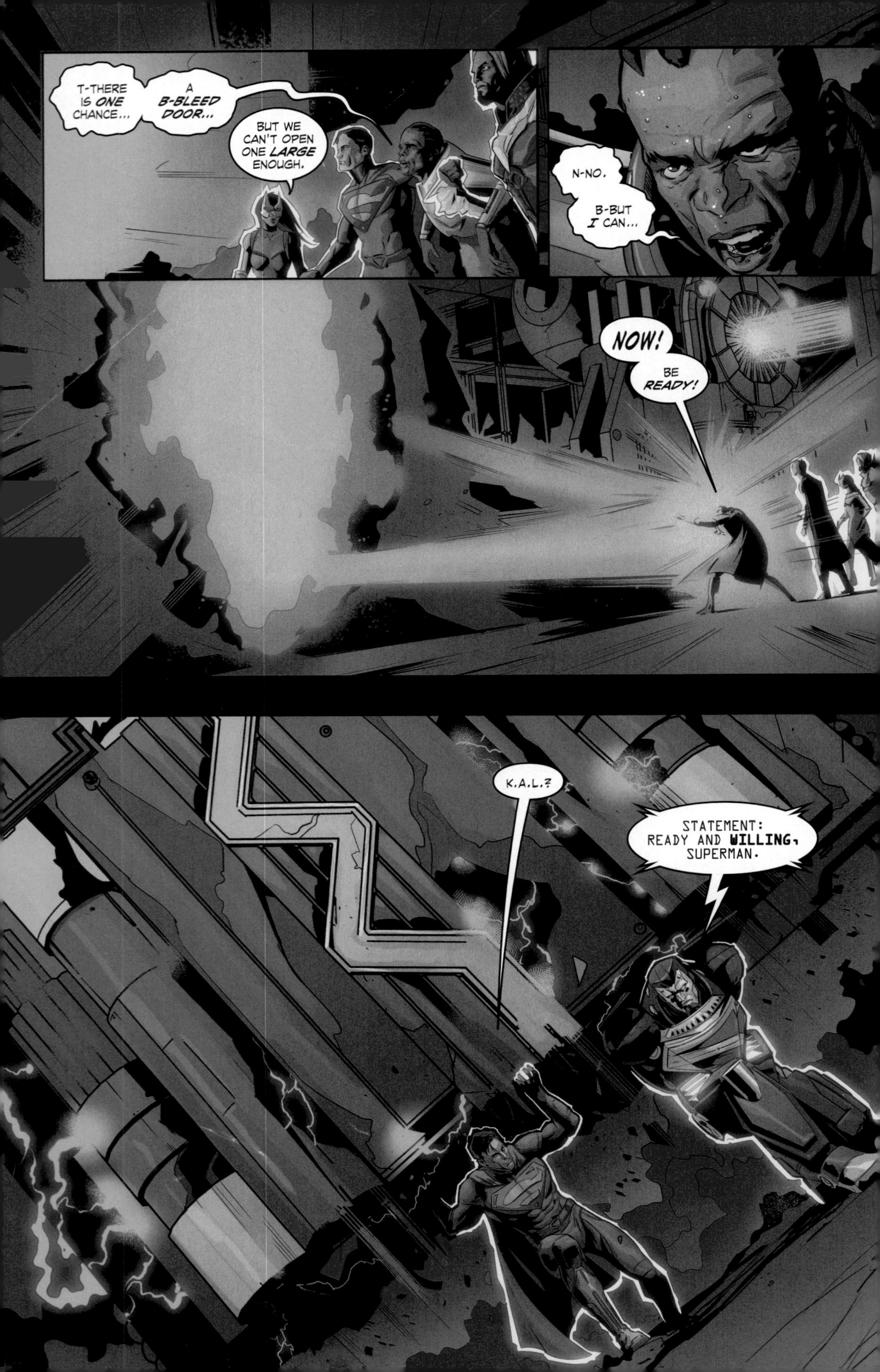
T-THERE IS ONE CHANCE...
A B-BLEED DOOR...
BUT WE CAN'T OPEN ONE LARGE ENOUGH.
N-NO.
B-BUT I CAN...
NOW!
BE READY!
K.A.L.?
STATEMENT: READY AND WILLING, SUPERMAN.

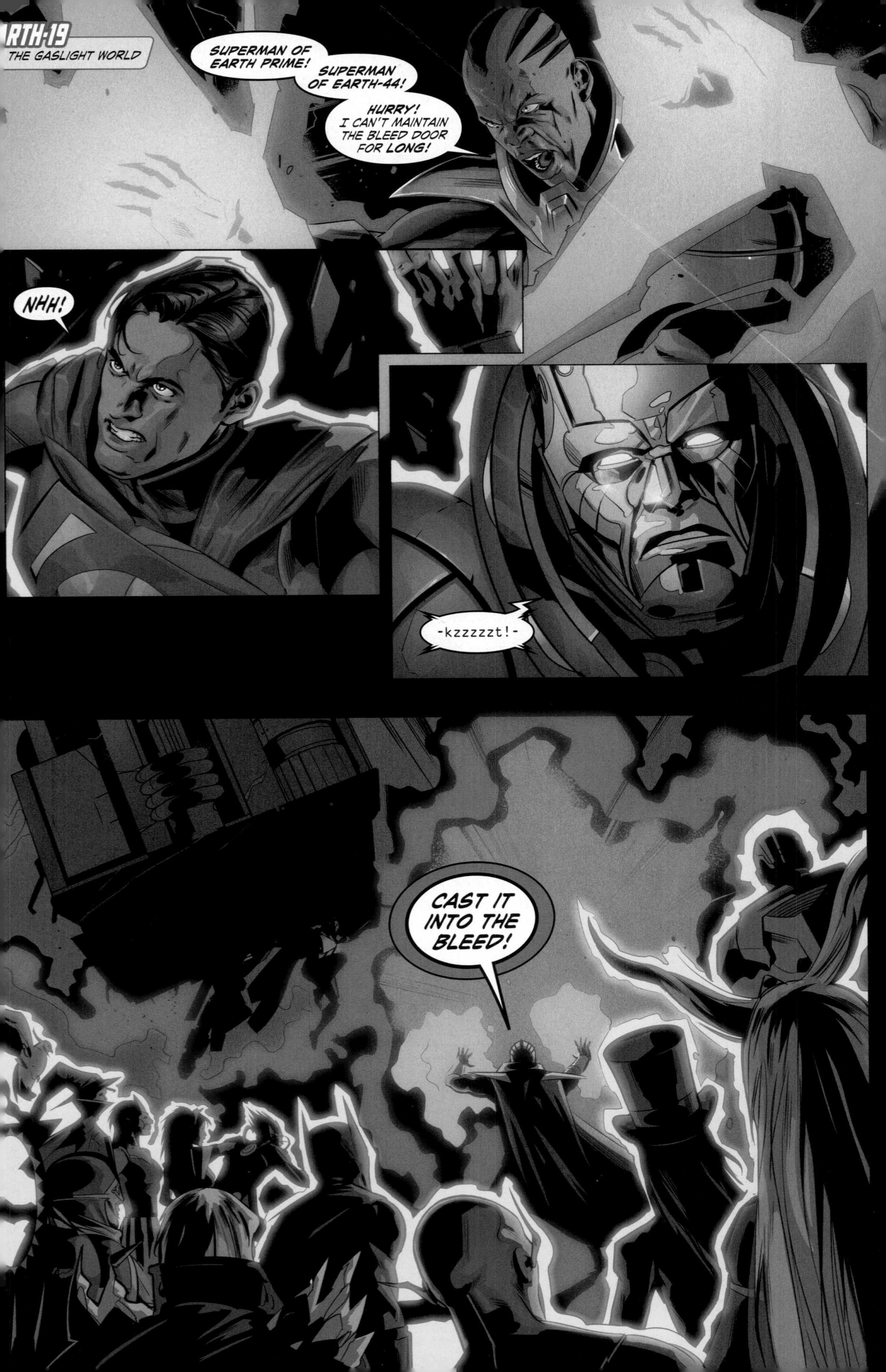
RTH-19
THE GASLIGHT WORLD
SUPERMAN OF EARTH PRIME!
SUPERMAN OF EARTH-44!
HURRY! I CAN'T MAINTAIN THE BLEED DOOR FOR LONG!
NHH!
-kzzzzzt!-
CAST IT INTO THE BLEED!

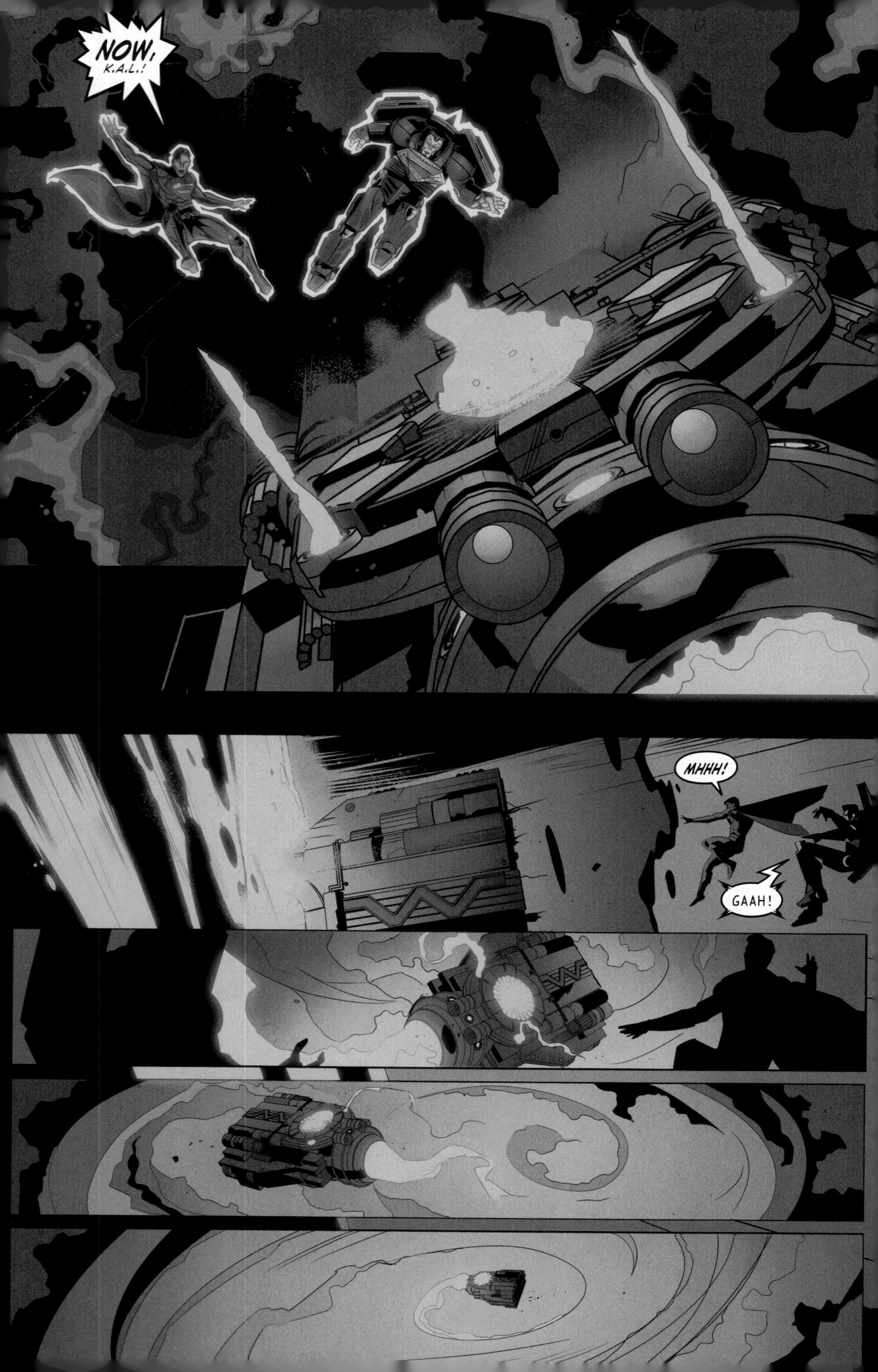
NOW, K.A.L.!
MHHH!
GAAH!

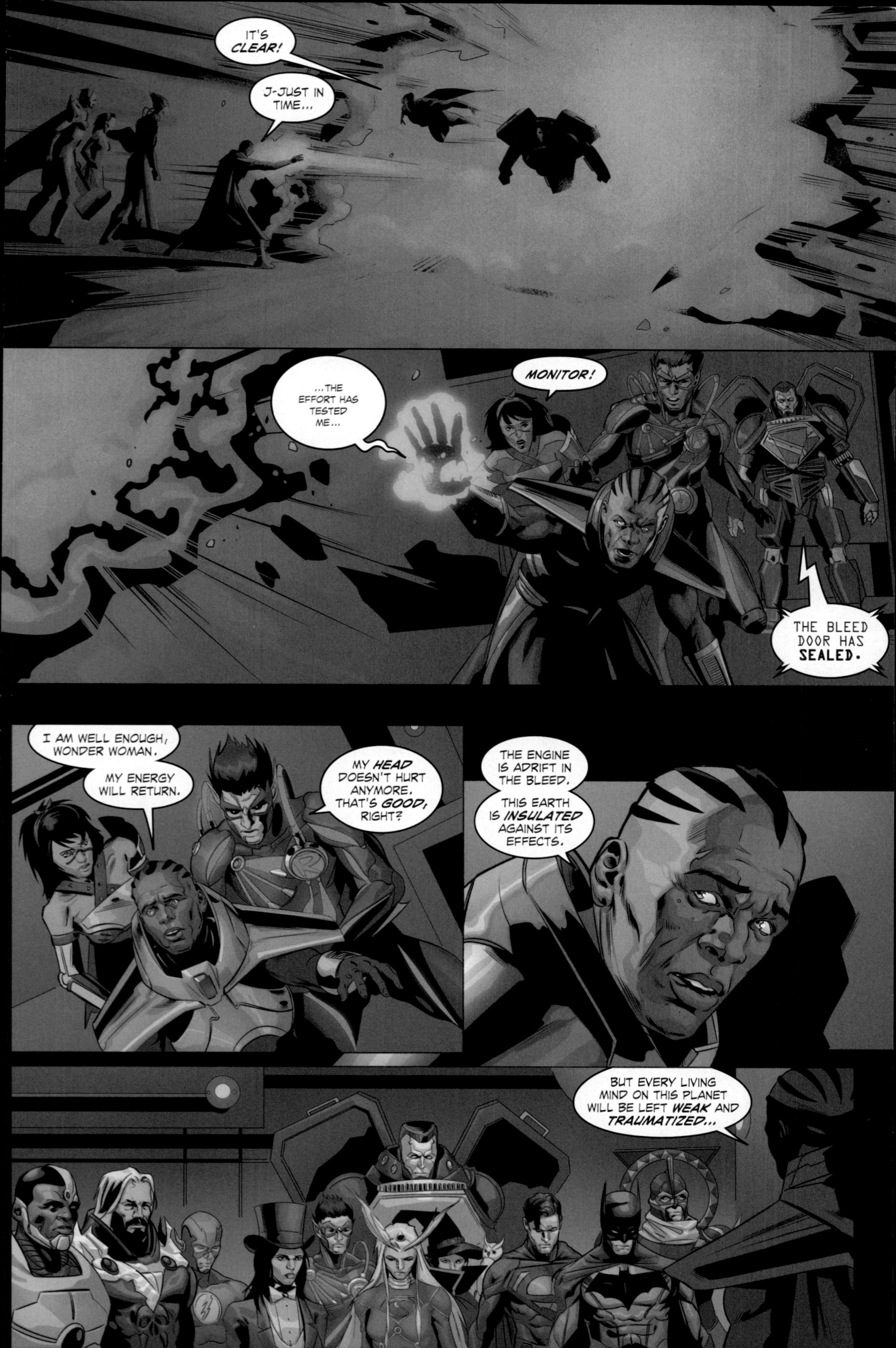
IT'S CLEAR!
J-JUST IN TIME...
...THE EFFORT HAS TESTED ME...
MONITOR!
THE BLEED DOOR HAS SEALED.
I AM WELL ENOUGH, WONDER WOMAN.
MY ENERGY WILL RETURN.
MY HEAD DOESN'T HURT ANYMORE. THAT'S GOOD, RIGHT?
THE ENGINE IS ADRIFT IN THE BLEED.
THIS EARTH IS INSULATED AGAINST ITS EFFECTS.
BUT EVERY LIVING MIND ON THIS PLANET WILL BE LEFT WEAK AND TRAUMATIZED...

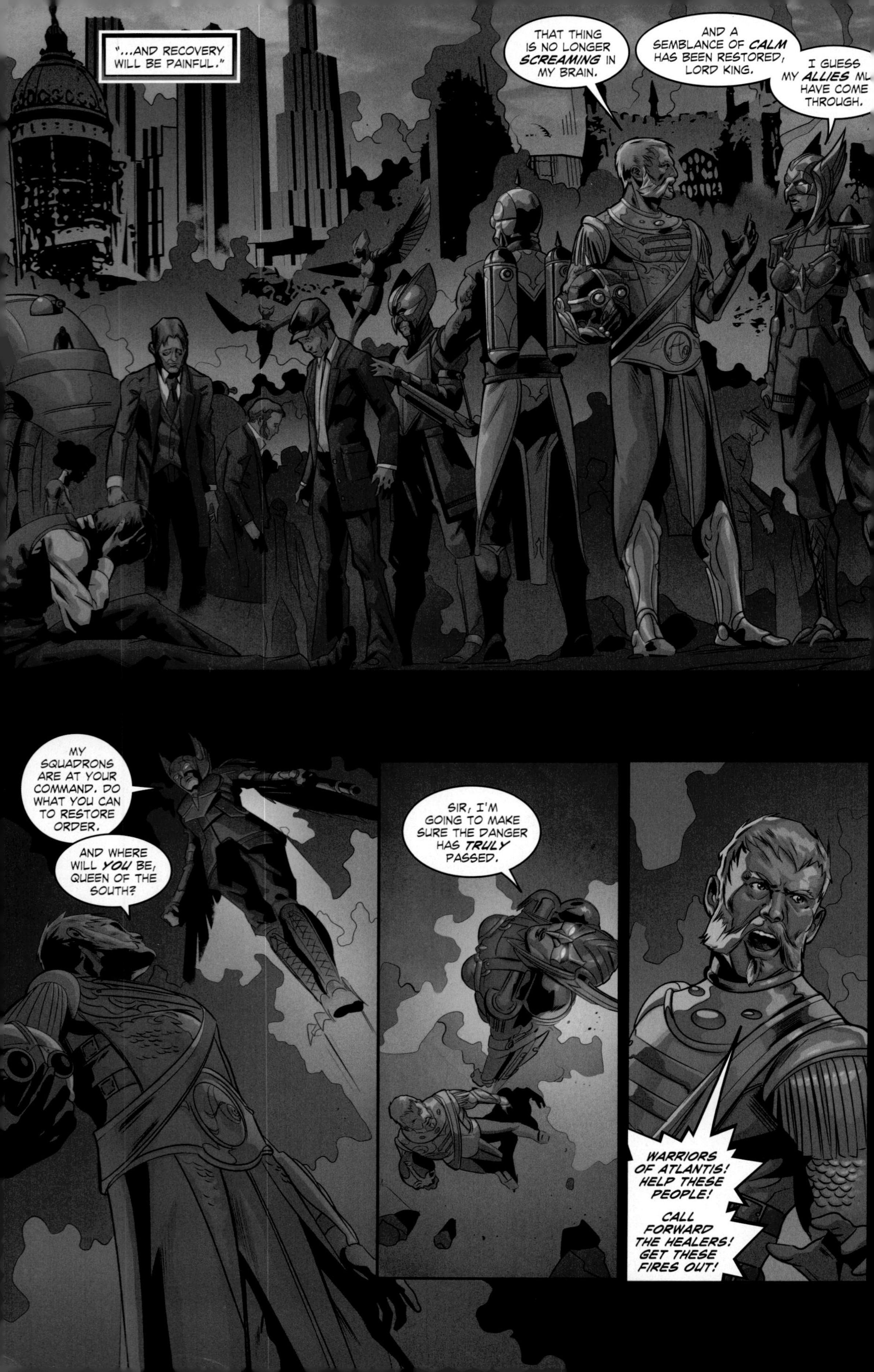
"...AND RECOVERY WILL BE PAINFUL."
THAT THING IS NO LONGER SCREAMING IN MY BRAIN.
AND A SEMBLANCE OF CALM HAS BEEN RESTORED, LORD KING.
I GUESS MY ALLIES MU HAVE COME THROUGH.
MY SQUADRONS ARE AT YOUR COMMAND. DO WHAT YOU CAN TO RESTORE ORDER.
AND WHERE WILL YOU BE, QUEEN OF THE SOUTH?
SIR, I'M GOING TO MAKE SURE THE DANGER HAS TRULY PASSED.
WARRIORS OF ATLANTIS! HELP THESE PEOPLE!
CALL FORWARD THE HEALERS! GET THESE FIRES OUT!

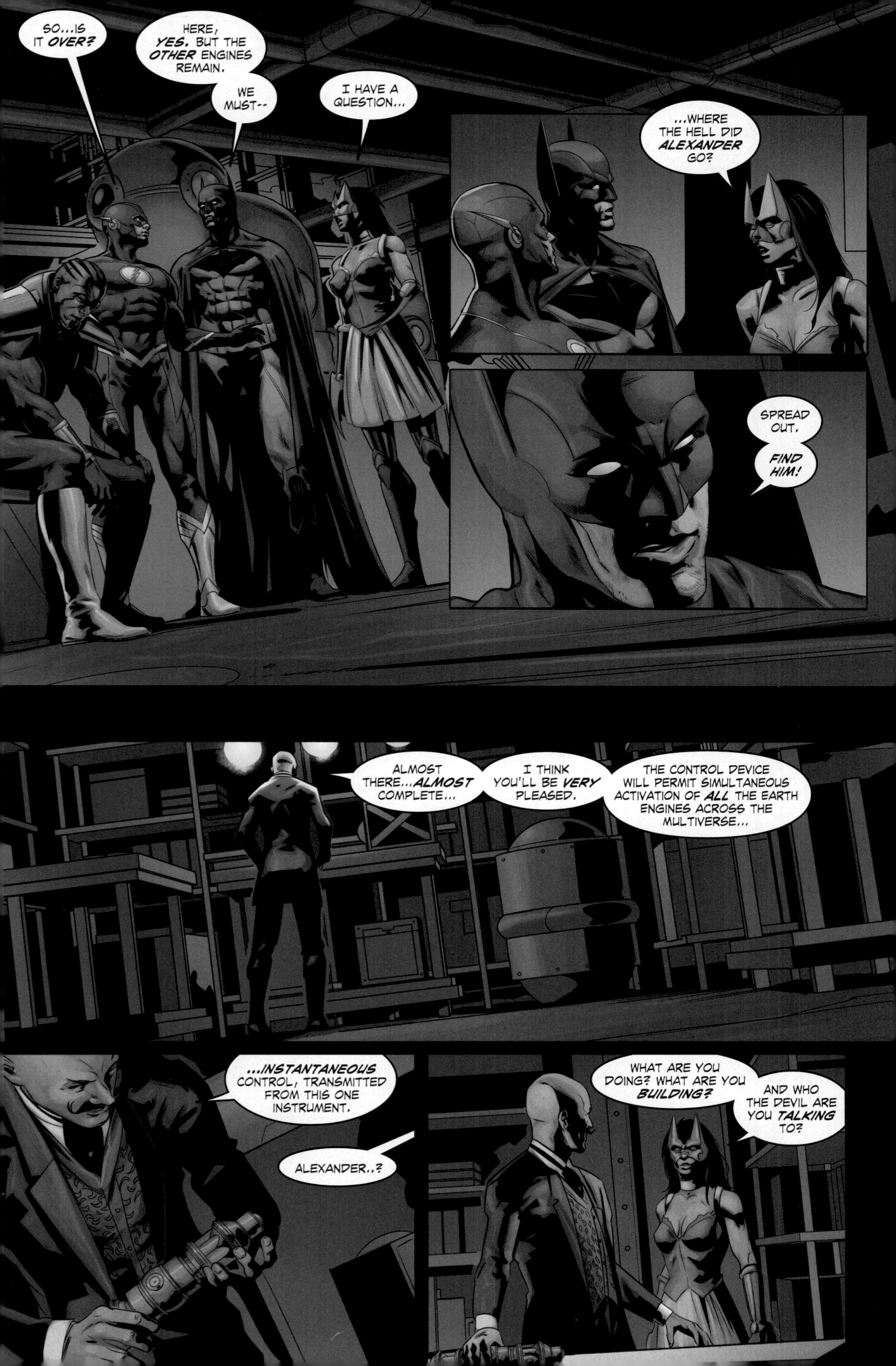
SO...IS IT OVER?
HERE, YES. BUT THE OTHER ENGINES REMAIN.
WE MUST--
I HAVE A QUESTION...
...WHERE THE HELL DID ALEXANDER GO?
SPREAD OUT.
FIND HIM!
ALMOST THERE...ALMOST COMPLETE...
I THINK YOU'LL BE VERY PLEASED.
THE CONTROL DEVICE WILL PERMIT SIMULTANEOUS ACTIVATION OF ALL THE EARTH ENGINES ACROSS THE MULTIVERSE...
...INSTANTANEOUS CONTROL, TRANSMITTED FROM THIS ONE INSTRUMENT.
ALEXANDER..?
WHAT ARE YOU DOING? WHAT ARE YOU BUILDING?
AND WHO THE DEVIL ARE YOU TALKING TO?

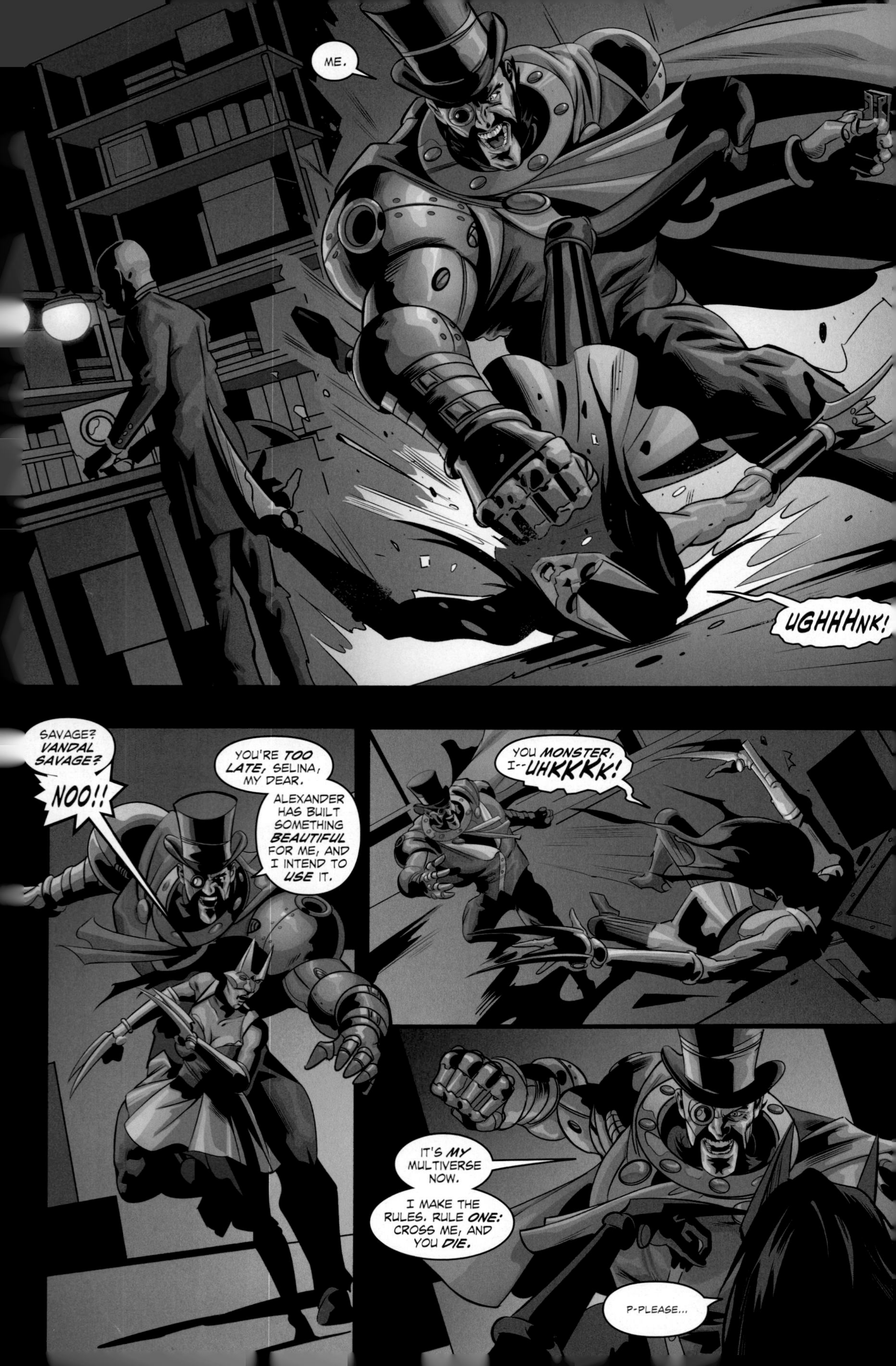
ME.
UGHHHNK!
SAVAGE? VANDAL SAVAGE?
NOO!!
YOU'RE TOO LATE, SELINA, MY DEAR.
ALEXANDER HAS BUILT SOMETHING BEAUTIFUL FOR ME, AND I INTEND TO USE IT.
YOU MONSTER, I--UHKKKK!
IT'S MY MULTIVERSE NOW.
I MAKE THE RULES. RULE ONE: CROSS ME, AND YOU DIE.
P-PLEASE...

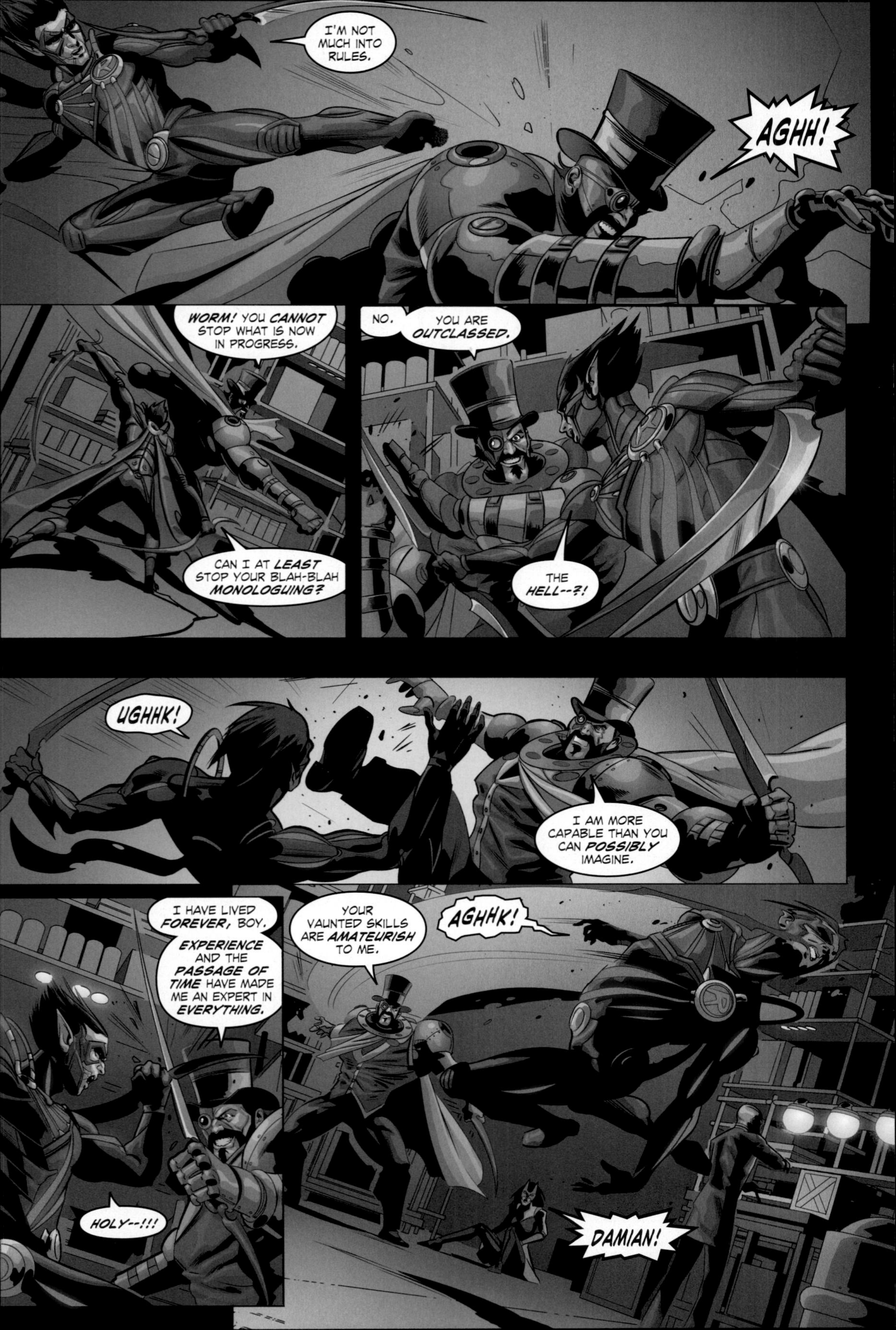
I'M NOT MUCH INTO RULES.
AGHH!
WORM! YOU CANNOT STOP WHAT IS NOW IN PROGRESS.
CAN I AT LEAST STOP YOUR BLAH-BLAH MONOLOGUING?
NO.
YOU ARE OUTCLASSED.
THE HELL--?!
UGHHK!
I AM MORE CAPABLE THAN YOU CAN POSSIBLY IMAGINE.
I HAVE LIVED FOREVER, BOY.
EXPERIENCE AND THE PASSAGE OF TIME HAVE MADE ME AN EXPERT IN EVERYTHING.
HOLY--!!!
YOUR VAUNTED SKILLS ARE AMATEURISH TO ME.
AGHHK!
DAMIAN!

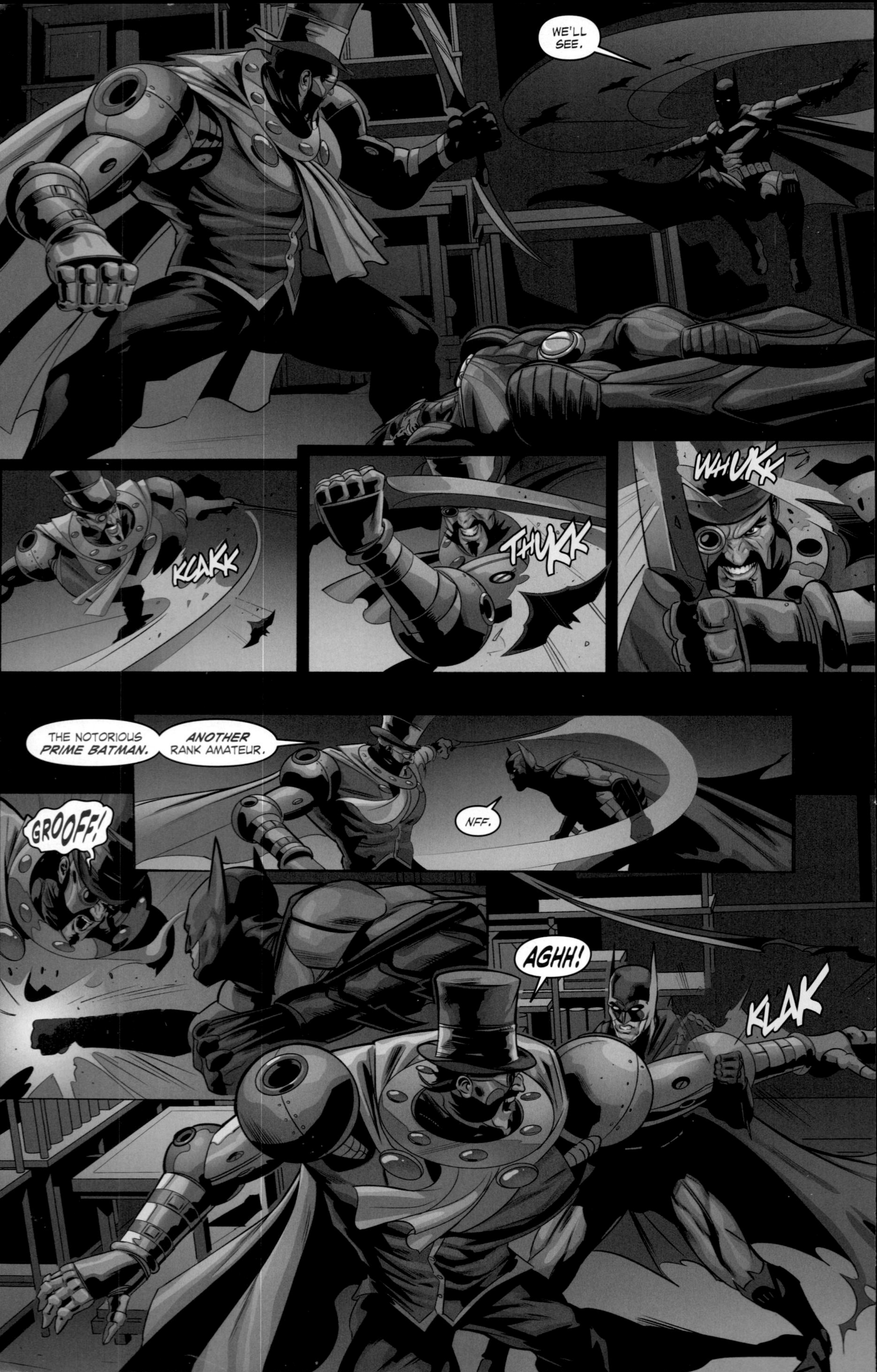
WE'LL SEE.
KLAKK
THUKK
WHUKK
THE NOTORIOUS PRIME BATMAN.
ANOTHER RANK AMATEUR.
NFF.
GROOFF!
AGHH!
KLAK

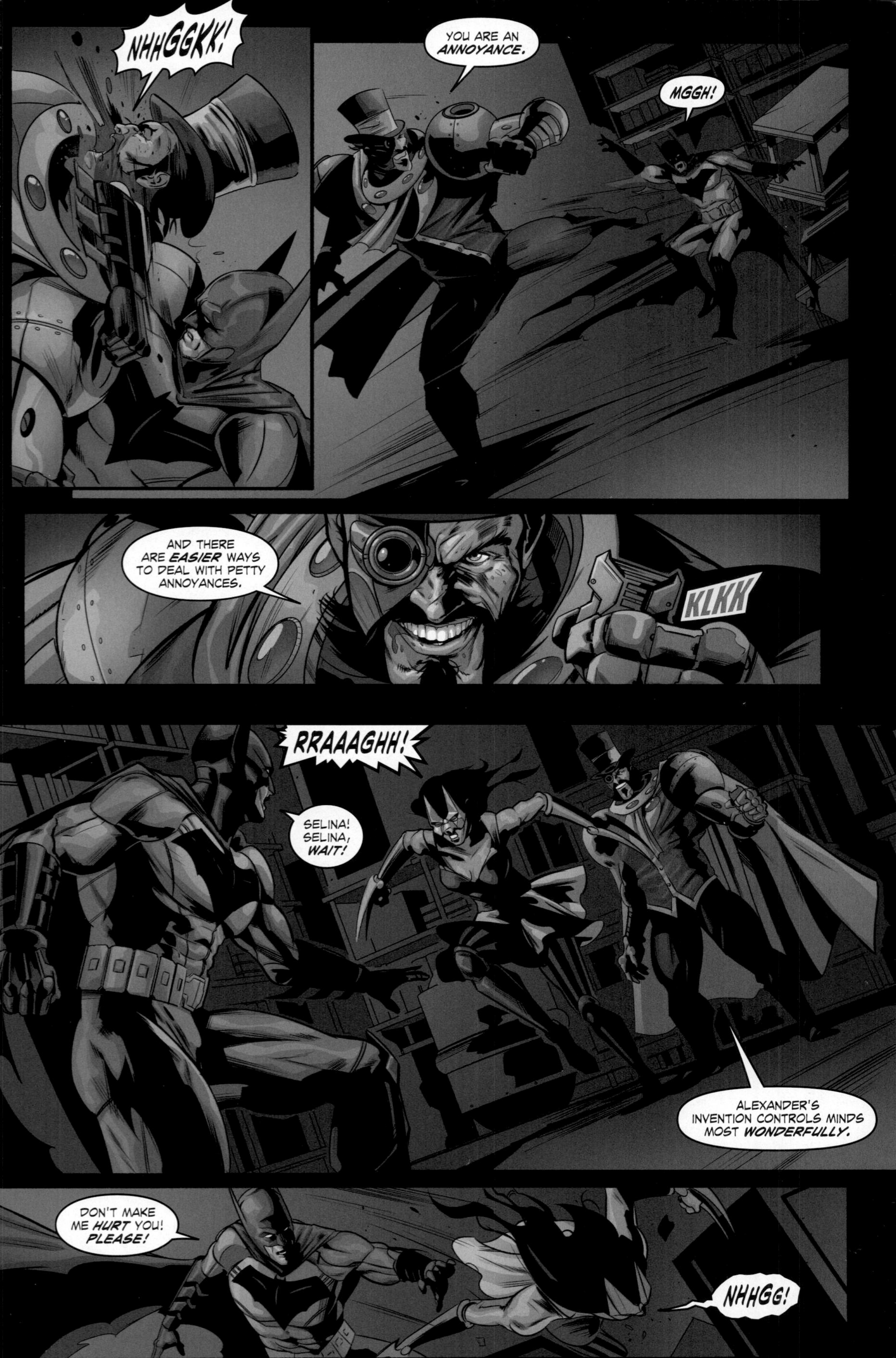
NHHGGKK!
YOU ARE AN ANNOYANCE.
MGGH!
AND THERE ARE EASIER WAYS TO DEAL WITH PETTY ANNOYANCES.
KLKK
RRAAAGHH!
SELINA! SELINA, WAIT!
ALEXANDER'S INVENTION CONTROLS MINDS MOST WONDERFULLY.
DON'T MAKE ME HURT YOU! PLEASE!
NHHGG!

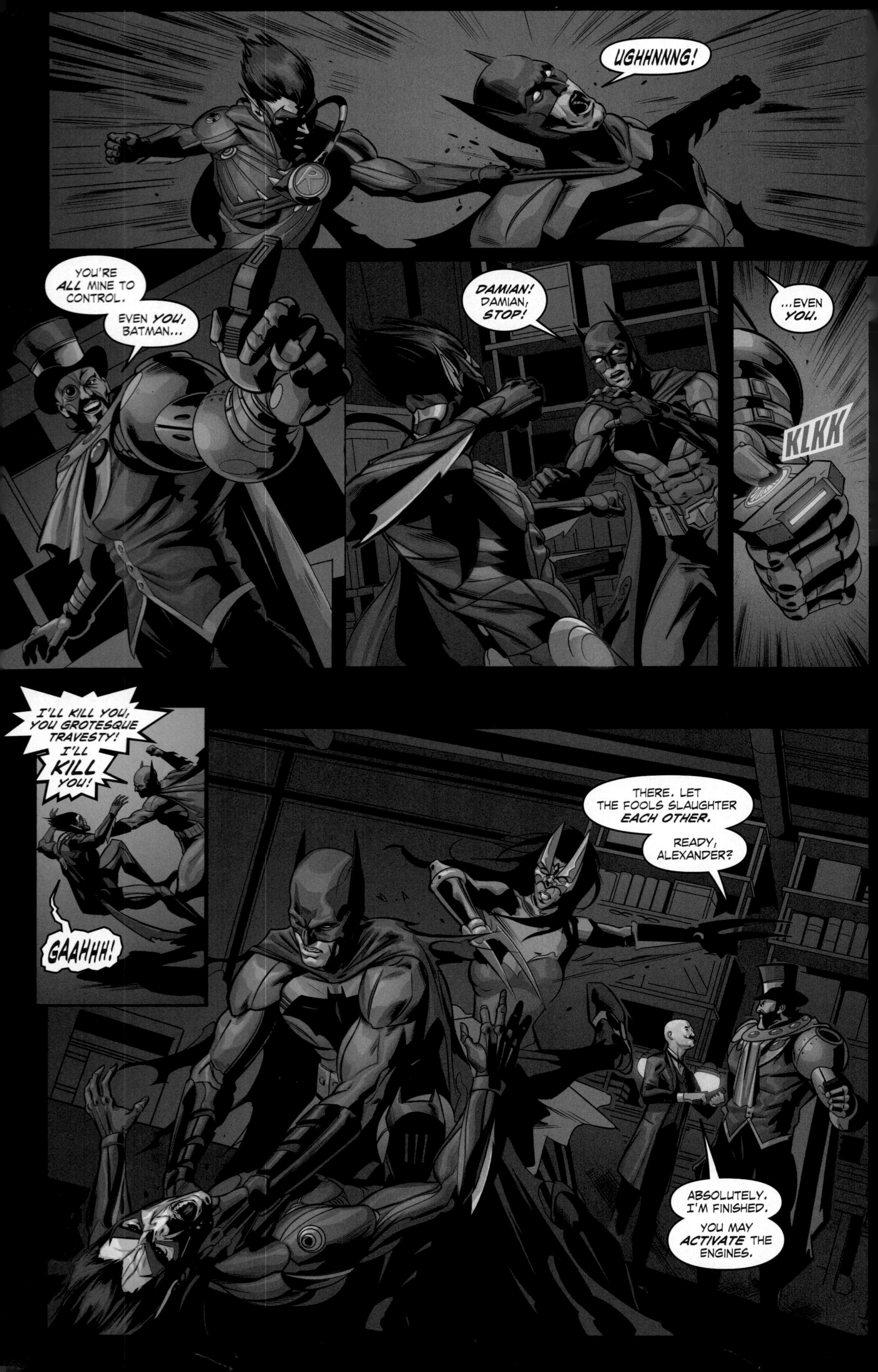

UGHHNNNG!
YOU'RE ALL MINE TO CONTROL.
EVEN YOU, BATMAN...
DAMIAN! DAMIAN, STOP!
...EVEN YOU.
KLKK
I'LL KILL YOU, YOU GROTESQUE TRAVESTY! I'LL KILL YOU!
GAAHHH!
THERE. LET THE FOOLS SLAUGHTER EACH OTHER.
READY, ALEXANDER?
ABSOLUTELY. I'M FINISHED.
YOU MAY ACTIVATE THE ENGINES.

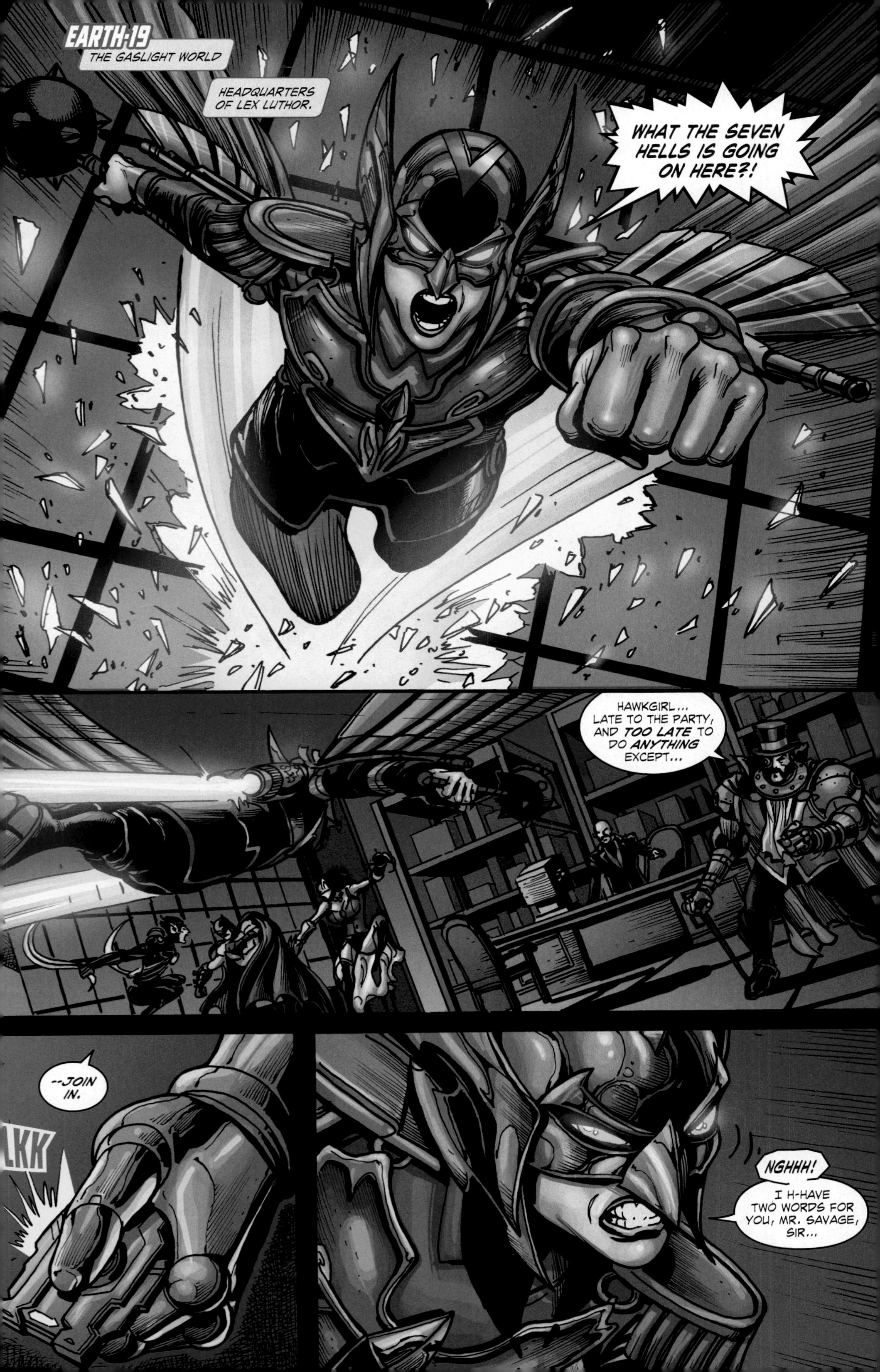

EARTH-19
THE GASLIGHT WORLD
HEADQUARTERS OF LEX LUTHOR.
WHAT THE SEVEN HELLS IS GOING ON HERE?!
HAWKGIRL... LATE TO THE PARTY, AND TOO LATE TO DO ANYTHING EXCEPT...
--JOIN IN.
LKK
NGHHH!
I H-HAVE TWO WORDS FOR YOU, MR. SAVAGE, SIR...

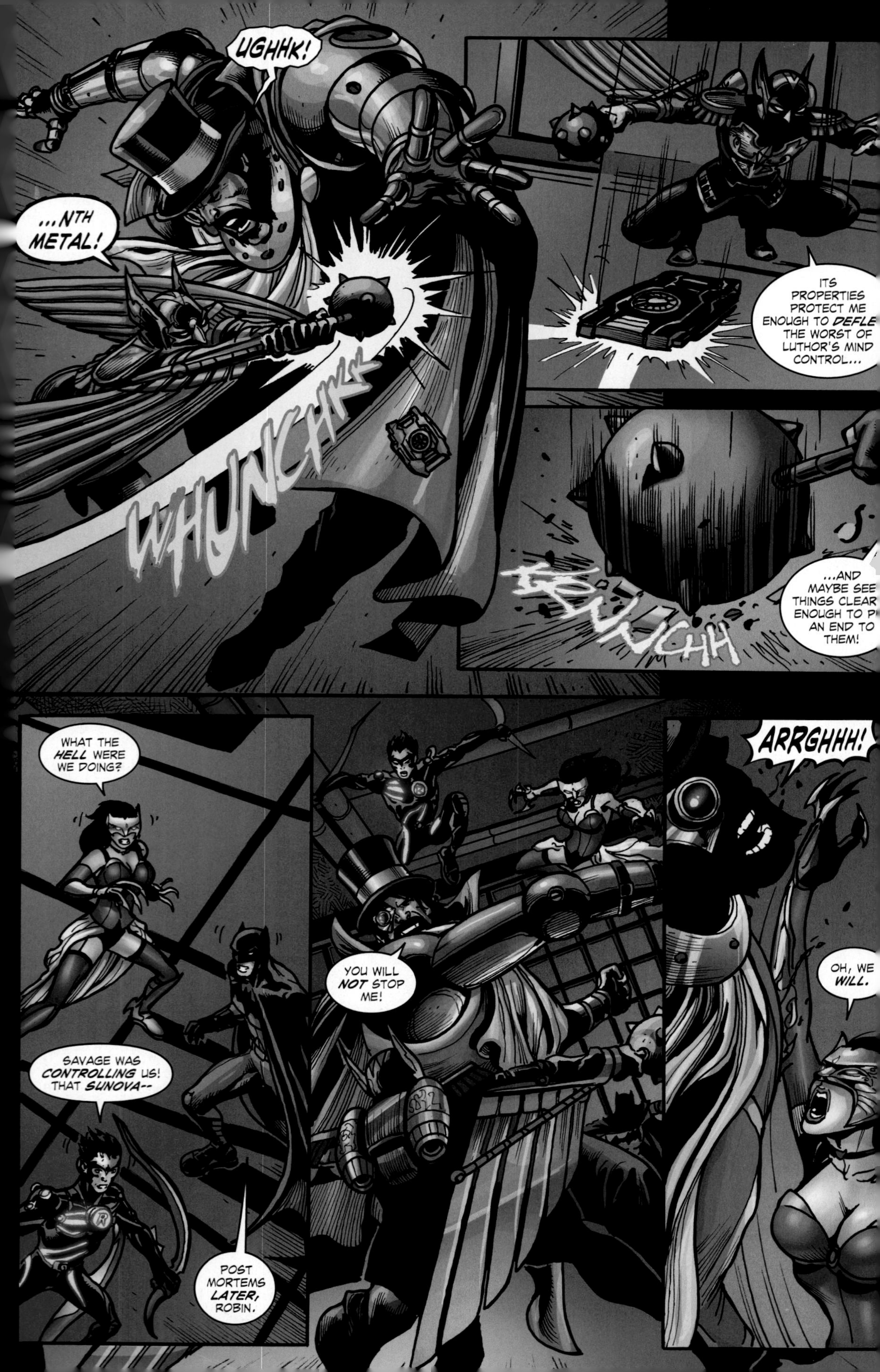
UGHHK!
...NTH METAL!
WHUNCHKK
ITS PROPERTIES PROTECT ME ENOUGH TO DEFLE THE WORST OF LUTHOR'S MIND CONTROL...
KRUNNCHH
...AND MAYBE SEE THINGS CLEAR ENOUGH TO P AN END TO THEM!
WHAT THE HELL WERE WE DOING?
SAVAGE WAS CONTROLLING US! THAT SUNOVA--
POST MORTEMS LATER, ROBIN.
YOU WILL NOT STOP ME!
ARRGHHH!
OH, WE WILL.

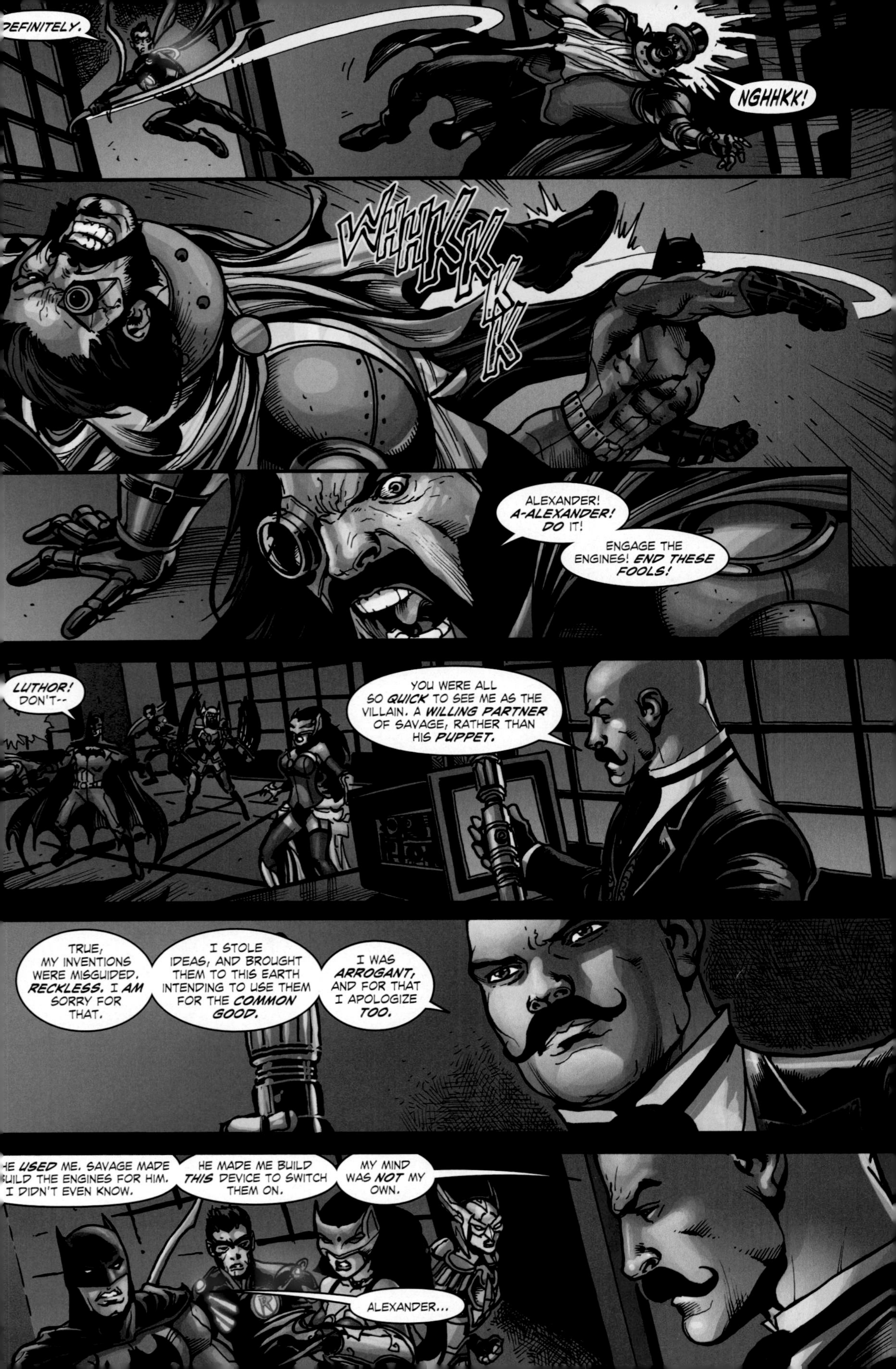
DEFINITELY.
NGHHKK!
WHHKKKK
ALEXANDER! A-ALEXANDER! DO IT!
ENGAGE THE ENGINES! END THESE FOOLS!
LUTHOR! DON'T--
YOU WERE ALL SO QUICK TO SEE ME AS THE VILLAIN. A WILLING PARTNER OF SAVAGE, RATHER THAN HIS PUPPET.
TRUE, MY INVENTIONS WERE MISGUIDED. RECKLESS. I AM SORRY FOR THAT.
I STOLE IDEAS, AND BROUGHT THEM TO THIS EARTH INTENDING TO USE THEM FOR THE COMMON GOOD.
I WAS ARROGANT, AND FOR THAT I APOLOGIZE TOO.
HE USED ME. SAVAGE MADE BUILD THE ENGINES FOR HIM. I DIDN'T EVEN KNOW.
HE MADE ME BUILD THIS DEVICE TO SWITCH THEM ON.
MY MIND WAS NOT MY OWN.
ALEXANDER...

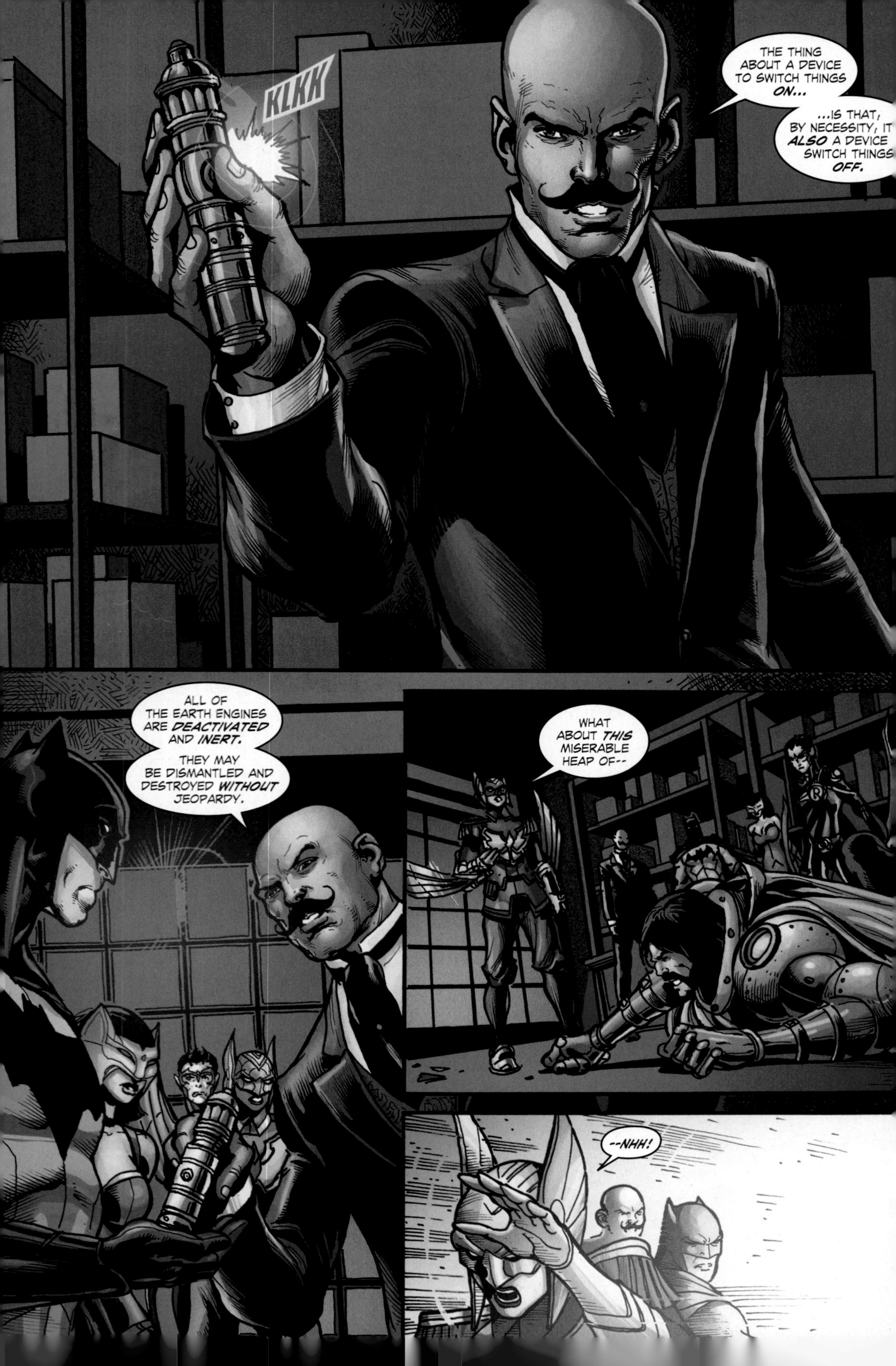
KLKK
THE THING ABOUT A DEVICE TO SWITCH THINGS ON...
...IS THAT, BY NECESSITY, IT ALSO A DEVICE SWITCH THINGS OFF.
ALL OF THE EARTH ENGINES ARE DEACTIVATED AND INERT.
THEY MAY BE DISMANTLED AND DESTROYED WITHOUT JEOPARDY.
WHAT ABOUT THIS MISERABLE HEAP OF--
--NHH!

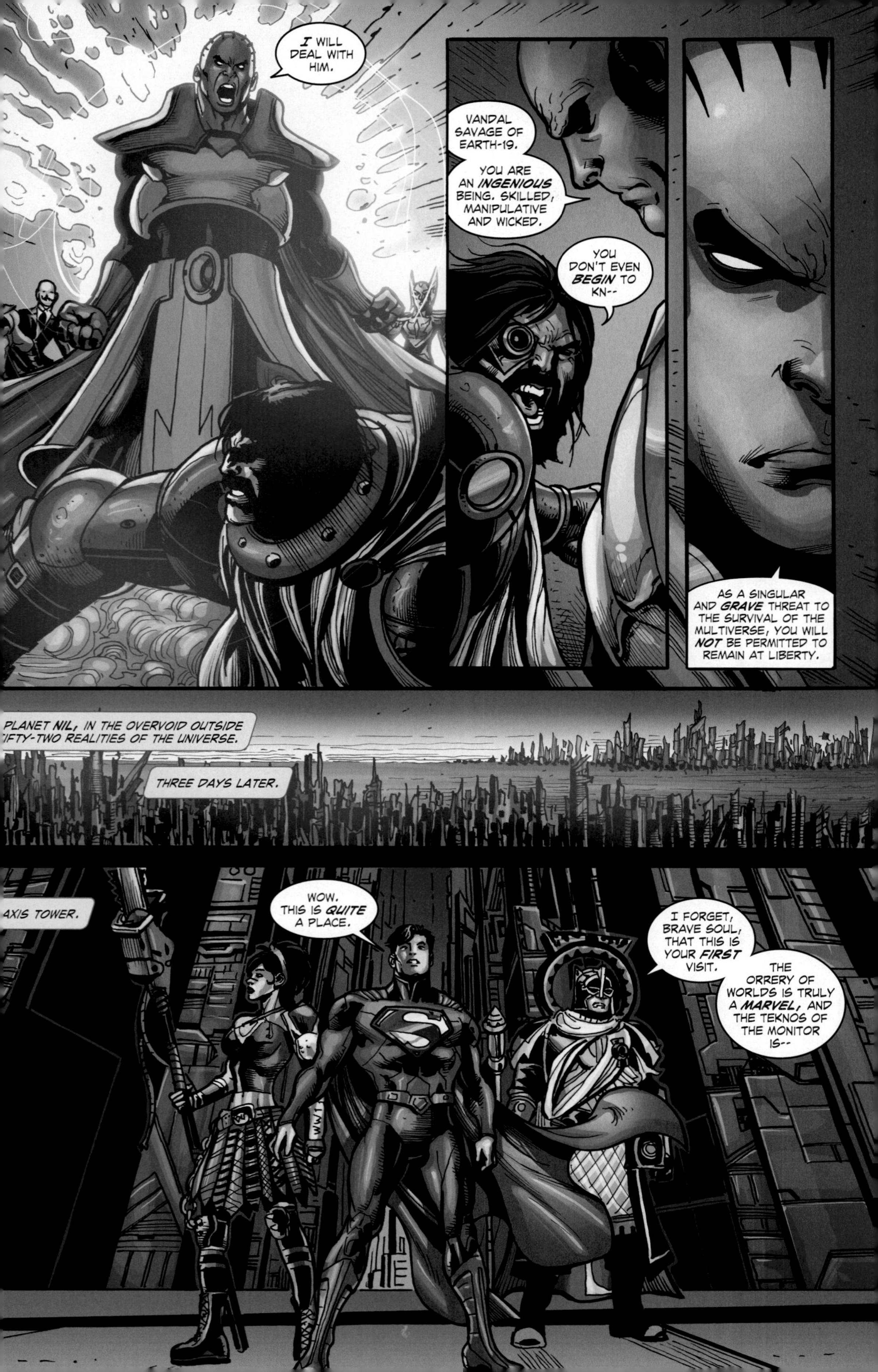
I WILL DEAL WITH HIM.
VANDAL SAVAGE OF EARTH-19.
YOU ARE AN INGENIOUS BEING. SKILLED, MANIPULATIVE AND WICKED.
YOU DON'T EVEN BEGIN TO KN--
AS A SINGULAR AND GRAVE THREAT TO THE SURVIVAL OF THE MULTIVERSE, YOU WILL NOT BE PERMITTED TO REMAIN AT LIBERTY.
PLANET NIL, IN THE OVERVOID OUTSIDE FIFTY-TWO REALITIES OF THE UNIVERSE.
THREE DAYS LATER.
AXIS TOWER.
WOW. THIS IS QUITE A PLACE.
I FORGET, BRAVE SOUL, THAT THIS IS YOUR FIRST VISIT.
THE ORRERY OF WORLDS IS TRULY A MARVEL, AND THE TEKNOS OF THE MONITOR IS--

FRIENDS. CHAMPIONS OF THE MULTIVERSE. *WELCOME.*

MONITOR, WE'RE PLEASED TO REPORT THAT *ALL* THE ENGINES HAVE BEEN DISMANTLED.

SAVAGE'S THREAT IS *OVER.*

GOOD NEWS INDEED.

HAVE YOU BEEN ABLE TO ESTABLISH WHO HE WAS WORKING FOR?

NO, SUPERMAN OF EARTH PRIME...

...HE APPEARS TO HAVE BEEN AN *OPPORTUNIST.*

HIS FORMIDABLE INTELLECT, COUPLED WITH HIS UNFORTUNATE ACCESS TO LUTHOR'S TECHNOLOGY, PRESENTED HIM WITH A CHANCE TO BECOME A *MAJOR POWER* IN THE MULTIVERSE.

AN OPPORTUNITY HE SEIZED WITH *RELISH.*

THAT IS ALL HE HAS *ADMITTED* TO ME.

OF COURSE IT IS POSSIB[L]E THAT HE WA[S] BUT A PAWN [OF] THE MYSTERIO[US] ADVERSARY W[HO] DRIVES THE[?] CRISIS.

IF SO, HE IS *PROTECTING* THOSE SECRETS.

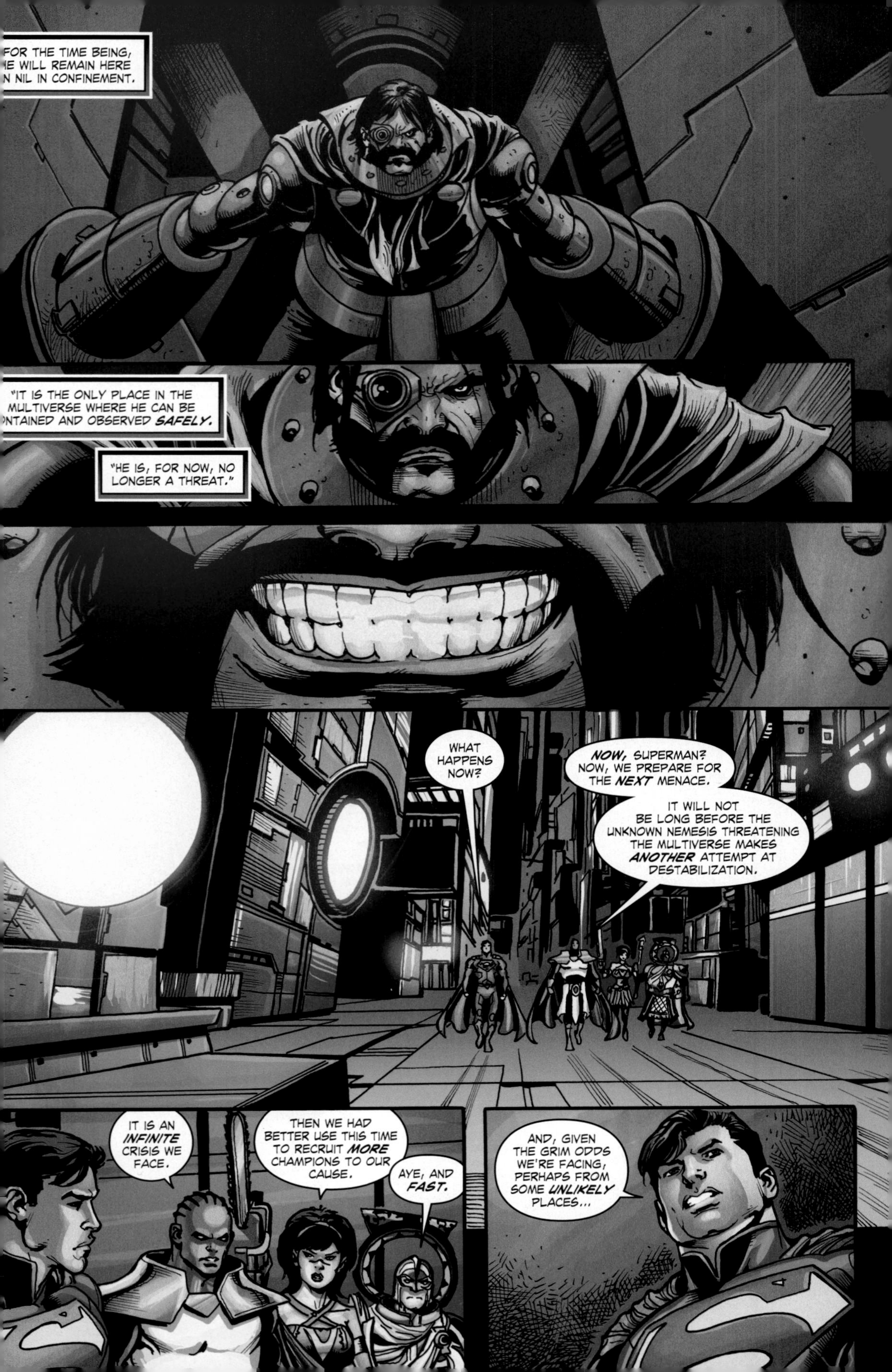
FOR THE TIME BEING, HE WILL REMAIN HERE N NIL IN CONFINEMENT.
"IT IS THE ONLY PLACE IN THE MULTIVERSE WHERE HE CAN BE ONTAINED AND OBSERVED SAFELY.
"HE IS, FOR NOW, NO LONGER A THREAT."
WHAT HAPPENS NOW?
NOW, SUPERMAN? NOW, WE PREPARE FOR THE NEXT MENACE.
IT WILL NOT BE LONG BEFORE THE UNKNOWN NEMESIS THREATENING THE MULTIVERSE MAKES ANOTHER ATTEMPT AT DESTABILIZATION.
IT IS AN INFINITE CRISIS WE FACE.
THEN WE HAD BETTER USE THIS TIME TO RECRUIT MORE CHAMPIONS TO OUR CAUSE.
AYE, AND FAST.
AND, GIVEN THE GRIM ODDS WE'RE FACING, PERHAPS FROM SOME UNLIKELY PLACES...

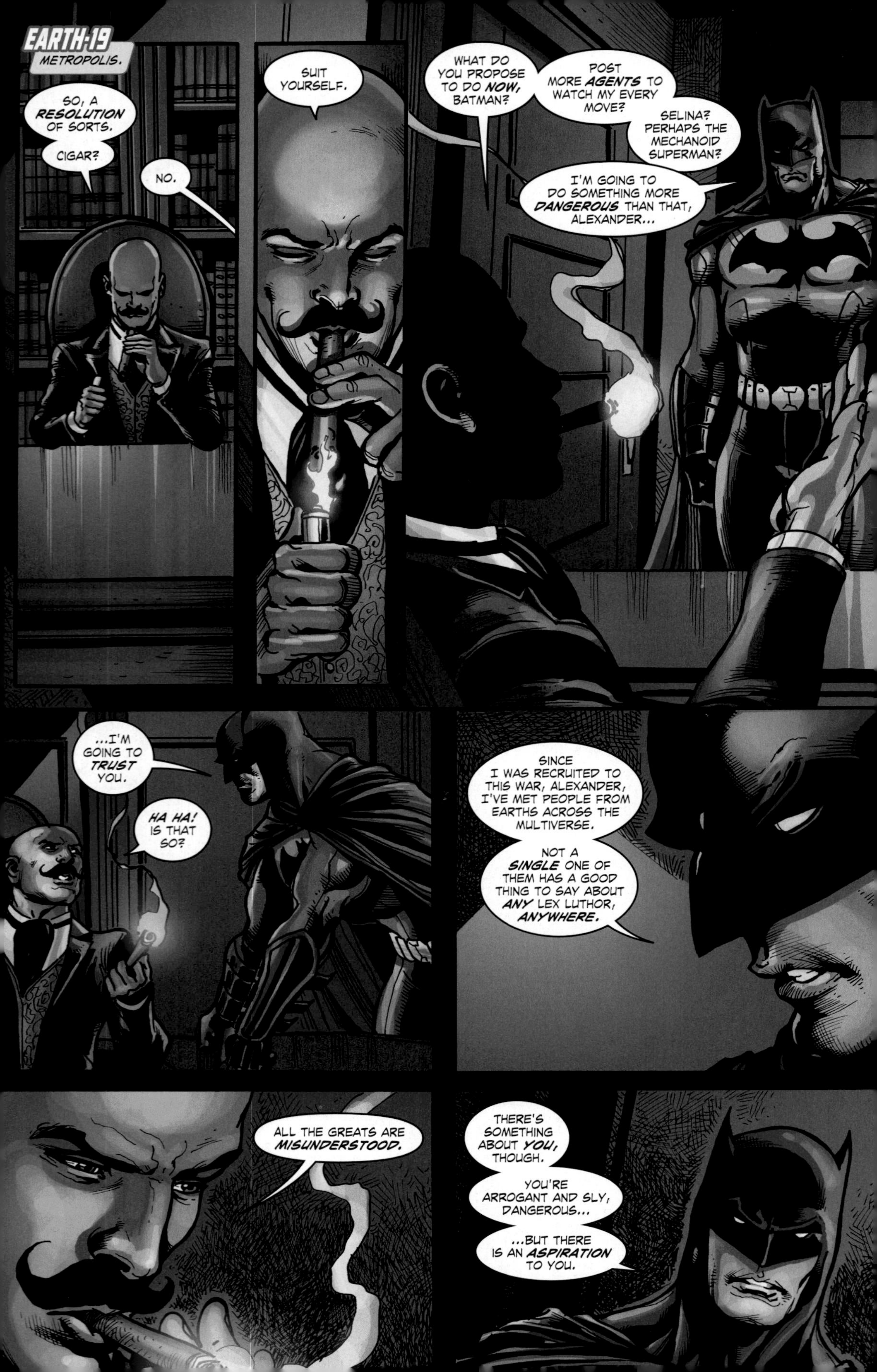
EARTH-19
METROPOLIS.
SO, A RESOLUTION OF SORTS.
CIGAR?
NO.
SUIT YOURSELF.
WHAT DO YOU PROPOSE TO DO NOW, BATMAN?
POST MORE AGENTS TO WATCH MY EVERY MOVE?
SELINA? PERHAPS THE MECHANOID SUPERMAN?
I'M GOING TO DO SOMETHING MORE DANGEROUS THAN THAT, ALEXANDER...
...I'M GOING TO TRUST YOU.
HA HA! IS THAT SO?
SINCE I WAS RECRUITED TO THIS WAR, ALEXANDER, I'VE MET PEOPLE FROM EARTHS ACROSS THE MULTIVERSE.
NOT A SINGLE ONE OF THEM HAS A GOOD THING TO SAY ABOUT ANY LEX LUTHOR, ANYWHERE.
ALL THE GREATS ARE MISUNDERSTOOD.
THERE'S SOMETHING ABOUT YOU, THOUGH.
YOU'RE ARROGANT AND SLY, DANGEROUS...
...BUT THERE IS AN ASPIRATION TO YOU.

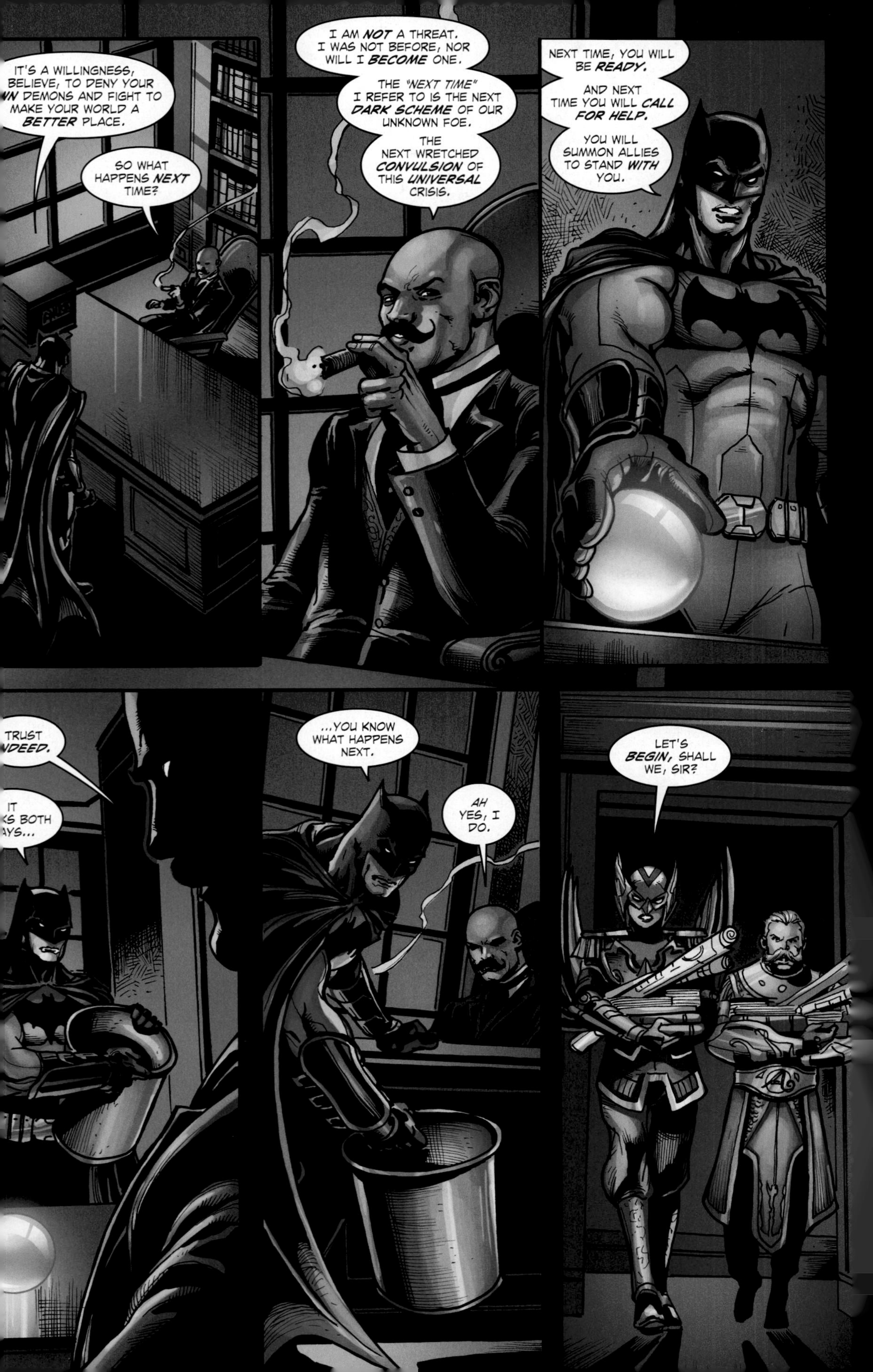

IT'S A WILLINGNESS, BELIEVE, TO DENY YOUR WN DEMONS AND FIGHT TO MAKE YOUR WORLD A BETTER PLACE.
SO WHAT HAPPENS NEXT TIME?
I AM NOT A THREAT. I WAS NOT BEFORE, NOR WILL I BECOME ONE.
THE "NEXT TIME" I REFER TO IS THE NEXT DARK SCHEME OF OUR UNKNOWN FOE.
THE NEXT WRETCHED CONVULSION OF THIS UNIVERSAL CRISIS.
NEXT TIME, YOU WILL BE READY.
AND NEXT TIME YOU WILL CALL FOR HELP.
YOU WILL SUMMON ALLIES TO STAND WITH YOU.
TRUST NDEED.
IT KS BOTH AYS...
...YOU KNOW WHAT HAPPENS NEXT.
AH YES, I DO.
LET'S BEGIN, SHALL WE, SIR?

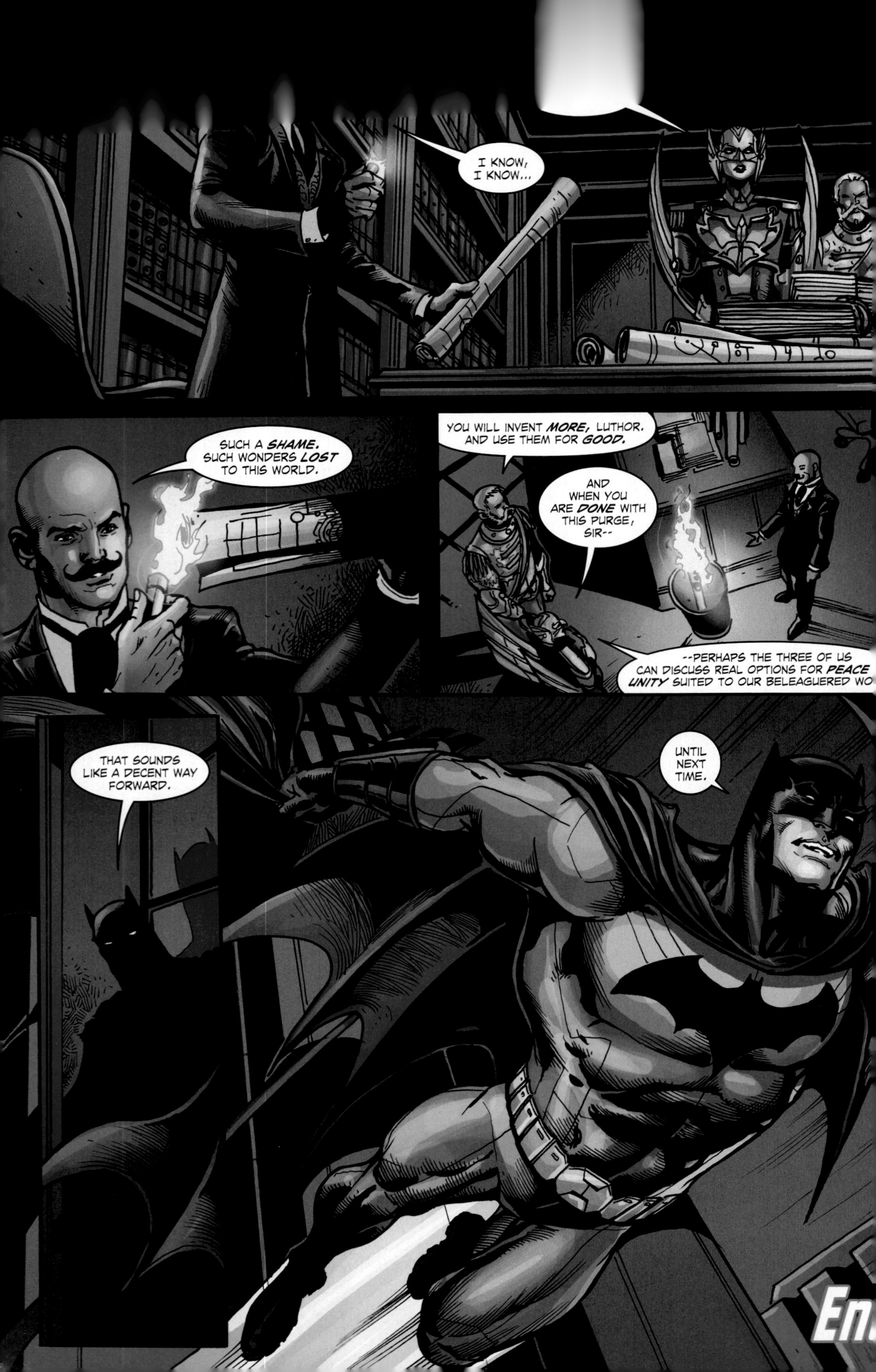
I KNOW, I KNOW...
SUCH A SHAME. SUCH WONDERS LOST TO THIS WORLD.
YOU WILL INVENT MORE, LUTHOR. AND USE THEM FOR GOOD.
AND WHEN YOU ARE DONE WITH THIS PURGE, SIR--
--PERHAPS THE THREE OF US CAN DISCUSS REAL OPTIONS FOR PEACE
UNITY SUITED TO OUR BELEAGUERED WO
THAT SOUNDS LIKE A DECENT WAY FORWARD.
UNTIL NEXT TIME.
En

START AT THE BEGINNING!
JUSTICE LEAGUE
VOLUME 1: ORIGIN
GEOFF JOHNS and JIM LEE

JUSTICE LEAGUE VOL. 2: THE VILLAIN'S JOURNEY

JUSTICE LEAGUE VOL. 3: THRONE OF ATLANTIS

JUSTICE LEAGUE OF AMERICA VOL. 1: WORLD'S MOST DANGEROUS

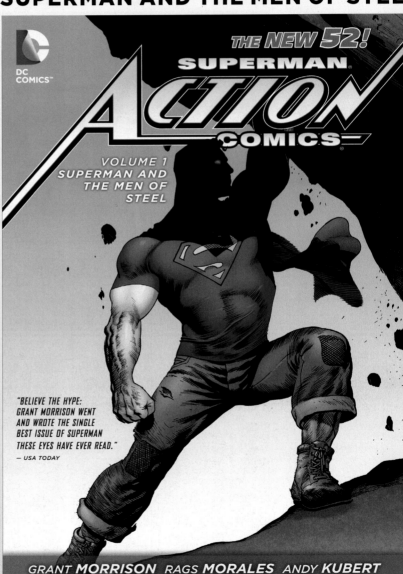

START AT THE BEGINNING!

BATMAN VOLUME 1: THE COURT OF OWLS

BATMAN & ROBIN VOLUME 1: BORN TO KILL

BATMAN: DETECTIVE COMICS VOLUME 1: FACES OF DEATH

BATMAN: THE DARK KNIGHT VOLUME 1: KNIGHT TERRORS

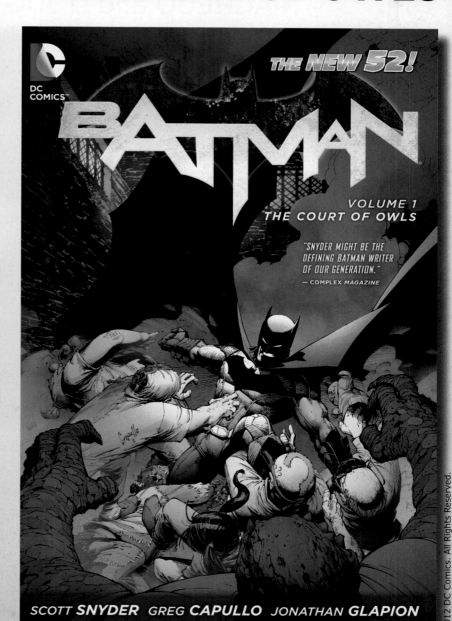

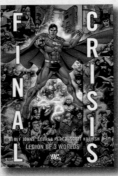